D1083069

CIVILIANS UNDER
MILITARY JUSTICE

SIR CHARLES GOULD, 1782
(After 1792, SIR CHARLES MORGAN, BART.)
Deputy Judge Advocate General, 1747–1769
Judge Advocate General, 1769–1806

From the portrait by Thomas Gainsborough in the possession of
The Equitable Life Assurance Society (of London)
and here reproduced with their permission

CIVILIANS UNDER
MILITARY JUSTICE

The British Practice since 1689
Especially in North America

FREDERICK BERNAYS WIENER

THE UNIVERSITY OF CHICAGO PRESS
Chicago and London

THE UNIVERSITY OF CHICAGO PRESS
CHICAGO & LONDON
The University of Toronto Press, Toronto 5, Canada

© 1967 by The University of Chicago
Published 1967

Library of Congress Catalog Card Number: 67–25530

Printed in the United States of America

TO
THE MEMORY OF
FELIX FRANKFURTER

PREFACE

A number of years ago, after participating as counsel in a series of litigated cases that established the invalidity under the Constitution of the United States of military trials of civilians in time of peace, I sought to assemble consecutively all of the materials that had been presented in a whole series of briefs filed in the several cases; and I had in mind supplementing at least in some measure the historical research that under the pressure of time had up to then been necessarily undertaken on a once-over-lightly basis. One part of the contemplated project, tentatively entitled "Appeal to History," was planned as a collection of historical materials in two chapters, the first dealing with the British background beginning with the first Mutiny Act of 1689, the second dealing with the American practice, preferably starting with the colonial wars against the French, but commencing in any event at the time that George Washington assumed command of the Continental Army in June 1775.

A fellowship grant from the John Simon Guggenheim Memorial Foundation made it possible to undertake the required research. At that juncture the teaching of the lawyers' best evidence rule joined with the historians' admonition to dirty one's hands with the documents: I started with the original entries reflecting the exercise of military jurisdiction, first the headquarters order books of the British Army in North America preserved in the William L. Clements Library of the University of Michigan at Ann Arbor, then the records of trial recorded in the War Office court-martial books in the Public Record Office in London.

Those basic documents, examined in connection with the first historical chapter originally projected, at once disclosed the exercise of a military jurisdiction over civilians, in the territories taken from France and Spain in the Seven Years War, as well as in the American cities occupied by British forces during the War of American Independence, that was far different from—and far broader than—the jurisdiction over camp followers that had been the subject matter of the series of litigated cases. From that point forward, further researches turned up so much more, in manuscript (notably in the correspondence of the Judge Advocate General), in print, and in the secondary sources that were essential to place the basic records in their setting, that what had been planned as a single chapter on the British background became, without padding but simply because of the bulk of the newly discovered materials, a sizable book.

I say, "newly discovered," because, however startling the assertion may appear, it is the fact, not only that the basic manuscript sources have never before been intensively examined, either by historians or by lawyers, but also that the subject matter of the present volume is treated neither by Holdsworth, the historian of English law; nor by Fortescue, the historian of the British Army; nor by Clode, the chronicler of British military institutions. This is, accordingly, in a very real sense, a pioneer work—no doubt with all the inescapable shortcomings of such an enterprise.

In due course I hope in implementation of my original plan to follow the present work with one on the American practice in the same area. But such a sequel is still some years in the future.

It seems appropriate here to explain certain features of the pages that follow.

1. This book is a legal history narrating and analyzing the development of legal doctrines governing the exercise of British court-martial jurisdiction. Those doctrines are relevant in the United States, not only because such jurisdiction was exercised while the Thirteen Colonies were still under British rule either *de jure* or *de facto*, so that this account is a part of American history, but also and indeed primarily because the Constitution of the United States is rooted in the common law of England as that law stood at the time the two countries separated.

Much of the book deals with the activities of the British Army in North America between the years 1765 and 1783, and thus is equally of interest to English and to American readers. I have in consequence been at some pains to make the substantive treatment of the conflict in question—in some quarters now euphemistically called the American and Bourbon War—sufficiently impartial in order not unduly to flutter patriotic sensibilities on either shore of the Atlantic Ocean. And, to ease the path of contemporaries in Britain, there have been added clarifying references to explain idiosyncrasies of a geographical or historical nature that, while perfectly familiar to most Americans, may at first glance seem confusing to English readers.

2. Nonetheless, since the work appears under the auspices of an

American university press, American spelling and style have prevailed—except in respect of documents, which are meticulously quoted from the originals. Along with Mr. Justice Holmes, "I believe in exact transcripts." (Holmes to Pollock, 9 August 1926, in 2 M. D. Howe, ed., *Holmes-Pollock Letters* [Cambridge, Mass., 1941] 188). Accordingly, the spelling and capitalization of every document quoted in the text or set forth in the Appendixes have been exactly reproduced, with only four concessions to modern usage—and technology: (*a*) The thorn has been eliminated (i.e., "ye" is rendered as "the"). (*b*) The capital "F" in secretary hand has been modernized (i.e., "ff" is rendered as "F"). (*c*) Periods have been substituted for short dashes at the ends of sentences. (*d*) Periods under superior letters have been uniformly omitted, as it is unnecessary to inflict that particular refinement on the Linotype machines on which this book was composed.

It should be added that, while dates are in Old Style throughout, without correction of days, the year is invariably given in New Style, viz., with the year beginning on 1 January rather than on 25 March.

3. Since this is a work of legal history and hence a law book, tables of statutes and of cases have been included, and the citations follow lawyers' rather than historians' conventions. The principal differences in consequence are that the number of the volume precedes the title of the work cited and that this is followed by the page number, without any punctuation and without any abbreviation for "page." But in view of the wide scope of the references, a few additional explanations may prove helpful.

a) The guideline of lawyers' conventions has necessarily entailed rejecting the schoolboy nonsense of the law reviews' *A Uniform System of Citation;* I have heeded the late Professor Mark Howe's admonition to stand up to the barbarians.

b) The book follows Holdsworth's system of citing English statutes without using commas to set off the chapter number from the regnal year (or, after 1962, the calendar year), and has similarly embraced the present practice of the Statute Law Committee, see 82 L.Q.R. 24, which gives the short title of every English statute without using a comma between its words and its calendar year.

c) The numbering of every Article of War, British and American alike, adheres faithfully to that of the originals—which were pretty consistently inconsistent in respect of Roman and Arabic numerals.

d) Unlike the British Articles of War, which were promulgated by the Crown as long as there were any, American Articles of War were always enacted by the legislature. The statutory citation to each American compilation accordingly appears in the Table of Statutes. But in order to save space and to avoid a proliferation of citations, particular American Articles of War are cited only by number and date, without individual page references to the *Journals of the Continental Congress* or to the *Statutes at Large*.

e) Finally, whenever any publication renumbers its volumes anew in successive series, or repages its issues within each volume, then series, volume, and page (or volume, issue, and page) are set off by colons (e.g., Force 4:2:968).

4. In the interest of brevity, I have abbreviated freely and have used short titles for almost every work cited more than once. A separate section lists the several abbreviations to repositories, to serials, and to military and official titles, while all of the short titles are fully expanded in the bibliography.

That bibliography collects every printed work cited, with the exception of standard works of reference, calendars and collections of official documents, and legal references (law reports, statutes, treaties, and parliamentary and other legislative proceedings, papers, and reports). I have explained in some detail the manuscript sources consulted, if only to supply later workers in the field with points of departure. But I have deliberately excluded from these listings the many references, in print and manuscript alike, that yielded up nothing save the experience and the discipline of examining them.

This course has the advantage of shortening perceptibly what is still a formidable collection of authorities, though it entails the disadvantage that learned readers may attribute to ignorance or oversight omissions intended simply to reflect critical judgment. This is a risk that in the circumstances must be assumed.

5. A lifetime spent in the practice of law has trained me never to make an undocumented assertion; the present work is therefore liberally footnoted. The reader who objects to footnotes is of course free to ignore them; the reader who likes footnotes will find them on the same page as the text—where they belong—and will, in the event of questioning the text, be able to determine for himself the strength of its supporting authorities. Every author owes as much to those for whom he writes, particularly when, as in this instance, he treads in fields that hitherto have remained essentially unexplored.

6. Many institutions and individuals have helped to make the present volume a reality, and in order that my very heartfelt gratitude for their assistance will not in any sense appear perfunctory, their names are separately set forth in the section that follows.

ACKNOWLEDGMENTS

Interdependence is not only the law of nature, it is a reality of literary endeavor in any field; even the searcher working alone, who eschews the current development of scholarship by committee, owes much to the generosity and helpfulness of friends and institutions. So it was in this instance.

My first thanks are due the John Simon Guggenheim Memorial Foundation, whose liberal fellowship grant made possible the trips to distant repositories that contained the unpublished manuscript materials on which the present work is primarily based.

Next in order are expressions of appreciation for permission to quote from those documents.

The excerpt in Chapter I from the Cumberland Papers in Windsor Castle appears by gracious permission of Her Majesty Queen Elizabeth II.

The transcripts of Crown-copyright records in the Public Record Office appear by permission of the Controller of H.M. Stationery Office.

Transcripts from the Gage, Clinton, and Carleton Papers in the William L. Clements Library of the University of Michigan at Ann Arbor are reproduced with the permission of that institution; transcripts of documents in the Boston Public Library appear with permission extended by its Trustees.

Grateful thanks are due the staffs of the many libraries in which the materials collected below were studied: The Public Record Office in London, and particularly Mr. H. C. Johnson, C.B.E., now Keeper of the Public Records, and Dr. Patricia M. Barnes, Assistant Keeper; the Ministry of Defence Library (Central and Army), also in London, and especially its Librarian, Mr. D. W. King, O.B.E., F.L.A.; the New-York Historical Society, and especially its Curator of Manuscripts, Mr. Wilmer R. Leech.

The Boston Public Library, the Massachusetts Historical Society, the John Carter Brown Library in Providence, the Folger Shakespeare Library in Washington, the Library of the Peabody Institute in Baltimore, and many divisions of the Library of Congress, all proved unfailingly helpful. I owe much, also, to numerous divisions of the New York Public Library, and particularly to Mr. Robert W. Hill, Keeper of Manuscripts; and to the staff of the William L. Clements Library, whose chiefs are individually thanked below. My thanks likewise go, in most ample measure, to the staff of the Library of the Supreme Court of the United States, every member of which has borne my many importunities not only with understanding but also with fortitude.

I must also express my gratitude to The Equitable Life Assurance Society, whose incomparable Gainsborough portrait of Sir Charles Gould appears as the frontispiece to this work, with permission extended by their President, Mr. H. J. Tappenden, F.I.A., and their Actuary, Mr. M. E. Ogborn, F.I.A., F.S.S.

The present Judge Advocate General of the Forces, Oliver C. Barnett, Esq., C.B.E., Q.C., has been more than generous in extending assistance. He supplied information concerning recent developments in British military law that no outsider could possibly have found on his own, and was also most helpful in furnishing memoranda prepared by and data preserved in his office. Without his help Chapter X on the Army and Air Force Acts 1955 could not have been written, and Chapter VII on the early Judge Advocates General would have been substantially less informative in respect of his eighteenth-century predecessors in office.

Professor Emeritus Verner W. Crane of the University of Michigan, my teacher of many years ago when he was George L. Littlefield Professor of American History at Brown University, very kindly consented to read several chapters in typescript.

Major N. P. Dawnay, Hon. Sec. of the Society for Army Historical Research, called my attention to a passage in the Cumberland Papers at Windsor Castle.

Mr. K. Howard Drake, Secretary of the Selden Society, was unfailingly helpful throughout. I particularly desire to acknowledge his hospitality in the course of my London trips.

This book owes a very great deal to Dr. Sylvia L. England of London. With her ingenuity, indefatigable zeal, and knowledge of the manuscript sources, she located many documents, arranged for even more to be copied—and helped immeasurably in checking the not inconsiderable number of references that on returning home I found unhappily incomplete in my own notes.

Mr. William S. Ewing, Curator of Manuscripts at the William L. Clements Library, called my attention to numerous significant papers, and was helpful far beyond the call of duty—or even friendship—in checking references and supplying copies, all over a period of several years.

Mr. F. S. Filby, then Assistant Librarian at the Peabody Institute of Baltimore, greatly assisted my work there.

Colonel Edward P. Hamilton, Director of Fort Ticonderoga, generously provided pertinent transcripts from the Monypenny Orderly Book preserved there.

Mr. William G. Keir, an Assistant Deputy Clerk of the New York Supreme Court for New York County, was most kind in facilitating reference to the early post-Revolutionary records in his care.

Miss Laetitia Kennedy-Skipton of the Folger Shakespeare Library transcribed the court-hand of the 1720 Gibraltar charter.

Professor Philip B. Kurland of the Law School of the University of Chicago was the catalyst who helped combine author and publisher—a result that I hope will be as pleasing to the latter as it has been to the former.

Major-General C. T. D. Lindsay of Stoke-in-Oxney, Kent, was unfailingly helpful in supplying proper English equivalents of current American military jargon.

Miss Dorothy E. Mason, Librarian of the Folger Shakespeare Library, made its vast store of historical materials readily available.

The Hon. Ewen E. S. Montagu, C.B.E., Q.C., D.L., Judge-Advocate of the Fleet, very kindly responded to my inquiries concerning the exercise of naval jurisdiction over civilians under the provisions of the Naval Discipline Act 1957.

Professor Howard H. Peckham, Director of the William L. Clements Library, was most helpful and hospitable.

Mr. G. D. Squibb, Q.C., generously shared his extensive (and, I strongly suspect, unsurpassed) learning of the civil law in England in response to numerous agonized inquiries on my part.

Mrs. L. E. Tilley of the Rhode Island Historical Society supplied a reference to the later career of Joseph Aplin, the Loyalist lawyer who defended Captain Lippincott and then helped prosecute the counterfeiters.

Mr. Ian D. Turner, T. D., of the Law Commission's staff, then a Deputy Judge Advocate, provided essential references to the legislative development of successive Acts of Parliament that I could not possibly have located without assistance.

Mr. S. G. P. Ward, of Lower Bourne, Farnham, Surrey, author of *Wellington's Headquarters* and of a recent short biography of the Duke, generously consented to read the chapter on Wellington's Army; made a series of helpful suggestions that were gratefully adopted; and supplied a number of initials and Christian names for the list of civil officers tried by court-martial that appears in Appendix III.

Mrs. Hazel Shadix Whitehead, my secretary, typed the manuscript, with accuracy—which was required—and with apparent pleasure—which was not, and for which I continue to be grateful.

Professor L. Kinvin Wroth of the Law School of the University of Maine, the co-editor of the *Legal Papers of John Adams*, very generously volunteered to read the proofs. I am under the deepest obligation to him for offering to undertake this chore, which I should never have dreamed of suggesting to him.

Finally, I must acknowledge the assistance of my wife, Doris Merchant Wiener, in two vital respects: First, for the impeccable critical sense that she brought to bear on each draft as it was written; to the extent that the text as it now stands reflects due proportion and avoids alike ellipsis and obscurity, a substantial part of the credit is hers. Second, for assisting in the essential but laborious task of checking references. She undertook that drudgery because she shares my strongly held view (which, I can say from personal examination, not every otherwise eminent, not to say pre-eminent, historian does) that it is never safe to neglect that essential policy—that essential insurance policy—of scholarly writing: "Verify citations."

In England, it would seem, the marriage vows have long included a covenant that, if the husband thereafter writes a book, his wife will compile its index. America, however, is a matriarchy, and consequently any married man smitten with the urge to produce non-fiction will jolly well construct his own. And that is precisely what I did. I hope the result proves serviceable.

CONTENTS

TABLE OF STATUTES

2. *Commonwealth Statutes*

3. *Constitution of the United States*

TABLE OF CASES

ABBREVIATIONS

1. *In general*. Familiarity with the recognized and conventional abbreviations for all legal references to the materials of Anglo-American law is assumed, inasmuch as this is a legal history. Similarly, there seems no need to expand common and even obvious designations such as DNB for the *Dictionary of National Biography*, HMC for the Historical Manuscripts Commission, DAB for the *Dictionary of American Biography*, Coll. for Collections, Proc. for Proceedings, and the like.

2. *Repositories*. Since the primary purpose of any abbreviation is to save time, it must be intelligible. The Library of Congress Union Catalogue designations of repositories, however appropriate for their particular use, do not meet this test; who but a professional bibliographer—or a clairvoyant—could possibly infer from the "NN" of that system that it stands for the New York Public Library? Accordingly, this book uses familiar and hence readily recognizable abbreviations for repositories, as follows:

BM British Museum
LC Library of Congress
MDL Ministry of Defence Library (Central and Army) —the former War Office Library
MHS Massachusetts Historical Society
NYHS New-York Historical Society
NYPL New York Public Library
PRO Public Record Office. For the most part, the several classes of documents will be cited without the PRO prefix, as follows:
 c Chancery
 co Colonial Office
 KB King's Bench
 PRO Used to designate gifts or deposits, as in the case of the Carleton or British Headquarters Papers, PRO 30/55
 SP State Papers
 wo War Office
WLCL William L. Clements Library, Ann Arbor, Michigan.

3. *Serials.* Serials with lengthy titles that are frequently cited are abbreviated as follows:

JSAHR Journal of the Society for Army Historical Research

MPHC Michigan Pioneer and Historical Collections

NEHGR New England Historical and Genealogical Register

PMHB Pennsylvania Magazine of History and Biography

SCHGM South Carolina Historical and Genealogical Magazine

4. *Titles, military and official.* The following abbreviations are used throughout:

ADC Aide de camp

ADQMG Assistant Deputy Quarter Master General

AG Adjutant General

CRA Commander Royal Artillery

CRE Commander Royal Engineers

DAG Deputy Adjutant General

DJA Deputy Judge Advocate

DJAG Deputy Judge Advocate General

JAG Judge Advocate General

MGO Master-General of the Ordnance

NAAFI Navy-Army-Air Force Institutes, "the official Canteen Organisation for H. M. Forces," i.e., the current British equivalent of the American post exchange

OB Order or Orderly Book

O.C. in C. Officer commanding in chief

SS Secretary of State

SW Secretary at War

5. *Military law references.* The abbreviations used by military lawyers are normally not overly familiar to most other members of the profession, hence the present section:

AW Article of War

GO General Orders

MAFL Manual of Air Force Law (more complete references in Short-Title Index portion of Bibliography)

MML Manual of Military Law (same)

UCMJ Uniform Code of Military Justice

CIVILIANS UNDER
MILITARY JUSTICE

INTRODUCTION

When, a few years back, the Supreme Court of the United States ultimately held—after some preliminary pulling and hauling—that individuals without military status could not consistently with the Constitution of the United States be subjected to trial by court-martial in time of peace,[1] the result appears to have occasioned considerable surprise in England, among lawyers in practice, lawyers at the universities, and serving lawyers in uniform.

Learned friends there have asserted that American constitutional law is beyond the ken of an English lawyer, a disclaimer reflecting, one strongly suspects, relief rather than dismay. But in this instance the governing principles are in no sense esoteric. It is a commonplace in the United States that "the provisions of the Constitution are not mathematical formulas having their essence in their form; they are organic living institutions transplanted from English soil. Their significance is vital not formal; it is to be gathered not simply by taking the words and a dictionary, but by considering their origin and the line of their growth."[2] It is further a settled princi-

---

[1] At first the constitutionality of such trials was sustained. *Kinsella* v. *Krueger*, 351 U.S. 470; *Reid* v. *Covert*, 351 U.S. 487. Thereafter a rehearing was granted in both cases (352 U.S. 901), following which the earlier opinions were withdrawn, and military trials in time of peace of civilian dependents charged with capital offenses were held unconstitutional. *Reid* v. *Covert* and *Kinsella* v. *Krueger*, 354 U.S. 1. A few years later, in a series of cases involving civilian dependents committing non-capital offenses (*Kinsella* v. *Singleton*, 361 U.S. 234), and civilian employees committing both capital (*Grisham* v. *Hagan*, 361 U.S. 278) and non-capital offenses (*McElroy* v. *Guagliardo* and *Wilson* v. *Bohlender*, 361 U.S. 281), all military trials of civilians in time of peace were held invalid, the test of military jurisdiction except in time of war being declared to depend on the military status or otherwise of the accused.

Mention of the fact that the author appeared as counsel for the relators in the *Krueger, Covert, Singleton, Grisham,* and *Wilson* cases should be regarded as an admission required by candor rather than as an assertion impelled by immodesty.

[2] *Gompers* v. *United States*, 233 U.S. 604, 610.

ple that "The language of the Constitution cannot be interpreted safely except by reference to the common law and to British institutions as they were when the instrument was framed and adopted." [3] And, particularly in connection with the Constitution's double guaranty of a jury trial,[4] it has long been the law that "the word 'jury' and the words 'trial by jury' were placed in the Constitution of the United States with reference to the meaning affixed to them in the law as it was in this country and in England at the time of the adoption of that instrument; . . ." [5] Consequently, if the final American decisions had actually marked a sharp departure from what had been settled English practice in the past, they would indeed have been surprising.

In fact, however, the ultimate result in the United States reflects with surprising fidelity what had long been the approved practice in the British service. For examination of the available materials, drawn in large measure from manuscript sources, demonstrates that, from the first Mutiny Act of 1689 [6] down to the Army Act 1955 [7] and its counterpart, the Air Force Act 1955,[8] persons not subject to military law, which is to say, persons not specifically named in the Mutiny Act and its statutory successors prior to the effective date of the two Acts last cited, were held not triable by court-martial in time of peace, whether in England or abroad.

The only recognized exceptions were camp followers in war or on active service. Even non-military persons who under currently accepted doctrines of international law are plainly subject to military jurisdiction—namely, civilians of every description, whether connected with the forces or simply inhabitants, who are physically present in areas taken from the enemy and militarily occupied—were in the 1760's ruled by the Judge Advocate General's Office not triable by court-martial. As will be pointed out below in more detail, not only did the rules of belligerent occupation not

---

[3] *Ex parte Grossman,* 267 U.S. 87, 108–109.

[4] Art. III, Sec. 2, cl. 3: "The Trial of all Crimes, except in Cases of Impeachment, shall be by Jury; and such Trial shall be held in the State where the said Crimes shall have been committed; but when not committed within any State, the Trial shall be at such Place or Places as the Congress may by Law have directed."

Sixth Amendment: "In all criminal prosecutions, the accused shall enjoy the right to a speedy and public trial, by an impartial jury of the State and district wherein the crime shall have been committed, which district shall have been previously ascertained by law, . . ."

[5] *Thompson* v. *Utah,* 170 U.S. 343, 350; *Patton* v. *United States,* 281 U.S. 276, 289.

[6] 1 Will. & M. c. 5.

[7] 3 & 4 Eliz. II c. 18.

[8] 3 & 4 Eliz. II c. 19.

develop until the nineteenth century, but the extent to which the King's prerogative permitted the creation of military tribunals to try crimes committed by the inhabitants of territory newly conquered by British arms seems never to have been specifically considered judicially—and the cognizant Secretary of State took inconsistent positions. Similarly, the extent to which military jurisdiction could be exercised when the enemy consisted of domestic rebels who had been accorded belligerent rights was unclear even to the most learned during the American Revolution; the governing principles in that area, also, were not formulated until much later.

In sum, the rulings in England at the time that the Thirteen Colonies went their separate way reflected a municipal military jurisdiction quite as limited as that now obtaining in the United States, and a jurisdiction under the laws of war far narrower than is now deemed appropriate by both countries. Moreover, with very limited exceptions of narrow application,[9] the statutory scope of municipal military law in England in time of peace and not on active service never exceeded the limits laid down at the Horse Guards in the third quarter of the eighteenth century until the 1955 Acts became effective on 1 January 1957.[10]

---

[9] Followers in foreign countries offending against the property or persons of foreign residents from 1813 to 1879, *infra*, pp. 202–203, 211–212; followers of the Indian Army and its sutlers from 1824 to 1879, *infra*, pp. 213–215; certain civil officers accompanying the forces until they were all fully militarized shortly after the close of the Crimean War, *infra*, pp. 202, 208–209.

[10] The first settlers in New South Wales in 1788 were subjected to an essentially military jurisdiction, but that was of course exceptional. See the article by Mr. Justice Windeyer of the High Court of Australia, *"A Birthright and Inheritance." The Establishment of the Rule of Law in Australia*, 1 Tasmanian Univ. L. Rev. 635.

CHAPTER I

FROM THE FIRST MUTINY ACT TO THE FIRST CAMP FOLLOWER ARTICLE OF WAR

This study seeks to trace the boundary between military and civil jurisdiction in English law, to ascertain where the line was drawn over the years between the lawful power of a court-martial to try soldiers and military officers, and its power if any to deal with civilians who though accompanying or present with the forces were quite without military status.

The starting point of this inquiry in time is the first Mutiny Act,[1] not because court-martial jurisdiction sprang into being full blown in consequence of that enactment—the fact was quite otherwise— but rather because in seeking to ascertain the recognized limits of military jurisdiction, it is not helpful doctrinally to explore the practices of any period earlier than the one when the standing army was first legalized by Parliament, of the years when military trials of even undoubted soldiers were deemed illegal.[2] Accordingly, the present volume starts from the time when the constitutional as distinguished from the organizational history of the British Army commences. That period, according to all authorities, coincides with the settlement effected by the Glorious Revolution, and, more specifically, with the effective date of the first Mutiny Act, on 12 April 1689.[3]

The inquiry as to persons starts with and includes all those varieties of civilians who, in 1689 and thereafter, accompanied a British army in the field. Three classes are principally in question.

---

[1] 1 Will. & M. c. 5. For the circumstances surrounding the adoption of this measure, see 3 *Lord Macaulay's History of England* (C. H. Firth, ed., London, 1914) 1346–1353; D. Ogg, *England in the Reigns of James II and William III* (rev. ed., Oxford, 1963) 230–231; 1 Clode M.F. 142–143; 1 Fortescue, 334–336. Its text appears at 6 Stat. Realm 55, but is no doubt more conveniently available in 1 Clode M.F. 499–501; 8 Eng. Hist. Doc. 812; Winthrop *1446–1447; or E. N. Williams, *The Eighteenth-Century Constitution, 1688–1815* (Cambridge, 1960) 34–36.

[2] As a matter of interest, however, the practice in the earlier period may be examined in Clode M.L. ch. 1; Walton 535 and ch. XXVI; 6 Holdsworth 225–230; C. H. Firth, *Cromwell's Army* (4th ed., London, 1962); C. G. Cruickshank, *Elizabeth's Army* (2d ed., Oxford, 1966).

[3] 1 Holdsworth 577; 6 *id.* 241; 10 *id.* 378; 1 Clode M.F. iv; Walton 529, 531, 534.

The first of these were the retainers to the camp: officers' servants; volunteers, i.e., young gentlemen awaiting commissions; and
women and children. It should be pointed out here once for all
that, pursuant to settled military practice and military orders and not
at all by way of individual escapade, women regularly accompanied British troops on active service through the end of the Crimean War.[4] Generally these were soldiers' wives, though searching
inquiry into their precise matrimonial status was probably rarely
made; the fact that they cooked, washed, sewed, and helped in
hospital quite overshadowed the wholly incidental circumstance
that their presence in camp also constituted confirmation of that
ancient and so enduring alliance between Mars and Venus.

The second group consisted of the sutlers, precursors of NAAFI
and the like, who ministered to soldiers' comforts—for a price; the
commodity primarily supplied was liquor.

The third group comprised the civil departments of the Army as
well as the civil officers and civilian employees of the military
portions of the Army. These individuals will be dealt with as they
emerge, and as they were given military status over the years; the
process of militarization began in the 1770's and was completed
soon after the end of the Crimean War.

Although the present discussion starts with 1689, the military
jurisdiction of that year and thereafter had its roots deep in the
past. The forces of William III grew out of those that were in
being during the Restoration, just as the regiments that General
Monck turned over to Charles II were, literally, out of Cromwell's
Army.[5] So too, the Mutiny Act of 1689 recognized rather than
created courts-martial,[6] and its counterparts in 1702 and 1717 rati-

---

[4] Ch. XI, "The Soldier's Wife," in H. De Watteville, *The British Soldier*
(London, 1955); E. J. Martin, *Women's War Work with the Army*, 23 JSAHR
54; 25 *id*. 21.

[5] E.g., Davies C.G. *passim;* 1 D. Ogg, *England in the Reign of Charles II* (2d ed.,
Oxford, 1956) 31–34, 253–254; G. Davies, *The Early Stuarts, 1603–1660* (2d ed.,
Oxford, 1959) 256–260; G. Clark, *The Later Stuarts, 1660–1714* (2d ed., Oxford,
1955) 3.

[6] As said at §12 of the first (1872) edition of Clode M.L., there was "no
difference of principle, and little of practice, in the administration of justice by
Courts-martial before and after the Mutiny Act of 1689."
But Clode is in error in stating (1 M.F. 475) that the court-martial books (which
were then in the War Office) begin with 22 Feb. 1684. The first complete trial by
court-martial recorded in those books commences with a warrant dated 11 May
1666, from the Duke of York to Dr. Samuel Barrow, Judge Advocate of H.M.'s
Land Forces, directing him to convene a court-martial for the trial of Thomas
Hanslope, a soldier, for speaking mutinous and opprobrious words against Sir
Thomas Daniell, his Captain (WO 89/1/11–28). The trial lasted from 20 May to 4

fied more than they authorized the framing of Articles of War by the Crown.[7] Except only during the years 1698–1702, an annual Mutiny Act was always in force,[8] with the result that anyone examining the printed statutes can trace, section by section and clause by clause, the development and elaboration of the Mutiny Act over the years as long as that measure was annually re-enacted.[9] It is hardly necessary to add that, except for Clode, who did so partially and in essentially desultory fashion nearly a century ago, only to make the obvious discovery that the task was "tedious," [10] no one has undertaken to cover the same ground since.

Indeed, it is difficult in the extreme to explain all the changes effected in the Mutiny Act over the years, inasmuch as the abbreviated debates in the *Parliamentary History* do little but record the periodic grumblings of those who, by way of virtual knee-jerk reflex, automatically inveighed against the dangers of a standing army, and, in the process, went so far as to assert the illegality of the law martial even as enacted by Parliament.[11]

June 1666. The Duke returned the sentence for revision downwards, with a view to letting the accused make submission. But Hanslope refused, and the court-martial adhered to its sentence, which on 17 September 1666 was put into execution: "That Thomas Hanslope (for Satisfaction to S[r] Thomas Daniell and Contempt of this Court [refusing to name the witnesses]), do Ride the Wooden horse for six days together during the time of the mounting of the Guards having his crimes written upon his Breast and back [the writing specified by the Court]. That he run the Gantlope, and be Cashier'd and render'd incapable to serve in his Majesty's Armies."

Similarly, one of the earliest proceedings in WO 71/121, dated "8 Aprill 1670," records that "Corporall Pye of Capt. Armstrong's Troope in his Majesty's Regiment of Horse Guards commanded by the Earl of Oxford" was sentenced to be cashiered.

[7] By §39 of 1 Anne St. 2 c. 20, the Crown was empowered to erect courts-martial within the kingdom to enforce the articles at home, and to try offenses against them committed abroad; by §41 of 3 Geo. I c. 2, the Crown was further empowered to make articles of war both at home and abroad, and to erect courts-martial to try any crime. See Clode M.L. 25–30; 1 Clode M.F. 146–148. Articles of War of 1689 for Ireland and of 1706 for the Low Countries are in the MDL, while Walton 809 *et seq*. prints the Articles of War of 1692 for the Low Countries. See also Scouller 257–258.

[8] MML 1914, p. 12; see the listing of the several Mutiny Acts until the accession of George I in 1 Clode M.F. 389–391. However, 7 Anne c. 2, listed at 1 Clode M.F. 390, was not a Mutiny Act. See also Scouller 255 and n. 3.

[9] As is pointed out in detail in Chapter IX below, the Mutiny Act and the Articles of War were superseded in 1879 by the Army Discipline and Regulation Act, 42 & 43 Vict. c. 33, which in turn gave way to the Army Act 1881, 44 & 45 Vict. c. 58.

[10] Clode M.L. 28.

[11] "Had Parliament not expressly sanctioned the change of dynasty, the punishment of the Soldier for Mutiny or Sedition against William III. would have been impossible. Hence the Mutiny Act of 1689, with its annual renewal, always

But the military lawyer who would trace the development of the Articles of War in detail, a project that Clode in turn dismissed as "a long digression," [12] is beset by an even greater difficulty, one that is well-nigh insuperable. It is impossible even by combining the resources of numerous repositories to reconstruct a complete set. The Public Record Office has a good run of the earlier Articles, the old War Office Library—now, after an intermediate change of name, designated the Ministry of Defence Library (Central and Army)—is strong on the later ones, but there are still tantalizing gaps,[13] and inquiry has revealed that there are no old Articles of War at Windsor Castle, none in the libraries of the Brigade of Guards or of the Royal Artillery Institution, and none of the missing ones either in the British Museum, in the library of the Royal United Services Institution, in the Library of Congress, or in the Harvard Law School Library. Occasionally, by happenstance, one thought to be lost will turn up.[14] But, barring a succession of lucky finds, it seems unlikely that an unbroken progression will ever become available.

Responsibility for effecting changes in the Articles of War over the years was at the outset nowhere clearly fixed. In 1715, the law officers were called upon for comment,[15] and, simultaneously, King George I asked the Board of General Officers, a body then and for many years thereafter annually reconstituted,[16] "to peruse the Arti-

---

encountered a strenuous opposition for many years at the hands of the Jacobites." Clode M.L. 19. See, e.g., 1 Clode M.F. 151–153; 2 Fortescue 18–20, 261, 562.

[12] 1 Clode M.F. 149.

[13] The most satisfactory listing is that in W. Y. Baldry, *Early Articles of War*, 4 JSAHR 166, 167 (1924), as corrected and supplemented at 6 *id.* 188 (1926). In addition, the MDL since 1926 acquired the Articles of War used in the Low Countries dated 1706, and a domestic set for 1725. The listing at Clode M.L. ix fails to reflect the collection now contained in PRO, WO 72/2.

Beginning with 1718, the only years not available in either the MDL or in the PRO are 1719, 1720, 1738, 1741, 1745 (Britain and dominions), 1746, 1752, 1754, 1758, 1766, 1770, and 1809.

Clode erred in stating that the 1720 Articles were in a War Office Miscellany Book; the compilation there copied (WO 26/16/116) contains only the 1721 Articles. (The foregoing comment does not involve confusion of Old and New Styles for the commencement of the year; the Articles in question are preceded and followed by items dated 10 April 1721. WO 26/16/115, 136.)

[14] If it is permissible to obtrude a personal note, the author in the spring of 1965 found a set of the domestic Articles of War for 1745 at a London bookseller's. No doubt it is not possible every day to obtain for a mere 15 shillings an item not available either in the PRO, the MDL, the British Museum, Windsor Castle, the Library of Congress, or the Harvard Law School Library.

[15] 1 Clode M.F. 505–506.

[16] For the Board of General Officers, see 2 Clode M.F. 257–258, 724–725; Scouller 44–51. Their proceedings are recorded in WO 71/1–12.

cles of War, and to give Their Opinion with respect to What Alterations or Additions They shall Judge Necessary to be made therein." The addressees, faithfully if not indeed instinctively reflecting the innate conservatism of their profession, dutifully replied that "the late Articles of War, Which having been Experienced for Two Wars, and found to Answer all Ends for the Government of the Army, the Board is unanimously of Opinion, That it would be for Your Maj"s Service to Continue the Same." [17] A request the next year for a similar examination brought no action whatever; [18] in 1717, a renewed request produced only a suggestion that the Attorney General be asked "to compare The said Articles with the Act of Parliament and Other Laws and Report his Opinion wherein they are Repugnant to the Same"; [19] but in 1718, the Board at last transmitted a revision on its own.[20] Unhappily, we do not know whether the 1718 Articles now extant [21] reflect the Board's work or its revision by another hand.

Thereafter, changes in the Mutiny Act and of the Articles of War dependent thereon were effected on an *ad hoc* basis, as deficiencies were disclosed in particular cases, frequently in consequence of a law officers' report.[22] In 1729, when the Judge Advocate General's views were not even sought, that official felt greatly aggrieved.[23] But as the military jurisdiction came more generally to be accepted as part of the law of the land, responsibility both for preparing the annual Mutiny Bill and the annual Articles of War gravitated as a matter of well-understood routine from the law officers [24] to the Secretary at War, and to the Judge Advocate General—at least after the latter was a lawyer.[25] Normally, the

---

[17] WO 71/3/143. There are fugitive references to the 1715 Articles of War in 1 Clode M.F. 505–506, and in PRO, WO 30/25/191, 287 and WO 71/17/5–6, but no complete set of the 1715 Articles has been found.

[18] WO 71/3/189–193.

[19] WO 71/3/215, 281, 282; WO 81/1, 11 Sept. and 18 Oct. 1717.

[20] WO 71/3/290–291, 294–299, 301, 327–328.

[21] There is a set in WO 72/2, which is briefly summarized at Scouller 391. The text of the 1717 Articles of War, appearing at 18 Com. J. 708–713 (4 Feb. 1718 [N.S.]), is summarized somewhat more fully at Scouller 389–391. Cf. 25 Com. J. 736 (10 Feb. 1748, humble address seeking copies of all Articles of War made *tempore* Charles II to the end of William III).

[22] Clode M.L. 98; 1 Clode M.F. 158–160, 508–509; the original report is at PRO, WO 26/16/176. See *infra*, p. 14.

[23] See WO 71/17/1–6, an acrimonious correspondence on numerous matters in October and November 1729 between Edward Hughes, JAG, and Henry Pelham, SW.

[24] 1 Clode M.F. 513–515, and references cited in n. 22 above.

[25] E.g., WO 81/12/142.

changes effected passed without incident, although once during the War of American Independence the Judge Advocate General frankly admitted that the failure to conform the Articles of War to an amendment of the Mutiny Act was an inadvertence attributable to the pressure of other business.[26]

It is now appropriate to examine successive versions both of the Mutiny Act and of the Articles of War to trace the extent that each undertook to place civilians under military law, and, in the process, to inquire whether the Articles of War were considered simply to implement the heads of military jurisdiction set forth in the Mutiny Act, or whether they were deemed an independent source of power competent to confer such jurisdiction in respect of classes of civilians who were enumerated only in the Articles.

Turning first to the statute law, we find that, until early in the nineteenth century, the only civilians whom Parliament specifically subjected to the provisions of the Mutiny Act were the "Officers and Persons imployed in the Trains of Artillery." Such a provision first appeared in 1702,[27] was continued for a number of years,[28] and then was dropped.[29] In 1739 it reappeared and thereafter was regularly continued.[30] In the intervening period, Judge Advocate General Edward Hughes in 1724 advised that, since the Mutiny Act empowered the Crown to make Articles of War, and since AW 45 rendered the artillery subject to the Articles thus made, a gunner could be tried for desertion by a court-martial half of whose members were officers of the Train of Artillery.[31] There is recorded in 1734, no doubt on the strength of this rationale, the trial by general court-martial of the Master Gunner of the Island of Scilly.[32]

---

[26] "It had escaped the attention of the War Office, in the Multiplicity of their business last Year, to make an Alteration in the Articles of War agreeable to the Amendment in the Mutiny Act. I took the liberty of noticing it, but it was then too late to call in several Copies which had been delivered out: However the Oath prescribed by the Act would of course controul the other form." Charles Gould, JAG, to Capt. S. P. Adye, DJA of the Troops in Boston, 27 Mar. 1776 (WO 81/13/77, 78). This was in response to Adye's inquiry, dated Boston, 12 Dec. 1775 (WO 72/7), though at the time Gould replied, of course unbeknownst to him, Howe and his entire force had evacuated Boston for Halifax. Howe OB, 16 Mar., 30 Mar. 1776.

[27] 1 Anne St. 2 c. 20, §46.

[28] 2 & 3 Anne c. 17, §44; 3 & 4 Anne c. 5, §46; 7 Anne c. 4, §58; 9 Anne c. 13, §57.

[29] It does not appear either in 12 Anne c. 13 or in 13 Anne c. 4.

[30] Beginning with §60 of 13 Geo. II c. 10; see 1 Clode M.F. 178.

[31] WO 81/2/43–44, set forth in Appendix IB, *infra*, p. 247.

[32] WO 26/18/180 and WO 71/17/91.

Meanwhile, in 1716, the Train of Artillery had been organized into the Royal Artillery;[33] in 1717, the Court of King's Bench had ruled in *Johnson* v. *Louth*[34] that a gunner was a soldier within an Act of Parliament ordering those "listed" as soldiers to be discharged from arrests for debt; in 1724, King George I peremptorily brushed aside the protest of officers of foot at Gibraltar who refused to sit at the court-martial table with officers of artillery when gunners or matrosses were to be tried;[35] and by Royal Warrant in the next reign, in 1751, the officers of artillery were given military rank.[36] But despite this cumulative process of assimilating the artillery into the Army, the Articles of War continued year after year solemnly to recite that they were applicable to the artillery as well as to officers and soldiers generally.

Civilians accompanying the Army on active service in the Irish campaign of 1691 were tried by court-martial.[37] That sutlers and servants were tried by court-martial during the War of the Spanish Succession appears inferentially from §50 of 13 Anne c.4, which provided indemnity for any officer "by reason of any Corporal Punishment inflicted by him or his Order" before 1 May 1714 "upon any Soldier Sutler or Servant under his Command beyond the Seas for any Matter or Cause relating to Military Service or Discipline."[38]

---

[33] And, in 1727, formed into the Royal Regiment of Artillery. See ch. VI, "The Formation of the Regiment," in O. F. G. Hogg, *English Artillery, 1326–1716* (London, 1963); 2 Fortescue 48–49; ch. VII, "The Birth of the Regiment," in 1 Duncan; 1 Clode M.F. 267.

[34] 1 Str. 7; s.c., 10 Mod. 346.

[35] H. Pelham, SW, to the Lt. Gov. or O.C. in C. at Gibraltar, 4 May 1724, in WO 72/1.

[36] 1 Clode M.F. 584; the original appears twice, in WO 26/21/488 and WO 71/9/133.

[37] 2 G. Story, *An Impartial History of the Wars of Ireland* (London, 1693) 187 (sutler condemned, 22 Aug. 1691, for buying goods from troopers guilty of robbery thereof); 2 *id.* 205 (woman condemned, 2 Sept. 1691, for inciting soldiers to desert).

[38] Neither the general index to, nor the synoptic tables of contents at the front of each of the five volumes of, G. Murray, ed., *The Letters and Dispatches of John Churchill, the first Duke of Marlborough from 1702–1712* (London, 1845) mention camp followers, women, or trials by court-martial. These letters and dispatches, over half of which are in French, extend to 3,342 printed pages by actual count. I have not read them.

Ch. VI, "Discipline and Morale," in Scouller, an admirable work on the administration of the armies of Queen Anne, while packed with interesting information, does not focus on the jurisdictional problems that are the concern of the present book.

There are references to and quotations from the 1691 Articles of War for Ireland in J. H. Leslie, ed., *A General Court Martial in 1708*, 4 JSAHR 161, a

Generally speaking, however, military jurisdiction was narrowly construed throughout the period of Marlborough's wars. Thus, when an English officer serving in Portugal was cashiered in 1706 after an altercation with a brother officer, but continued to accompany the forces and then killed his antagonist while renewing the quarrel, Judge Advocate General Thomas Byde ruled that he was not subject to trial by court-martial and could be dealt with only by the courts of Portugal.[39] Two years later, the 1708 amendment to the Mutiny Act specifically made volunteers amenable thereto,[40] but whether this was a consequence of the foregoing ruling may be doubted, since Byde had proceeded on the premise that the ex-officer was not a volunteer.[41]

Turning now to the Articles of War promulgated by the Crown, we find that, in the reign of George I—who showed considerably more interest in the military affairs of his new kingdom than in most other aspects of its government [42]—those Articles for many years reflected a narrow scope for court-martial jurisdiction. For instance, AW 2 provided that any sutler selling anything during divine services or sermon "shall be deliver'd over to the Civil Magistrate to be punished according to Law." [43] Similarly, AW 4 directed that any officer or soldier guilty of blasphemy or of speaking "against any known Article of the Christian Faith" was in like manner to be delivered over to the civil magistrate.[44] AW 16

---

transcript that records many cases the proceedings in which were approved on 13 June 1708 by the Duke of Marlborough.

[39] WO 30/18/27.

[40] 6 Anne c. 18; see 1 Clode M.F. 178.

[41] "It is my Opinion, That a Volunteer Serving Her Majesty in Her Army's (as a Soldier) may be punish'd as a Soldier, But Crimes Committed by others (not Soldiers) being Her Majesty's Subjects, as the Crime in the Case mentioned, must be punish'd by the Ordinary Methods of Law, and (A) for this Murder may be Try'd according to the Course and Law of that Country where it was Committed." WO 30/18/28.

[42] Williams *Whig Sup.* 18–19, 217–218; 2 Fortescue 29–31, 51. The circumstance that many of the proceedings of general courts-martial held in the years 1717 to 1723 contained in PRO, WO 30/25, are recorded in contemporary French doubtless reflects the fact that George I, who could neither speak nor read English, was well versed in French.

Interestingly enough, at the time of Haldane's reforms nearly two centuries later, "the state of the army" still "touched the Hanoverian heart" of King Edward VII. Heuston 203. See also J. Hayes, *The Royal House of Hanover and the British Army, 1714–1760*, 40 Bull. J. Rylands Lib. 328.

[43] This provision remained through 1740—no copy of the 1741 Articles has been located—and in the domestic Articles (i.e., Great Britain, Ireland, and the Dominions beyond the Seas) from 1742 through 1745.

[44] Again, this remained unchanged as long as AW 2 was repeated; see the preceding note.

required commanding officers to deliver to the civil magistrate all military personnel accused of crimes punishable by the known laws of the land. It was however provided in AW 44, which rested on §46 of the Mutiny Act for 1720,[45] that if no application for civil proceedings were made within eight days, the offender might be tried by court-martial for any offense made punishable by the Articles of War.

Both provisions bear on the jurisdiction of courts-martial over common law felonies. By 1716 it had been authoritatively ruled that no soldier could be tried by court-martial in England for murder or other common law felony.[46] Then, in 1720, while the "within eight days" provision was in effect, the law officers held that, in the absence of a civil complaint within the eight days, the court-martial could lawfully try a soldier for murder.[47] In the following year, the "within eight days" section was dropped[48]—a consequence, one is inclined to suspect, of the foregoing ruling— and AW 16 of 1722 was varied accordingly.[49] Thereafter it was only "in our Garrison of Gibraltar, Island of Minorca, Forts of Placentia and Annapolis Royal, . . . or in any other Place beyond the Seas, . . . where there is no form of Our Civil Judicature in Force" that crimes not mentioned in the Mutiny Act could be tried by court-martial.[50]

But even the provision last quoted was limited by reports of the law officers. Attorney General Sir J. Willes ruled in 1733 that soldiers charged with homicide at Placentia in Newfoundland, where there were insufficient officers to constitute a general court-martial, could not be tried by court-martial in England, to which they had been brought, but must stand trial at the assizes under the provisions of 10 & 11 Will. III c. 25, § 13.[51] Again, in 1734,

---

[45] 7 Geo. I c. 6.

[46] See SW to JAG, 3 Oct. 1716, 1 Clode M.F. 519; JAG letters, 23 Aug. 1717, 6 Oct. 1719, and 15 Oct. 1719, in PRO, WO 81/1.

[47] WO 30/25/158 (19 Nov. 1720), set forth in Appendix IA, *infra*, pp. 245–246. This ruling is neither mentioned nor quoted by Clode.

[48] 8 Geo. I c. 3.

[49] 1 Clode M.F. 158–160, 508–509; Clode M.L. 98. AW 16 was amended by requiring each commanding officer "to use his utmost endeavour to deliver over such accused Person to the Civil Magistrate," in addition to the earlier direction to "be aiding and assisting to the Officers of Justice in the Securing and apprehending such offender in order to bring him to trial." Similarly, to the earlier penalty, "under Pain of Our Highest Displeasure," there was added, "and suffer such other Penalty as by the Act of Parliament for that purpose is inflicted."

[50] AW 46 of 1717 through 1721; AW 45 of 1722 through 1740; AW 45 of 1743 through 1745 (Britain and dominions); see Prichard 238.

[51] 1 Clode M.F. 529; the original report is in PRO, WO 72/3.

he ruled that while soldiers at Gibraltar could be tried by court-martial under the Article of War last quoted, civilians could not be:

> But if any of the inhabitants or others in that place (being not military persons) should offend in like manner, I am of opinion that they cannot be tryed by a Court-martial, though there is no form of a Civil Judicature there established. For though the words of that paragraph seem to be general, and to extend to all criminals, yet, as they refer to the 16th Article,[52] cannot be taken in a more extensive sense. And the rather since the Articles have their authority only from the Act against Mutiny and Desertion, which plainly relates only to military persons.[53]

This opinion may have been the basis for the action mentioned by Lord Mansfield in the course of his judgment in *Mostyn* v. *Fabrigas:* [54]

> I remember, early in my time, being counsel in an action brought by a carpenter in the train of Artillery, against Governor Sabine, who was Governor of Gibraltar, and who had barely confirmed the sentence of a court-martial, by which the plaintiff had been tried, and sentenced to be whipped. The Governor was very ably defended, but nobody ever thought that the action would not lie; and it having been proved at the trial, that the tradesmen who followed the train, were not liable to martial law; the Court were of that opinion, and the jury accordingly found the defendant guilty of trespass, as having had a share in the sentence; and gave 500*l.* damages.

---

[52] *Supra,* n. 49.

[53] 1 Clode M.F. 532–533; the original, said by Clode to be in WO Letter Book 721, has not been located. Intensive examination of the PRO indexes indicates that no volume answering that description is now in the Public Record Office, a fact confirmed by manful search on the part of its staff in February 1964. It seems likely that this volume was never turned over to the PRO by the War Office, and, in all probability, that it was no longer in the War Office when all its other records were transferred.

Earlier, in 1727, women at Gibraltar who offended were put either in the pillory or in the whirligig. See ch. I, "Gibraltar under Siege," in J. W. Fortescue, *Following the Drum* (Edinburgh and London, 1931) 5–6, 16, 20–21. For the whirligig, see 2 F. Grose, *Military Antiquities* (2d ed., London, 1812) 111: "this was a kind of circular wooden cage, which turned on a pivot; and when set in motion, whirled round with such an amazing velocity, that the delinquent became extremely sick, and commonly emptied his or her body through every aperture."

[54] *Mostyn* v. *Fabrigas,* 1 Cowp. 161, 175–176; s.c. *sub nom. Fabrigas* v. *Mostyn,* 20 How. St. Tr. 81, 232. The latter version of Lord Mansfield's judgment differs slightly from that quoted in the text.

The actual record of this case has now been located.[55] The plaintiff, Stephen Conning, Master Carpenter of the Office of Ordnance, alleged that he had been imprisoned for twenty days, then given three hundred lashes, then imprisoned for two months more, and finally deported, "to the Damages of the said Stephen of Ten Thousand Pounds." (The sentence complained of was within the competence of a garrison court-martial, which no doubt tried him, as no prosecution of Conning is entered in the War Office books that record the proceedings of general courts-martial.)

When the action came on for trial, Governor Sabine defaulted, whereupon the jury on 15 February 1738 awarded £700 damages, to which was added £96 costs. Inasmuch as the Governor was represented by counsel, it can only be surmised that he and his legal advisers deemed the question of his liability too clear to be contested.[56]

In 1742, with the outbreak of the War of the Austrian Succession, two sets of Articles of War were issued for a number of years.[57] One, limited to Great Britain and Ireland and the Dominions beyond the Seas, continued the provisions theretofore promulgated "for the better Government of the Horse and Foot Guards and all other His Majesty's Land Forces." A second set was "for the better Government of our Forces Employed in Foreign Parts." The latter compilation provided that sutlers carrying on business during divine service would "forfeit the full value thereof for the use of the Poor," [58] that sutlers selling or keeping open after 9 P.M. or before reveille would do so "under pain of being Dismissed from all future Suttling," [59] and that military persons guilty

---

[55] PRO, K.B. 122/165 (Rot. 482). I owe this reference to the industry and ingenuity of Dr. Sylvia L. England. Counsel in the later case correctly cited the earlier one as occurring in Michaelmas Term, 11 Geo. II, but incorrectly named the plaintiff as *Comyn* in one report (1 Cowp. at 169), and as *Conner* in the other (20 How. St. Tr. at 218).

[56] The roll is indorsed "Writt of Error Allowed," and counsel in *Mostyn* v. *Fabrigas* asserted (1 Cowp. at 169; 20 How. St. Tr. at 218) that the judgment was affirmed on writ of error. But search in the PRO has failed to locate any further proceedings in the Exchequer Chamber, and inquiry at the Record Office of the House of Lords reveals nothing further, either as a case heard or as a case lodged and withdrawn.

[57] Clode (M.L. x) notes the existence of the two sets, but does not comment further on that phenomenon, and he nowhere discusses the differences between the two in either of his works on military law.

[58] AW 2. This provision was substantially identical with that contained in the last previous compilation for use abroad that has been found, for 1706.

[59] AW 24. Under AW 50 of the Articles of War of 1692 for the Low Countries (Walton 815), a sutler thus offending was to be punished at discretion.

of blaspheming should be tried by court-martial.[60] The foreign parts set also contained articles denouncing murder, willful killing, robbery, and theft "committed by any Person in, or belonging to, or attendant upon the Army." [61] But those provisions appear to have been limited by AW 47, which required observance of the foreign parts Articles of War only by "all Officers and Soldiers in Our Service, and also by Our Royal Regiment of Artillery, Engineers, Gunners, Matrosses and all other Military Officers and Persons Employed in the Train of Artillery."

Nonetheless, it was probably pursuant to AW 44, which denounced robbery and theft, that a female camp follower was "convicted of petty larceny" within the year; here is how General Pulteney described the proceedings to the Duke of Cumberland's secretary:

> For the ladies at first setting out behaved like devils; one lady being convicted of petty larceny, her tail was immediately turned up before the door of the house where the robbing was committed, and the Drummer of the Regiment tickled her with one hundred very good lashes, since which time they have behaved like angels. The sex is not the worse for correction.[62]

But formal trial was not a prerequisite for punishment of camp followers at this period; the Duke of Cumberland's orders in France in 1745 and then in Scotland in 1746 reflect both formal and informal means of dealing with offending civilians:

> John Crosley Surgeon's mate to Brig^r Johnsons Reg^t to be cashiered, & drum^d out of both Lines of the British Army, w^h a Halter about his neck, & not return again, either in Camp or Garrison, on pain of severe punishm^t, for having unjustly and ignominiously aspers'd the character of Lieut. Sampson & Lieut. Collis.

> The Following disorderly women being try'd are to be drumm'd from Guard to Guard out of Camp:

---

[60] AW 4. In the foreign parts Articles of 1706, the punishment prescribed for a blasphemer was that "he shall have his Tongue Bored through with a Red-Hot Iron."

[61] AW 43 (murder and unlawful killing), AW 44 (robbery and theft). The corresponding provisions in the overseas Articles of 1706 were AW XIX and AW XX, respectively.

[62] Maj.-Gen. Pulteney to Sir Everard Fawkener, Secretary to H.R.H. the Duke of Cumberland, Audenbosch, 28 Sept. 1745 (Cumberland Papers, 5/139, Windsor Castle). I am indebted for this reference to Major N. P. Dawnay, Hon. Sec. of the Society for Army Historical Research.

Elizth Phillips, Elizth Lupton, Margaret Power, to be drum^d in the same manner, & receive 200 Lashes w^h a Cat of Nine Tails, & none of these women ever to return again into the British Army.

Joseph Lee Servt to Com^t Beaumont of Genl Honeyworls Reg^t [1st Dragoon Guards] being tryd & condemnd for Robery, to be hang'd tomorrow at the head of the said Reg^t the Piquet of the Reg^t to be present at the Execution.

All Suttlers to be examin'd over again, & all those who do not belong to some Reg^t, or can shew no protection, to be turn'd away, & told if they are found in the Camp hereafter, they shall be hangd.

Any man that is found morading will be hang'd without a Court Martial.

By order of H.R.H. Elizabeth Williams convicted of endeavouring to inveigle men to the French Service, is to be put into a Cart sitting backwards, that she may see the punishment inflicted on Peter M'Conachy who is to be tyd to the said Cart, strip^d to his waste, with a Label tyd about his neck, specifieing his Crime, & to be whipd for spreading false intelligence by the youngest drum of each Reg^t from the South end quite thro' the Town of Strathbogie till over the Bridge beyond the Castle, when the Serj^t who conducts them is to dismiss them, & acquaint them th^t if they are ever seen among his Majesty's Troops, it is H.R.H. pleasure that they be hanged imediately without a Court Martial. This to be put in execution at 12, and 2 drums of each Reg^t to beat the Pioneers march dureing the Punishm^t.

There is no meal to be sold to any person but Soldiers, their wives are not alow'd to buy it, if any soldier soldiers wife or other person belonging to the Army, is known to sell or give any meal to any Highlander, or any person of the Country, they shall be first whipd severely, for disobeying this order, & then put upon meal & water in the Provost for a fourthnight.

Any Sutler or woman who presumes to take money for changeing gold into silver will be severely punished & Drumd out of Camp.

Whereas complaint has been made that Several men as well as women, who have been Indulg^d w^h liberty to remain w^h

their husbands in their Quarters have struck and abused their Landlords & Landladies, any soldier guilty of the like misbehaviour will be most severely punished, and the women, if guilty, will not be allowed to remain in their Quarters: where they have no Right to be, but by Indulgence.[63]

On occasion, at this same period, punishment was adjudged *in absentia.* Thus, in 1747, following the first capture of Louisbourg,[64] one Daniel Buckley, a private in Captain Winslow's company of Massachusetts troops, was tried by general court-martial for the murder of Serjeant John Gorman. The accused admitted the act, but justified on the ground that the serjeant had been keeping company with and debauching his wife while he, the prisoner, was posted on guard; complaints lodged with the serjeant's commanding officer had produced only promises to desist, and those had not been kept. On this state of facts the court-martial found the accused guilty and formally sentenced him to death;

> but in consideration of the great and frequent Provocation the prisoner had received from the said John Gorman, the many warnings he had given him in order to Desist from his Criminal Conversation with his Wife, his long Confinement in Irons, since the 11th of August 1746, and other Circumstances which appearing to the Court he has proved,
>
> The Court do therefore Adjudge that the said Daniel Buckley receive no further Punishment, and he be set at Liberty.
>
> And that as Lydia Buckley (the Prisoner's Wife) was the chief Cause of this Misfortune that has happened,
>
> The Court Recommend it to the President & Commander in Chief to Order her to be Drummed out of the Fort at the Cart's Tail, be Duck'd and sent to Boston, from whence she came to this Place, by the first convenient opportunity, and that in the mean time the man be kept in the Fort, and She be not Suffer'd to come into it.[65]

This particular instance can doubtless be shrugged off as achieving substantial if somewhat inelegant justice. Indeed, Fortescue characterizes this first capture of Louisbourg as "one of the curiosities of military history," which, effected as it was by New England

---

[63] Maclachlan 210, 212, 232, 237, 279, 282–283, 324–325, 328, 342.

[64] In 1745; see 2 Fortescue 257–259; 2 Parkman H.C.C. 78–185; Peckham C.W. 99–106. In 1748, Louisbourg was returned to the French by the Treaty of Aix-la-Chapelle, but in the next war it was recaptured by Gen. Amherst in 1758. 2 Fortescue 314–321; Peckham C.W. 169–172; 7 Gipson B.E. 176–207.

[65] WO 71/38/263–268. The trial did not take place until 23 October 1747.

irregulars, he dismisses as "no part of the story of the British Army." [66] Certainly that expedition was marked by a lusty informality in discipline as well as in sanitation, the latter with results fatal to many. [67]

But there was another informality prevalent then and continued long thereafter, not in colonial levies but in the Regular Army, one that will in all likelihood shock even the most hardened advocates of the "give-'em-a-fair-trial-and-hang-'em" school of law enforcement. That was the practice of requiring a group of prisoners, all of whom had been duly condemned to death, to draw lots to determine which among them should in fact be executed. Clode and Walton give an instance of this on order of King William III. [68] The custom appears to have been that, where all of several condemned were equally guilty, they should throw a die at the place of execution. [69] In 1746, King George II directed that twenty-four convicted deserters, who were taken prisoner while in the French service, "should cast Lotts for their Lives, so that only Five of them should suffer." In the event, however, all were pardoned on condition of joining "Regiments serving in the Plantations." [70] But the drawing of lots continued to appear in the court-martial books for many years, the latest instance found occurring in the Peninsular War in December 1813, on orders of the Marquess of Wellington (as he then was). [71]

Meanwhile, on the other side of the Atlantic from Louisbourg, at Ghent in February 1745, a sutler and a farrier, both of them followers of the army, were tried "on Suspicion of Clipping of

---

[66] 2 Fortescue 258.

[67] Parkman H.C.C. 129–134, 162–185; Peckham C.W. 105–106.

[68] 1 Clode M.F. 503–504; s.c., Walton 825. Scouller 267 n. 4 has a similar example from the reign of Queen Anne.

[69] WO 71/36/285 (1734); *id*. 288 (1735).

[70] William Yonge, SW, to the JAG or his Deputy, 26 May 1746, in WO 72/1.

[71] E.g., WO 71/38/263 (1747); WO 71/46/13; s.c., 2 Knox 310 (1759); WO 71/68/44 (1761); WO 71/77/417–418 (1771); and see 7 Well. *Disp*. 177: "I desire that —— and —— may be pardoned; that ——, ——, and ——, may be executed by being shot; and that the remainder of the prisoners should first draw lots for one more to be executed, by being shot, according to the sentence of the General Court Martial" (St. Jean de Luz, 3 Dec. 1813).

Apparently only the reviewing authority could direct the drawing of lots. When Attorney General Ryder was asked in March 1752 whether a court-martial could legally adjudge "That the several Persons so Convicted Shall draw lots, and that he, upon whom the Lot shall fall, Shall Suffer Death," he replied that "Upon the Penning of the [Mutiny] Act I think a Court Martial cannot pronounce Such Sentence unless Usage would warrant it which I am not sufficiently acquainted with." PRO, WO 72/3.

Ducats." The members of the court resolved that, this being no offense against the British Crown, it was not cognizable by a general court-martial.[72] Nonetheless, since Lieutenant-General Hawley, commanding in Flanders, appears to have been of opinion that hanging pursuant to the sentence of a British court-martial would be preferable to boiling in oil, which was the penalty imposed after conviction in the local civilian tribunal, the matter was referred to the law officers, Sir D. Ryder and Sir W. Murray.

They ruled that the generalized terms of AW 46 extended to clipping, but that the applicability of the Articles of War to non-military persons depended on usage in the Army.[73] This report had several consequences. First, no person of a class not specifically named in the Mutiny Act was thereafter ever tried by court-martial in Britain.[74] Next, out of an abundance of caution, AW 46 of the 1745 Articles for foreign parts was expanded to denounce specifically "Coining, Clipping, or in any other way diminishing the Coin of Great Britain, or any foreign coin, which shall be current in the Country." Finally, AW 48 of the same compilation was expanded to make those Articles binding, not only on the artillery and the engineers, but, in terms, on "all other Persons belonging to or attendant upon, our Forces employed in Foreign Parts."

No copy of the 1746 Articles of War has been found. But, beginning in 1747, the two sets first promulgated in 1742 were combined, into a single compilation that was entitled "Rules and Articles for the better Government of our Horse and Foot Guards and all other Our Forces in Our Kingdoms of Great Britain and Ireland, Dominions beyond the Seas and Foreign Parts." [75] On this occasion, the several Articles were no longer numbered consecutively, but were arranged in twenty sections.[76] The overly com-

---

[72] WO 30/29/6–12.

[73] 1 Clode M.F. 534–536. Here again, the original is in the missing WO Letter Book 721.

[74] Clode M.L. 94.

[75] The MDL has a set of MS Articles of War dated 1748, a note on which states that they appear to be those of 1747. The correctness of the note is confirmed by a printed copy of 1749 Articles in the same library in which the changes from 1748 Articles are clearly set out; from the latter compilation it appears that the 1748 Articles had included Art. 27 of Sec. XIV, a provision not found in the 1747 manuscript.

[76] The State Papers, Domestic, Military, in the PRO, covering the years 1742 through 1747 (SP 41/13–18) cast no light either on the promulgation of the two sets of Articles of War in 1742 nor on their later combination into one. Possibly the considerations underlying the revision are articulated somewhere in

mercial sutler was punished by terminating his activities, as in the foreign parts Articles of 1742,[77] the blaspheming officer or soldier was to be dealt with by delivery to the civil magistrate,[78] and the Gibraltar-Minorca-no-form-of-civil-judicature article remained unchanged.[79] Moreover, a new provision was added, Article 23 of Section XIV, the camp follower article that read:

> All Suttlers and Retainers to a Camp, and all Persons whatsoever Serving with Our Armys in the Field, tho' no inlisted Soldiers, are to be Subject to Orders, according to the Rules & Discipline of War.[80]

This provision remained in the British Articles of War through 1828.[81] Meanwhile, in the United States, where Articles of War have been legislative enactments from the beginning,[82] the same

---

the sixty or so uncalendared boxes of Cumberland Papers in the Royal Library at Windsor Castle. Unfortunately it has not been found possible to examine those documents.

[77] Sec. VIII, Art. 1.

[78] Sec. I, Art. 3.

[79] Sec. XX, Art. 2.

[80] Clode erred (M.L. 94) in attributing the first appearance of this provision to 1744. It is in neither set of Articles for 1744 or 1745; as has been indicated (n. 13 and p. 21, both *supra*), no Articles for 1746 have been located; and the earliest set in which it has been found are those for 1747.

Clode's errors have been adverted to before. ". . . it is unfortunate that any statement of fact made by Clode cannot be accepted without reserve: the more one investigates any question, particularly any matter of a date or reference, the more one is led to conclude that Clode neither read his proofs not entrusted them to any competent person." Capt. H. Bullock, 5 JSAHR at 203–204.

[81] In its final form, it was Art. III of Sec. XXIV of 1828, and its introductory words read as follows: "All Serjeants and Non-commissioned Officers and Persons employed on the Recruiting Service, and receiving regular Pay in respect of such Service, and all Suttlers and Retainers to a Camp," etc.

[82] The second Continental Articles of War, adopted on 20 Sept. 1776 (5 J. Cont. Cong. 788; Winthrop, *1489), were drafted by John Adams, later the second President of the United States. Here are the reasons why this very revolutionary American statesman simply copied the Articles that governed the forces then arrayed against him (3 Adams D. & A. 409–410):

"It was a very difficult and unpopular Subject: and I observed to Jefferson, that Whatever Alteration We should report with the least Ennergy in it, or the least tendency to a necessary discipline of the Army, would be opposed with as much Vehemence as if it were the most perfect: We might as well therefore report a compleat System at once and let it meet its fate. Some thing perhaps might be gained. There was extant one System of Articles of War, which had carried two Empires to the head of Mankind, the Roman And the British: for the British Articles of War were only a litteral Translation of the Roman: it would be in vain for Us to seek, in our own Inventions or the Records of Warlike nations for a more compleat System of military discipline: It was an Observation founded in undoubted facts that the Prosperity of Nations had been in proportion to the discipline of their forces by Sea and Land: I was therefore for reporting the

camp follower article was copied verbatim, and indeed was carried on the statute book in that identical form for over 140 years, from 1775 to 1917.[83]

In England, however, the camp follower Article of War did not rest on any corresponding statutory expansion of the Mutiny Act. Neither did the revision of the Gibraltar-Minorca-no-form-of-civil-judicature provision first effected by Article 2 of Section XX for 1749, which then and for many years afterwards provided that at such places—new language then added is italicized—

> the Generals or Governors or Commanders respectively, are to appoint General Courts-Martial to be held, who are to *try all Persons guilty of wilful Murder, Theft, Robbery, Rapes, Coining, or Clipping the Coin of Great Britain, or of an foreign Coin, current in the Country or Garrison, and all other Capital Crimes or other Offenses and* punish offenders *according to the Known Laws of the land, or* as the Nature of their Crimes shall deserve.[84]

As will appear throughout the narrative, not only commanders in the field but their legal advisers and members of general courts-martial regularly construed literally the words of that article, "to try all Persons," for nothing could be more clear to the military mind than the proposition that "all Persons" could only mean "all Persons." [85] But the Judge Advocate General's Office at the Horse Guards, with equal regularity, followed the reasoning of

---

British Articles of War, totidem Verbis. Jefferson in those days never failed to agree with me, in every Thing of a political nature, and he very cordially concurred in this. The British Articles of War were Accordingly reported and defended in Congress, by me Assisted by some others, and finally carried. They laid the foundation of a discipline, which in time brought our Troops to a Capacity of contending with British Veterans, and a rivalry with the best Troops of France."

[83] AW XXXII of 1775; Sec. XIII, Art. 23, of 1776; AW 60 of 1806; AW 63 of 1874. The cited provisions are conveniently available in 2 Winthrop, at, respectively, *1482, *1497, *1516, and *1531. The 1874 Articles of War remained in force until 1 Mar. 1917, the effective date of the 1916 revision of the Articles of War. See §4 of the Act of Aug. 29, 1916, c. 418, 39 Stat. 619, 670.

[84] Art. 2 of Sec. XX; see Prichard 238. Clode (M.L. 99) erroneously attributes this change to the year 1750.

[85] The proper scope of the word "all" continues to bedevil military law. In a recent American case, an officer who had resigned from the Navy because of chronic and incurable seasickness and then had been commissioned in the Army, successfully applied to the Army Board for the Correction of Military Records to obtain credit for his naval commissioned service "for all purposes." But it required a suit in the Court of Claims to overcome a ruling by the Comptroller General that this correction did not extend to pay and allowances. *Darby v. United States,* 146 C. Cls. 211, 173 F. Supp. 619.

Attorney General Sir J. Willes' 1734 opinion,[86] and ruled consistently that "all Persons" comprised only "all Persons subject to the Mutiny Act."

Thus, in 1755, when a Clerk of the Works at Gibraltar, under appointment from the Board of Ordnance, assaulted an officer on the Parade, subsequent to his arrest by that officer for boarding a vessel without the Governor's permission, Deputy Judge Advocate General Charles Gould advised the Secretary at War that this civilian functionary was not subject to trial by court-martial.[87]

A word regarding the jurisdictional position at Gibraltar, where three of the instances already cited arose, can hardly be deemed a digression, the less so since no consecutive account is available anywhere.[88] Once the records are looked to, it becomes plain that the consistent recital in the Articles of War that "there is no Form of Our Civil Judicature in Force" at Gibraltar,[89] as well as the suggestion in a number of judicial opinions that Gibraltar was merely a garrison,[90] are severally erroneous.

On 4 November 1720, by letters patent, there was created at Gibraltar a court with jurisdiction over civil pleas of debt, account, contract, trespasses, and all manner of personal pleas. This court was composed of the judge advocate of the garrison for the time being, together with two merchants selected by him, the judge

---

[86] *Supra*, pp. 14–15.

[87] Lt.-Gen. Thomas Fowke, Governor of Gibraltar, to the Rt. Hon. Henry Fox, SW, 19 Sept. 1755, WO 81/7/11, *infra*, Appendix IC1, pp. 247–249; Charles Gould, DJAG, to the Rt. Hon. Henry Fox, SW, 18 Oct. 1755, WO 81/7/13, *infra*, Appendix IC2, pp. 249–250. In the next year, Gen. Fowke was relieved of command for disobedience of orders in refusing a regiment for the relief of Minorca, tried by court-martial (WO 71/22/334), and dismissed by the King. 2 Fortescue 293, 295.

For a plan of the Gibraltar Parade where the act took place, see the plate facing 2 James 350. That book was written while James was a Lieutenant-Colonel R.A. He died a Colonel Commandant R.A. and a Major-General in the Army, either in 1780 or in 1782 (1 Duncan 308, 378), but actually attained his most enduring fame while a Major in New York in 1765: His house was sacked by a mob protesting the Stamp Act. 1 Duncan 339; Shy 211–212; 10 Gipson B.E. 304–306; Gipson C.R. 103, 167 n. 18; C. L. Becker, *The History of Political Parties in the Province of New York, 1760–1776* (Madison, Wis., 1909) 31; Major James to the Marquis of Granby, 1765, 4 HMC Rutland 235; same to same, 7 Dec. 1766, requesting appointment as Fire Master for North America, 2 *id.* 289.

[88] "There exists no adequate study of the history of the internal development of Gibraltar from a military fortress to its present status of a colony under the Colonial Office. Historians have written at length on its sieges and on its diplomatic history but have made only passing references to the stages of its institutional and constitutional development." Preston 403.

[89] *Supra*, pp. 14–16, 22.

[90] *Lubbock* v. *Potts*, 7 East 449, 455; *The Nemesis*, Edw. Adm. 51.

advocate and one merchant to constitute a quorum; from this tribunal an appeal would lie to the Governor; and, in cases where the demand exceeded the value of £300, another appeal lay to His Majesty in Council.[91]

The law officers, reporting in December 1722, deemed that arrangement unsatisfactory, because "this is too great a power to be entrusted with a single person, especially with one who is an officer of the garrison, and subject to the command of the military governor, and upon that account the more improper." [92] But nothing was then done to implement their recommendation to fix the laws and the courts of justice at Gibraltar on a firm basis. Moreover, the prevailing lack of precise information available in England concerning Gibraltar was emphasized by the proposal "for erecting a Civil Magistracy there," published by "a Gentleman of the Navy" at London in 1725, which urged the establishment of a tribunal for the determination of "all Disputes depending between Merchants, and such other Controversies as relate to Civil Matters." [93] This was all very sensible, to be sure—but the author was plainly unaware that just such a court was then in fact functioning at Gibraltar.

A second charter, dated 10 May 1740, created the Court of Civil Pleas at Gibraltar, and named Robert Robinson, barrister at law, the first Chief Judge, and Richard Holroide and William Chalmers, Esquires, to be the other two judges.[94] This charter conferred jurisdiction over all civil causes and pleas, likewise over "all Murders, Felonies, Trespasses, and other Crimes, of what Nature or kind soever (Treasons excepted) arising within the Town of *Gibraltar* and Lands thereunto belonging; unless the Offender be a Person in actual Pay, as a Member of the Garrison, and the Offence be punishable by Virtue of the *Articles of War*." [95] A right of

---

[91] PRO, C 66/3540, No. 3, located by Dr. England, and apparently never printed. I am greatly obliged to Miss Laetitia Kennedy-Skipton of the Folger Shakespeare Library for transcribing the court hand of the original, this charter having been enrolled before the further use of that so unintelligible form of writing was rendered illegal by 4 Geo. II c. 26.

[92] 1 G. Chalmers, *Opinions of Eminent Lawyers* (London, 1814) 169, 175 (Sir R. Raymond and Sir P. Yorke).

[93] Philalethes, *Gibraltar a Bulwark of Great Britain* (London, 1725) 33, 34–35, 41–42.

[94] *The Royal Charter for Establishing a Civil Government at Gibraltar &c.* (London, 1742). This is dated 10 May, 13 Geo. II; inasmuch as King George II's accession took place on 11 June 1727, the charter was issued in 1740, and not in 1739 as stated in 4 *Laws of Gibraltar* (rev. ed. 1950) i, in 4 *id.* (rev. ed. 31 Dec. 1935) ix, and at Preston, 407.

[95] Arts. VI and XIX, respectively.

appeal in civil cases involving £ 200 or upwards was granted, to the Court of Appeals at Gibraltar, also constituted by the charter, which was composed of the Chief Justice of the Civil Pleas and of four additional named gentlemen.[96] Finally, Article XXIV provided in rounded terms for the supremacy of the civil power:

> And further, we do, by these Presents, for Us, our Heirs and Successors declare, That the Governor, or Lieutenant Governor, or Commander in Chief for the Time being, have not any Right, Title, or Authority to Arrest, Imprison, Try, Judge, or Condemn, by Military Law, or Articles of War, any of the Inhabitants of *Gibraltar*, or within the Limits aforesaid, not being Persons actually in Pay as Members of the Garrison, except only during such Time as *Gibraltar* shall be actually Besieg'd, or in such Cases as concern the Safety of the Town during a War with *Spain*.

Alas for these flowing phrases! Chief Justice Robinson never left England, the courts mentioned in the charter were never erected, and in consequence, according to one actually present in Gibraltar in 1748, "the governor was the only magistrate, and his will was the sole law by which he governed." [97] Not only were the civilians—fewer than 800 in 1730, but about 1,800 in 1753—"wretchedly misgoverned," but the members of the garrison were dealt with tyrannically by governors who flouted the Articles of War.[98]

Still—there was indeed a fully functioning court of civil judicature in operation at Gibraltar, a fact emphatically demonstrated by the record of trial by general court-martial of Mr. James Penman, Surgeon Major of the Garrison.[99] This gentleman was tried at Gibraltar on 19 February 1752 "for publickly Disturbing and Interrupting the Administration of Justice, by the Civil Court of

---

[96] Arts. XII, XV, XVI; the other four judges of the Court of Appeals named in the charter were Edward Pearson, William Jenkins, William Graves, and James Reed, Esquires.

[97] 27 *Gentleman's Magazine* 105 (March 1757), quoting from *Three Letters relating to the Navy, Gibraltar, and Portmahon* (London, 1757) 118. "These letters were wrote in the years 1747, and 1748, at the request of a worthy member of the house of commons." *Id.* at iii. A manuscript note on the copy in the New York Public Library identifies the M.P. as Charles Gray, Esq., Member for Colchester, and the writer as Dr. Lind, minister of Wivenhoe in Essex.

[98] Population in 1730, S. Conn, *Gibraltar in British Diplomacy in the Eighteenth Century* (New Haven, 1942) 132. Population in 1753, 2 James 320. "Wretchedly misgoverned," Sayer 260. Disregard of Articles of War, Sayer 467–472; 2 James 367–381.

[99] WO 71/40/99–120.

Judicature established in This Town and Garrison by Royal Authority, and endeavouring to Stir up and excite others to the like behaviour, Contrary to good Order and Discipline, and in Contempt of His Majesty's Authority."

What happened was that the accused's father-in-law had a cause pending before the court composed of the judge advocate and the two merchants erected under the letters patent of 1720; the father-in-law lost, and appealed to the Governor; and when the Governor confirmed the sentence, Penman enthusiastically embraced the cause of his wife's family by putting up an advertisement on the Parade asserting that the loss of the property to the winning party was a robbery. Inasmuch as the "practice familiar in the long history of Anglo-American litigation, whereby unsuccessful litigants and lawyers give vent to their disappointment in tavern or press," [100] seems not at that time to have taken root at Gibraltar, Surgeon Major Penman was convicted and sentenced to be cashiered, a sentence which was duly confirmed by Their Excellencies the Lords Justices.[101]

Later that year, on 1 August 1752, new letters patent enlarged the jurisdiction of the judge-advocate-plus-two-merchants court, conferring power to adjudicate matters pertaining to real estate and to probate and administration, and granting a criminal jurisdiction, "Excepting Soldiers or others in Actual pay as Members of the Garrison," over "all Murders Felonies, Forgeries perjuries Trespasses and other Crimes whatsoever committed in or at Gibraltar and the Territorys thereto belonging (Excepting Treasons and Misprisions of Treason)." [102] Curiously enough, the 1752 letters, though specifically referring to those of 1720, made no mention whatever of the charter of 1740. Yet in 1835, the Judicial Committee of the Privy Council held in *Jephson* v. *Riera* [103] that it was in consequence of the 1740 charter that English law had replaced Spanish law at Gibraltar in respect of real property there.

During the Seven Years War a Vice-Admiralty court made its

---

[100] *United States* v. *Morgan*, 313 U.S. 409, 421, *per* Frankfurter, J.

[101] Charles Gould, DJAG, to Gov. Bland, 28 April 1752, WO 81/5/43. Perhaps modern readers need to be reminded that the Lords Justices of the late seventeenth and first half of the eighteenth centuries were the regents of the kingdom while King William III was absent in Holland and Kings George I and II tarried in Hanover.

[102] PRO, C 66/3687, No. 8, also located by Dr. England, and likewise apparently never printed.

[103] 3 Knapp P.C. 130, noted though not cited at Preston 407. This decision contains the first informed judicial discussion of the legal position at Gibraltar.

appearance, primarily to condemn prizes.[104] Much later, in 1802, Governor H.R.H. the Duke of Kent (father of Queen Victoria) presided over a "civil session" as judge, and sentenced three Spaniards to be hanged for stealing.[105] But the inhabitants at the Rock had no enforceable right to civil liberty until, by the Charter of Justice in 1830, a Supreme Court and a civil magistracy were established there.[106]

The recital just concluded, which carries the account of military jurisdiction over civilians to the outbreak of the Seven Years War, suggests serious doubts concerning the weight to be accorded the Articles of War.

It is of course always a source of error to read later legal concepts into the thinking of an earlier age; Maitland is the great teacher in that respect;[107] and simply because Clode in 1869 asserted unhesitatingly that "The Crown, in framing the Articles of War, must . . . confine their operation strictly within the terms of the Mutiny Act, both as to the persons liable to punishment and as to the powers to be exercised thereunder,"[108] it by no means follows that this was the view of the War Office a century or more earlier.

Judge Advocate General Hughes plainly did not think so in 1724 when he ruled the artillery subject to military law at a time when it was not named in the Mutiny Act;[109] neither Judge Advocate General Morgan nor his Deputy, King Gould, both of whom held office during the expansion of jurisdiction over civilians that was asserted in the Articles framed in the late 1740's, expansion that is nowhere reflected in the corresponding Mutiny Acts, apparently thought so either.[110] But none of these three was a lawyer. It is only when Charles Gould became Judge Advocate General *de facto*, in

---

[104] Sayer 245. It seems to have been particularly active after 1793. J. Bell, *The History of Gibraltar* (London, 1845) 190.

[105] Sayer 428. The Duke's tour of duty was not a happy one. E. Neale, *The Life of Field-Marshal H.R.H. Edward, Duke of Kent* (2d ed., London, 1850), chs. VIII–X; 7 Martin 36–53.

[106] *Laws of Gibraltar, supra* n. 94; Sayer 437; 7 Martin 93. Preston considers in detail the development of government at Gibraltar in the nineteenth and twentieth centuries.

[107] "But if Maitland brought law to bear on history, he brought history to bear on law. Again and again he emphasised the danger of imposing legal concepts of a later date on facts of an earlier date. . . . We must not read either law or history backwards." H. M. Cam, ed., *Selected Historical Essays of F. W. Maitland* (Cambridge, 1957) xi.

[108] 1 M.F. 149–150.

[109] *Supra*, p. 11; *infra*, Appendix IB, p. 247.

[110] *Supra*, pp. 14, 17, 22–24.

1747 or thereabouts,[111] that the latter notion made its appearance. Significantly, as will be seen in Chapter VII, he was the first lawyer ever to serve in the Judge Advocate General's office.

Moreover, the Articles of War over the years reflect vestigial survivals, which no one apparently thought necessary or desirable to delete or revise with a view to modernization. The documents already cited leave no doubt that Charles Gould, who as Deputy Judge Advocate General reviewed the record of trial of Surgeon Major Penman in 1752 and in the same capacity ruled the Clerk of the Works not amenable to trial by court-martial in 1755, was surely aware that there was in fact a "form of Our Civil Judicature in Force" at Gibraltar. Yet the Gibraltar Article of War continued solemnly to recite the contrary well into the 1830's.[112]

Any suggestion that such a recital was still necessary because neither the 1720 nor the 1740 charter created courts with jurisdiction to try members of the garrison, so that no tribunal in Gibraltar could deal with soldiers as did the courts at home,[113] does not survive examination. The language of the Article of War was, "where there is *no form* of Our Civil Judicature in Force"—italics added—not "where there is no Civil Judicature in Force competent to try Persons in actual Pay, as Members of the Garrison."[114] Moreover, when the clause in question first appeared in the Articles of War, by 1717 at the latest,[115] there was in fact no civil judicature of any kind at Gibraltar; as has been seen, the first tribunal created there was established by the charter of 1720.[116]

The Gibraltar Article of War, then, was simply a survival, mechanically repeated year by year. The same approach was reflected in other Articles. Thus, for more than 130 years after the artillery was regularly named in the Mutiny Act as subject thereto,[117] it continued to be specifically mentioned in the Articles of War—for as long as they were promulgated.[118]

---

[111] The first letter in the JAG Letter Books signed by Charles Gould is dated 14 Aug. 1747 (WO 81/4/26). At this time he was in residence at Lincoln's Inn, but his call to the Bar was still more than three years distant. See p. 175, *infra*.

[112] See AW 102 of 1830 through 1837.

[113] *Supra*, pp. 14–15, 23–26; *infra*, Appendix IC2, pp. 249–250.

[114] The second quotation incorporates the exclusionary paragraph of the 1740 charter, *supra*, p. 25.

[115] *Supra*, p. 14. Gibraltar passed to Great Britain by the Treaty of Utrecht in 1713, but the first set of Articles of War framed thereafter that has been found is that for 1717. See note 21, *supra*.

[116] *Supra*, pp. 24–25.

[117] *Supra*, p. 11.

[118] E.g., AW 187 of 1873 and §2 of the Mutiny Act for that year, 36 Vict. c. 10.

In addition, the provision fixing the relative rank of provincial officers in North America was repeated year by year in the Articles of War long after its terms ceased to have any subject matter on which they could operate. This Article of War first appeared in 1755, at which time it ranked all provincial officers of every grade below junior Regular captains [119]—an arrangement that had a well-nigh disastrous effect.[120] Whether William Pitt or Lord Loudoun was responsible for the change that soon became necessary is not here material,[121] but it is the fact that by the Articles of War of 1759, which made provincial officers junior only to Regular officers of the same grade,[122] colonial pride was salved, and colonial military effectiveness correspondingly enhanced. The same scheme was continued after the close of the Seven Years War, when it might have had application to the colonial troops requested to assist in suppressing Indian disturbances,[123] and through the War of American Independence, where it regulated the relative rank of the very substantial provincial forces that were raised from the Loyalists.[124] After 1783, however, when the United States were recognized as independent, this provision was, very plainly, *functus officio*. Nonetheless, it was solemnly continued in the Articles of War through 1828.[125]

One cannot safely be dogmatic concerning eighteenth-century English military law. But the developments recounted in the present chapter certainly leave the strong impression that, at least partially, the Articles of War involved less a source of law than "a

---

[119] Art. 2 of Sec. 19 of 1755. Although the 1754 Articles of War have not reappeared, it is possible to fix the year with certainty, because troops raised in America were not subjected to the British Articles of War until the Mutiny Act for 1755. 28 Geo. II c. 4 (last clause).

[120] 2 C. H. Lincoln, ed., *Correspondence of William Shirley* (New York, 1912) 492–498, 501–519; and see, for the impact of the older provision on one of the most outstanding provincial officers, 2 Freeman 12–13, 138–139, 148–149, 153–156.

[121] 1 B. Williams, *The Life of William Pitt* (London, 1913) 368–369; Pargellis *Loudoun* 85–93; 7 Gipson B.E. 177–179.

[122] Art. 2 of Sec. 19 of 1759.

[123] Ch. VI, "The Conquest of the West," in Alden *Gage;* ch. V, "The Great Indian Uprising, 1763," in 9 Gipson B.E.; H. H. Peckham, *Pontiac and the Indian Uprising* (Chicago, 1947).

[124] Smith L. & R. *passim;* 12 Gipson B.E. 369; W. H. Siebert, *Loyalist Troops of New England*, 4 New Eng. Q. 108; W. O. Raymond, ed., *Winslow Papers*, A.D. *1776–1826* (St. John, N.B., 1901). Winslow was a Lieutenant-Colonel and Muster Master General of the Loyalist Forces. For Sir Henry Clinton's difficulties in the matter of provincial rank, see Willcox 285–287, 317–318.

[125] Art. I of Sec. XXI.

curious cabinet of antiquities" [126]—on a par with the continuation of the French fleur-de-lis in the Royal Arms until 1801,[127] or the Royal Welch Fusiliers' flash that even today still memorializes the departed queue.[128]

---

[126] 2 F. Pollock & F. W. Maitland, *History of English Law* (2d ed., Cambridge, 1898) 365.

[127] E.g., C. W. Scott-Giles and J. P. Brooke-Little, *Boutell's Heraldry* (rev. ed. London, 1963) 214–215, and Plate V.

[128] Appendix IX, "The 'Flash,'" in 2 A. D. L. Cary & S. McCance, *Regimental Records of the Royal Welch Fusiliers* (London, 1923) 399–406.

CHAPTER II

THE SEVEN YEARS WAR

Lord Macaulay's much quoted comment on Frederick the Great—". . . in order that he might rob a neighbour whom he had promised to defend, black men fought on the coast of Coromandel, and red men scalped each other by the Great Lakes of North America"[1]—referred of course to the War of the Austrian Succession that followed the Prussian King's seizure of Silesia. Now, however, it is more generally considered that the First World War began, not with that conflict, not with the guns of August 1914, but with the Seven Years War, which lasted officially from 1756 until 1763.[2]

The geographical extent of the last-named struggle is reflected in the War Office court-martial books, which record trials all over the globe—in Germany, at Belle Isle, in the American colonies, in both Indies, East and West, in Africa, and in the territories taken from the enemy: Canada, Florida, Cuba, and the island of "Luconia" in the Philippines (now, after two later wars in that archipelago, better known as "Luzon"). Names later famous and infamous alike are recorded—Colonel George Washington of the 1st Virginia Regiment sits as president of a general court-martial,[3] Lord George Sackville acts upon sentences,[4] Horatio Gates, later gloriously victorious at Saratoga and in turn ingloriously vanquished at Camden, appears holding the King's commission as Captain of H.M.'s Independent Company of New York.[5] Here, however, we are concerned only with the civilians who were tried by court-martial during the conflict.

---

[1] "Frederic the Great," in 6 Lady Trevelyan, ed., *The Works of Lord Macaulay* (London and Bombay, 1897) 645, 660–661.

[2] See ch. XI of Bk. VIII, "The First World War," in 3 W. S. Churchill, *A History of the English-Speaking Peoples* (New York, 1957); S. E. Morison, *The Oxford History of the American People* (New York, 1965) 164; Savory vii.

[3] WO 71/66/450.

[4] WO 71/67/94, 103; 8 HMC *Var. Coll.* 519, 558, 562–563, 566.

[5] WO 71/44/307. See S. M. Pargellis, "The Four Independent Companies of New York," in *Essays in Colonial History Presented to Charles McLean Andrews by His Students* (New Haven, 1931) 96–123, an account of military mismanagement unusual even by eighteenth-century standards.

GERMANY AND FRANCE

Although it was Britain's basic policy to leave fighting on the continent of Europe to its Prussian ally, there was a British army in Germany from 1758 through 1763, a period marked by the famous victory at Minden.[6] That encounter led to Lord George Sackville's trial by court-martial for disobedience of orders after he had been dismissed the service, an exercise of military jurisdiction then approved by both the law officers and the judges, even though, once dismissed, Sackville had become a civilian.[7] This rule, with statutory sanction at least in part, has been adhered to in the British service ever since.[8]

Other courts-martial of civilians took place in the theater of war. During the campaigns in Germany, there were tried officers' servants,[9] drivers of waggons,[10] a stall master to the artillery,[11] a hospital steward,[12] a "Schaffer" in the bakery train,[13] and a servant to "a Merchant attending the Army."[14] Two seemingly suspicious characters were charged, brought up for trial, not prosecuted, but reconfined; no further proceedings appear. One was a Jew,[15] the other is described simply as "a Foreigner"[16]—a classification of course inherently suspicious. The crimes charged included mur-

---

[6] Savory *passim;* 2 Fortescue 485–497.

[7] Simmons 22–23; 1 Clode M.F. 183–184; *Proceedings of a General Court-Martial held . . . upon the Trial of Lord George Sackville* (London, 1760).

[8] Army Act 1881, §158(1) (trial by court-martial authorized for three months following separation, for a limited number of offenses); Army Act 1955, §131 (a somewhat broader provision). See *Marks* v. *Frogley,* [1898] 1 Q.B. 888 (determinative factor is whether accused was subject to military law when offense was committed); *Rex* v. *Governor of Wormwood Scrubs Prison; Ex parte Boydell,* [1948] 2 K.B. 193 (*aliter,* where the prosecution under the earlier Army Act was commenced more than three months after separation).
The only doubt ever expressed in England is at 1 Clode M.F. 185. In America the rule of the Sackville trial has never been law (Winthrop *117); efforts to exert military jurisdiction following re-entry into the service proved unavailing in *United States* v. *Cooke,* 336 U.S. 210; and the subsequent attempt to overcome the decision last cited by legislation similar in substance to Army Act 1881, §158(1), failed on constitutional grounds. *Toth* v. *Quarles,* 350 U.S. 11. See Appendix IV, *infra,* at pp. 307–309.

[9] WO 71/67/94, WO 71/69/31; 8 HMC *Var. Coll.* 432, 450.

[10] WO 71/67/216, WO 71/69/231, WO 71/70/268, WO 71/72/122.

[11] WO 71/68/44.

[12] WO 71/69/227.

[13] WO 71/70/246.

[14] WO 71/72/115.

[15] WO 71/67/216.

[16] WO 71/67/220.

der,[17] fraud,[18] assault,[19] theft,[20] sale of H.M.'s stores,[21] embezzlement,[22] and, in the case of drivers, desertion.[23] Of the fourteen proceedings reported, five resulted in acquittals, two more (already
noted) in confinement pending further action, and one in pardon—hardly a notable season for the prosecution. How many more
civilian camp followers were tried by regimental courts-martial
or were summarily dealt with by the provost marshal does not
appear.

In 1761, a British force seized Belle Isle off the coast of France
and held the island until the peace.[24] Three civilians were there
tried during that period by general courts-martial of the British
Army: a soldier's wife, charged with complicity in the robbing of
an officer's tent, and acquitted;[25] a sailor from a transport, accused
of plundering a French ship employed in the King's service, and
also acquitted;[26] and finally an officer's servant, tried under the "no
Form of Our Civil Judicature" article because "he contradicted
himself in his evidence and prevaricated with the Court," who
upon conviction was sentenced to five hundred lashes in the usual
manner.[27]

CUBA, THE PHILIPPINES, AND THE FLORIDAS

Spain declared war on Britain in 1762, a most unwise act that
eventually lost her Minorca and both Floridas, East and West,
during the twenty years that followed the end of the war. While
the struggle still lasted, the British captured Havana and Manila,
returning Cuba and the Philippines at the peace, the latter only
because news of its capture had not reached Europe until after
signature of the preliminary treaty.[28]

Manila was taken early in 1762 by an expedition that set out

---

[17] WO 71/67/94, WO 71/70/246.
[18] WO 71/67/216.
[19] WO 71/67/220.
[20] WO 71/69/31, WO 71/72/115, WO 71/72/122; 8 HMC *Var. Coll.* 432
(marauding); *id.* 450 (stealing and selling a coat; acquitted of theft, but found
guilty of the sale; adjudged "to make good what he has sold and turned out of the
line as a vagabond").
[21] WO 71/68/44.
[22] WO 71/69/227.
[23] WO 71/67/216, WO 71/69/231, WO 71/70/268.
[24] 2 Fortescue 521–522; 8 Gipson B.E. 178–185; 1 Duncan 227–240.
[25] WO 71/69/167.
[26] WO 71/69/221.
[27] WO 71/69/223.
[28] Williams *Whig Sup.* 372; Whitworth 371.

from Madras.[29] Only a single civilian was tried there by court-martial, one Francisco Hinerequez De Villacourta, charged with "High Treason, by carrying on a Traiterous Correspondence with the Enemies of His Britannic Majesty, in violation of his Oath of Allegiance Solemnly Sworn to his said Majesty"; he was acquitted.[30]

There were more trials of non-military persons by court-martial in Havana, half a world away, a place likewise taken from the Spaniards in 1762.[31] The first of these was a surgeon on a transport, accused by a naval officer of marauding in conjunction with a soldier. The surgeon was convicted under the camp follower article and sentenced to three hundred lashes, the soldier was found to be an idiot, in consequence of which the court declined passing sentence on him.[32] A few months later a Spaniard was tried on suspicion of murder; fortunately for him, if unfortunately for the history of military law, he escaped from the provost guard in the course of the trial.[33] The last trial in 1762 dealt with a soldier's wife, charged with robbery and acquitted.[34]

Early in 1763, the servant to a local merchant, the latter apparently English, was haled before a court-martial for committing rape upon a seven-year-old girl and then infecting her. He was tried under the "no Form of Civil Judicature" Article of War, Article 2 of Section XX, "but from the 18th Statute of Queen Elizabeth [the court] find the Prisoner not guilty of the Rape." (Section 4 of 18 Eliz. I c. 7 declared carnal knowledge of "any Woman Childe under the Age of Tenne" to be felony, a provision thereafter interpreted to mean that such an act did not constitute rape.) [35] For the other offense, however, he was sentenced to receive one thousand lashes "and to pay all charges attending [her] Cure, and afterwards to be drummed out of the Garrison with his Crime on his Breast." [36]

In April 1763, two Spaniards were separately tried on charges of inducing British soldiers to desert. One was acquitted; [37] the second,

[29] 2 Fortescue 544–545; 8 Gipson B.E. 275–282; Whitworth 363.
[30] WO 71/74/8.
[31] 2 Fortescue 541–544; 8 Gipson B.E. 260–268; Mante 397–465; Whitworth 364–367.
[32] WO 71/71/271.
[33] WO 71/72/24.
[34] WO 71/72/32.
[35] 4 Bl. Comm. *212; 1 Radzinowicz 631–632.
[36] WO 71/73/101.
[37] WO 71/73/149.

charged also with disobeying the British Governor's proclamation, was convicted of both accusations and then sentenced to death, the severity of the sentence probably stemming from the fact that he had sought to persuade the deserters to enter the Spanish service.[38] A third inhabitant, a local Captain of Militia with the imposing name of Don Pablo Peres Mancha Justiniani, accused of harboring deserters, was honorably acquitted.[39]

One trial remained before Cuba was evacuated, that of a Spaniard charged under Article 2 of Section XX with the murder of two English merchants. Upon conviction, the court-martial adjudged "that he be hanged by the Neck untill he be dead, and then to have his Head sever'd from his Body and fixed up on the most public place, there to remain, and his Body to be thrown into the Sea." [40] As long as the Union Jack waved over the Pearl of the Antilles, there would be no open season on British merchants.

Yet, curiously enough, the terms of the capitulation surrendering "the Havanna" specifically provided that all of the inhabitants there "shall preserve and keep the rights and privileges which they have hitherto enjoyed, and they shall be governed in his Britannic Majesty's name, under the same laws and administration of justice, and under such conditions as they have done hitherto in the dominion of Spain, in every particular, appointing their justices and officers of justice, agreeable to their usual custom." [41] The eyewitness historian of the siege and occupation of Havana, who noted that the commander of the British Army forces put the articles of capitulation in force,[42] does not mention the trials of inhabitants by court-martial that have been noted, all of which were duly recorded in the War Office books.

At the Peace of Paris of 10 February 1763, Cuba and the Philippines were returned to Spain, but, in exchange, Britain obtained East and West Florida, under provisions permitting adherents of the Spanish cause to leave within eighteen months thereafter.[43]

St. Augustine in East Florida was accordingly occupied in July 1763 by a small British force under command of a Major Ogilvie, who served as virtual governor until the civil government es-

[38] WO 71/73/130.
[39] WO 71/73/154.
[40] WO 71/73/183.
[41] Art. XII, Mante at 453, dated 12 Aug. 1762.
[42] Mante 463. The author was Assistant Engineer during the two months' siege.
[43] By Art. XX of the Treaty, 10 Eng. Hist. Doc. 936, 941.

tablished by the Proclamation of 1763 [44] could be constituted; Governor Grant landed in August 1764, and under him the civil government commenced functioning on 31 October.[45] No record of military trials of inhabitants in the fifteen-month interval of military rule has been found.

That portion of the new domain west of the Apalachicola and Chattahoochee rivers was organized into the separate Province of West Florida, a region that was under a military government from 8 August 1763 when the troops landed, until 21 October 1764 when the first civil Governor arrived.[46] During that period, on 12 January 1764, one John Lucas, a baker and inhabitant of Pensacola, was tried by court-martial for buying and receiving stolen provisions and assisting a soldier to desert. He was sentenced to receive one thousand lashes, "and afterwards to be Drumm'd out of the Garrison and it's Districts, never to return." [47]

Included in the new British Province of West Florida was the area around Mobile known as British Louisiana; there also a military government functioned in fact. Here the principal controversy concerned the contention of the first civil Governor, Sir G. Johnstone, that he had the right to review the civil cases that had been tried in the interval of military government by the military commandant, Major Farmer, assisted by the DJA of the post at Mobile.[48]

CANADA

Following the battle on the Plains of Abraham where both Wolfe and Montcalm fell, Quebec was surrendered on 18 September 1759. Thereafter the British under General James Murray

---

[44] 9 Eng. Hist. Doc. 639.

[45] C. L. Mowat, *East Florida as a British Province, 1763–1784* (Berkeley and Los Angeles, 1943) 7–14; ch. VIII, "East Florida as a British Province, 1763–1765," in 9 Gipson B.E. 177–199.

[46] Cecil Johnson, *British West Florida, 1763–1783* (New Haven, 1943) 8–23; ch. III, "The Interval of Military Government," in C. N. Howard, *The British Development of West Florida, 1763–1769* (Berkeley and Los Angeles, 1947); ch. IX, "West Florida as a British Province," in 9 Gipson B.E. 200–231; W. H. Siebert, *How the Spanish Evacuated Pensacola in 1763*, 11 Fla. Hist. Q. 48.

[47] WO 71/74/141, a case noted by neither Johnson nor Howard.

[48] C. N. Howard, *The Military Occupation of British West Florida 1763*, 17 Fla. Hist. Q. 181, 187–196; and see ch. IV, "The Quarrels of the First Governor with the Military Officers," in Howard's work cited in n. 46, *supra*.

Documents relating to the civil-military struggle in West Florida appear in Gage *Corr. passim*, and in 1 D. Rowland, ed., *Mississippi Provincial Archives 1763–1766* (Nashville, 1911); the matter is also discussed at Shy 150–158.

spent a difficult winter in the city, fought and nearly lost a second battle, and were saved only by the timely appearance of their fleet. But in 1760, three columns directed by General Jeffery Amherst successfully converged on Canada, with the consequence that on 8 September Vaudreuil surrendered not only Montreal but also all of Canada and of New France down to but not including New Orleans.[49] Title to this vast new domain did not pass until the Treaty of Paris was signed on 10 February 1763.[50] During that lengthy interval, and indeed until the expiration of the eighteen months within which adherents of the French cause were by the terms of the treaty permitted to leave the country, Canada was occupied territory under military rule; the period between 1759 and 1764 is accordingly known in Canadian history as the *Règne Militaire*.[51]

During the first winter, while the British maintained their precarious foothold in Quebec, General Murray "established a civil jurisdiction for the inhabitants, and appointed Colonel Young chief judge";[52] similarly, in January 1760 he appointed one Jacques Allier "civil and criminal judge to execute justice in the parishes of Berthier and beyond."[53] The precise distribution of jurisdiction over inhabitants charged with offenses, between these judges and general or garrison courts-martial of the British Army, does not clearly appear. Contemporary journals disclose several instances of inhabitants, and also of women presumably belonging to the Army—there were many of these, and numerous orders relating to them[54]—whipped through the town.[55] General Murray's own journal records at least three hangings without trial, one of a soldier

---

[49] 2 Fortescue 366 *et seq.*; ch. VII, "The Capitulation of Canada, 1759–1760," in Stanley. The Articles of Capitulation signed at Quebec on 18 Sept. 1759 appear at Shortt and Doughty 1–7, and at 2 Knox 126–132.

The Montreal Articles of Capitulation, 8 Sept. 1760, are at Shortt and Doughty 7–36, and at 2 Knox 566–589. For the number of women and children included in that surrender of the French forces, see J. C. Webster, ed., *The Journal of Jeffery Amherst* (Toronto and Chicago, 1931) 249–250.

[50] Shortt and Doughty 113 *et seq.*; 10 Eng. Hist. Doc. 936–942.

[51] Doughty, App. B, "Ordinances of the Règne Militaire"; Viger 87–139, "Législation du Gouvernement de Montréal durant le Règne Militaire"; *id.* 145–296, "Législation du Gouvernement des Trois Rivières durant le Règne Militaire."

[52] Doughty, App. B, p. 3, ¶4 (Proclamation of Gov. Murray, 16 Nov. 1759); Murray Journal 8, entry for 12 Nov. 1759; Mahon 204, 277; Burt 20–21.

[53] Murray Journal 18; Shortt and Doughty 36–37, commission dated 16 Jan. 1760; Mahon 277.

[54] 2 Knox 337–338 (recording, Feb. 1760 in Quebec, 569 women accompanying 9 regiments, the artillery, and the rangers); 2 *id.* 271, 293, 302, 337, 348, 365, 400, 403, 408, 410, 453, 464, 530, 531 n.

[55] 2 Knox 280, 289, 306.

in terrorem.[56] (Was this why his engineer called him "a mad-man"?) [57] One record of the trial of a soldier's wife by general court-martial toward the end of this period has been found; she was sentenced to two hundred lashes and banishment.[58] It is probably accurate to conclude that British rule in Quebec during the winter of 1759–1760 operated on an essentially *ad hoc* basis.[59]

Certainly it is plain that, immediately after the final surrender in 1760, General Amherst made other arrangements. He constituted three military governments, at Quebec under General Murray, at Montreal under General Gage, and at Trois Rivières under Colonel Burton (who had previously been General Murray's Lieutenant-Governor at Quebec), stating specifically that "the Whole Country Should be on the same footing, and under One and the Same Regulations." [60] So far as a judicial system was concerned, all criminal cases would be tried by courts-martial; all civil cases were to be heard by the captains of the Canadian militia in the several parishes, with a right of appeal, first to the British officer locally in command, and then to the cognizant governor. This basic arrangement is of course tolerably familiar.[61] But in view of the assertions of one

---

[56] (*a*) Frenchman "for having enticed some of our soldiers to desert" (Murray Journal 10 [entry for 16 Nov. 1759]; 2 Knox 277 [18 Nov. 1759]); (*b*) drunken soldiers breaking into houses, "ordered one to be hung for an example to the rest" (Murray Journal 33–34 [entry for 30 Apr. 1760]; 2 Knox 401 ["one man was hanged this evening *in terrorem,* without any trial"]); (*c*) 2 Knox 453–454 (30 May 1760; "a native of the parish of St. Michel was hanged yesterday, in sight of his own hamlet, for having exerted his utmost endeavours to spirit up his countrymen to revolt, and drawing several of his own company, he being a Captain of the militia, to join the late French army.") The last entry is not noted in the continuation of General Murray's Journal, 3 Knox 307.

[57] Montrésor 116. The younger Montrésor, then a Lieutenant, served as Gen. Murray's Engineer at Quebec.

[58] WO 71/46/309–314 (20 Aug. 1760).

[59] Ch. II, "The First Winter of the British in Canada," in Burt; ch. IX, "Quebec—the First Winter," in Mahon.

[60] Amherst to Murray, 23 Sept. 1760, WO 34/3/25. This and later references in the present chapter to the Amherst Papers, WO 34, are to volume and folio rather than to volume and page. For Burton as Lieutenant-Governor at Quebec during the winter of 1759–1760, see 2 Knox 241 and Burt 13–14.

[61] Proclamation of Gen. Amherst, 22 Sept. 1760, Shortt and Doughty 38–41, also Doughty, App. B., pp. 86–87; Proclamation of Gen. Gage, 26 Oct. 1760, Doughty, App. B, pp. 32–33; Ordinance of Gen. Murray establishing courts, 31 Oct. 1760, Shortt and Doughty 42–46, also Doughty App. B, pp. 14–16; Ordinance regarding appeals, 19 Mar. 1761, Doughty, App. B, pp. 42–43; Regulation for the administration of justice, 13 Oct. 1761, Doughty, App. B, pp. 48–50; Proclamation of the establishment of courts, 5 June 1762, Doughty, App. B., pp. 128–131; Suspension of Justice [because of the harvest], Aug. 1762, Doughty, App. B., p. 134. For secondary references, see Alden *Gage* 55, 57; ch. III, "The Canadians under Military Rule," in Burt; ch. VII, "Canada becomes a British Province," in 9 Gipson

frequently quoted Canadian historian that the expression *Règne Militaire* "is in all respects a misnomer" [62] and that "criminal cases were submitted to a court of military officers" [63] (as though "court-martial" were a dirty word); in view of the conclusion of a distinguished Canadian constitutional commentator that Governor Murray "was not bound by Amherst's instructions to Burton and Gage" and that throughout the *Règne Militaire* there was "in Quebec a type of military rule quite different from that in Three Rivers and Montreal"; [64] and, pre-eminently, in view of the later ruling of the Deputy Judge Advocate General in England that none of the trials of inhabitants by court-martial during the *Règne Militaire* was warranted in law, [65] it seems appropriate to turn to and quote from the basic documents.

Here is what General Amherst wrote General Murray on 23 September 1760:

> The following is the Rule I have laid down. That with respect to Thefts & Murder, it is absolutely Necessary the Military Law should take place: but with regard to Differences between the Inhabitants, I would have them Settled among themselves, agreeable to their own Laws and Customs: for which purpose You will Authorize the Several Captains of Militia, within Your Government, to preside over the Different Parishes & Districts to Which they belong, and to terminate all Such Differences. And When it Shall so happen that any of these Captains cannot Settle the same; then the Parties Must Apply, to the Officer Commanding His Majesty's Troops within the said District, to Whom You will give Such limitted power as You Judge proper for his Examining, and pronouncing thereon, According to the best of his Judgment; but if the Affair should prove so Intricate as to Make him Decline the Decision, the Same is then to be brought before You, that either thro' Yourself, or with the Advice of Councill (consisting of as many Field Officers as You shall think

B.E.; ch. XI, "An Empire for the Crown," in J. C. Long, *Lord Jeffery Amherst: A Soldier of the King* (New York, 1933); ch. XIII, "The Military Government of Quebec, 1761–62," in Mahon; Riddell *Br. Cts.*; Stanley 98–99. Chapter IV, "The 'Régime Militaire,'" in Kennedy, must be used with caution, for reasons noted immediately below; while J. M. LeMoine, *Quebec, Past and Present* (Quebec, 1876) 187, reflects primarily the tradition of French-Canadian discontent.

[62] 4 Kingsford 440.

[63] 4 Kingsford 442. But compare n. 98, *infra*. Curiously enough, Kingsford began life as a British soldier. DNB Supp.

[64] Kennedy 26–27.

[65] *Infra*, pp. 55–62.

proper, Which You will Assemble for that purpose, as often as You shall see Occasion) You may finally determine there-upon.[66]

Substantially verbatim instructions went to General Gage and Colonel Burton,[67] while Mr. Secretary Pitt was fully advised, receiving copies of the instructions sent all three governors, as well as a copy of General Murray's new appointment as Governor over the district of Quebec, the earlier one having covered only the city and its fortifications.[68]

In fact, Pitt gave up the seals the day after Amherst wrote, and it was not until more than a year later that the Earl of Egremont, Pitt's successor, conveyed to General Amherst the royal approval of his 1760 arrangements:

> As to the Plan which You have laid down to the Gov⁷ˢ of Trois Rivieres, Montreal, & Quebec, for the Government of His Majesty's Conquests, You will have the Satisfaction of Seeing, that What I have now in Command from His Majesty, on that Head, Implies his Gracious Approbation of the prudent Arrangement, which You have made for that purpose.[69]

General Amherst immediately sent copies of that communication to the three military governors.[70]

Once the records of trial are looked to, and most historians of Canada seem never to have examined them,[71] it is clear, not only

---

[66] Amherst to Murray, 23 Sept. 1760, WO 34/3/25, a letter noted at Mahon 277, 278.

[67] Amherst to Gage, 21 Sept. 1760, WO 34/7/1; Amherst to Burton, 16 Sept. 1760, WO 34/7/206; same to same, 23 Sept. 1760, WO 34/7/217.

[68] Amherst to Pitt, SS, 4 Oct. 1760, PRO, CO 5/59/Pt. I, f. 125 (printed in part at 2 Kimball 335). The instructions to the three governors are inclosures 30–33 to this letter, the new commission to Gen. Murray is inclosure 34. CO 5/59/Pt. II, ff. 30–41.

See also Mahon 285–286, who quotes from Gen. Murray's Commission as Military Governor of the Town of Quebec, 27 Oct. 1759, signed by Pitt: "And you are to observe and follow all such orders and directions from time to time as you shall receive from Us according to the rules of war."

[69] Earl of Egremont, SS, to Gen. Amherst, 12 Dec. 1761; I have quoted from the copy in the Haldimand Papers, BM Add. MS. 21697, f. 9, cited at Burt 30 and at 9 Gipson B.E. 157–158.

[70] Amherst to Murray, 9 Feb. 1762, WO 34/3/132; Amherst to Gage, same date, WO 34/7/81; Amherst to Burton, same date, WO 34/7/263.

[71] Burt, characterized at 9 Gipson B.E. 157, as the author of the "standard account of the history of Canada, 1760–1791," does not cite a single War Office court-martial record. Viger (as to whom see *infra*, pp. 42, 46–48) is the only historian of Canada who seems ever to have examined any court-martial records. Pargellis, whose accounts stop with the recall of Lord Loudoun and the dismissal

that the captains of militia exercised no criminal jurisdiction what-soever,[72] but also that to speak of "military government," a term now so generally familiar after two World Wars, is not to indulge in retrospective reading of history, but is simply to repeat an expression that was used contemporaneously. Here is what ap-peared in the order book of General Gage, commanding at Mont-real, under date of 7 October 1760: "As this country is at present under a military government, courts-martial are to take cognisance of all persons and crimes brought before them." [73]

Consequently British courts-martial in Canada in 1760–1764 tried not only followers of the army and soldiers' wives charged with criminal offenses [74] but also inhabitants who had no military connection whatever. That is to say, such courts-martial exercised, not a mere jurisdiction over accompanying civilians and depend-ents, but what today would be considered a full-blown military government jurisdiction over all inhabitants of occupied territory held by right of military conquest.

Vaudreuil's surrender in 1760, as has been said, comprised a vast wilderness, including the post at Detroit; the latter did not become a part of the Province of Quebec until 1774.[75] (Perhaps it should be noted here that Detroit became American soil *de jure* after the second Peace of Paris in 1783, and, ultimately, following Jay's

of the Duke of Cumberland, did not reach the period of the *Règne Militaire;* he noted, however, that court-martial records "reconstitute the intimate details of army life more satisfactorily than any other kind of document." Pargellis *Loudoun* 370. Shy similarly did not deal with Canada, and moreover appears not to have examined the courts-martial recorded in WO 71/37–62, Home and Foreign Stations. Shy 344 n. 72, 363 n. 140; cf. Bibliography, *infra*, p. 315, "Court-martial books".

[72] ". . . les délits, tant petits que grands, d'une nature criminelle, se portait au conseil de guerre, autrement dit *Cour Martiale.* . . . Il ne paraît pas que les chambres des milices aient exercé aucune jurisdiction criminelle." Viger 33–34, 40.

[73] Hervey 132. Captain Hervey of the 44th Foot, appointed Major of Brigade on 5 May 1759 (1 Knox 459), kept an order book for General Gage's brigade from 1 June 1760 through 17 May 1763. Here again, Pargellis seems to be the only historian aware of the existence of Hervey's order book. Pargellis *Loudoun* 309 n.

[74] WO 71/49/207 (soldier's wife; receiving stolen goods; acquitted); WO 71/68/125 (soldier's wife; theft; acquitted); WO 71/71/97 (4 soldiers, a follower of the army, and 5 women in the 60th Regt.; buying stolen goods; acquitted); and case cited in n. 58, *supra*.

[75] 7 Gipson B.E. 466; Riddell *Mich.* 10–13. Taking possession of this vast new wilderness presented difficult problems. See, e.g., 2 Kimball 336–337, 404; N. V. Russell, *The British Regime in Michigan and the Old Northwest, 1760–1796* (Northfield, Minn., 1939) 1–30; ch. I, "The Interregnum, 1760–1763," in L. P. Kellogg, *The British Regime in Wisconsin and the Northwest* (Madison, Wis., 1935); *The British Regime in Wisconsin*, 18 Wis. Hist. Soc. Coll. 223; Carter *Illinois passim;* Shy 419–421.

Treaty and General "Mad Anthony" Wayne's victory over the Indians at Fallen Timbers, American soil *de facto* in 1796.)

The point relevant in the present connection is that, in consequence of a particularly barbarous murder of a Detroit trader committed by his two "Panis" (i.e., Pawnee) slaves in the summer of 1762,[76] General Amherst authorized and required the commandant there, Major Gladwin,

> to Collect as many of the Officers belonging to His Majesty's Troops as you conveniently can, who are Hereby Empowered to Hear & Examine, by Oath, or Otherwise, all such Evidences as can be found, for or against the Two Panis Slaves, Confined for the Murder aforesaid, or any other Person, or Persons, whether Indian, or White, that are anyway Suspected of having been concerned in that Inhuman Act: And according to the Opinion given by a Majority of the Court, after hearing the Information or Evidence, given for & against the Prisoners, You will give immediate Directions, for putting the Sentence or Sentences, into Execution, Even if they should Extend to Death, provided You think proper to approve of the Same; And You are further Required to See that the said Sentence, or Sentences, are Executed in the most Exemplary & publick manner, that thereby Others may be Deterred from Committing such Cruelties for the Future.[77]

By the time the court was convened, the male Pawnee prisoner had escaped, but the Pawnee woman was duly sentenced to be hanged, a judgment that Major Gladwin "put in Execution in the most Publick Manner." [78] General Amherst, being notified, wrote to say that "I am only Sorry the Chief Perpetrator did not meet with the same Punishment, for then the Example would have been Compleat." [79]

The tribunal concerned resembled a court of inquiry far more closely than a court-martial,[80] and assuredly the proceeding that it

---

[76] 3 Johnson 887; *Bouquet Papers*, 19 MPHC 27, 160–161.

[77] Warrant from General Amherst to Major Gladwin, 15 Sept. 1762, in *The Gladwin Manuscripts*, 27 MPHC 674–675. General Amherst wrote (3 Johnson 896), "I most Sincerely Wish that this may be the last occasion I may ever have for ordering a Tryal for such Offenders; but I am firmly Determined, while I have the Honor to Command, to make Examples of Every One, whether Indian or White, that are Guilty of that Horrid Crime of Murder, in Districts where the Civil Law cannot take place."

[78] Gladwin to Amherst, 20 Apr. 1763, 4 Johnson 95–96.

[79] Amherst to Sir W. Johnson, 29 May 1763, 4 Johnson 98, 100.

[80] Compare the warrant issued in Nov. 1757 for a court of inquiry set forth at Adye (8th ed. 1810) 63–65 and at Mil. L. Eng. 298–300.

conducted was no trial by general court-martial; accordingly, this case is not entered in the War Office court-martial books.[81] But, certainly under modern concepts, military government jurisdiction can be exercised by any form of tribunal thereunto authorized by the commander.[82]

Some of the offenses for which inhabitants were tried by court-martial in Canada were not only ordinary common law felonies, but were crimes by the standards of any civilized community; e.g., murder,[83] theft,[84] rape,[85] receiving stolen goods,[86] robbery,[87] extortion,[88] assault,[89] perjury,[90] subornation of perjury,[91] "knowing of a murder" (i.e., either misprision of felony or being

---

[81] It is noted in, and the citations are taken from, Riddell *Mich.* 29–31, 397. In view of the tenor of Gen. Amherst's warrant, however, it is submitted that the author erred in characterizing this event as a trial by court-martial.

Later in the *Règne Militaire*, in Jan. 1764, two inhabitants of Detroit, accused of carrying messages to and joining in arms with the Indians during Pontiac's war, were specifically ordered to be tried by court-martial. Gage to the Earl of Halifax, SS, 7 Jan. 1764, 1 Gage *Corr.* 9.

[82] F..g., *Madsen* v. *Kinsella*, 343 U.S. 341, sustaining military government jurisdiction exercised by courts of the occupying power that were manned by civilians and that derived their authority from a civilian High Commissioner.

[83] WO 71/68/131 (former French soldier; charged also with robbery; death); WO 71/68/203 (inhabitant; acquitted); WO 71/73/240 (2 women; suspicion of murder; acquitted).

[84] WO 71/68/130 (female slave; charged also with running away; 30 lashes); WO 71/69/19 (2 inhabitants; acquitted); WO 71/73/284, 287 (2 separate acquittals).

[85] WO 71/68/136 (inhabitant; charged also with robbery and attempted murder; acquitted).

[86] WO 71/49/207 (soldier's wife; acquitted); WO 71/68/127 (2 women, one a Negro slave; both acquitted); WO 71/70/217 (public house keeper; sentenced to banishment); WO 71/71/178 (3 inhabitants; purchasing military supplies; 8 days' confinement in provost marshal's custody).

[87] WO 71/69/21 (inhabitant of New Jersey; death, but pardoned); WO 71/69/23 (inhabitant; suspicion of robbery; acquitted because no evidence presented); WO 71/70/228 (Canadian servant; 1,000 lashes); WO 71/70/276 (former soldier; suspicion of robbery; acquitted); WO 71/73/273 (female inhabitant; acquitted); WO 71/73/281 (inhabitant; 500 lashes and restitution; property to be forfeited to motherless children of soldier and former soldier; corporal punishment remitted by convening authority).

[88] WO 71/70/206 (extorting money and goods from the inhabitants "under pretence of being employed in H.M.'s Service"; 1,000 lashes and banishment).

[89] WO 71/49/223 (5 inhabitants; abusing and assaulting an officer; held to be an attack upon discipline and military government; all convicted and adjudged to ask pardon; 3 ordered to pay £100 New York currency each, to be disposed of for charitable uses; mitigated to £30 each, to be paid to the Town Major); WO 71/71/179 (inhabitant; assault on a serjeant of militia; acquitted).

[90] WO 71/49/196 (see *infra*, p. 54).

[91] WO 71/73/277 (woman; 200 lashes and afterwards to be branded; 100 lashes remitted "and to receive the rest by the hands of the executioner").

an accessory after the fact),[92] and abusing other inhabitants.[93] A charge of treason by an Englishman in arms against his own countrymen could not be considered unusual as a matter of law,[94] and, in a country that recognized human slavery, a slave running away necessarily committed a criminal offense.[95]

The punishments inflicted were consistent with contemporary military standards, however severe they may appear two centuries later. Thus it was said of a sentence of one thousand lashes imposed upon conviction of robbery, "The youth of the Offender being the sole Cause of the Court's inflicting so mild a Punishment on so heinous a Crime." [96] An older person, found guilty of extortion, was directed by the convening authority to receive a like punishment "on public Parade at three several Times, till the Number of 1000 Lashes shall be compleated. The Punishment to be Given by the Hands of the public Executioner, and the Provost Marshal to attend." [97]

But the case that doubtless brought home to the inhabitants of occupied New France better than any other a full realization that the common law of England was indeed the perfection of reason was that of "St. John otherwise called St. Paul, late a Soldier in the French Regiment of LaSarre," who was accused of robbery, murder, and setting fire to the house of an inhabitant of the Parish of St. François. The sentence of the court-martial, which General Gage duly approved for execution on 18 March 1761, was "to be hanged by the Neck, near the City of Montreal Until his Body be dead. After which his Body to be Carried from the place of Execution, to the most Convenient Place near the place where this Horrid Crime was Committed, and there to be Hung in Irons on a Jibbet, in the same manner as practiced in England, Until his Bones shall drop asunder, as a Terror to all evil minded People." [98]

It should be noted here that hanging in chains and gibbeting were common practices in England at this time, nor were they

---

[92] This is the case noted below, pp. 53–54. For varying views of the precise nature of this imprecisely alleged offense see Adye (1st ed. 1769) 56–58, and Riddell *Br. Cts.* 578.

[93] WO 71/74/213 (former French soldier and former British soldier; both acquitted).

[94] WO 71/68/147 (death).

[95] WO 71/68/130 (and stealing; 30 lashes).

[96] WO 71/70/229.

[97] WO 71/70/207.

[98] WO 71/68/131, 136, a punishment noted at 4 Kingsford 445.

abolished until 1834.[99] Court-martial sentences passed on soldiers in the next conflict, the War of American Independence, occasionally specified both, and, in one instance, alternative delivery of the bodies for dissection, the latter in conformity with the English law from 1752 to 1828.[100]

General Gage's brigade order book, from soon after the surrender of Montreal until May 1763,[101] announces the results of trials of inhabitants by garrison courts-martial for lesser offenses, the most usual one being the sale of liquor without a license or to soldiers contrary to orders; this accounts for nearly half of the cases recorded. Other offenses run the gamut of police court matters—petty fraud, use of false weights, keeping a disorderly house, minor thefts and assaults, insulting a sentry, insulting an officer. The punishments are correspondingly lighter—small fines, short terms of imprisonment, and, for a number of camp followers, male and female, drumming out of the garrison without more. Liquor sold without license and beef sold with false weights were severally confiscated. A Canadian found guilty of cutting another with a sword was sentenced "to pay the surgeon's bill and 80 livres to [the victim] for loss of time and the pain he has occasioned him, and not to wear a sword any more under the English Government." The most savage sentence of the lot was passed on a Canadian for "being concerned in taking down his Majesty's declaration of war against Spain and treating the same with the highest insolence and indignity"; for this the prisoner was flogged through the town at the cart's tail by the executioner, to the tune of one hundred lashes at each of four places. But about one-third of the prisoners tried were

---

[99] The grisly details of both are fully documented in 1 Radzinowicz 213–220. For those whose interests lie in that direction, it may be noted that an actual gibbet can be seen in the White Tower at the Tower of London.

[100] Two soldiers sentenced to be hanged and gibbeted, 1 Kemble 624–625 (1 June 1778); same sentence, Clinton OB, 23 Oct. 1779; two soldiers sentenced to death, "and their Bodies afterwards, to be Hanged in Chains, or delivered to the Surgeons for Dissection, as his Excellency the Commander in Chief shall please to direct," WO 71/93/195 (18 Feb. 1781). For dissection of a murderer's body, see 1 Radzinowicz 206–209.

[101] Hervey 140–182. In view of the narrow compass of these orders, it has seemed unnecessary to make more detailed references to the several trials involved, particularly since the editor (p. 65) abbreviated the entries relating to courts-martial.

Viger 30–33 prints numerous cases from a similar order book that records many of the same trials, but (p. 65) desists from reciting more because of the severity of the sentences.

acquitted, and on one occasion the garrison court-martial was directed to sit "to examine into the debts of the debtors now in prison."

Insofar as ordinary civil offenses were concerned, the high percentage of acquittals of French inhabitants by general and garrison courts-martial of the British conqueror appears to reflect a most conscientious consideration on the part of the officers who deliberated on the cases. The real difficulties appeared when the boundaries of ordinary civil offenses were passed. For example, "Mr. Thomas Gamble, late belonging to the 44th Regiment"—a lieutenant, he had been dismissed the service a few months earlier for having called out (i.e., challenged) Major John Beckwith, his commanding officer[102]—was charged with thereafter insulting this same Major Beckwith "by demanding satisfaction of him, in a most Insolent manner, reproaching him with being a Villain, and abusing him in a most Scandalous manner." A finding of guilty resulted in the court's adjudging "said Mr. Gamble publickly to ask Major Beckwith's Pardon, before any number of Officers, whom H.E. the Governour shall appoint." General Gage approved this sentence, ordering "the same to be put in Execution at Longueil in the presence of as many Officers of the 44th Regiment, as Major Beckwith can conveniently Assemble."[103]

Similarly, two Montreal merchants, William Grant and Edward Chinn—who obviously were not Frenchmen—were tried for abusing, assaulting, and otherwise mistreating Ensign Nott of the 60th Foot. Both were sentenced to apologize, and to pay sums of money for the distressed poor. General Gage reduced the fines but directed each of the two to apologize "in the presence of one Field Officer, 2 Captains, and 4 Subalterns at least of the Garrison."[104] Another non-Frenchman, Forrest Oakes, also tried and convicted of insulting Ensign Nott—the latter apparently a very touchy young man—was sentenced publicly to ask pardon, and then to be confined for fourteen days. General Gage remitted the apology, the insults having been reciprocal, and directed Oakes's release

[102] Hervey 143; PRO, WO 71/46/152.

[103] WO 71/68/196. Here is the apology adjudged to be asked (*id.* at 201): "Major Beckwith, I am very Sorry, that in my Passion I expressed myself to you, in insulting Terms, and beg your Pardon for the same, before these Gentlemen Present."

[104] WO 71/70/181–194. Viger, 33, records the apology as follows: "Enseigne Nott, je suis très-fâché de m'être rendu coupable d'assault à votre égard, et je vous en demande très-humblement pardon."

after twenty-five hours upon finding security for future good behavior.[105]

So far, so bad; but more confusion was in store a few months
later. John Raab and David King, two indentured servants to Lieutenant-Colonel Gabriel Christie, were tried by court-martial for,
among other things, "having absented themselves from his Service
without Leave . . . and also giving out, they were discharged from
said Colonel's Service." The court found "a Neglect, of perform-
ing, and fulfilling the Articles of Indenture" on both sides. It
therefore found the prisoners not guilty of any punishable crime,
and adjudged that they "stand acquitted from the Service of said
Colonel Christie, as tho' no such Indentures had been made, or
passed between them." But General Gage upheld the indentures,
and ordered that the two servants "shall be delivered up to their
Master Lt. Col. Christie, to serve out their Time of Service, as
Stipulated by said Indentures." [106] Christie, Deputy Quarter Master
General of the command,[107] who is shown from other sources to
have been a most difficult individual,[108] appears to have been
equally difficult as a master. Two other indentured servants of his
had also run away,[109] while this was the second time that Raab and
King had done so, their first escape having been punished by a
garrison court-martial with three hundred lashes each, of which
half were remitted.[110]

During the last year of the military government of Canada, other
essentially civil causes engaged the attention of British general
courts-martial. Thus, in July 1763, there was considered the case of

---

[105] WO 71/70/195–205.

[106] WO 71/71/158–160.

[107] Doughty, App. B, p. 36. Christie first appears as Acting ADQMG at Albany
in Lord Loudoun's time. Pargellis *Loudoun* 291.

[108] See Christie to Gage, 10 Oct. 1763; same to same, 10 Oct. 1764; same to same,
18 Sept. 1765; same to same, 18 Mar. 1766; all in Gage Papers (American Series),
WLCL. And see Sir J. Amherst to Marquis of Granby, 27 Aug. 1769 (dispute
between Maj.-Gen. Prevost and Lt.-Col. G. Christie), 2 HMC Rutland 311.
In the following decade, Generals Howe and Carleton successively—and successfully—resisted Lord George Germain's urging that they appoint Christie to be
Quarter Master General. Valentine 142, 152–153, 184, 330.

[109] Viger 208–209; Doughty, App. B, p. 115 (quoting a notice by Col. Burton,
Governor at Trois Rivières, 29 Nov. 1761, regarding Thomas Lloyd and Jean
Mora).

[110] Viger 32–33; Hervey 158 (trial by garrison court-martial, 31 Jan. 1762); Viger
231; Doughty, App. B, p. 126 (notice by Col. Haldimand [temporary successor to
Burton as Governor at Trois Rivières], 23 May 1762, that Raab and King have run
off again). Their trial by general court-martial, noted in the text, then followed on
2 Aug. 1762.

a child that had been run over and severely injured. The court adjudged that the two persons responsible should pay the surgeon all his fees, past and present; that they "be further answerable upon their Bail, in case the Child dies, by means of the above hurts it has received"; and that the child's father be paid "thirty Dollars." [111] (Was this *de facto* military recognition of the action of trespass *per quod servitium amisit?*)

In December 1763, two inhabitants—of English nationality to judge from their names, Todd and Knaggs—were among a group of five who had been convicted by court-martial of abusing and assaulting an officer, at a trial where they were allowed counsel in their defense.[112] A week thereafter they were charged with forcing their way into the apartment of a Mme. LaCote, in consequence of which she jumped out of a window and was injured. To press her charges, the injured lady was permitted the services of M. Panet, Greffier of the City of Montreal. Knaggs was acquitted, but Todd was sentenced to pay £40 New York Currency to Mme. LaCote for her surgeon and other extraordinary expenses, an additional £60 as the Governor might direct, and to find security for keeping the peace in the ensuing three months. The £60 fine was reduced to £40 by Colonel Burton, General Gage's successor as Governor at Montreal, who confirmed the sentence in all other respects.[113]

A little later, the same general court-martial heard a complaint

---

[111] WO 71/73/263.

[112] WO 71/49/223 (counsel allowed at 239). In 1769 and in 1779, Adye wrote that the judge advocate "is generally expected to assist the prisoner in his defence," footnoting the word "generally" with the comment that "I say generally for there have been instances of a prisoner being admitted to plead by his own Council." Adye (1st ed. 1769) 37; (3d ed. 1779) 46.

But by 1810 Adye's text had been revised to say (8th ed. 1810, p. 103) that "counsel, or at least *amici curiae*, have been allowed to prisoners at courts martial, in all cases." Cf. Sullivan 40–41.

[113] WO 71/49/241. Burton was not promoted to brigadier-general until the fall of 1764. 1 Gage *Corr.* 44; 2 *id.* 256.

With respect to the allowance of counsel to the prosecutrix, the following letter from a somewhat later period may be illuminating (Gould, JAG, to Joseph Collins, Esq., DJA at Minorca, 8 Aug. 1777, WO 81/13/154, 155–156):

"In trials for Military Crimes it has certainly not been usual, nor does it seem at all essential to Justice, to admit the open interference of any Council or Attorney; but when by reason of the want of an established Civil Judicature Courts Martial exercise the power of determining upon other Offences, and that upon the plaint of persons not military (more specially as in the present instance where a Woman prosecuted) it may be reasonable, for the sake of bringing the matter more fully before the Court, to give rather more latitude; provided always, that the persons permitted to afford that assistance conduct themselves with decency."

brought against Edward Chinn—doubtless the identical individual who nearly two years earlier had insulted that thin-skinned young warrior Ensign Nott [114]—alleging that Chinn had withheld wages from canoe men. There was much testimony concerning the custom of Canada in like cases, after which the court concluded that

> as the present case is an affair of Commerce, that may be attended with the utmost bad Consequences, to alter the Established Rules, the Court Martial is of opinion the same should be continued and that the defendant has a right in Equity and usage to retain the Wages for the Navigation of the Canoes, untill such times as he receives Satisfaction for his proved Losses from such Navigations.

Governor Burton approved this sentence, adding that he would "soon make publick the Established Rules, between Merchants and their hyred Canoe Men, employ'd in the Traffic, to and from the upper Countries." [115]

The probable reason why so many of these civil matters came before general courts-martial is suggested by the correspondence between the first Military Governor at Montreal, General Gage, and the Commander in Chief for North America, General Amherst, whose headquarters were in New York. From these letters [116] it appears that a number of British subjects in occupied Canada insisted that they were not subject to French law. Gage's later letter suggests that this was rather less a claim of extraterritorial immunity than an unwillingness on the part of British subjects present in the occupied province to submit their disputes with its French inhabitants to the civil tribunals presided over by the captains of Canadian militia. After all, General Amherst had constituted those tribunals simply for the settlement of differences among such inhabitants, not to adjudicate between French and British Canadians.[117] At any rate, the arguments necessitated resort to General Gage as Governor for ultimate adjudication of disputes involving property substantial in value.

"That Military Law, takes place here in Criminal Matters, I suppose there is no doubt," wrote Gage, but it was different in civil matters; he inclosed a "Case & Queries," requesting General Am-

---

[114] *Supra,* n. 104.
[115] WO 71/49/255.
[116] See letters cited in nn. 121 and 122.
[117] *Supra,* pp. 40–41. See Gage to Gould, DJAG, 10 Apr. 1764, Appendix ID6, *infra,* at p. 255.

herst "to get the same laid before the most eminent Lawyers in York, for their Opinions thereupon." [118] A fortnight later Gage wrote again, hoping "that I shall soon have answers, from the Learned at York, to the very ignorant Lawyers of Montreal. I am got into it, and don't know how to get out. And two such obstinate, Quibbling, Chicanning fellows, as the two Disputants are, I never met with. . . . I depend on your goodness, to help us out of a Labyrinth of the Law, in which we are all lost, and have argued one another out of the little Common Sense, Nature had bestowed upon Us." [119]

General Amherst, however, thought that while a legal opinion might be appropriate "if it was a Commencement instead of nearly the Close of the present form of Government," under present circumstances "it really appears to me unnecessary."

> I can't but think it is law, I am sure it is plain Reason, that the Form of Government, that was established, and had the King's thorough Approbation, remains in force, 'till His Majesty is pleased to change it . . . surely your Form of Government must be as valid, as any other Government is, and I may undoubtedly conclude, that every Subject, of whatever Country he may be, who comes into Canada, is not less liable to the present established Laws of that Country, than he would be to those of every other Country he might go to.

But, since the Secretary of State had advised that there would soon be received "the King's Commands relative to the Form of Civil Government to be established, . . . it is better not to lay your Queries before the learned in the Law of this Place, nor to make any change before His Majesty's orders arrive." [120]

Gage replied that he had no doubt of the legality of the existing government, it was the pendency of a particular quarrel over a very valuable property that had occasioned his queries. "I could meet only with one out of four, who choose to cooperate, agreeable to the Dictates of Sense & Reason, or the common nature of All proceedings in a Country so circumstanced as this is. On the contrary we had harangues upon prosecutions, retailing Bits & Scraps of Law, which the Retailers did not understand and only served to terrify & Confound, & not to enlighten. . . . I have got into a Scrape,

---

[118] Gage to Amherst, 19 July 1763, Gage Letter Book II, WLCL.
[119] Gage to Amherst, 31 July 1763, Gage Letter Book II, WLCL.
[120] Amherst to Gage, 20 Aug. 1763, WO 34/7/160; original in Amherst Papers, WLCL.

which I must get out of, as well as I can, but I hope it will be the last of Matters of Law." [121]

A month later Gage recurred to his problems: "my greatest trouble is with the British Subjects, and greatest Opposition from the Military who get in Civil Suit with the Inhabitants, about property. . . . I have been threatened by a Military person, with a prosecution, for presuming to try a Civil Cause, betwixt him, & an Inhabitant about property. Neither your Instructions or the King's Approbation of them, were allowed to be Sufficient." But, added Gage, he would continue to pursue his instructions, "which I hope will be no longer, than 'till the Arrival of the packet." [122]

This last letter was written in October, just a few days after the Proclamation of 1763 was issued in London; that historic document empowered the British Governor to establish a civil government, with civilian courts for the trial of criminal as well as civil cases.[123] Before the year was out, General Gage went to New York as Commander in Chief in North America vice General Amherst,[124] while General Murray remained at Quebec to function as Captain General and Governor in Chief of the newly created Province of Quebec when the Proclamation went into effect.[125] That event did not take place until 10 August 1764, at the expiration of the eighteen-month period prescribed by the Treaty of Paris.[126] It was not until the latter date that the *Règne Militaire* came to a close,[127] and ten years more were to pass until, in 1774, the Quebec Act for the first time established the government of Canada on a statutory basis, with English law to be applied in criminal causes and French law in civil ones.[128]

British military rule in Canada might accordingly have remained

---

[121] Gage to Amherst, 8 Sept. 1763, Gage Letter Book II, WLCL.

[122] Gage to Amherst, 12 Oct. 1763, Gage Letter Book II, WLCL.

[123] 7 Oct. 1763, *supra*, n. 44; for its text, see 9 Eng. Hist. Doc. 639, and Shortt and Doughty 163.

[124] Alden *Gage* 61; Montrésor 253; Amherst to Murray, 11 Oct. 1763, WO 34/3/216; Amherst to Gage, 11 Oct. 1763, WO 34/7/178; same to same, 17 Nov. 1763, WO 34/7/184.

[125] Shortt and Doughty 173; 9 Gipson B.E. 162; ch. XIV, "The First British Governor of Canada," in Mahon.

[126] See Art. IV of the Treaty, Shortt and Doughty 115; 10 Eng. Hist. Doc. 937. By Art. VIII, British subjects were similarly allowed 18 months within which to depart from Guadeloupe, Martinique, and Belle Isle.

[127] Doughty, introduction to App. B, and App. C, p. 1.

[128] The Quebec Act is 14 Geo. III c. 83. The establishment of civil government and the adoption of the French civil law belong to the history of Canada, while the effect of the Proclamation of 1763 and of the Quebec Act on American sensibilities, by closing the area between the Alleghenies and the Mississippi to further settlement by the American colonists and by permitting toleration for the

simply an interesting chapter in that nation's past, had there not come to light contemporaneously a case which both in facts and ultimate denouement seems more characteristic of today's detective fiction than of actual events occurring two centuries ago.

On 29 March 1763, a general court-martial convened at Quebec for the trial of Joseph Corriveaux for the murder at St. Vallier of his son-in-law Louis Helene Dodier, and of Marie Josephe Dodier née Corriveaux, widow of the deceased, as an accomplice; [129] the court-martial appointed M. Saillant to defend the prisoners.[130]

It appeared from the evidence that both accused had quarreled and been on bad terms with Dodier, who was found dead early one morning in his stable. A coroner's inquest drawn up by the Captain of Militia, also named Corriveaux, with the aid of the local curé, "from Motives of Charity, to cover the disgrace of a whole Family," declared that the deceased had been trampled to death by his horses. But the animals were not shod, the deceased's wounds could not in any event have been made by horses' hoofs, and there had been great and apparently unseemly haste to bury the remains. Moreover, Isabella Silvain, Corriveaux's niece and servant, told inconsistent stories; sometimes she said her uncle had arisen during the night and that she had heard "a great Scriech"; on other occasions she denied both events.

"Summoned again to tell the whole truth from first to last, she delivered herself in so indistinct, incoherent, and contradictory a manner, there was no possibility to take down the same." Then, "being advised to Recollect herself, she was informed the Court would indulge her to the next day, but that if she did not then give a full, clear, and explicit account of what she knew she would be tried for her Life, for the Crime of Perjury."

In the morning, being "still obstinate and inconsistent, the Court committed her Prisoner to Stand her Trial for Perjury." And M. Saillant in his closing arguments twice urged that she could not be believed.[131]

Catholic religion in Canada, to that of the United States. See, for excellent treatments with differing emphases, Burt; Gipson C.R.; Sosin; and R. Coupland, *The Quebec Act: A Study in Statesmanship* (Oxford, 1925).

[129] WO 71/49/147. The second accused appears variously in the same proceeding, as Mary, Marie, and Maria.

[130] Saillant's appointment, WO 71/49/173, 174. Right to counsel at military law, see n. 112, *supra*. Later English texts reflect a willingness to permit counsel to be present at courts-martial, but as advisers only, not as speakers. 2 McArthur 41–43; A. F. Tytler, *An Essay on Military Law, and the Practice of Courts Martial* (1st ed., London, 1800) 253–255; *id.* (2d ed., London, 1806) 250–252.

[131] References to Silvain, WO 71/49 at 166–167, 173, 177, 188.

The court found Corriveaux guilty of murder, and sentenced him to be hanged; it found his daughter "guilty of knowing of the said Murder, and doth therefore adjudge her to receive sixty Lashes with a Cat and Nine Tails upon her bare back, at three different places, viz., under the Gallows, upon the Market place at Quebec, and in the Parish of St. Vallier, twenty Lashes at each place, and to be Branded in the Left hand with the Letter M."

Thereupon Isabella Silvain was brought in, to be tried for perjury; she declared that she had nothing to say, whereupon the court-martial convicted her and sentenced her to receive thirty lashes, "Ten at the same time and place as Maria, and to be branded in the Left Hand with the Letter P." [132] All these cases were approved by the Governor, General James Murray, on 9 April 1763.[133]

"When a man knows he is to be hanged on the morrow," Dr. Johnson was quoted as saying, "it concentrates his mind wonderfully." So it was with Corriveaux; imprisoned and meditating his imminent departure from this transitory world, he thought better of the whole affair, and on the twelfth of April, "having Offered His Excellency the Governor, thro' the means of his Confessor, to reveal the Guilty if his Life was saved, His Excellency ordered him to be informed, that provided he had not committed the Fact, or advised the same, and had no part therein, his Life should be granted him."

Joseph, examined by the Judge Advocate and M. Panet, declared that it was his daughter who killed her husband in his bed with a blunted hatchet. On the next day, this declaration being read to his daughter, she admitted it to be true: she had indeed killed Dodier, after which her father helped carry the body into the stable. On the day following, the fourteenth, Maria's mother and daughter severally retracted their testimony.[134]

Retribution was swift. On the fifteenth, Maria was haled before the court-martial, charged with her husband's murder; she pleaded guilty, and declared that "she Murdered her Husband . . . in the Night, that he was in Bed asleep, that she did it with a Hatchet; That she was neither advised to it, assisted in it, neither did any one know of it; She is conscious that she deserves death, only begs of the Court, she may be indulged with a little time to Confess, and make

---

[132] WO 71/49/196.
[133] WO 71/49/208.
[134] WO 71/49/210–212.

her Peace with Heaven; adds that it was indeed a good deal owing to the ill Treatment of her Husband, she was Guilty of this Crime."

Whereupon she was sentenced to death, "by being Hanged in Chains wherever the Governor shall think proper," a sentence that was approved on the same day.[135] Actually, so local tradition has it, she was gibbeted.[136] In England, women who were hanged for felony were never subjected to the additional punishment of either hanging in chains or gibbeting—but at this time the English law still deemed the killing of husband by wife not felony but petty treason, for which the punishment was burning.[137] In retrospect, therefore, La Corriveaux was luckier than she knew.[138]

But when these several proceedings reached England, Charles Gould, then and for some fifteen years past the Judge Advocate General in fact, was aghast. Neither Corriveaux nor his daughter nor his niece were military persons; under the rulings since 1734 they could not be tried by court-martial;[139] there was thus no military jurisdiction, and hence General Murray's pardon was ineffectual; Corriveaux must receive a royal pardon for his exculpation to be effective; and, pre-eminently, no such trials of non-military persons must be had hereafter.

Gould swung into action accordingly. Late in July 1763, he forwarded a warrant for Corriveaux's pardon, suggesting that "possibly a quickening Fee to the Clerk may not be amiss."[140] (If

---

[135] WO 71/49/213–214.

[136] P. A. de Gaspé, *Les Anciens Canadiens* (1961 reprint, Montreal and Paris, of 2d Montreal ed., 1864) 294–299; Riddell *Br. Cts.* 579.

[137] Burning as punishment for petty treason, 1 Radzinowicz 209–213; not abolished until 1790, by 30 Geo. III c. 48. Women not hanged in chains, 1 Radzinowicz 217.

The Proclamation of 1763 recited (Shortt and Doughty at 165; 9 Eng. Hist. Doc. at 641) that "We have given Power . . . to erect and constitute . . . Courts of Judicature and public Justice within our Said Colonies for hearing of and determining all Causes, as well Criminal as Civil, according to Law and Equity, and as near as may be agreeable to the Laws of England." Even if this language sufficed to make applicable to Canada *eo nomine* the common law of and penalty for petty treason, a matter of admitting of substantial doubt, it is clear that these provisions were in any event ineffective until the end of the *Règne Militaire* in August 1764. *Supra,* p. 52.

[138] Up to this point, the story is told by De Gaspé, *loc. cit. supra,* n. 136, substantially as it appears in the court-martial records, except for minor inaccuracies. Riddell *Br. Cts.* 578–579, simply cites and summarizes De Gaspé.

[139] *Supra,* pp. 14–16, 23–24.

[140] "Herewith I put into your hands a Warrant for a Pardon to Joseph Corriveaux an Inhabitant of St. Vallier in Canada, and now a Prisoner at Quebec as an accessary in a Murder, or rather Petit Treason, Committed there. You will oblige me in expediting it in the proper Channel, until it has passed the Great Seal:

such a fee was in fact paid, it may have expedited matters; a pardon was issued for Corriveaux on 8 August 1763, "in consideration of his having discovered the Person, who actually committed the Murder," though the document itself was not transmitted to Canada for another month.) [141] Next, Gould wrote to Mr. Cramahé, the DJA at Quebec who had presided at the trial and had assisted in taking the several post-trial declarations, expounding the by then settled jurisdictional views of the Judge Advocate General's Office,[142] and at the same time wrote General Murray in similar vein.[143]

Gould's letter to the Military Governor of Quebec is a strange document. First, Gould says that he writes separately, "not choosing that any thing should appear officially concerning [Corriveaux's] case," and because Lord Egremont, the Secretary of State, "preferred it's passing in a private manner through me, rather than Signifying the King's Commands from his Office." Next, he reports that Lord Egremont "saw the Matter in the same light"; this was the minister who, only a year and a half earlier, had conveyed the royal approval of General Amherst's instructions to the Governors of Trois Rivières, Montreal, and Quebec, "That with respect to Thefts & Murder, it is absolutely necessary the Military Law take place." [144] Finally, Gould stated that "Although there has been no Substantial injustice done in this case, . . . you are so well apprised, how many there are in this Kingdom, who view the Military Arm with a jealous Eye and are ever ready to take advantage of the least mistaken excess of Power"—as though this were of itself a basis for denying the existence of power to govern a conquered province through military means.

I believe Mr. Attorney General, whom I have apprised of it's coming before him, will be disposed to give it dispatch, but possibly a quickening Fee to the Clerk may not be amiss. It is very material, that I should be able to transmit it by the first opportunity. I know the Fees are large, and I have inclosed a Draught for £50.—.—; but if more is wanted, you will be kind enough to advance it or give me notice that I may send you a farther order." Gould, DJAG, to Mr. Francis, 26 July 1763, WO 81/10/201. The addressee was probably Philip (later Sir Philip) Francis, then first clerk at the War Office, and later the reputed author of *The Letters of Junius*. DNB.

[141] Memorandum of the pardon, WO 71/49/214; transmission to Canada, WO 81/10/223 (10 Sept. 1763).

[142] Gould, DJAG, to H. T. Cramahé, Esq., 11 Aug. 1763; WO 81/10/204; Appendix ID1, *infra*, pp. 250–251.

[143] Gould, DJAG, to Gov. Murray of Quebec, 11 Aug. 1763, WO 72/5; Appendix ID2, *infra*, pp. 251–252.

[144] *Supra*, pp. 40–41.

General Murray's response was in terms grateful rather than otherwise: [145] "I think it was lucky we did not Know, how limited our Jurisdiction has been here for four years past." But he could not forbear to mention the instance of the Canadian hanged for murder at Montreal by General Gage,[146] or the approval conveyed by Lord Egremont in 1761: "I certainly must do you the Justice to believe that the Proceedings of that Court Marshal were never sent to Your Office, but I can with difficulty reconcile Lord Egremonts Letter, to His Lordships seeing the Affair of Corrivaux in the same light that you do."

Gould's embarrassment is reflected by the badly blotted retained draft of his reply to the points made by General Murray.[147] "Though my Opinion is still the same, as to the Strict legality," he had written, going on to add, "At the same time I must admit, that the Extract of Lord Egremont's Letter might reasonably be thought to extend"—but that letter had been so explicit that contrary reasoning based upon it could hardly be pursued. So Gould simply crossed out the second passage. By this time, the Earl of Egremont was dead; he had in fact died on 21 August 1763,[148] shortly after Gould conferred with him; it may well be doubted whether he had even then been able either to recall his prior communication or to concentrate on the problem in hand.

As for the case tried by General Gage—well, that proceeding though duly recorded in the court-martial books by the clerks had never in fact been examined by the Judge Advocate General or his Deputy. Here again the scratched-out draft suggests the painfulness of this admission. "However," Gould concluded, "with this one and the other they have had their good effect, and that they may have no other, I shall endeavor as far as in me lies, by keeping the matter to myself."

But the question preyed greatly on his mind, so that he simply could not keep the matter to himself. A month later he was constrained to recur to the issue, writing this time to General Gage:

> Upon looking into some late Proceedings of General Courts
> Martial . . . I observe some Trials, and those in capital cases,
> of Persons confessedly not Military. These in my humble

---

[145] Governor Murray of Quebec to Gould, DJAG, 12 Nov. 1763, WO 72/5; Appendix ID3, *infra*, pp. 252–253.

[146] *Supra*, p. 45.

[147] Draft, Gould, DJAG, to Governor Murray of Canada, WO 72/6; Appendix ID4, *infra*, pp. 253–254.

[148] DNB.

apprehension (and indeed it does not rest upon my private opinion only) are not Strictly warranted in Law.[149]

When that communication reached New York, General Gage exploded. Military trials of civilian criminals in militarily occupied territory illegal? Impossible; Gage had a copy of Lord Egremont's letter that conveyed the King's approval of General Amherst's plan of trying criminal cases under military law, and, only within the year, in the several letters concerning civil litigation at Montreal that have been quoted at length, Gage and Sir Jeffery Amherst were in complete accord regarding the validity of this system of administering criminal justice.[150] Now this lawyer in London, this Deputy, was blandly and flatly asserting the contrary.

Gage composed a holograph letter, without retaining any copy among his own papers, the pages of which two centuries later still seethe with barely restrained wrath. Anticipating Mr. Justice Holmes's mordant dissent by some 140 years—"I also think that the statute is constitutional, and but for the decision of my brethren I should have felt pretty clear about it"[151]—Gage replied to Gould: "till the Receipt of your letter, I must own to you, I had not the smallest Doubt of [those court-martial proceedings] being consistent with Law."[152] Gage continued in the same vein:

> In Canada, all Justice ceased upon the Conquest, for every Court of Civil or Criminal Judicature left the Country. The Gen' therefore constituted new Courts of Judicature, and criminal Cases were ordered to be tried by Gen' Courts Martial only. This Method was approved of by the King, and was accordingly followed.
>
> If this Method was not strictly Warranted in Law, I should think it worth asking the opinion & advice of the Heads of the

---

[149] Gould, DJAG, to Gen. Gage, late Governor of Montreal, 11 Feb. 1764, MS, Gage Papers, WLCL; Appendix ID5, *infra*, p. 254. Mr. William S. Ewing, Curator of Manuscripts, WLCL, first called this document to my attention. There is no copy in the PRO, and it should be noted here that, where any of the correspondence in connection with jurisdictional matters is cited only to the JAG Correspondence (WO 72) and not to the JAG Letter Books (WO 81), the communication in question was not copied into the latter.

[150] Egremont's approval of Amherst's plan, *supra*, pp. 40–41; Amherst and Gage in accord on legality of military trials of civilian criminals, *supra*, pp. 50–52.

General Amherst was created K.B. in 1761. DNB.

[151] *Adair* v. *United States*, 208 U.S. 161, 190.

[152] Gen. Gage, C. in C. North America, to Gould, DJAG, 10 April 1764, WO 72/6; Appendix ID6, *infra*, pp. 254–255.

Law, how Canada in such Circumstances, ought to be governed, . . .

I tell you what has passed, and the Difficulty and Questions which have been started. What ought to have been done,
or what ought not to have been done, I must leave to your
better Judgment, as I am not ashamed to own myself at a Loss
in a matter, which has puzzled those, who should be more
knowing in these Affairs.

Civil Judges we hear are appointed for Canada, It's to be
hoped they will arrive soon, and put an End to the Trouble
and Perplexity, which the Governors have undergone ever
Since the Capitulation of Montreal.

Gould climbed down as best he could; he submitted Gage's letter
to the Earl of Halifax, the new Secretary of State, who in turn took
refuge in the comforting observation that since Governor Murray's
instructions under his new civil commission as Captain General and
Governor in Chief authorized him to constitute civil courts, the
problem no longer existed.[153] "This makes it unnecessary for me,"
Gould could accordingly write Gage, "to trouble you with a more
particular answer to your letter." Or, one may fairly add, to trouble himself with the formulation of such an answer.

The controversy over criminal jurisdiction ended, not with
General Gage's shout, but with Colonel Burton's whimper. In view
of the fact that the proceedings questioned by Gould, wrote Gage's
successor at Montreal, "met with His Majesty's most gracious Approbation, it is to be hoped that in case any Sentence given here,
should come to be litigated in Great Britain, the Circumstances of
these Governments and the good Intentions of those, who carry on
that part of the Service, will be taken into Consideration." [154] (Burton's concern may have reflected the circumstance that in Montreal
civilians had been tried by court-martial as late as May 1764.) [155]

Today's lawyers, reading the foregoing correspondence in its
entirety in Appendix ID, will immediately wonder why it was that

[153] Gould, DJAG, to Hunter Sedgwick, Esq., 30 May 1764, WO 81/11/12;
Appendix ID7, *infra*, pp. 255–256; Gould, DJAG, to Gen. Gage, 7 June 1764, WO
81/11/14; Appendix ID8, *infra*, pp. 256–257. For the pertinent paragraphs in Gov.
Murray's commission and instructions, respectively, see Shortt and Doughty
176–177 and 187.

[154] Gov. Burton of Montreal to Gould, DJAG, 3 July 1764, WO 72/6; Appendix
ID9, *infra*, p. 247.

[155] WO 71/74/213 (trial of two bakers, one a German formerly a French soldier,
the other "a Switzer" late of the 60th Foot; held on 14 May 1764; both accused
acquitted). This is the last such trial in Canada recorded in the War Office
court-martial books.

Gould, an exceedingly competent lawyer, should never have per-
ceived the obvious difference between a municipal military law
jurisdiction over accompanying civilians, who plainly would not
be subject to the Mutiny Act unless particularly named therein,
and a military government jurisdiction over all inhabitants of militarily occupied territory taken from the enemy, who are subject to
trial by military tribunals under that branch of international law
known as the law of war. Individual status is the touchstone of
military jurisdiction under municipal law, territorial status under
international law.[156] Nothing could be more obvious to a lawyer
today; why was it not equally obvious to Charles Gould?

The answer to this apparent paradox is one of time: the distinction just noted was not known in 1763–1764. The law of belligerent occupation was not clearly formulated until Wellington's time,
nor did it develop fully until the middle of the nineteenth
century.[157] Charles Gould, DJAG, ruling as he did in 1763, cannot
be convicted of error for not anticipating legal developments that
did not materialize until much later.

In Gould's lifetime, the case that came closest to dealing with the
question of military jurisdiction in Canada was *Campbell* v. *Hall*,[158]

---

[156] This distinction was recently illustrated in dramatic fashion by the trial of
Mrs. Madsen, convicted in 1950 by an American military government court in
occupied Germany of killing her airman husband. The Supreme Court of the
United States sustained that jurisdiction under familiar military government
principles. *Madsen* v. *Kinsella*, 343 U.S. 341. Thereafter, following the release of
Mrs. Covert, convicted by an American court-martial of a similar offense in
England in 1952, and of Mrs. Smith, convicted by an American court-martial of
killing her husband in Japan following termination of the American occupation
there, *Reid* v. *Covert* and *Kinsella* v. *Krueger*, 354 U.S. 1, Mrs. Madsen sought
release on habeas corpus; but to no avail. *Madsen* v. *Overholser*, 102 U.S. App.
D.C. 146, 251 F. 2d 387, certiorari denied, 356 U.S. 920. She also sought to reopen
the original proceeding, which had been decided in April 1952, by a motion to file
a petition for rehearing out of time; but this also was denied, in March 1958.
Madsen v. *Kinsella*, 356 U.S. 925.

[157] "Martial law as applied to any persons, excepting the officers, soldiers, and
followers of the army, for whose government there are particular provisions of
law in all well regulated countries, is neither more nor less than the will of the
General of the army. He punishes, either with or without trial, for crimes either
declared to be so, or not so declared by any existing law, or by his own
orders. . . .

"The Commander in Chief, or the government, has been authorised to proceed
by military process, that is, by Court Martial or Council of War, to try persons
offending against certain laws, or against their own orders, issued generally, for the
security of the army, . . ." Lt.-Gen. Visc. Wellington to Minister Stuart at Lisbon,
19 Apr. 1810, 4 Well. *Disp.* 23, 24. And see 2 Oppenheim 432–433; 14 Holdsworth
38–39.

[158] 20 How. St. Tr. 239; s.c., 1 Cowp. 204, Lofft 655.

Lord Mansfield's judgment in 1774 on the scope of the prerogative in relation to conquered and settled colonies. But that decision simply held that, once the Crown had created a legislative assembly in newly ceded territory, the prerogative power of levying taxes in that territory lapsed. Nothing therein throws any light on the issue over which the Earl of Egremont vacillated in his last month on earth: May the King, before his prerogative powers have lapsed, erect military tribunals to try criminal offenses in territory taken from but not yet ceded by the enemy, and in which all other forms of judicature have ceased to function?

One of Lord Mansfield's resolutions in *Campbell* v. *Hall* suggests an affirmative answer:

> No question was ever started before, but that the King has a right to a legislative authority over a conquered country; it was never denied in Westminster-Hall; it never was questioned in Parliament. Coke's report of the arguments and resolutions of the Judges in *Calvin's case* lays it down as clear. If a King (says the book) comes to a kingdom by conquest, he may change and alter the laws of that kingdom; . . .[159]

Another resolution leans toward a negative response:

> 6thly, If the king has power (and, when I say the king, I mean in this case to be understood "without concurrence of parliament") to make new laws for a conquered country, this being a power subordinate to his own authority, as a part of the supreme legislature in parliament, he can make none which are contrary to fundamental principles; . . .[160]

According to Holdsworth, Lord Mansfield by the latter passage "probably meant that [the Crown] could make no laws which shocked the moral sense of Englishmen of the day." But, Holdsworth added, "This principle is necessarily somewhat vague. What will be regarded as contrary to the moral sense of the nation varies from age to age." [161] Specifically, was a direction that criminal cases be tried by court-martial in territory conquered from the enemy but not yet ceded to the Crown abhorrent to Englishmen in the 1760's? Plainly, it was not so regarded by Lord Egremont in 1761, and in 1763 Gould did not examine the matter as one involving the scope of the prerogative.

---

[159] 1 Cowp. at 211; Lofft at 742; cf. 20 How. St. Tr. at 324.
[160] 20 How. St. Tr. at 323; 1 Cowp. at 209; Lofft at 741–742.
[161] 11 Holdsworth 246.

Campbell v. *Hall* did not in any sense decide that issue, because there Lord Mansfield was simply not addressing himself to the question earlier debated by Generals Gage and Murray with Deputy Judge Advocate General Gould. Nor was that question resolved in any English tribunal during their time.

It should perhaps be added that the discussion above accepts the view, held by Lord Mansfield and by Blackstone, that the law of nations is part of the law of England.[162] But the law of nations had not then developed so as to include the law of belligerent occupation in its present form, and hence the scope of the prerogative in respect of conquered territory was correspondingly unclear.

That the *Règne Militaire* in Canada was indeed a military administration is too plain from the documents to be controverted; that it was an enlightened rule by comparison with that of Louis XIV and Louis XV in Canada and with some of the military occupations of the present century may well be true also,[163] notwithstanding the sentiments of those in Canada who still feel unable to accept the events of 1759 and 1760; that the trials of Canadian inhabitants by court-martial during the *Règne Militaire* were consistent with modern doctrines of international law must likewise be conceded.[164] The foregoing pages have set forth the scope of those

---

[162] 10 Holdsworth 372–373; 14 *id*. 23–24.

[163] "On an appelé cette periode, qui va du 8 septembre 1760 au 10 août 1764, le Régime Militaire et il l'était par le fait de l'occupation des troupes anglaises, mais je ne vois pas qu'il ait été plus rigoureux que le régime pacifique dont la colonie souffrait depuis cent cinquante ans. Il n'avait rien de la dureté allemande ni de l'absolutisme français que ces deux mots semblent exprimer: régime militaire. C'était plutôt le gouvernement du bon père de famille. . . . Après tout, est-ce que la colonie n'avait pas toujours été sous le regime militaire? Où était sa liberté civile 'du temps des Français'?" B. Sulte, *Le Régime Militaire 1760–1764*, Proc. & Trans. Roy. Soc. Can., 2:XI: xxvii, xlviii, lxix.

Benjamin Sulte (1841–1923) was a prolific author of works on Canadian history, and in his lifetime was sufficiently regarded to be a charter Fellow of the Royal Society of Canada and to be elected its President for 1904–1905. But he was self-taught, without any academic background, and early in his literary career was bitterly attacked for reaching conclusions at variance with deeply cherished French Canadian beliefs. Proc. & Trans. Roy. Soc. Can., 3:XVIII: iv–vii; *Les Histoires de M. Sulte. Protestation par J. C. Taché* (Montreal, 1883). Today, no doubt for both reasons in varying degree, some Canadians regard him as "no authority."

[164] 2 Oppenheim 432–456; 3 C. C. Hyde, *International Law Chiefly as Interpreted and Applied by the United States* (2d ed., Boston, 1945) §§688–702A.

Military government jurisdiction such as was exercised in Canada from 1760 to 1764 is clearly recognized in pars. 12 and 13 of Dr. Francis Lieber's *Instructions for the Government of Armies of the United States in the Field* (GO 100, War Dep't, Washington, 24 Apr. 1863), and in pars. 47 and 48, MML 1884, as derived from the common law of war. In the first authority mentioned, such jurisdiction is spoken

trials as reflected in documents that most writers on the period have never consulted, and have additionally disclosed an earlier English view which, prior to the development of the law of military government, held those trials to be expedient but illegal.[165]

The civil proceedings conducted under General Amherst's plan for the military government of Canada were ratified by one of the first Ordinances promulgated by the successor civil government, subject to a right of appeal that was later extended.[166] The criminal proceedings conducted under the same plan have also been ratified, not indeed by legislation, but rather by the legal consensus of successor generations of international lawyers.

---

of as exercised by military commissions, in the second by special tribunals. In the United States, general courts-martial have since 1916 been granted military government jurisdiction by statute. AW 12 of 1916, 1920, and 1948; Art. 18 UCMJ.

[165] Shy 198, published in 1965, contains the first reference to the Gould opinion that has been seen in print. But his discussion (pp. 197–198), which all too obviously lacks a sufficient legal and jurisdictional background, cannot fairly or even hopefully be regarded as adequate.

[166] Ordinance of 20 Sept. 1764, "For ratifying and confirming the Decrees of the several Courts of Justice established in the Districts of Quebec, Montreal, and Trois-Rivieres, prior to the Establishment of Civil Government throughout this Province, upon the tenth Day of August, One Thousand Seven Hundred and Sixty-Four," in *Ordinances, Made for the Province of Quebec, By the Governor and Council of the said Province, since the Establishment of the Civil Government* (Quebec, 1767) 16; Ordinance of 12 Nov. 1764, enlarging the time for appeals, *id.* at 20.

CHAPTER III

RESTRICTIONS ON MILITARY JURISDICTION OVER NON-MILITARY PERSONS

The records of the 1760's and 1770's reflect further restrictive rulings and determinations concerning the jurisdiction of British Army courts-martial over persons not named in the Mutiny Act, rulings that, as in the Seven Years War, ranged over a wide geographical area.

As has been seen, British soldiers could not be tried by court-martial for common law felonies committed on British soil, except where no form of civil judicature was asserted to be in force, and except in foreign parts (where of course such soldiers would not be stationed except in time of war).[1] But this sharp jurisdictional line became blurred in the forests of North America, in areas where the King's writ often ran only in theory.

CIVILIANS IN THE AMERICAN WILDERNESS

In 1755, a general court-martial sitting at Oswego on Lake Ontario refused to pass sentence in two separate cases of murder. In the first, "The Court having considered the nature of [the prisoner's] Crime, and finding it to be committed at Schenectady in the County of Albany and Province of New York where a Civil Court of Judicature is held once a Year, is of Opinion, that they have not a Power to try a Prisoner."[2] In the other, the court was "of Opinion, that they have no Power to try [the prisoner], as Oswego, where the Fact was Committed, is in the Province of New York in the County of Albany."[3]

Similarly, when Lord Loudoun was Commander in Chief in America in 1757, he insisted that, at Schenectady, soldiers committing civilian offenses be turned over to the civil magistrate.[4] Later

---

[1] *Supra*, pp. 14–15, 23–24.
[2] WO 71/42/196, 213.
[3] WO 71/42/214, 238.
[4] Pargellis *Loudoun* 334–335. Also in 1757, strangely enough, Lord Loudoun committed to the provost marshal a New York baker who had used sour flour in bread intended for the Army, justifying his action "by the principle that a power

in the same year, however, a general court-martial at Albany presided over by Lieutenant-Colonel Thomas Gage tried and convicted three offenders of theft.[5] (Albany and Schenectady were then of about the same size.) [6] And in 1759, Gage, by then a brigadier-general, wrote as follows from Albany to Lord Loudoun's successor, General Amherst, at the latter's headquarters in New York—which at that time was a virtual metropolis with a population of 18,000 persons: [7]

> Upon several Complaints of Thefts committed by the Soldiery, I intimated a design of trying that Crime for the future by general court-martial; but finding many Officers scrupulous in this Point, I assembled the Field Officers and Captains of the Garrison to know their Opinions. They told me in General, That they perceived the great Necessity of it, but were so tyed down by the *Oath*, That they could not pass Sentence of *Death* on any Persons tryed for such Crimes, and only inflict Corporal Punishments. That the Articles of War & Act of Parliament, which the Oath binds every Member religiously to follow, has so fully explained, That *Thefts* were only cognizable by Court Martials, where The Civil Judicature was not in Force. They could not in Conscience inflict Death, unless out of the Inhabited Country. If I mistake not, there was another Oath taken by Court Martials in Flanders, & other Articles, termed *Field Articles*, used there, & in Scotland during the Rebellion.[8]

The difficulties adverted to increased greatly after the peace, when not only Canada but all of the North American continent between the Appalachian Mountains and the Mississippi River passed to Great Britain. This was a vast wilderness peopled by Indians, which the French had held with the aid of scattered mili-

---

was seated in the commanding officer during war for the preservation of the troops." *Id.* 294.

[5] WO 71/66/113, 126.

[6] Schenectady had about 300 houses in 1758, Albany about the same number in 1765. E. B. Greene and V. D. Harrington, *American Population before the Federal Census of 1790* (New York, 1932) 101 n. t, 102. The authority last cited gives no population figures on Oswego, which at this time appears to have been little more than a garrison that may have included a few traders. See "Papers Relating to Oswego," in 1 N.Y. State Doc. (Albany, 1849) 441–506, and the contemporary engraving of Oswego that faces 29 *London Magazine* 232 (1760). A reproduction similarly faces 5 Gipson B.E. 98.

[7] Bridenbaugh 5. In 1756, Albany had 329 families within the town. Pargellis *Loudoun* 195.

[8] WO 34/46A/15.

tary posts and in which French hunters, traders, and missionaries had roamed. The British took over the posts soon after the surrender, only to abandon them within less than a decade, largely because of expense,[9] but no doubt also because of the potentiality of endemic Indian wars foreshadowed by Pontiac's conspiracy.[10]

While the posts were still garrisoned, however, there loomed large the problem of maintaining law and order among the variegated civilians, whose misdeeds could easily trigger further Indian uprisings. In March 1762, General Gage, then still Military Governor at Montreal, suggested to General Amherst that "in each of these Posts" the officers should be "Authorized, either solely by themselves, or assisted by such other persons as may be found in the posts, to exercise a Judicial power." [11]

Nothing came of the proposal, and then followed a number of events that quite altered the position: the Proclamation of 1763 setting up new civil governments, Gage's appointment as Commander in Chief in succession to Amherst, and Gould's ruling that courts-martial could try only persons specifically named in the Mutiny Act.[12]

The Proclamation of 1763 had specifically required all officers in the newly acquired wilderness, "as well Military as those Employed in the Management and Direction of Indian Affairs," to seize all fugitives from justice who might seek refuge there, and "to send them under a proper guard to the Colony where the Crime was committed of which they stand accused, in order to take their Trial for the same." [13] This was entirely adequate as far as it went, but it plainly did not deal with offenses committed in the vast area reserved for Indian settlement, which was not only outside the boundary of any organized government, but which under other provisions of the same Proclamation was barred to white settlement.

The obvious solution, particularly in the light of Gould's recent animadversions, was to amend the statute law.

Accordingly, on 22 January 1765, General Gage pointed out to

---

[9] There is an extensive literature on this point. Ch. VIII, "The Western Problem," in Alden *Gage;* Gage *Corr. passim;* 11 Gipson B.E. 419–421, 438–440; Shy 223–231, 236–237; Sosin *passim.* British troop dispositions in North America in 1760, 1763, 1766, 1772, and 1775 are graphically shown on the maps at Shy 97, 112, 238, 328, and 419.

[10] *Supra*, p. 30, n. 123 of Ch. I.

[11] Gen. Gage's Report of the State of the Government of Montreal, 20 Mar. 1762, Shortt and Doughty 91, 94.

[12] *Supra*, pp. 52, 55–59.

[13] 9 Eng. Hist. Doc. at 643.

Secretary at War Welbore Ellis the difficulties encountered because the Mutiny Act did not apply to North America.[14] Further, under the heading "Additions proposed to be made to the Mutiny Act, to suit the Circumstances of the Troops, and Inhabitants of America," he submitted a proposal to deal with conditions in the wilderness, as follows:

> After the 60th Clause,—But if such Crime or Trepass, be committed at any of the posts, not in the inhabited parts of the Country, and where the Civil Judicature hath not taken place; Be it enacted by the Authority aforesaid, that the person accused, may be there proceeded against, and tried, and convicted by a Regimental or General Court-Martial according to the degree of the Offence.[15]

Ellis passed this letter to the Earl of Halifax, the Secretary of State, with a comment that throws a revealing light on Whitehall's ignorance of even formal conditions in America:

> The addition proposed to the 60th clause being new, and an extension of military jurisdiction over crimes and persons not military, can give no opinion relative thereto. All the posts in North America are within some civil jurisdiction.[16]

The noble lord showed himself far better informed:

> With regard to the legality and expediency of the addition proposed to be made to the 60th clause of the Mutiny Act, his Lordship can only refer him to the advice of His Majesty's lawyers. But as he seems to think that all the posts in North America are within some civil jurisdiction, and therefore that such additional clauses will be unnecessary, his Lordship incloses for his information an extract from H.M.'s proclamation of Oct. 7, 1763, by which he will see that the several military posts in the lands and territories reserved for the Indians are not within any civil jurisdiction; and that although provision is made therein for apprehending and bringing to justice such criminals as may take refuge at those posts, yet no mode is established for the punishment of crimes committed at those posts, or in the reserved territories.[17]

---

[14] 2 Gage *Corr.* 262. See also, to the same effect, Gage to Earl of Halifax, SS, 23 Jan. 1765, 1 Gage *Corr.* 47, 49.

[15] 2 Gage *Corr.* 266.

[16] SW to Mr. Sedgwick, 7 Mar. 1765, 1 *Cal. Home Office Pap. 1760–1765* (London, 1878) 529. See Shy 191–192.

[17] Earl of Halifax, SS, to SW, 11 Mar. 1765, 1 *Cal. Home Office Pap. 1760–1765*, p. 534.

A Mutiny Act for North America was duly enacted in 1765,[18] with provisions for quartering soldiers that seriously exacerbated relations between Britain and its American colonies.[19] Here, however, there is relevant only the fate of General Gage's proposal to try offending civilians in the wilderness by military courts. This was felt to be medicine too strong to be administered anywhere, and in the Act as passed there was substituted a much milder remedy.[20] In order to deal with "Crimes and Offences . . . committed by several Persons, not being Soldiers, at several Forts or Garrisons, and several other Places within His Majesty's Dominions in *America*, which are not within the Limits or Jurisdiction of any Civil Government there hitherto established; and which Crimes and Offences are not properly cognizable, or triable and punishable, by a Court-martial, but by the Civil Magistrate," commanding officers were charged to convey and deliver such offenders "to the Civil Magistrate of the next adjoining Province . . . to be committed and dealt with by such Civil Magistrate . . . according to law," there to be prosecuted "in the same Manner as if such Crime or Offence had really been committed within the Jurisdiction of such Court." [21]

The foregoing provision was regularly renewed, until well into the War of American Independence.[22]

Interestingly enough, after the same wilderness became American soil consequent upon the second Peace of Paris twenty years later, in 1783, a similar proposal to try civilian offenders there by court-martial, then made by an American general, was in turn rejected by the American legislature.

On 11 July 1787, General Henry Knox, the American Secretary at War, suggested to the Continental Congress that the commanding officer of troops in the "Territory Northwest of the river

---

[18] 5 Geo. III c. 33.

[19] The details of those provisions, which caused the measure to be known in America as the Quartering Act, have been treated at length elsewhere. Ch. II, "New York and the Quartering Act," 11 Gipson B.E. 39–69; Gipson C.R. 129–132, 134, 135, 149, 152–153; Alden *Gage* 35, 109, 122, 153–154; Shy 163–181, 184–187, 250–258; Gage *Corr. passim.* For the quartering problem in the war just concluded, see ch. VII, "Quartering," in Pargellis *Loudoun.*

[20] The difference between the provision as recommended and the one ultimately adopted is quite missed by C. E. Carter, *The Significance of the Military Office in America, 1763–1765*, 28 Am. Hist. Rev. 475, 479.

[21] Sec. 25. (This provision appears as §24 in some versions; at this time statutes as printed by the King's Printer were not divided into sections.)

[22] 6 Geo. III c. 18; 7 Geo. III c. 55; 8 Geo. III c. 19; 9 Geo. III c. 18; 10 Geo. III c. 15; 11 Geo. III c. 11; 12 Geo. III c. 12; 13 Geo. III c. 24; 14 Geo. III c. 6; 15 Geo. III c. 15; 16 Geo. III c. 11 (extension into the year 1778).

Ohio" should be empowered to try all persons who should "injure or kill any of the indians or otherwise infract the treaty." [23] A committee of the Congress proposed that, until the civil government authorized by the Northwest Ordinance [24] was established, such offenders should be tried and punished "by law martial in the same manner as the regular soldiers are tried and punished for the like offences." [25] But, despite further committee recommendations to the same effect,[26] no action was taken thereon by Congress. In fact, the civil government of the Northwest Territory did not begin to function until July 1788, a full year later.[27] Otherwise stated, Congress chose a hiatus of law on the frontier in preference to subjecting civilians there to even an interim military jurisdiction. In this respect it was faithfully following in the steps of His Majesty's Government in 1765, an administration which, though it was responsible for the notorious Stamp Act,[28] after which reconciliation with the colonies was in fact never again really possible,[29] still refused to suffer wilderness civilians to be tried by court-martial.

MEMBERS OF THE ROYAL NAVY

In the course of the Seven Years War, the British captured the French islands of Martinique and Guadeloupe.[30] Both were returned at the peace, though, as is well known, the question whether to retain those islands in preference to Canada was hotly controverted.[31] The incident presently relevant concerns a trial by an Army court-martial had in May 1763 in Martinique of one Daniel McDonald, Boatswain of H.M.S. *Foudroyant*, for the murder of Private William Sampey of the 76th Foot, which resulted in conviction and a sentence of death.[32]

When that sentence was sent home for confirmation by the King, Charles Gould ruled that the court-martial lacked jurisdic-

---

[23] 32 J. Cont. Cong. 327, 330.
[24] 32 J. Cont. Cong. 334 (13 July 1787), also at 2 *Terr. Pap. U.S.* 39.
[25] 32 J. Cont. Cong. 370, 374.
[26] 33 J. Cont. Cong. 410–411; 2 *Terr. Pap. U.S.* 56–57. The debates preceding this second report are at 32 J. Cont. Cong. 376; 33 *id.* 385–387.
[27] 3 *Terr. Pap. U.S.* 263; 2 *id.* 133. No crimes act was adopted for the area until 6 Sept. 1788. See 1 *Stat. Ohio & N.W. Terr.* (S.P. Chase ed. 1833) 97–101.
[28] 5 Geo. III c. 12.
[29] Morgan *passim.*
[30] 2 Fortescue 349–356; ch. V, "Island Hopping in the French West Indies, 1759," in 8 Gipson B.E. (Guadeloupe); M. Smelser, *The Campaign for the Sugar Islands, 1759* (Chapel Hill, 1955); 8 Gipson B.E. 185–196 (Martinique in 1762).
[31] Williams *Whig Sup.* 368–369; 9 Gipson B.E. 233–235; Watson *Geo. III* 86–87.
[32] WO 71/49/120–146.

tion.[33] The "all Persons" provision in the familiar "no Form of Our Civil Judicature" article of war, under which the court had proceeded, was insufficient; "this expression must be understood of such Persons, as are the objects of Military Law and Articles of War." McDonald could not be included therein, since he was neither officer nor soldier nor under the command of any commanding officer named in the Mutiny Act. But Gould invoked another and to modern minds a curious argument based on consent:

> But I even go a Step farther, and should humbly apprehend, that, if the words of the Article were clearly extended to all Persons Civil, as Well as Military, nevertheless this would not conferr a Legal Jurisdiction over the former, because they have never done any Act, nor entered into any engagement, which Subjects them to the Articles of War, nor are they bound to take notice of them.

Since, at this juncture, no royal pardon was forthcoming "untill the Offence shall have been tried by a Court having a competent Jurisdiction, I conceive, it will be advisable, that the Prisoner be sent over to England in order to his being tried by a Jury upon an Indictment to be preferred in the King's Bench."

The balance of the correspondence deals with Gould's efforts to notify, under eighteenth-century conditions of communication, the commanding officers concerned; his application to the Admiralty upon learning that McDonald had been sent home; and his advice to the captain of the man-of-war on which the prisoner was being detained in respect of making return to the writ of habeas corpus that was about to be served in order to bring McDonald before the Court of King's Bench.[34]

In the event, McDonald was pardoned on 28 October 1763, probably without a retrial; the facts indicated only manslaughter, for which the punishment was burning in the hand, and this made it inadvisable to convene the only tribunal competent to try the case, a special commission under 33 Hen. VIII c. 23.[35]

Over the years, the jurisdiction of one armed force to try members of another has been, if possible, even more jealously limited

---

[33] Gould, DJAG, to Welbore Ellis, SW, 2 June 1763, WO 81/10/169; Appendix IE1, *infra*, pp. 257–258.

[34] Appendixes IE2–5, *infra*, pp. 258–261.

[35] The Attorney General's report explaining why a pardon would be desirable was written on 22 Sept. 1763 (1 *Cal. Home Office Pap. 1760–1765*, 306); Gould's last letter (Appendix IE5, *infra*, pp. 260–261) is dated 31 Aug., while the pardon itself (WO 71/49/144–146) bears date of 28 Oct.

than that of courts-martial to try civilians. Throughout the eighteenth and nineteenth centuries, Army courts-martial could not try
sailors, and Army courts-martial could not sit on board naval vessels to try soldiers embarked thereon.[36] The first breach in the wall
between the British services came in 1795, since which time military personnel serving on board H.M's ships have been subject to
naval law and triable by naval courts-martial.[37]

The Royal Marines, then as now *sui generis*, constituted perhaps
the only consistent exception to the wall of separation. When
originally raised, in 1694, they were governed when on board ship
by the Naval Discipline Act then in force, and when on land by the
Mutiny Act and the Articles of War.[38] Later, from 1755 through
1878, they were subject while on shore to a Marine Mutiny Act,
which was annually adopted precisely in the same manner as the
Army's annual Mutiny Act.[39] Since that time the Royal Marines
have at all times been subject to the law governing the Army, the
position today, except that they still come under the Naval Discipline Act when, but only when, they are "borne on the books of
any of Her Majesty's ships or naval establishments." [40]

---

[36] 1 McArthur 206–212, 424–430; Simmons 18; Mil. L. Eng. 228.

[37] 1 McArthur 201–204, 421–424; Simmons 18–21; Clode M.L. 45–46; Mil. L.
Eng. 228; Army Act 1881, §186; for the implementing Orders in Council, see
MML 1914, pp. 728–733; *id.* 1929, pp. 818–824; *id.* 1951, pp. 592–597. Under Army
Act 1881, §188, Army courts-martial could be held afloat only on ships not
commissioned by H.M.

[38] 1 Clode M.F. 75, 264; Clode M.L. 38. The first Naval Discipline Act, 13 Car. II
c. 9, passed in 1661, which—unlike the later Mutiny Acts governing the Army—
was permanent legislation, remained in force for over eighty years, until superseded
in 1749 by 22 Geo. II c. 33. The substance of the latter statute remained in force
until supplanted in 1861 by a new Naval Discipline Act, 23 & 24 Vict. c. 123. Clode
M.L. 42–44; 10 Holdsworth 381.

[39] 1 Clode M.F. 265; Clode M.L. 38–39. The first Marine Mutiny Act was 28
Geo. II c. 11, the last was 41 Vict. c. 11.

[40] Army Act 1955, §§210(1), 210 (3); Naval Discipline Act 1957, 5 & 6 Eliz. II. c.
53, §112. As summarized in Art. 1810, Queen's Regulations and Admiralty Instructions, "Members of the Royal Marine forces are at all times subject to military
law. They are also subject to the Naval Discipline Act when borne on the books
of any H.M. ships or naval establishments. Certain provisions of military law and
of the Naval Discipline Act are inappropriate to the Royal Marine forces and the
necessary modifications are contained in the Seventh Schedule to the Army Act
1955 [Provisions as to Royal Marines] and the First Schedule to the Naval
Discipline Act [Application of Act to Marine Forces]. When travelling as
passengers in H.M. ships members of the Royal Marine forces are subject to the
Naval Discipline Act in the same way as members of the military and air forces in
those circumstances. When travelling as passengers in other ships or aircraft they
are subject to the disciplinary code of the Service by which the ship or aircraft is
administered." Double jeopardy is precluded by Army Act 1955, §134(1).

After the Royal Air Force became an independent armed force in 1918, such of its members as were attached to the Army became subject to the Army Act.[41] Today, when combined operations are the rule, members of one armed force are frequently attached to another, a formal act resulting in all becoming subject to the law governing the service to which they are attached.[42] Thus, at the present time, there is universal and reciprocal inter-service jurisdiction in the British armed forces.

The trend in the United States has been in the same direction. At first there was rigid separation, with the Marine Corps likewise the only exception for many years. Unlike the position in England, however, the United States Marine Corps has always been a part of the Navy.[43] But the British jurisdictional arrangement was followed in substance, so that marines were normally subject to the Articles for the Government of the Navy except when detached for service with the Army, in which latter status they became subject to the Articles of War.[44] Nonetheless, until the effective date of the 1916 Articles of War, marines committing offenses against the Army's code while subject thereto could not be thereafter tried for such offenses by naval courts-martial.[45] And it was not until the Uniform Code of Military Justice went into effect in 1951 that the jurisdictional barriers between the several American armed forces were finally eliminated.[46]

---

[41] Army Act 1881, §§175(1A), 176(1A); cf. §184A (World War II provision regulating relations between military, naval, and air forces acting together).

[42] Army Act 1955, §208 and Sixth Schedule, Application of Military Law to attached Members of Naval and Air Forces; Air Force Act 1955, §208 and Sixth Schedule, Application of Act to attached Members of Naval and Military Forces; Naval Discipline Act 1957, §113 and Second Schedule, Application of Act to attached Military and Air Forces. The mechanics of attachment are governed by §179 of both the Army and Air Force Acts, and by the Naval, Military and Air Forces (Attachment) Regulations, 1964 (MML 1965, pp. 805–808).

[43] For the American marines of the War of Independence, see 3 J. Cont. Cong. 348, 393, 405, and 6 id. 913. There were no marines from the end of that conflict until 1798, when they were once more authorized by the Act of July 11, 1798, c. 72, 1 Stat. 594. Rulings from 1798 through 1951 concerning the status of the United States Marine Corps are collected in the annotations to R.S. §1621 in 34 U.S.C.A. §715. The provision presently in force is 10 U.S.C. §5011.

[44] Sec. 4 of the Act of July 11, 1798, c. 72, 1 Stat. 594, 595; Sec. 2 of the Act of June 30, 1834, c. 132, 4 Stat. 712, 713; R.S. §1621. Under a provision in the Act of August 29, 1916, c. 417, 39 Stat. 556, 573, Navy medical personnel serving with marines so detached were similarly subject to the Articles of War.

[45] AW 2(c) of 1916, legislatively overruling U.S. ex rel. Davis v. Waller, 225 Fed. 673 (E.D. Pa.).

[46] Art. 17 UCMJ. The older jurisdictional provision governing the Marine Corps, R.S. §1621, was repealed by §14(e) of the act establishing the UCMJ.

In the case of Boatswain McDonald at Martinique, however, modern doctrines independent of statutory innovations would have validated his trial: He was physically present in Martinique, which was then occupied territory, and hence he could have been tried there by an Army court-martial sitting as a tribunal of military government. Indeed, General Amherst did not scruple to deal summarily with sailors in Canada committing depredations ashore immediately after the surrender,[47] and General Gage tried members of the Royal Navy by garrison court-martial during the *Règne Militaire*.[48] But when McDonald was tried, in 1763, as has been seen in connection with Canada, military government jurisdiction had not yet been articulated or rationalized. It was only in the conflict following, when courts-martial of the British Army sitting in the American cities that were occupied by the King's forces tried various varieties of seagoing individuals for misconduct, that members of the Royal Navy were similarly dealt with in routine fashion.[49]

CIVILIANS ON MINORCA

Even under recognized twentieth-century concepts of international law, however, there would have been no justification for the next group of military trials to be considered, involving civilians haled before courts-martial on Minorca after the island had been restored to Britain by the 1763 Peace of Paris. For, at that time, the amenability of non-military persons to military jurisdiction would once more have become purely a question of municipal law.

A few words regarding the status of Minorca properly belong here. It passed to Britain, together with Gibraltar, by the Treaty of Utrecht in 1713, and it remained in British hands until the French captured it in 1756. This was the setback for which Admiral Byng paid with his life. At the end of the Seven Years War, Minorca was returned to Great Britain and it is then that the instances about to be discussed arose. Thereafter, late in the next conflict, Minorca fell once more, and Spain reacquired it pursuant to the 1783 Peace

---

[47] Amherst to Gov. Murray, 14 Sept. 1760, WO 34/3/13, concerning complaints of R.N. sailors who in conjunction with sailors from transports have been plundering inhabitants: "That I may put an entire stop to any further Disorders I am determined the Provost Martial, who has Orders to go his Rounds and take up Stragglers, shall have an Officer to Attend him, and whoever is found in the fact of plundering the Inhabitants Shall be hung immediately."

[48] Hervey 127 (larceny by sailors from H.M.S. *Alcide*, tried by garrison court-martial, 16 Sept. 1760).

[49] *Infra*, pp. 108, 109.

of Paris. Except for intervals during the Napoleonic wars, Minorca has remained Spanish ever since.[50]

During all of the more than sixty years that the island was British soil, it was named in the Articles of War, along with Gibraltar, as a place "where there is no Form of Our Civil Judicature in Force." But, precisely as in the case of Gibraltar,[51] that recital was not true in fact.

Spanish law remained in force in Minorca, law that was administered by the Court of Royal Government. In theory, the Governor was the presiding judge, and all proceedings were in his name; in fact, he rarely if ever sat in civil cases, and, certainly in the second period of British rule, never in criminal cases.

The theoretical Governor in criminal cases was assisted by two officers of the court, the assessor (sometimes called the chief justice criminal), and the fiscal. The first was the Governor's counsellor, to manage the trial, and to preside as judge in fact. In theory, the assessor only gave his advice, which the Governor could follow or not as he wished, and certainly the judgment was not valid until signed by the Governor. During the trial, the fiscal acted as advocate for the Crown, but when sentence was passed, he had a voice together with the assessor; if the two agreed, the Governor was bound to confirm; if they disagreed, the Governor had the casting voice. There was also a *Procurador-Real*, "to attend the Court, and inform them of such Matters as are to be brought before them, and to push on the Tryal."

Minor criminal cases were delegated to the magistrates or jurats, or, in the royalty or arraval of St. Phillip's, to the *Almutazen* or *Mustastaph*. In civil cases, the views of another assessor (sometimes called the chief justice civil, and senior in rank to the assessor in criminal cases) were decisive, and binding on the Governor.[52]

---

[50] See 2 Fortescue 291–295 ("The unfortunate admiral was shot because Newcastle deserved to be hanged"); ch. XIII, "The Loss of Minorca," in 6 Gipson B.E.; 3 Fortescue 305–306, 351, 416–418 (second capture); Watson *Geo. III* 255, 379, 409 (subsequent disposition).

For recent works on the first loss of Minorca by the British, see H. W. Richmond, ed., *Papers Relating to the loss of Minorca in 1756* (Nav. Rec. Soc., 1913, vol. 42); W. C. B. Tunstall, *Admiral Byng and the Loss of Minorca* (London, 1928); D. Pope, *At Twelve Mr. Byng Was Shot* (Philadelphia and New York, 1962); G. French, *The Martyrdom of Admiral Byng* (Glasgow, 1961).

[51] *Supra*, pp. 24–27, 29.

[52] This description of the Minorquin judicial system is based on J. Armstrong, *The History of the Island of Minorca* (London, 1752) 101–102, 107 (Letter IX, dated 27 June 1741), and on the testimony and the uncontroverted statements of counsel in *Fabrigas* v. *Mostyn*, 20 How. St. Tr. 81, 100–102, 110–114, 119–124, 127, 137, 140, 168, 196.

All of the foregoing involved the Governor's civil jurisdiction over the inhabitants of the island, as distinguished from his military jurisdiction over the garrison. The problem to be discussed arose when civilians connected with the garrison were accused of criminal offenses; two of them were tried by courts-martial.

The first of these, Dennis Fogharty, "Executioner to the Island," was tried at St. Phillip's in February 1764, together with four soldiers, for "Coining false Coin, or being Aiding and Abetting to the Coining thereof; and for Uttering false Coin, knowing it to be such." Fogharty was acquitted, and hence does not figure further in legal history, a circumstance that doubtless caused him no regret whatever.[53]

Then, at the same place in January 1765, there were tried "John McLearen, William Rogers, and Mary the wife of the said William Rogers, all of the 11th Regiment of Foot," charged with "being concerned in Murdering & Robbing Joseph Peloutier, a French Shopkeeper at Ciudadella" on Christmas Day, 1764. All were convicted and sentenced to death, McLearen to be "afterwards hung in Chains," William Rogers to be hanged without more. Those two were duly executed, but Mary Rogers was pardoned by the Governor.[54]

Charles Gould's reaction when these proceedings came to his attention was predictable; the court-martial lacked jurisdiction to try the woman, and "the Pardon of the Commanding Officer Granted upon a Supposition of his having Authority to Confirm or remit the Sentences of Courts Martial is mistaken and insufficient." Writing thus to the Earl of Halifax, Secretary of State, Gould suggested a royal pardon for Mary Rogers, "who is represented to have made the first discovery of the Murder and of the persons concerned in it; and the rather, as She does not appear, tho' present in Company with her Husband, to have been actually assisting in the perpetration of the Murder." [55]

In another letter to Governor Townshend of Minorca, Gould repeated his by now familiar ruling that the words "All Persons" in the Minorca Article of War meant only persons—

> who are Subject to the Articles of War, and who have Sworn or Subscribed to their observance:—and even supposing this Woman to have been considered in some Sort, as a part of the

---

[53] WO 71/74/106–117.
[54] WO 71/75/1–5.
[55] Gould, DJAG, to the Earl of Halifax, SS, 7 Mar. 1765, WO 81/11/66; Appendix IF1, *infra*, p. 261.

Garrison and attached to the Corps, which she followed, and that instances might be produced of Courts Martial animadverting upon some irregularities committed by Persons within that description, but which is perhaps connived at, rather than expressly warranted, I think no Usage or Construction can be supported in that latitude as to punish Capitally, and upon a Charge purely Civil.

Accordingly, the Governor's pardon was ineffectual; a royal pardon was required; the King had indicated to the Earl of Halifax his assent to this course; "And His Lordship approved the method suggested by me of the Pardon passing through my hands, as upon a private Sollicitation, rather than that he should signify the King's Commands to you officially, as Secretary of State." Then "Mary Rogers may receive it at your hands, as the Royal Confirmation obtained by you of the Pardon, which you had in the King's Name assured her of." [56]

Apparently, however, the question of trying soldiers' wives by court-martial would not stay at rest; in 1770, the new DJA at Minorca, Henry Schomberg, "Captain 110th late Regiment," sent a series of questions to Gould (by that time JAG *de jure*), in one of which he asked about the prospective trial of a soldier's wife by court-martial. Gould's reply was drily to the point:

I should by no means recommend the Trial of a Woman, Wife to a Soldier, by a Court Martial for Felony. You mention their being included in the Mutiny Act; but I do not recollect any Clause which extends to such. And the Article of War, which says, that in the Island of Minorca and other places specified, All *Persons* guilty of Murder, Robbery, &ca—are to be tried by Courts Martial, must necessarily be understood to speak of Military Persons. [57]

Poor Schomberg! His is a story that might warrant further inquiry; here is what Governor Mostyn (soon to be mulcted in

---

[56] Gould, DJAG, to Col. Townshend, Gov. of Minorca, 28 Mar. 1765, WO 81/11/71; Appendix IF2, *infra*, pp. 262–263.

The Earl of Halifax, SS, on 13 Mar. 1765 signed a warrant to the law officers to prepare a bill for the pardon of Mary Rogers (WO 72/6). The actual pardon, dated 20 Apr. 1765, appears as Appendix IF3, *infra*, pp. 263–264.

[57] Gould, JAG, to Capt. Schomberg, DJA at Minorca, 22 Sept. 1770, WO 72/6; Appendix IF4, *infra*, p. 264. Schomberg announced his appointment as DJA and Commissary of Musters at Minorca in a letter to Gould on 13 Oct. 1769 (WO 72/6).

£3,000 damages by "Red Tony" Fabrigas) [58] wrote about him to Gould in 1771:

> I much fear, that We shall scarce be able to send from hence, any Proceedings of Courts Martial, free from Informalities at least, if not with more material Errors: Our Judge Advocate being so utterly incapable of the Office. Poor Man! I really wish Him well, & think His Heart good; but His Head is not at all calculated for so warm a Climate. He is really, as has been represented, by General Johnston, before I came here, & since by me, to Lord Barrington, as mad as Bedlam.[59]

Even after Schomberg had a successor, the question of rendering amenable to court-martial civilians at Minorca who were connected with the garrison once more arose; this time, in 1777, it concerned the storekeepers, clerks, and artificers of the ordnance. The Judge Advocate General advised that "If the several persons in the Service or employ of the Ordnance in Minorca are desirous of being considered as Military, and to be alike Subject to discipline and trial by Courts Martial, it is probable, a representation through the Master and Principal Officers would be attended to." [60]

Interestingly enough, when the Supreme Court of the United States in 1960, nearly two centuries later, was dealing with the assertion that civilian employees of the armed forces must as a matter of necessity be subject to military jurisdiction, it gave the same answer, namely, if such a step is indeed necessary, then the solution is to incorporate these employees into the armed forces, either by compulsory induction or by voluntary enlistment, so as to give them a military status.[61]

---

[58] *Fabrigas* v. *Mostyn*, 20 How. St. Tr. at 175. Gov. Mostyn was also required to pay £159 in costs. *Id*. at 238.

[59] Gov. Mostyn of Minorca to Charles Gould, JAG, 3 July 1771, WO 72/7. Viscount Barrington was then Secretary at War. Schomberg's many letters to Gould in WO 72/6 and 72/7 reflect a distinctly unstable personality.

[60] Charles Gould, JAG, to Joseph Collins, DJA at Minorca, 23 Sept. 1777, WO 81/13/157; Appendix IF5, *infra*, pp. 264–265.

[61] *McElroy* v. *Guagliardo*, 361 U.S. 281, 286–287.

Minorca should not be left without two closing remarks. First, the correspondence in CO 5/174 may repay examination for those interested in this island. Second, in 1781 there was tried at that place a private soldier who later became world famous, namely, Thomas Atkins (of the 61st Foot; WO 71/94/201). Is this not his first appearance anywhere?

CHAPTER IV

MILITARY RELATIONS WITH CIVILIANS AND THE CIVIL POWER IN AMERICA, 1765–1775

General Gage continued as Commander in Chief in North America until after the War of American Independence actually commenced. His headquarters were in New York until June 1773, when he sailed home on leave.[1] Upon his return late in the spring of 1774 he went to Boston,[2] having while in England been given a civil appointment as Governor of the Province of Massachusetts Bay in addition to his military command. He held both posts during the affair at Lexington and Concord in April 1775 and at the Battle of Bunker Hill in June. He was called home in September of the same year, which is to say, just as soon as Lord North's administration could communicate its reaction to the latter so disastrous engagement, in which over 40 per cent of the British troops engaged became casualties.[3]

But General Gage's correspondence in the interim quite belies the bloodthirsty image of him that was limned by generations of American patrioteer historians. Whatever may be said of his purely soldierly abilities, and assuredly he will never be ranked among

---

[1] Alden *Gage* 192–193. Gage had to await receipt of a special Act of Parliament to permit Maj.-Gen. Haldimand, the next senior officer but a Swiss Protestant, to assume command. This enabling Act was 13 Geo. III c. 25; Haldimand and a host of others similarly situated had been first enabled to serve in America by 29 Geo. II c. 5, pursuant to which there were formed the Royal Americans, later the 60th Foot. See 1 L. Butler, *The Annals of the King's Royal Rifle Corps* (London, 1913) 16–18, 31–33; Pargellis *Loudoun* 61–67; 1 Clode M.F. 90–92. Gen Haldimand's first orders at New York are dated 10 June 1773. PRO, WO 36/1.

[2] He arrived in Boston Harbor on 13 May and landed on the 17th. Alden *Gage* 204, 206. But his first military orders thereafter that have been found are dated 10 June. PRO, WO 36/1.

[3] There is of course an extensive literature on Bunker Hill, but probably the best account is in French F.Y. 211–255. A good recent version, alike readable and well documented, is T. J. Fleming, *Now We Are Enemies* (London and New York, 1960).

The British casualties are discussed in 3 Fortescue 161; 1 C. Ward 96; French F.Y. 256–257. Gen. Gage's contemporary estimate, written nine days after the battle, was that "The loss we have Sustained, is greater than we can bear." Gage to Viscount Barrington, SW, 26 June 1775, 2 Gage *Corr.* 686.

Britain's great captains, his correspondence reveals him to have been up to then a thoughtful, temperate, and law-abiding administrator.

Thus, agreeable to the policy laid down in the Mutiny Acts for North America,[4] he regularly ordered malefactors apprehended in the wilderness to be sent for trial to settled areas,[5] although he recognized fully that, in fact, no frontier jury would convict a white man for maltreating Indians.[6]

The instructions sent him, that he was not to employ troops in aid of the civil power, except on the express request of that power,[7] were not only scrupulously obeyed, but were regularly impressed by him on numerous royal officials in the colonies.[8] In fact, until the final conflagration he was called on to employ troops against civilian rioters only in connection with the disturbances in Albany and Dutchess Counties in New York in 1766.[9]

In the dispute between the civil and military power in West Florida in 1766 he supported the former;[10] his view that the Bermuda Assembly was not empowered to enact a Mutiny Act applicable to any but local levies was confirmed by disallowance of that body's legislation;[11] and he rejected a proposal to place his district

---

[4] *Supra*, p. 68.

[5] Gage to Earl of Hillsborough, SS, 7 Oct. 1769, 1 Gage *Corr.* 238, 239; same to same, 1 July 1772, 1 *id.* 328, 329; s.c., Sir William Johnson to same, 29 June 1772, 8 N.Y. Col. Doc. 300; Gage to Earl of Dartmouth, SS, 7 Apr. 1773, 1 Gage *Corr.* 347, 349.

[6] Gage to Gen. Conway, SS, 6 May 1766, 1 Gage *Corr.* 89, 91.

[7] Gen. Conway, SS, to Gage, 24 Oct. 1765, 2 Gage *Corr.* 27, 28–29; War Office Instructions, 24 Oct. 1765, 2 *id.* 47, n. 30; Earl of Shelburne, SS, to Gage, 11 Dec. 1766, 2 *id.* 47–48; Earl of Hillsborough, SS, to Gage, 12 Oct. 1768, 2 *id.* 75, 77.

[8] Gage to Earl of Halifax, SS, 7 Jan. 1764, 1 Gage *Corr.* 9; Gage to Gen. Conway, SS, 16 Jan. 1766, 1 *id.* 80; Gage to Viscount Barrington, SW, 16 Jan. 1766, 2 *id.* 334; Gage to Gov. Bernard of Mass., 11 July 1768, 2 *id.* 77, note; Gage to Earl of Hillsborough, SS, 31 Oct. 1768, 1 *id.* 202, 205; same to same, 26 Apr. 1770, 2 *id.* 102; same to same, 7 July 1770, 1 *id.* 262, 263. In strict accord with the foregoing are Gen. Haldimand's orders for 22 Oct. and 20 Dec. 1773 in WO 36/1, as well as Gage OB, 20 July 1774.

[9] Gage to Earl of Halifax, SS, 10 Aug. 1765, 1 Gage *Corr.* 62, 64; Gage to Gen. Conway, SS, 24 June 1766, 1 *id.* 93, 95; same to same 15 July 1766, 1 *id.* 99; Gage to Duke of Richmond, MGO, 26 Aug. 1766, 1 *id.* 102; same to same, 13 Sept. 1766, 1 *id.* 107; Gage to Earl of Shelburne, SS, 11 Nov. 1766, 1 *id.* 112, 114; same to same, 23 Dec. 1766, 1 *id.* 115, 117–118; 11 Gipson B.E. 49–50, 337–338; Morgan 172; Shy 217–223.

[10] Gage to Gen. Conway, SS, 26 Mar. 1766, 1 Gage *Corr.* 85, 87–89; Earl of Shelburne, SS, to Gage, 13 Sept. 1766, 2 *id.* 44, 45–46; Gage to Earl of Shelburne, SS, 11 Nov. 1766, 1 *id.* 112. See also Shy 151, 153–159.

[11] Gage to Earl of Shelburne, SS, 19 Oct. 1767, 1 Gage *Corr.* 154; Earl of Hillsborough, SS, to Gage, 12 Mar. 1768, 2 *id.* 58, 60.

commanders under civil officers lest there be a recurrence of "the Broils that have happened between the Civil Governors and the military Commanders." [12]

He wrote General (and Mr. Secretary) Conway in June 1766 that he would "particularly avoid giving Encouragement to any idle pretensions of exclusive priviledges in the Military Service. I know of no exclusive priviledges that the Military are entitled to, or indeed have I ever heard that they had claimed any." [13] In November of the same year he reassured Lord Shelburne "that I shall do every thing which depends upon me, to make the Burthen of quartering the Troops as light upon every Province, as shall be possible for me to do." [14]

The problem of law and order in the wilderness, i.e., in what was then known as the Illinois country, a matter already adverted to in the preceding chapter, continued to trouble Gage for many years. In March 1766, probably before being advised that his plan for military jurisdiction there had been rejected, he urged "that a military Governor should be appointed for the Ilinois as soon as possible." [15] Two years later he wrote that "Courts sh'd be also erected, for the trial of Civil, as well as Criminal Causes, but how proper Jurys can be impannelled, out of such small numbers as will for some time compose these Governments, I can't devise." In the meantime he suggested that the officer commanding should also be Governor for the time being with additional allowances, on the Gibraltar pattern. [16]

In 1769, after Lieutenant-Colonel Wilkins of the 18th Regiment, who commanded at Fort Chartres (located on the Mississippi River, in what is now the southwestern portion of the State of Illinois), had established a court of judicature for the settlement of all civil disputes, [17] Gage dispatched a warning in which one hears an echo of the disputants before him at Montreal, about whom he had complained to General Amherst a few years earlier: [18]

> You are doing everything you can that some sort of Justice may be carried on in the Settlements. I would advise in

[12] Gage to Viscount Barrington, SW, 6 July 1770, 2 Gage *Corr.* 545; same to same, 8 Mar. 1771, 2 *id.* 570.
[13] Gage to Gen. Conway, SS, 24 June 1766, 1 Gage *Corr.* 96, 98.
[14] Gage to Earl of Shelburne, SS, 11 Nov. 1766, 1 Gage *Corr.* 112.
[15] Gage to Gen. Conway, SS, 28 Mar. 1766, 1 Gage *Corr.* 85, 86.
[16] Gage to Viscount Barrington, SW, 15 May 1768, 2 Gage *Corr.* 473.
[17] Carter *Illinois* 64–72; 11 Gipson B.E. 421–424.
[18] *Supra,* pp. 50–52.

whatever is done, to let the Inhabitants carry those matters on themselves, and not to appear yourself in them, but when your authority shall be necessary to restrain injustice. There cannot be many nice affairs of great Consequence to determine. But I would have you avoid giving any handle to Litigious People, who might hereafter endeavor to hamper you with tricks of Law.[19]

Colonel Wilkins' tribunal, which sat alternately at Chartres and Kaskaskia, was abolished in 1770, while military courts of inquiry, also designed to settle civil disputes, proved unsatisfactory.[20]

Accordingly, in August 1771, following those efforts, and also after five years of experience with the scheme of the Mutiny Act for North America, General Gage wrote that "there has been wanting Judicial Powers to try and determine" causes; accordingly, he recurred to the example of Gibraltar, suggesting adoption of whatever plan of government was in force there, "which place occurrs to me, as I think it in Situation and Circumstances, the most similar to the Ilinois, of any other."[21] In 1772 and again in 1773 he forwarded suggestions for plans of civil government in Illinois.[22]

Thereafter, following his return from home leave with the burden of his new civil office, General Gage's correspondence records the growing exacerbation of relations between the colonists and the Crown. Thus, while Lord Dartmouth in August 1774 warned of the extreme caution to be used in sending persons to England for trial under the provisions of 35 Hen. VIII c. 2,[23] the same official's emphasis by April 1775 had shifted from the caution to a reminder of the power.[24]

But, as long as there was still no fighting, General Gage's own

---

[19] *Some Letters & Papers of General Thomas Gage*, John P. Branch Hist. Pap. of Randolph-Macon College, 4:2:86, 95, 96.

[20] Carter *Illinois* 71–72; 11 Gipson B.E. 423–424. Wilkins was subsequently relieved of command after becoming financially interested in the profits of a commercial firm's trade in Illinois. Shy 281–282.

[21] Gage to Earl of Hillsborough, SS, 6 Aug. 1771, 1 Gage *Corr.* 304, 306.

[22] Gage to Earl of Hillsborough, SS, 4 Mar. 1772, 1 Gage *Corr.* 317, 318–319; Gage to Earl of Dartmouth, SS, 6 Jan. 1773, 1 *id.* 342; same to same, 7 Apr. 1773, 1 *id.* 347, 348; same to same, 5 May 1773, 1 *id.* 351, 352. See also L. P. Kellogg, *A Footnote to the Quebec Act*, 13 Can. Hist. Rev. 147.

[23] Earl of Dartmouth, SS, to Gage, 23 Aug. 1774, 2 Gage *Corr.* 171, 172.

[24] Earl of Dartmouth, SS, to Gage, 15 Apr. 1775, 2 Gage *Corr.* 190, 191, 196.

Perhaps the reader should be reminded here of the coincidence of Gage's civil appointment and the passage of the Boston Port Act (14 Geo. III c. 19); the latter, Parliament's reply to the Boston Tea Party, assuredly contributed to the exacerbation. See 2 Adams *Leg. Pap.* 105–106, 243–246.

orders reflect a wholehearted desire to avoid quarrels with the colonists, and breathe a scrupulous regard for legality. On 12 June 1774 he directed that the commanding officer will order his men "from having as little intercourse or Conversation with the Inhabitants as possible." [25] On 20 July, he declared out of bounds the business of "one Stephen Harris a Baker living at the Sign of the Three Wheat Sheaves," because that individual "has behaved himself in a Lawless & insolent manner, deceiving & abusing the Soldiers & otherwise hurting the King's Service." [26] On 26 September he directed that "All Officers & Soldiers will avoid any Altercations whatever with the Inhabitants & enter into no Disputes or abuse, or any conversation tending thereto," [27] an order that was repeated a month later.[28] On Guy Fawkes Day, traditionally and uproariously celebrated in Boston as "Pope's Day," soldiers were forbidden to appear in the streets, "As this is a day of Riot among the Towns People." [29]

A week later General Gage directed that "No Soldier or others are allowed to take their own Satisfaction for injustice received but to apply to legal Authority for redress," listing the names and addresses of six magistrates, as well as the names and addresses of six constables, the latter as persons "who may be Applyed to Occationally." [30] And on the next day he ordered that no soldier unless on duty was to be permitted to wear sidearms, and that "The Centinels when in Town are not to Challenge any Person going thro' the Street." [31]

But neither General Gage's good intentions nor his implementing orders were proof against the inevitable propensity of junior officers to overindulge in liquor on occasion; late in January 1775, just three months before Lexington and Concord, a number of subalterns assaulted members of the watch.[32] The General was much displeased, and convened a court of inquiry.[33] A few days later, he admonished all concerned in orders: "The Attacking the Watch of any Town, in all parts of the World, must be attended with bad Consequence, for as they are Appointed by Law, the

---

[25] Gage OB, 12 June 1774.
[26] Gage OB, 20 July 1774.
[27] Gage OB, 26 Sept. 1774.
[28] Gage OB, 25 Oct. 1774.
[29] Gage OB, 5 Nov. 1774; see 1 Adams D. & A. 322 n. 3.
[30] Gage OB, 12 Nov. 1774.
[31] Gage OB, 13 Nov. 1774.
[32] This was on 20 Jan. 1775. 1 Mackenzie 4–5; Andrews 395–396; Barker 21–22.
[33] 1 Mackenzie 4–5.

Laws will protect them, & no Person that Quarrells with them, will get Satisfaction for Injuries he may Receive, but on the Contrary will be condemned." [34] In actual fact, the officers involved in that fracas were put on trial before Justices of the Peace.[35]

The principle implicit in General Gage's orders was that all civilians who accompanied his Army were to be dealt with by the civil government, precisely like all other civilians in the province, nor did he ever apply military means of enforcement until after the shooting had actually started. Thus, when complaints were received, two and a half months before the first fighting, of soldiers' wives keeping dram shops,[36] he directed that, should "the liquor Sold in such houses prove fatal to many Soldiers, the Commanding Officers will direct such Persons to be carried before a Magistrate with proper witnesses, who will order them to be fined & proceeded against in other Respects according to Law." [37] It was only after Lexington and Concord that military sanctions were employed; then the "Women of Different Corps" who still sold rum to soldiers were ordered "to be Immediately Seiz'd & put on Board Ship." [38] The penalty at that point imposed on women who refused to serve as nurses in the hospital was to be "struck off the Provision list," [39] that for women who broke into private houses infected with smallpox was to be ordered "on Board Ship & Sent away." [40]

Finally, on 12 June 1775, just five days before Bunker Hill, General Gage as Governor of the Province of Massachusetts Bay and in conformity with its charter declared martial law, the assigned reason being the non-functioning of the civil courts.[41] That

---

[34] Gage OB, 24 Jan. 1775.

[35] Andrews 397; Willard 58.

Some of the riotous officers were bound over to appear at the April Assizes—but never tried, because by then all the courts were closed. Barker 23; 1 L. H. Butterfield et al., eds., Adams Family Correspondence (Cambridge, Mass., 1963) 179–181. I am indebted to Professor L. Kinvin Wroth for the reference last cited.

[36] Gage OB, 2 Feb. 1775.

[37] Gage OB, 10 Feb. 1775.

[38] Gage OB, 9 May 1775; Barker 44.

[39] Gage OB, 29 May 1775.

[40] Gage OB, 6 June 1775.

[41] Force, 4:2:968, 970; Gage to Earl of Dartmouth, SS, 12 June 1775, 1 Gage Corr. 404, 405; Gage to Viscount Barrington, SW, 12 June 1775, 2 id. 684. The Governor's powers in this regard had been earlier pointed out to him. Earl of Dartmouth, SS, to Gage, 27 Jan. 1775, 2 id. 179, 183: same to same, 15 Apr. 1775, 2 id. 190, 191–192.

The proclamation itself was drafted by Burgoyne, then the recently arrived junior major-general, who admitted his authorship. E. B. de Fonblanque, Political and Military Episodes . . . derived from the Life and Correspondence of the Rt.

reason was neither makeweight nor subterfuge. In consequence of the dispute over the source of the judges' salaries—were they to be dependent on the provincial legislature for their pay, or could they properly accept emoluments from the Crown?—Chief Justice Oliver was impeached in February 1774, and the superior courts of law indeed stopped functioning.[42] Thereafter, in February 1775, "the history of royal justice in Massachusetts came to an end." [43]

Until the proclamation of martial law was actually issued, however, the numerous civilian dependents and followers of the army were never tried by court-martial, despite the many entries concerning them and their regulation that appear in the order books.[44] It was only after the town of Boston had been subjected to the law martial, and its communications by land cut off by the encircling American army, that the first woman was there haled before a British court-martial for trial.

This doubtful honor fell to "Winifred McCowan, a Retainer to the Camp, . . . accused of having stolen the Town Bull, and caused him to be killed." (The lady's preference for fresh beef was understandable; Boston during the siege was on short commons; salt pork and little else had been the unvarying fare for days on end.) [45] Following findings of guilty, the court adjudged that she "be tied to a Carts-tail, and there receive one hundred lashes on her bare

---

Hon. John Burgoyne (London, 1876) 136. But contemporaries recognized Burgoyne's style without any need for that admission. French F.Y. 202–204, 317; see Alden *Gage* 263–264.

There is no mention of this proclamation in either of the order books that contain Gen. Gage's military orders for 12 June 1775. Waller OB; Gage OB, WO 36/1.

[42] 12 Gipson B.E. 139–145, 163–164; 1 Adams *Leg. Pap.* lxxxviii–xc.

[43] 1 Adams *Leg. Pap.* xc.

[44] A complete listing of the relevant order books appears in the Bibliography. There seems no need to make special reference to the entries therein that deal with the many civilians of every description who followed the army.

[45] ". . . fresh provisions are scarce, and what we have, not of the best quality. Vegetables, we have none." W. Carter 8 (23 July 1775). "We are now reduced to live upon Salt pork and peas as fresh provisions are not to be got for Money." *Concord Fight: The Narrative of Jeremy Lister* (Cambridge, Mass., 1931) 55 (15 July 1775). "For my part, & indeed most of the Subalterns, are obliged to live on their Rations, which is 7 lb of Bread, 7 lb of Salt Pork and 4 oz of Butter, for which we pay 1/7 per week. We have neither Pease, Rice, nor Oatmeal allowed us, which we used to have till this two months past." 1 A. M. W. Stirling, *Annals of a Yorkshire House* (London, 1911) 351–352. See also 2 *id.* 14–16, but according to the *Army List*, the officer mentioned there was Major F. B. Sill, not Major I. R. Till as stated in the author's transcription.

The statement in Alden *Gage* 276, that "According to a tradition which seems to have no foundation in fact, even the town bull, an aged animal, was turned into steaks and roasts," overlooks this documented instance, which has several times been noticed in print.

back in different portions in the most public parts of the town and Camp, and afterwards be imprisoned for three months." General Gage approved that sentence on 25 September 1775.[46] On the next day he received orders to return to England, relieved of command in fact, though this bitter pill was sugar-coated for a few months by talk of his going home for consultation.[47]

Gage was, in a very real sense, "the Cassandra of the first British empire," [48] who had repeatedly pointed out to his official superiors that any war with the colonies would be long and costly:

> . . . if you will resist and not yield, that Resistance should be effectual at the Beginning. If you think Ten Thousand Men sufficient, send Twenty, if one Million is thought enough, give two; you will save both Blood and Treasure in the End. A large Force will terrify and engage many to join you, a middling one will encourage Resistance, and gain no Friends. The Crisis is indeed an alarming one, & Britain had never more Need of Wisdom, Firmness, and Union than at this Juncture.[49]

But Lord North's administration followed instead a policy of too little and too late, and when, after Bunker Hill, it became apparent that this policy was wrong, Gage was the obvious scapegoat. Yet his only major shortcoming was that, like almost all his contemporaries at home, he had utterly misunderstood the nature of the American Revolution.[50]

---

[46] WO 71/81/393–399, Gage OB, 25 Sept. 1775. The testimony suggests that the accused was a soldier's wife. This is case No. 140 in Appendix II.

[47] Ch. XVI, "Recall," in Alden *Gage;* H. Clinton 22–23; Frothingham 247. Gen. Gage sailed from Boston on 10 Oct. 1775, on which day Gen. Howe assumed command. Howe OB; 1 Kemble 60; Barker 65.

Gage's authority as Commander in Chief in North America was not formally revoked until the following April, and even then he was permitted to continue in office (and receive pay) as Governor of the Province of Massachusetts Bay. Lord G. Germain, SS, to Gage, 18 Apr. 1776, 2 Gage *Corr.* 206.

[48] Alden *Gage* 187.

[49] Gage to Viscount Barrington, SW, 2 Nov. 1774, 2 Gage *Corr.* 658, 659.

[50] "A man of good abilities and executive capacity, with a steady head and much self-control in the face of great provocation, in the times before the war [Gage] held the balance even between the Bostonians and his own men as long as any man could have done. His one error then was that he did not learn the temper and the abilities of his adversaries. But this error was serious, and unfitted him for either judgment or action. A bolder governor would have struck earlier; a wiser one would have measured the Americans better. But it is not possible to say that among his major-generals any one would have done better, for each in succession failed in the war. A peaceful solution of the situation called for a man who did not exist: an English administrator in advance of his times, who could perceive the justice and the common-sense of a change in political theory, and could persuade the home government to a constitutional readjustment. Failing such a prodigy, backed by prodigies at home, war was inevitable." French F.Y. 528.

CHAPTER V

THE WAR OF
AMERICAN INDEPENDENCE
—PART ONE

If Benjamin Franklin indeed remarked to his fellow members of the Continental Congress, just after the adoption of the Declaration of Independence, that all must hang together lest all hang separately,[1] he was but emphasizing an obvious municipal law aspect of the American Revolution. But that conflict, like the American Civil War in the following century, was a revolt of such proportions that the opponents of constituted authority were early granted belligerent rights,[2] so that upon capture they were treated as prisoners of war rather than as traitors.[3]

CIVILIANS WITH THE BRITISH ARMY

On the British side, the ration strength during this period included what today would be considered an amazingly high proportion of civilians, amounting in some places to over 35 per cent of the whole. Thus, when Ethan Allen (and Benedict Arnold) captured Fort Ticonderoga and its subposts in May 1775, the ninety-three British prisoners they took included two civilian officials and thirty-four women and children.[4] When the British Army sailed out of Boston in March 1776, its 8,906 officers and men were accompanied by 667 women and 553 children belonging to the

---

[1] Van Doren *Franklin* 551–552.

[2] E.g., *Williams* v. *Bruffy*, 96 U.S. 176, 186–187. See Carleton to Washington, 20 June 1782, 8 Sparks *Wash.* 537, 538: "In a civil war between people of one empire, there can, during the contest, be no treason at all." As early as 1758, Vattel had urged that the parties to a civil war should observe the established rules of war (E. de Vattel, *The Law of Nations* [1758] Bk. III, ch. XVIII, §§293–294; Fenwick tr., p. 338).

[3] The first exchange of prisoners took place on 22 May 1775. Barker 49. Throughout most of the war, the British Army's Commissary of Prisoners was Joshua Loring, Jr., Esq., the complaisant husband of Sir William Howe's notoriously affectionate "Sultana," who mitigated the lonely isolation of high command, first in Boston, and later in New York and in Philadelphia. It would unduly extend the documentation of the present volume, already fully and perhaps even fearsomely documented, to collect only a portion of the existing printed references to Mrs. Loring.

[4] A. French, *The Taking of Ticonderoga in 1775* (Cambridge, Mass., 1928) 55.

several corps.[5] And in the summer of 1781, a muster of the British forces in and about New York disclosed 9,686 British troops, 3,512 non-military persons in the civil departments of the Army, and 10,251 German troops, plus an aggregate of 3,615 women and 4,127 children attached to these three groups.[6]

For at this time the Army comprised, both in its military branches as well as in its civil departments, many officials and individuals who in the course of time became militarized. The civil officials included the Deputy Paymaster General and the Commissary General with his deputies and assistants.[7] The Royal Artillery had its conductors and drivers, its own Commissaries who were under the Board of Ordnance, and its numerous varieties of non-military artificers, i.e., civilians skilled in various crafts.[8] The Quar-

[5] French F.Y. 672–673. This figure is exclusive of the thousand or so Loyalist inhabitants who left Boston with the British Army. *Infra*, p. 95.

[6] *Proceedings of a Board of General Officers of the British Army at New York, 1781* (NYHS Coll., 1916). The Board's proceedings provide a mine of information regarding the number and classes of civilians in the employ of the British Army in and around New York at this time. But they embroiled General Clinton with the Treasury at home, and, what made the position more painful, had been initiated by the Commissary of Accounts, Major Drummond, his former ADC, who had become estranged and antagonistic. Willcox 285–288, 448–450, 476–478; H. Clinton 365–366.

[7] This enumeration is based on Sir Henry Clinton's List of the General and Staff Officers, &c., for 1779 and for 1781 (WLCL). The civil departments listed in the 1781 Board of General Officers' investigation included the Barrack Master's Department, the Commissary General of Stores and Provisions, the Quarter Master General's Department, and the Engineer's Department. The public departments included also the Adjutant General, the Physicians and Surgeons of the Hospital, the Deputy Judge Advocate, the Deputy Paymaster General, the Commissary and Paymaster of Artillery, and the Commissary of Musters. All of the Commissaries and Paymasters were civilians and are listed as "Esq."; the Barrack Master General was a Lieutenant-Colonel at the time. Thereafter a Major was announced as Waggon Master General. Carleton OB, 1 July 1782. The gradual militarization of these several civil departments is considered below in chs. VIII and IX.

[8] The Board of Ordnance, which controlled both the Engineers and the Artillery, continued to have its own commissaries and its own stores for many years to come. S. G. P. Ward 8. The correspondence of Gen. Pattison, CRA in North America in 1779 and 1780 (Pattison 1–218), is full of references to many civil officers (Paymaster, Commissary of Artillery, Ordnance Storekeeper, Clerk of Survey, Clerk of Cheque, Clerk of Stores, Conductor of Stores, Barrack Master to the Ordnance, Conductors of Horse, Overseer of the Works), as well as to numerous artificers (carpenters, smiths, wheelers, drivers, farriers, blacksmiths, coopers, collar makers, armourers).

During Gen. Braddock's time, in June 1755, the other ranks in the military branch of the Royal Artillery were Serjeants, Corporals, Bombardiers, Gunners, Matrosses, and Drummers, while the civil branch included a Waggon Master, a Master of Horse, a Commissary and his assistant, Conductors, and Artificers. S. M. Pargellis, ed., *Military Affairs in North America, 1748–1765* (New York, 1936) 90–91.

ter Master General had waggoners and storekeepers, all of them pure civilians,[9] as were the several varieties of artificers directed by the Engineer.[10] The medical officers were part of a civil department, but they had commissions from which they could be dismissed and cashiered, as in the case of Surgeon Major Penman at Gibraltar in 1752, which has already been noted.[11] A little later, another doctor was sentenced to dismissal in default of an apology.[12] Needless to say, none had military rank; their titles reflected a host of specialized functions.[13] Chaplains were similarly subject to trial by court-martial, and one chaplain was tried in New York in 1774.[14]

---

[9] See the enumeration in the 1781 Board proceedings, classifying the various kinds of Quarter Master General employees, and the reference in 2 Mackenzie 600 to "a general Muster this day [26 Aug. 1781] of all the Conductors, Artificers, Labourers, Drivers, horses, and Waggons belonging to the Quarter Master General's department."

[10] At the period now in question, from 1775 until 1778, the "Chief Engineer of America" was Captain John Montrésor. See the references in Montrésor to the "Contracted Company of Carpenters" (432, 434, 454, 480), "my artificers, labourers and waggoners" (454), and to the Engineer's paymaster, assistant in accounts, draughtsmen, and storekeepers (534).

[11] Supra, pp. 26–27.

[12] WO 71/75/6 (Mr. John Thompson, Surgeon's Mate of the 3d Regiment of Foot, tried at Minorca on 1 July 1765 "For giving the Lye to, & Striking Ensign Richard Warren of the 57th Regiment"; convicted; sentenced "To ask Pardon, and if he refuses, to be dismissed"). And see WO 71/28/177–221 (Mr. James Moore, Surgeon's Mate, 1st Foot Guards, tried 27 Mar. 1783; convicted of using disrespectful but not contemptuous language, and sentenced to a public reprimand in the presence of all the medical officers; the King's action on the proceedings declares that this dispute must cease). See also supra, p. 17.

[13] Physician & Inspector; Purveyor & Chief Surgeon; Physician; Surgeon; Apothecary & Deputy Purveyor; Apothecary; Purveyor; Mate; Deputy Chaplain. See "Return of the Staff Officers and Mates of H.M's Hospital at New York, July 24th 1777," WO 1/10/293.

[14] WO 71/80/1, 175 ("to be suspended for the space of 6 months from all Duty and Pay as Chaplain to the 18th or Royal Regiment of Foot of Ireland"). These proceedings were approved by Gen. Gage on 9 Sept. 1774; the case had earlier caused him much concern and an extensive correspondence (Gage Papers, WLCL). It will not occasion surprise that the individual involved is not mentioned in the regimental history. G. leM. Gretton, The Campaigns and History of the Royal Irish Regiment (Edinburgh and London, 1911).
Here is the provision pursuant to which the foregoing trial was held: "Whatsoever Chaplain to a Regiment, Troop, or Garrison, shall be guilty of Drunkenness, or of other scandalous or vicious Behaviour, derogating from the Sacred Character with which he is invested, shall upon due Proofs before a Court-Martial, be discharged from his said Office." Art. 6 of Sec. I, Articles of War for 1774. It should perhaps be noted that in May 1746, in the Duke of Cumberland's time, he twice threatened chaplains with trial by general court-martial for neglect of duty: "Chaplains to take their Turns in visiteing the Hospitals & attending the Condemned prisoners, & will be more diligent in doeing their duty for the Future, otherwise they shall be tryᵈ by a Gen¹ Court Martial." Maclachlan 56; also id. 307.

The other civilians accompanying the army included the retainers to the camp, principally officers' servants; many others, male and female, white and black, who are generically described in the records as "followers of the Army";[15] and finally, as has been noted, literally thousands of women and children, many of whom accompanied the army not only in its quarters but also on the march.[16]

All this was perfectly orthodox military practice at the time, so that the troops obtained by treaty from a whole series of German principalities brought their women with them, marched with them, and brought them back.[17] Some of these were lawfully married to the soldiers; more important than their status was the fact that they washed and mended, cooked and nursed,[18] with the result that their usefulness in garrison and in the field far outweighed their endemic pilfering, plundering, and other acts of disobedience.

The order books, the court-martial records, and a spate of private journals refer to various aspects of the regulation of the accompanying women and children—their rations, their quarters, restrictions on their movements, restrictions on their activities

---

[15] The 80 followers made prisoner after Yorktown in 1781 included purveyors, commissaries, conductors, a waggon master, waggoners, the provost marshal and his assistants, clerks and issuers, stewards, ward masters and assistants, and artificers. WO 36/3.

[16] References to women marching with the army appear in Howe OB 1 Oct. 1776; Clinton OB, 18 June 1778, 3 July 1778, 26 May 1779; and also in the record of the Burgoyne expedition, discussed *infra*, pp. 162–164. On Gen. Clinton's first expedition to South Carolina, 60 women and 12 servants accompanied each regiment. E. Robson, *The Expedition to the Southern Colonies, 1775–1776*, 66 Eng. Hist. Rev. 535, 541.

[17] Trip to America: Pettengill 163, 200; *Commissary Rainsford's Journal of Transactions, 1776–1778* (NYHS Coll., 1879) 369, 378, 394; Pausch 33, 41. Gen. Rainsford was a British officer stationed in Germany who made arrangements for the transportation of the several contingents to ports of embarkation; Capt. Pausch was the Chief of the Hesse-Hanau Artillery during the Burgoyne Campaign.

Marching: Fisher 450 (26 Sept. 1777, describing the British entry into Philadelphia: "Baggage wagons, Hessian women, & horses, cows, goats & asses brought up the rear."). See also Washington to Carleton, 21 Apr. 1783, 26 Washington 341, referring to the women and children with the Convention troops at Winchester and Fredericksburg.

Return home: Popp 253–254.

For women with the mixed British and German force that fought the French on the continent of Europe from 1758 to 1763, see Savory 55, 199 n. 1, 244 n. 1, 335 n. 1, 342, 355 n. 1, and 447.

[18] At punishment parade, "The Soldiers' wives attended with pails of Water saturated with salt, to wash the bloody backs of the sufferers; the pain of the remedy was equal to that of the punishment, but it cured them." Reminiscences of John Pintard (NYHS) 116.

(especially with reference to the sale of liquor), their embarkation and debarkation, their duty in hospitals.[19] Only occasionally does a visitor leer.[20] Some of these women became casualties themselves,[21] while a far greater number, with their children, were sent home as widows and orphans [22]—mute testimony to the marksmanship of the embattled Americans.

Sanctions for disobedience of orders on the part of these women and other followers included striking from the provision list, banishment from the camp or beyond the lines, and, from time to time, trial by court-martial. The extent to which they were additionally punished without trial does not appear, but there is no reason to suppose that the practice in this respect had changed much since the Duke of Cumberland's time.[23] Indeed, surviving records reflect consistency and continuity. During the time of General Braddock's ill-fated expedition in 1755, his order book contains several threats

---

[19] The most perceptive summaries, all recent, are in French F.Y., 105–108; 2 C. Ward 913 n. 20; and Glover 221.

The older and distinctly more embarrassed approach is reflected in E. E. Curtis, *The Organization of the British Army in the American Revolution* (New Haven, 1926) 10–11.

Contemporary attitude is shown by this 1776 comment on Lord Percy: "He had a large tent provided for every company at his own expense to accommodate their women, and he makes it a rule to receive no other servants into his family but soldiers and their wives." Evelyn 127.

Contemporary attitude may also appear in the circumstance that Capt. Evelyn of the 4th Foot, who died in New York in November 1776 of wounds received in action, left his entire estate to Peggie Wright, a woman servant who had accompanied him to Boston and Halifax. Evelyn 90–94. But other sources suggest that she was rather more than a servant. 1 Cowper 233.

[20] "Colnls. Reid and Cotton and me rode in a Baggage Wagon and made ourselves very merry with the different scenes that we saw amongst the soldiery and their ladies." *The Journal of Nicholas Cresswell* (2d ed., New York, 1928) 240, entry dated 21 June 1777, Bonum Town, New Jersey. Cresswell was a young English visitor.

[21] 1 André 43, entry for 20 June 1777: "They killed or wounded about twenty of our people and a woman, a Grenadier's wife." André, then a Captain, later became Major and Clinton's DAG; deeply concerned in Benedict Arnold's defection, he was captured and hanged as a spy. And see Willcox 172 for the injuries suffered by the wife of a provincial officer.

Earlier, an American raid on Charlestown, Mass., during the siege of Boston on 8 Jan. 1776, had netted six prisoners including one woman. *Letters illustrating the siege of Boston*, 14 MHS Proc. 276 (letter dated 9 Jan. 1776); J. D. Black and W. G. Roelker, eds., *A Rhode Island Chaplain in the Revolution* (Providence, 1949) 7 (letter dated 8 Jan. 1776).

[22] Gage to Viscount Barrington, SW, 15 Aug. 1775, 2 Gage *Corr.* 695; Gage OB, 6 May and 6 July 1775; Clinton OB, 4 Feb. 1779, 26 June 1780; Carleton OB, 29 Nov. 1782.

[23] *Supra,* pp. 17–19.

of both corporal and capital punishment without trial.[24] An order book kept by a brigade major a little later, in 1758 and 1759, reflects identical fulminations.[25]

Similar threats also dot the pages of the orders issued by Generals Howe and Carleton,[26] and, specifically directed at the women, appear in subordinate order books.[27] On at least one officially recorded occasion, the threat was translated into action.[28] For this was the era of the notorious "provost marshal" article that purported to legalize summary punishment *in terrorem*, a provision that remained in British military law until 1879.[29]

On the other side of the hill, Washington's Continentals had

---

[24] "If any officer, soldier or follower of the army shall dare to give any strong liquor, or money to the Indian Men or Women, . . . if a . . . follower of the army he shall receive 250 lashes without a C't Mart'l." *Major-General Edward Braddock's Orderly Books, from February 26 to June 17, 1755* (Cumberland, Md., 1880) xxxix (23 May 1775). "If any soldier is seen Drunk in Camp . . . the next morning he is to receive two hundred lashes without a Court Martial." *Id.*, xli (26 May). "Any person whatsoever that is detected in stealing shall be immediately hanged with[t] being brought to a Court Martial." *Id.*, xlix (11 June). And see the extracts from the Duke of Cumberland's orders in 1745 and 1746, *supra*, p. 18.

[25] E. P. Hamilton, *Fort Ticonderoga: Key to a Continent* (Boston, 1964) 74. Col. Hamilton, the Director of Fort Ticonderoga, has very kindly furnished transcripts of the Monypenny orderly book relating to disciplinary items, which show threats of punishment without trial on 31 May, 14 June, 1 July, and 14 July 1757, the last involving a threat of capital punishment.

[26] Howe OB, 31 Oct. 1776, 21 June, 17 July, 29 Aug., 24 Dec. 1777, 8 Jan. 1778; Carleton OB, 14 Sept. 1782, 2 Aug. 1783.

A typical order is Gen. Howe's dated 17 July 1777: "The Commander in Chief thinks it Incumbent Upon him Once More to Declare to the troops that he is Determin'd Upon no account what so Ever to pardon any man found Guilty of Plundering or of being About With out Leave from his post, the Provost Marshall has Receiv'd Warrants to Execute upon the Spot Any Soldier or Follower of the Army Detect'd in Depradation of Any Sort."

[27] "The Ord[r] respecting Bat Men Women, Serv[ts] & other followers of the Army is repeated, any person who may be again found out of the Line of March, will be punished on the Spot, in the most Exemplary Manner." A. R. Newsome, ed., *A British Orderly Book, 1780–1781*, 9 N.C. Hist. Rev. 57, 163, 183 (27 Dec. 1780). "The D:P: Marshal has likewise orders to Execute on the Spot any Negro Who is found quitting the Line of March in search of plunder." *Id.* 276 (6 Jan. 1781, repeating Lord Cornwallis' Orders of 27 Sept. 1780). "Women to attend all Roll Calls in the Rear of the Companies (Except such as are in the Service of Officers) any, and every one found absent, to be immediately Whipp'd & Drumm'd out of the Brigade. . . . NB: The Women to attend all Punishments." *Id.* 374 (2 Mar. 1781). The latter direction was withdrawn ten days later. *Id.* 386.

[28] Howe OB, 9 Sept. 1777: "The Commander in Chief by his own Authority orders for Immediate Execution Andrew Lawder private Soldier in the 10th Regt. of foot Guilty of the Crime of Marauding & Detect'd with plunder upon him & is Determin'd for the future to show no mercy to any man Guilty of that Crime."

[29] 2 Clode M.F. 662–666; and see *infra*, pp. 216–217.

their complement of women also, at least after the war was well under way, concerning whom the American commanders issued virtually identical orders.[30] The present work, however, is limited to the trials of such civilians as were brought before courts-martial of the British Army during the conflict.[31]

The records show that every class of civilian who served with or accompanied that army was so tried: civil officials (generally for embezzlement); male camp followers (more usually for less sophisticated offenses against property); waggoners, drivers, and conductors; one volunteer—sentenced to a thousand lashes for stealing cattle, he was, one may fairly infer, not thereafter commissioned;[32] and, in a number of instances, soldiers' wives and other female camp followers.[33] None of the foregoing trials should occasion surprise; all of them took place during what British military men today would call "on active service" (and in what their American opposite numbers would currently class as "the theater of operations").

SIX OCCUPIED CITIES

During the course of the war, the British Army at various periods and for varying lengths of time occupied the six largest American communities, displacing the civil power in the process. Civil government was restored in only one occupied province; in the other five, military rule held sway as long as the several occupations continued, and, in consequence, courts-martial tried not only civilian officials of the Army and its camp followers, but inhabitants of the country, together with mariners engaging in criminal conduct while working off their accumulated energies ashore. Individuals in both the latter categories were tried, not only for war offenses—corresponding with or aiding the enemy, forcing a safeguard,

---

[30] See the index references under "Women" in the Revolutionary War volumes of Washington. For a recent discursive account, drawn, however, from the records, see W. H. Blumenthal, *Women Camp Followers of the American Revolution* (Philadelphia, 1952). But at first there were very few women in the American camp. French F.Y. 165.

[31] In order to avoid a proliferation of references, all of the civilians tried by general court-martial during the war have been alphabetically listed, with full particulars of their status and trials, in Appendix II, *infra*, pp. 277–300. Where it seems appropriate to mention specific cases, reference will be made to the number assigned them in that Appendix. Generally speaking, only instances of more than routine interest will be thus noted.

[32] No. 195.

[33] Soldiers' wives: Nos. 107, 145, 190, 221. Female camp followers: Nos. 36, 39, 116, 140. Woman's precise status unclear: No. 32.

counseling or assisting desertion, sometimes of soldiers, sometimes of sailors—but, in a far greater number of instances, on charges of committing ordinary common law felonies.

The latter jurisdiction is mentioned only briefly if at all in local histories. The discussion that follows treats the trials and the other incidents of military government in the six occupied cities chronologically, from the date that each was captured by British arms.

BOSTON

As noted in the preceding chapter, General Howe in October 1775 took command in Boston, where General Gage in his capacity as civil Governor of the Province of Massachusetts Bay had declared martial law in June.

Shortly thereafter, in December, two soldiers' wives were tried jointly with their respective husbands: Isabella McMahan, spouse of Private McMahan of the 43d Foot, both accused of receiving stolen goods, and Ann Hennesey, married to Private Hennesey of the 52d Foot, both charged with breaking and entering. The two Henneseys were acquitted,[34] the two McMahans convicted, with Isabella sentenced (like Winifred McCowan a few months previously) "to receive one hundred lashes on her bare back at the Cart's tail in different portions in the most conspicuous parts of the town, & to be imprisoned for three months." [35]

"Boston under rigid martial rule," according to an earlier historian, "was like a prison." [36] For, as one of the besieged civilians wrote at the time, "No manner of business is carried on here but the military; the five churches are turned into barracks, and the people who have commodious houses, obliged to give them up for

---

[34] No. 107.

[35] No. 145.

[36] Frothingham 282. And see Leach 256: "The whole Town was a prison." There are numerous contemporary references to the town being a garrison. *Letters written from Boston, during its occupation by the British troops*, 16 MHS Proc. 182, 281; Sewall [last Royal Atty. Gen. of Mass.], 413, 414 (letter headed "Garrison at Boston, July 15th 1775," "this is the best of all possible worlds, & the garrison of Boston the best possible garrison").

Sewall was the last Royal Attorney General to appear in the courts. On the day before Gov. Gage received the orders that recalled him home, he appointed James Putnam of Worcester to be Attorney General. Gage to Earl of Dartmouth, SS, 9 Oct. 1775, 2 Gage *Corr.* 421. By this time the courts had long since been closed, the portion of the Province of Massachusetts Bay that was still under Royal government consisted only of one besieged city, and Capt. Adye, the army's DJA, undoubtedly handled far more law business than did the nominal Attorney General. Ironically enough, this same James Putnam was the lawyer in whose office John Adams had first studied law. Adams D. & A. *passim*.

the use of the soldiery."[37] Many buildings were pulled down for fuel[38]—"The King needs wood"[39]—and forced labor was required of some artisans.[40] Churches became not only barracks but stables.[41] The British commanders issued proclamations requiring all inhabitants to give in their names and residences, regulating the movements of such of those as wished to leave the beleaguered town, regulating the sale of provisions, and prohibiting the removal of specie.[42] Although the courts were closed, at least one coroner's jury was convened and rendered a verdict.[43] Contemporary letters and journals reflect the fact that numerous inhabitants were imprisoned in the provost on suspicion of aiding the rebels and indeed for expressing any discontent with existing conditions;[44] "since martial law has taken place, there is no such thing as saying any thing."[45] A garrison court of inquiry sat to consider the cases of prisoners suspected of overt disloyalty;[46] it acquitted one individual,[47] and seems to have sentenced another to death—who, however, was reprieved.[48] A similar tribunal had adjudged the Indian slave at Detroit to be hanged for murder,[49] and other records indicate that

---

[37] Willard 255, quoting the letter of a British officer's wife in Boston, 15 Jan. 1776. For other references to the requisitioning of houses, see *id.* 241; Cheever 95; Newell 270; W. Carter 17 ("Several Regiments have struck their tents, and got into houses allotted them in Boston, for winter quarters").

[38] Frothingham 252, 282, 293, 327; Evelyn 79; Newell 270, 271; Edes 129 *et seq.*

[39] Edes 129 *et seq.*

[40] Cheever 92; French F.Y. 339. But see the warrant from Gen. Howe, 31 Dec. 1775, to pay Lt. Robert Lindsey, 22d Foot, the sum of £204/16/6 for the pay of a company of laborers and Negroes for work between 16 Sept. and 30 Dec. 1775. 8 Mag. Am. Hist. 129.

[41] Cheever 95; Newell 269; Sewall 414 ("my pew in church is converted into a pork tub"); W. Carter 15 (". . . a meeting-house, where sedition has often been preached, is clearing out, to be made into a riding-house for the Light Dragoons").

[42] Frothingham 247, 252, 279–280; Howe OB, 20, 23, 25, and 30 Oct., 18 Nov. 1775, 14 Mar. 1776; *The Massachusetts Gazette and Boston Weekly News-Letter,* 9 and 16 Nov. 1775; G. E. Ellis, "Chronicle of the Siege," in *Centennial Anniversary of the Evacuation of Boston* (Boston, 1876) 119, 120, 164–165, 167, 170–172, 174–175; *Broadsides, Ballads, &c. Printed in Massachusetts, 1639–1800* (75 MHS Coll., 1922) 251, 252, 271 (Nos. 1819, 1821–1826, 1828, 1833, 1961); Force 4:3:1246–1247, 1379.

[43] *The Massachusetts Gazette and Boston Weekly News-Letter,* 4 Jan. 1776.

[44] Newell 264, 265; Cheever 92, 93; Leach 258 ("for speaking saucy to an officer"), 259 ("for Complaining of the soldiers for Robbing his Garden, which was his whole living"); Willard 190–191; and see, for the best secondary text, French F.Y. 339–344, 652.

[45] Letter, Isaac Smith of Boston, 1 July 1775, 16 MHS Proc. 291.

[46] Leach 257–258; Edes 96 *et seq.*

[47] Leach 261; Edes 105.

[48] Newell 264; Cheever 93; Willard 174.

[49] *Supra,* pp. 43–44.

garrison courts of inquiry were frequently convened in the British service during this period.[50]

But neither the British headquarters orders issued in Boston nor the War Office court-martial books at home reflect the trial of any inhabitant by general court-martial up to the time that Howe and his Army and over a thousand Loyalists left Boston on 17 March 1776.[51] That day was long celebrated in Boston as Evacuation Day, until, after about 1850, the many Irish immigrants who had settled there made it a double holiday, commemorating not only the spiritual glory of their patron, St. Patrick, but the more immediate and more tangible effulgence of a setback to the Sassenach as well.

NEW YORK

New York was longest under British military occupation, from 15 September 1776 when Howe's troops landed on Manhattan Island, until 25 November 1783 when Washington re-entered the city after the peace.[52] The latter event followed by over a year and a half Sir Guy Carleton's direction (contained in his letter of appointment) to withdraw the garrison,[53] and by nearly eight

---

[50] WO 71/44/382 (29 Mar. 1757 on the island of Antigua); 1 Mackenzie 4–5 (21 Jan. 1775 at Boston); E. G. Williams, ed., *The Orderly Book of Colonel Henry Bouquet's Expedition against the Ohio Indians, 1764* (Pittsburgh, 1960) 42–43 (2 Nov. 1764, Camp at the Forks of the Muskingum); *id.* 45 (7 Nov. 1764, same place); Illinois country, 1769–1770, see *supra*, p. 81; "Court of Enquiry of Field Officers," Savannah, 4 Aug. 1779 (Regimental OB, MS, LC).

Compare the following order, dated Münster, 9 Jan. 1759: "A garrison court-martial to assemble to-morrow at 9 o'clock at the main guard to examine into the conduct of Beard, who is accused of malpractices in his employment about the hospital. They are not required to pass any sentence, but to determine whether Beard is guilty of the charge alleged against him or not." 8 HMC *Var. Coll.* 532. And see the instance of the garrison court-martial at Montreal in 1761, directed to investigate the cases of the imprisoned debtors. Hervey 146, noted *supra*, p. 47.

[51] No record of any trials of inhabitants by garrison courts-martial has been found. For reprints of the texts of a number of original accounts of incidents of the siege, see H. S. Commager and R. B. Morris, eds., *The Spirit of 'Seventy-Six* (Indianapolis and New York, 1958) 147–150, 847–849. No reliance has been placed on *Boyle's Journal of Occurrences in Boston*, 85 NEHGR 5, 117, inasmuch as the author was not in Boston between 9 May 1775 and 18 Mar. 1776 (pp. 13, 119), a period covering almost the entire siege. For the number and many of the names of the Loyalists who left Boston with Howe, see 18 MHS Proc. 266–268, and 30 *id.* 360.

[52] 4 Freeman 176–203; 5 *id.* 460–464.

[53] "The first object of your attention must be to provide for withdrawing the Garrison, Artillery, Provisions, Stores of all kinds, every Species of Public property from New York and its Dependencies to Halifax. The same Steps are to be taken with respect to the Garrisons of Charles Town & Savannah. The Garrison of St. Augustine you will determine upon according to circumstances

months the latter's proclamation of the end of hostilities that was issued after the preliminary articles of peace had been signed.[54]

During the more than seven years of occupation, there was no civil government; the city and such of the adjacent counties as were within the lines were ruled by the British Army.[55] Those who held civil office, as Governor, Lieutenant Governor, Chief Justice, and Mayor, simply drew pay and obeyed military orders. When the British first entered the city, Governor Tryon deferred to General Robertson, the first Commandant, and "kept the executive powers of Civil Government dormant, leaving every thing to the direction of the Military." [56] Later, after General Robertson was himself commissioned Governor, he was instructed that "the orders

---

upon your arrival. The Execution of the whole both in point of *mode* and *time*, It is His Majesty's intention to leave to your discretion." Sir Guy Carleton's Letter of Appointment, CO 5/106/1, 2 (4 Apr. 1782).

These instructions reflected accurately the Cabinet's decision recorded in a minute dated 30 Mar. 1782, 5 Geo. III *Corr.* 435 (No. 3618), and followed by less than five weeks the House of Commons resolutions against further military operations directed at the colonies (38 Com. J. 861, 27 Feb. 1782; 38 Com. J. 868, 4 Mar. 1782).

[54] Carleton OB, 7 Apr. 1783; Carleton to Washington, 6 Apr. 1783, 8 Sparks *Wash.* 542; 26 Washington 334 (American orders for cessation of hostilities, 18 Apr. 1783).

The text of the preliminary treaty, the "Provisional Articles" signed on 30 Nov. 1782, appears at 8 Stat. 54, and 2 H. Miller 96.

The basic reason for the British Army's delay in leaving the city, from which by the terms of Art. VII of that treaty it was to withdraw "with all convenient speed" (8 Stat. 57; 2 H. Miller 99–100), was the problem of carrying away the nearly 30,000 Loyalists who after the earlier evacuations of Boston, Philadelphia, Newport, Savannah, and Charleston were within the British lines in New York in 1783. See "Return of Loyalists," Commissary General's Office, New York, 12 Oct. 1783, PRO, WO 36/3, last page; also Wertenbaker 265, and, generally, ch. XI, "Exile." Contemporary explanations of the delay are reflected in Gen. Carleton's letter to Gov. George Clinton of New York State, 18 June 1783 (8 G. Clinton 207).

[55] The most helpful works bearing on the subject matter of this section are ch. III, "Keeping Peace in the War-Time City," in Barck, and the two volumes of Jones, which include the carefully documented notes of his editor, Mr. E. F. de Lancey. The appearance in print of Judge Jones's history, which he wrote in the 1780's during his exile in England, evoked the bitter comment (H. P. Johnston, *Observations on Judge Jones' Loyalist History* [New York, 1880] 86) that "however true the Judge's statements may prove to be in any given case, *they still require confirmation.*" And, while Gen. Clinton's definitive biographer has pointed out several instances of the author's unreliability (Willcox 123 n. 2, 131 n. 1), preparation of the present book has demonstrated the accuracy of many of Judge Jones's factual statements regarding the British occupation of New York, Philadelphia, Charleston, and Savannah.

[56] Gov. Tryon to Lord G. Germain, SS, 24 Sept. 1776, in 8 N.Y. Col. Doc. 686; Schaukirk 257 (18 Nov. 1776; to avoid having the soldiers quartered in the meetinghouse of the Moravian Congregation, the pastor made application to Gen. Robertson and Gov. Tryon; "the latter received him kindly, but said he could do nothing in the matter, as now all the power was lodged with the army").

of the Commander in Chief must be the rule of your conduct";[57] in retrospect he remarked that he had exercised but few acts as a civil Governor, all his authority having been derived from the Commander in Chief.[58]

Details of administration were in the hands of a succession of Commandants, who issued proclamations regulating the conduct of the inhabitants, their business, and their entrance and egress into the city.[59] In form and substance both, these proclamations would be perfectly familiar to any British or American military government officer who served in either of the twentieth-century's two World Wars. A Department of Police and a city Vestry enforced the Commandant's orders,[60] a Superintendent of Exports appointed by the Commander in Chief functioned as Collector of Customs,[61] while an essentially ineffective council met periodically with the nominal Governor.[62]

All of the civil courts of general jurisdiction were closed. The Court of Vice-Admiralty remained open, to condemn prizes,[63] though this appears to have had specific statutory sanction.[64] The court for the trial of piracies, its commission grounded on 11 & 12 Will. III c. 7, met, and sentenced at least one person to be hanged.[65] Coroners' inquests were regularly held, down to the end;[66] the

[57] Lord G. Germain, SS, to Gov. Robertson, 9 July 1779, 8 N.Y. Col. Doc. 767.

[58] Gov. Robertson to Lt.-Gov. Elliot, 14 Apr. 1783, 4 HMC Am. MSS. 34.

[59] Pattison 221–430 (his letters as Commandant of New York); this general officer, who was also CRA in North America, was "The Gunner who Governed New York" (1 Duncan, ch. XXVIII); 2 Jones 413–414, 426–427, 454–455; Mackenzie Papers, Item D, WLCL.

[60] The Vestry, established by Gen. Robertson as Commandant on 27 Dec. 1777, consisted of the Magistrates of Police and some 19 citizens who had been appointed to collect alms for the poor. Dawson 154; Barck 55.

[61] 2 Jones 454–455. This was Andrew Elliot, who had been Receiver General and Collector of the Post under the Crown from 1764, who at this time was simultaneously Superintendent of Police, see text *infra*, and who became Lieutenant-Governor in March 1780. See E. Devereux, *Andrew Elliot, Lieutenant-Governor of the Province of New York*, 11 PMHB 129.

[62] Barck 54–55, 61–63, 66–69.

[63] 2 Jones 100, 103.

[64] See Lord G. Germain, SS, to Gov. Tryon, 3 Mar. 1777, 8 N.Y. Col. Doc. 704, 705; Gov. Tryon to Lord G. Germain, SS, 8 June 1777, 8 *id.* 711 (Vice-Admiralty Court not yet open); Lord G. Germain, SS, to Gov. Tryon, 6 Aug. 1777, 8 *id.* 716 (inclosing copy of sentence of Court of Admiralty in England, "that it may serve as a guide to the Court of V. Admiralty to be established in New York in similar cases"); and, pre-eminently, *Letter from Lieutenant Governor Andrew Elliot to Governor Robertson, January 19, 1781*, 37 PMHB 480, 484, stating that the admiralty court was established as soon as the Act authorizing the carrying of prizes into North America (17 Geo. III c. 40) arrived.

[65] *N.-Y. Royal Gazette*, 19 June 1782. No effort has been made to trace other sittings of this tribunal.

[66] E.g., 4 HMC Am. MSS. 221, 376, 414, 419, 443, 464.

Prerogative Court remained open throughout, while some justices of the peace and the Court of Common Pleas on Long Island functioned at least for a time.[67] General Howe in 1777 and General Robertson as Governor in 1780 established Courts of Police, each under a Superintendent, to try a limited class of civil cases—prewar debts were expressly excluded [68]—and which further had no jurisdiction over any military persons, whether soldiers or civil officers of the Army.[69] Minor offenses were dealt with by these Courts of Police, while for more serious ones the inhabitants were regularly tried by court-martial; those trials, in respect of status of the accused, offenses charged, and punishments imposed, are treated in detail below. On occasion, the persons accused were released without trial upon giving bail.[70]

Business disputes were submitted to the Chamber of Commerce, and there arbitrated,[71] and the awards were either performed voluntarily, or else enforced by the Commandant on a "pay up or else" basis.[72] On one occasion, when the losing party insulted the committee of arbitration, he was required by the Magistrates of Police to apologize in writing.[73] The Chamber co-operated with the Commandant in connection with the latter's price-fixing activities,[74] and with his regulation of licensed tradespeople.[75]

In October 1776, shortly after the Continental Army had been driven from New York City, some thousand or so Loyalists who remained petitioned General Howe for the restoration of civil government; their request was pigeonholed without action.[76] Then, considerably later, the Commissioners for Conciliation headed by the Earl of Carlisle, who came to America in June 1778, recommended the restoration of civil government.[77]

Thereafter, early in 1780, General Robertson, the first Comman-

---

[67] 2 Jones 100, 103–104, 119, 130–131.
[68] 2 Jones 2, 10, 12, 18, 30–32, and 120–142 (ch. VII, "The 'Courts of Police,' Military Courts with Quasi-Civilian Jurisdiction Created by Proclamations of British Commanders for Ruling New York").
[69] 2 Jones 21, 65, 72, 120–142.
[70] Pattison 240, 296.
[71] E.g., Stevens 204, 215, 219, 287–288; see index entries under "Arbitration Committee."
[72] Pattison 292, 406–407, 429–430.
For articulation of this technique, see Appendix IG2, *infra*, at p. 268.
[73] Stevens 264–267, 270.
[74] Stevens 210, 216–217, 223, 225–227, 275–277.
[75] Stevens 206–207, 237, 247–248, 261–263, 277.
[76] 2 Jones 433–453; Dawson 117–140.
[77] For the Carlisle Commissioners, see H. Clinton 86–88, 112–113; Alden A.R. 196–197, 199–202; Van Doren S.H. 63–116; ch. X, "The Carlisle Commission,

dant, returned to New York as civil Governor of the province, issuing on arrival a resounding proclamation:

> It is his Majesty's wish, by the Revival of the Civil Authority, to prove to all the Colonies and Provinces, that it is not his design to govern America by Military Law, but they are to enjoy all the Benefits of a local Legislation and their former Constitution. To this End I have brought out the Royal Appointments for forming the Council, and supplying the Places of Lieutenant Governor and Chief Justice. And in concurrence with the Commander-in-chief of the British Forces, who is also his Majesty's Commissioner for restoring Peace to the Colonies, I shall as speedily as the publick Exigencies permit, give order for opening the Courts of Judicature and convening the Assembly; and in general proceed to the Execution of the Powers reposed in me, for the free Course and complete Re-Establishment, both of the Legislative and Executive Authority.[78]

Here was indeed good news. But, unhappily for those who read his proclamation literally, Governor Robertson's directive to restore civil government was hedged about with self-defeating qualifications, namely, that restoration depended on the order of Sir Henry Clinton (who was strongly opposed),[79] and that the Assembly could not be convened until enough of the province had been reconquered to enable a majority of the prewar members to be returned (a practical impossibility, while Clinton stayed on the defensive in New York and sailed off to capture Charleston in South Carolina). Consequently, notwithstanding the assurances in the new Governor's proclamation, notwithstanding generalized encouragement from home, no change was made—a result that greatly chagrined the Loyalist population.[80]

1778," in W. A. Brown, *Empire or Independence* (University, La., 1941); Willcox 220–225, 229–232, 240–242, 254–255; A. S. Brown, *The British Peace Offer of 1778: A Study in Ministerial Confusion*, 40 Pap. Mich. Acad. Sci. Arts. & Ltrs. 249; and the several Acts of Parliament aimed at reconciliation. 18 Geo. III cc. 11, 12, and 13. For their proposals in the present connection, see Barck 61–63; Smith L. & R. 114. They arrived in Philadelphia on 6 June 1778, at which time the guard was turned out in their honor (1 Kemble 590)—small recompense for the hopelessly destructive effect on their mission of the British evacuation of that city 12 days after their arrival. See also references cited in note 39 of Chapter VI, *infra*, p. 145.

[78] 4 N.Y. State Doc. (Albany, 1851) 655 [quarto ed.]; *id.*, p. 1085 [folio ed.].

[79] Willcox 379–380.

[80] For the directives, see Lord G. Germain, SS, to Gov. Robertson, 9 July 1779, 8 N.Y. Col. Doc. 767; same to same, 5 July 1780, 8 *id.* 795; same to same, 6 Sept. 1780,

Late in 1781, Superintendent-General (and Lieutenant-Governor) Elliot expressed the hope that the arbitral duties of the Chamber of Commerce would soon be rendered unnecessary. "It has long been proposed (I hope Events are not distant that may admit of a Trial) to revive at least such part of the civil Authority by which Justice may be administered to the Community. Individuals will then be freed from the Burthen of adjusting Mercantile disputes, and I shall be relieved from a most fatiguing anxious situation." [81]

It was not to be. Cornwallis surrendered within the month, and the end was in sight, although evacuation of the city was still nearly two years away. By that time all of the foregoing procedures and policies had become not only well settled but indeed institutionalized, so that when one George Folliott sought relief in respect of debts that had been incurred before the war by persons within the lines—a class of obligation that, as has been seen, was expressly excluded from the jurisdiction of the Courts of Police—Elliot, Mayor Mathews, and one of the Magistrates of Police explained the reasons for this exclusion in a long report that set forth in detail the operation of the military government they were engaged in administering. That report, dated 4 December 1781, appears in Appendix IG2; it seems never before to have been printed. [82]

General Clinton simply forwarded both documents to the Secretary of State, to show "the Manner in which [the officers of the police] conduct this temporary Institution, which was established in May 1778 and with a View of affording the Citizens of this Garrison every possible Security to their property and Persons that would not cause Confusion in Real Estates, or give rise to Points the adjusting of which might at a future Day be troublesome to Government. . . . The Peace and good Order which has uniformly

---

8 *id.* 801, 802. When Gov. Robertson discovered that Sir Henry Clinton and the senior British admiral then at New York, Vice-Admiral Marriot Arbuthnot, thought differently on the subject (Willcox 379–380), he reported that "I have taken some pains to keep the question out of sight." Gov. Robertson to Lord G. Germain, SS, 1 July 1780, 8 N.Y. Col. Doc. 794. For the Loyalist reaction see ch. I, "Affairs in New York in 1780," in 2 Jones.

[81] To Isaac Low, President of the Chamber of Commerce, 2 Oct. 1781 (Stevens, 269).

[82] The Folliott memorial, listed but not calendared at 2 HMC Am. MSS. 353, is PRO 30/55 No. 3892. The answering report is CO 5/104/166, reproduced as Appendix IG2, *infra*, pp. 266–271. It is not noted in Barck, and represents the earliest known document signed by William Walton as a Magistrate of Police. See Stevens 362–363.

been kept up in this Garrison is solely to be attributed to the proper Manner in which this Temporary Establishment has been conducted." [83]

Not only was the limitation in respect of pre-existing debts proper, the entire governmental machinery should be continued, and early in 1782 Clinton and his advisers solemnly determined that any restoration of civil authority would be inexpedient.[84] And, by the time General Carleton arrived to assume command in May of that year, the end of offensive operations had been directed by resolution of the House of Commons.[85] It was then far simpler to continue existing arrangements pending final evacuation of the city,[86] and although Carleton did speak in June 1782 of considering "establishing a court of criminal law in this town," [87] that was probably little more than a pious hope induced by the complications of the Lippincott trial, which, as will be seen, were then at a particularly vexing level.

For, although General Carleton had said during his first month at New York that "he detested the thought of trying Citizens by Soldiers and that he sincerely wished to put all Criminals into the hands of the Law," he had added, almost in the same breath, "But what can I do . . . if I find no Courts open—are we all to live exposed to Murder?" [88] In actual fact, therefore, far more inhabitants were tried by general court-martial during the eighteen months of his command, relatively speaking, than in the more than five and a half years that Generals Howe and Clinton served as Commanders in Chief.[89]

---

[83] Clinton to Lord G. Germain, SS, 6 Dec. 1781; listed at 2 HMC Am. MSS. 361, full text in PRO 30/55 No. 3939.

[84] H. Clinton 592–594; 2 HMC Am. MSS. 385.

[85] See "The House of Commons repudiates the American War," in I. R. Christie, *The End of North's Ministry, 1780–1782* (London, 1958) 319–340. The resolutions are at 38 Com. J. 861 (27 Feb. 1782) and at 38 Com. J. 868 (4 Mar. 1782). The first of these was the decisive one. See Lord North to the King, 28 Feb. 1782, 5 Geo. III *Corr.* 374 (No. 3535). Gen. Carleton assumed command on 8 May 1782; see entries in both Clinton OB and Carleton OB for that day. Gen. Carleton and Adm. Digby communicated the House of Commons' resolution to Washington on 2 Apr. 1782. 8 Sparks *Wash.* 540.

[86] Barck 70–72.

[87] Carleton to Washington, 20 June 1782, 8 Sparks *Wash.* 537, 538; Barck 70–71.

[88] William Smith Diary (NYPL) 3 June 1782.

[89] Two women unconnected with the Army were tried in Gen. Howe's time, 8 in Clinton's, 4 in Carleton's. Seventeen persons unconnected with the Army were tried in and around New York under Gen. Howe (Sept. 1776–May 1778), 73 under Gen. Clinton (May 1778–May 1782), and 66 under Gen. Carleton (May

The legal justification for military rule in New York that was most generally asserted contemporaneously was the Prohibitory Act (16 Geo. III c. 5), which, it was contended on behalf of the military commanders, not only halted the colonists' trade but deprived them of all civil and political rights as well, by putting them out of the King's peace.[90] Judge Jones, the cantankerous Loyalist, challenged the soundness of this view.[91] He pointed out that this measure mentioned neither courts nor civil government; that the royal government of the province had been displaced, not by the Prohibitory Act when that statute became effective early in 1776, but only by the arrival in New York of Washington's army following the British evacuation of Boston; that he himself as a Justice of the Supreme Court of the Province of New York—one of H.M.'s judges—had continued after such arrival to hold court, and, with the approval of their officers, to try and to sentence American soldiers charged with civil offenses; [92] that only the Declaration of Independence had vacated his office under the Crown; that after General Howe had driven out the American forces and restored British authority, some royal courts continued to sit notwithstanding the Prohibitory Act; and that numerous public corporations other than the city itself—"The Mayor, Aldermen, and Commonalty of the City of New York"—continued to function.

Judge Jones would have been mightily surprised had he known that his own strongly held view, that the terms of the Prohibitory Act afforded no justification whatever for military rule in New York, was shared by the highest ranking civilian in the province. But it was the fact, though not published until over 130 years later, that Lieutenant-Governor Andrew Elliot had solemnly—and correctly—declared in January 1781 that "the Parliament of Great Britain has not passed any act by which the Power of the Officers

1782–Nov. 1783). This classification, drawn from the details in Appendix II, excludes soldiers' wives and civil officers and employees, because they were connected with the Army, but includes mariners and Royal Navy personnel, who were not.

[90] Barck 49–50; ch. VI, "Why the Laws of the Colony were Abolished and the Courts of Justice Shut up During the War," in 2 Jones. This legal theory was attributed to Joseph Galloway, who, see text *infra*, pp. 145–147, was Superintendent-General in Philadelphia during the British occupation. 2 Jones 109–110, 430–431. The parliamentary background of the Prohibitory Act is discussed in 12 Gipson B.E. 346–349.

[91] Ch. VI (*supra*, n. 90) in 2 Jones.

[92] 1 Jones 137; 2 Jones 135.

of Civil Government are suspended in the Revolted Provinces." [93]

But, although Judge Jones had thus accurately asserted the irrelevancy of the Prohibitory Act, his continually repeated tirades against the rapacity of "barrack masters, quarter masters, and commissaries" caused him to overlook significant aspects underlying and justifying the substitution of military for civil rule.

In point of fact—and, despite the purposeful destruction of many of the occupation records prior to evacuation,[94] the matter plainly appears—the real reason for the continuation of the military regime in New York was the stubborn but all-pervasive circumstance of a war whose progress had limited British authority in the Province of New York "to the three Islands"—Manhattan Island, Staten Island, and Long Island.[95] Hence Elliot, while conceding that the position might be different if additional territory were under royal authority, wrote that "whilst we continue in our present circumscribed situation, any attempt to Revive the Civil Power, would not only injure the Public cause, but also Private interest, by impeding the Military Operations, laying the foundation of future Province feuds, by calling a partial Assembly and create future confusion in Private property by decisions being made at such times." [96]

So far as Generals Howe and Clinton were concerned, continued military government in New York was, almost literally, a matter of military necessity. Facing Washington and his amazingly viable army; relying on a Ministry at home than never in fact provided the military means they so urgently besought and that "neither focused

---

[93] Lt.-Gov. Elliot to Gov. Robertson, 19 Jan. 1781 (*supra*, n. 64), 37 PMHB 480. This frank admission was disturbing to Gen. Robertson, who during his earlier duty in New York as Commandant had doubtless been indoctrinated to the contrary. Forwarding Elliot's letter home, he wrote Lord George Germain that "His opinion about civil Government is different from mine." Gov. Robertson to Lord G. Germain, SS, 28 Jan. 1781, 8 N.Y. Col. Doc. 809, 810.

[94] Barck 51, 252–253; Lt.-Gov. Elliot to Gen. Carleton, 15 Nov. 1783, 4 HMC Am. MSS. 457–458. It is true that Art. VII of the preliminary treaty (*loc. cit. supra*, n. 54) provided for the immediate restoration and delivery of "all archives, records, deeds and papers, belonging to any of said states, or their citizens . . . to the proper states and persons to whom they belong." The records of the occupation, clearly, were not within that description.

[95] "The means of escape to us, is become somewhat more difficult by our withdrawing our posts, and confining ourselves to the three Islands." Gov. Robertson to Lord G. Germain, SS, 1 Sept. 1780, 8 N.Y. Col. Doc. 799, 800.

[96] Elliot to Robertson (*supra*, n. 64), 37 PMHB 482; the qualification follows at 482–483.

on a raiding war nor provided the troops for a war of conquest";[97] unlikely to be unaware that they were fighting an unpopular war [98] —is it to be supposed that these commanders would consciously compound their woes by voluntarily adding to existing burdens the manifold complications of an independent civil government in their midst? [99]

For such a government, as Judge Jones envisaged it, would have included precisely the kind of rump Assembly that Whitehall for all its homilies about restoring "the civil Authority to it's former dignity" [100] was not prepared to accept,[101] yet which if functioning would have regulated the more than 2,500 militiamen within the British lines; [102] such a government would have included a restored municipal administration supervising the police of a garrison whose aggregate ration strength exceeded 30,000; [103] and it would have included a full complement of civil courts staffed by Loyalist judges entertaining fiercely traditional views of the subordination of the military to the civil power under the British constitution.[104] Every sentry shooting a nocturnal prowler would have been haled before a jury of civilians, just as Captain Preston and the soldiers concerned in the Boston Massacre of 1770 had been; [105] every

---

[97] Willcox 258.

[98] See 2 Mackenzie 551, written in the summer of 1781: ". . . this is an unpopular war, and men of ability do not chuse to risk their reputation by taking an active part in it."

"British officers were deserting America in droves. Lord Howe, Generals Pigot and Grey, Lord Cornwallis—all were either back in England or on the way; and even General Jones wanted to return for fear that the command would devolve upon him." Willcox 263, citing letters dated in October and December 1778. See also the documentation in Valentine 305 supporting his statement that "the number of military and naval officers who openly opposed the war is impressive."

[99] "In the summer of 1780 [Clinton] had claimed to be 'as much for civil government as any man . . . as soon as it consisted with the general good,' but by the end of the year he had decided that it would be disastrous; the bulk of the population was either covert rebels or merchants bent on exploiting the army, and if these men acquired political power 'I will no longer be answerable for military operations and I can no longer consent to conduct them, let the consequence be as it may.' " Willcox 379.

[100] Lord G. Germain, SS, to Gov. Robertson, 6 Sept. 1780, 8 N.Y. Col. Doc. 801, 802.

[101] *Supra*, p. 99.

[102] Pattison 147, 153.

[103] *Supra*, p. 87.

[104] 2 Jones 93, 116, 134–142.

[105] 11 Gipson B.E. 274–285; Gipson C.R. 201–202; 3 Adams D. & A. 291–296.

All previous discussions of the Boston Massacre are now superseded by vol. 3 of Adams *Leg. Pap.*, which is devoted in its entirety to the Boston Massacre trials—and which demonstrates (pp. 17–19) how the jury that acquitted Capt. Preston was substantially packed in his favor.

subaltern tangling with a constable in the course of off-duty carousing would have faced a civil magistrate, as did the officers who assaulted the Boston watch in January 1775;[106] every soldier unable to pay a heavy fine imposed by the local justices might well have been bound out as a servant, as so many soldiers in Boston had been;[107] and every official procuring supplies or quarters for the King's Army plainly risked actions at law for damages.

Had all this come to pass, then, assuredly, for every subject seeking redress from military spoliation there would have been a dozen suits—and prosecutions—brought against conscientious officers who were endeavoring to feed and house the troops in a war-torn, half-burned-out city.[108] Not even commanders of the caliber of Marlborough, Amherst, or Wellington—which Howe and Clinton, to both of whom the United States in such large measure owe their independence, very obviously were not—could have functioned under any such arrangement.

Judge Jones is less to be criticized for failing to anticipate the subsequently formulated legal basis for what the commanders whom he held in such disesteem were doing. That was the law of belligerent occupation, as it developed in the following century, with this variant, that in New York and in the other American cities during the War of American Independence, the British Army was present as a military occupant. The same situation precisely recurred ninety years later, when the United States Army militarily occupied portions of the seceded Confederate States as those were slowly and painfully reconquered.

Turning for a moment to the later struggle, which took place after the law had become fully articulated, the United States Army in the reoccupied Confederacy was administering military government and exercising military jurisdiction. It erected new courts,[109]

---

[106] *Supra*, pp. 82–83.

[107] Shy 313–314; see *Rex* v. *Moyse and Reader* (1769), 2 Adams *Leg. Pap.* 436–437.

[108] A large part of New York was burned shortly after the British entered, in September 1776; the Loyalists insisted that its cause was deliberate arson by the retreating Continentals, the Americans were positive the fire had been accidental. Wertenbaker 99–102; 3 Fortescue 190; Barck 79–82.

As late as 18 Oct. 1783, seven years after the event and a little more than a month prior to final evacuation, Gen. Carleton appointed a board of officers to inquire into the cause of the 1776 fire. 4 HMC Am. MSS. 416. Some of the evidence then taken is summarized at 5 I.N.P. Stokes 1168–1169.

[109] *The Grapeshot*, 9 Wall. 129; *Pennywit* v. *Eaton*, 15 Wall. 382; *Burke* v. *Miltenberger*, 19 Wall. 519; *United States* v. *Reiter*, Fed. Case No. 16,146 (U.S. Provisional Ct. for Louisiana); *State* v. *Jarvis*, 63 N.C. 556 (same, during Recon-

it immunized its military personnel from the jurisdiction of local courts,[110] it exercised authority theretofore vested in local municipal authorities,[111] and it treated as enemy property everything useful in the prosecution of the war that it found within its lines, whether owned by citizens of the United States or by aliens.[112] This was military government in fact because the Confederate States were at all times accorded belligerent rights.[113]

Actually, the position of the loyal army that reoccupied rebel territory in New York in 1776–1783 was identical to that of the loyal army that similarly reoccupied rebel territory in Louisiana and Tennessee in 1862–1865—once it is conceded that the American colonists had belligerent rights; and of course that concession underlay every exchange of prisoners from May 1775 until the end.[114] Therefore, much as the British Army had done in Canada and in Florida at the end of the Seven Years War, it could in the American cities in the following conflict, under presently accepted doctrines, close courts at will; erect new courts from whose process the members of its own forces and their dependents and followers would be immune; try inhabitants by courts-martial sitting as military government tribunals; and legislate by military order to regulate in minute detail the business, the affairs, and the police of the community.

The parallel between the War of American Independence and the later American Civil War is an exact one, as eminent historians on both sides of the Atlantic have long sensed. Henry Belcher, an Englishman, entitled his history of the earlier struggle "The First American Civil War"; [115] Edward Channing of Massachusetts called his account of the later one "The War for Southern Inde-

---

struction); *State ex rel. Kain* v. *Hall*, 6 Baxter (Tenn.) 3 (same); *Cronin* v. *Patrick County*, 89 Fed. 79 (C.C. W.D.Va.) (same).

[110] *Coleman* v. *Tennessee*, 97 U.S. 509; *Dow* v. *Johnson*, 100 U.S. 158.

[111] *New Orleans* v. *Steamship Co.*, 20 Wall. 387; *Keely* v. *Sanders*, 99 U.S. 441; *State ex rel. O'Hara* v. *Heath*, 20 La. Ann. 518 (Reconstruction case); *Clegg* v. *State*, 42 Tex. 605 (same).

[112] *Mrs. Alexander's Cotton*, 2 Wall. 404; *Miller* v. *United States*, 11 Wall. 268; *Lamar* v. *Browne*, 92 U.S. 187; *United States* v. *Diekelman*, 92 U.S. 520 (property of Prussian subject); *Ford* v. *Surget*, 97 U.S. 594. As most of these cases show, a United States citizen able to establish his loyalty could recover the value of his seized property by suit in the Court of Claims.

[113] *Supra*, n. 2.

[114] *Supra*, n. 3.

[115] London, 1911.

pendence." [116] And Professor Gipson, author of the definitive multivolume study *The British Empire before the American Revolution*, has pointed out that both wars involved an identical political problem, namely, the use of coercion by a state to restrain its subordinate units.[117]

Judge Thomas Jones, sometime Justice of the Supreme Court of H.M.'s Province of New York, should not be unduly criticized today because, dying in exile in 1792,[118] he was insufficiently clairvoyant to invoke the same comparison.

It is now appropriate to return to the matter in hand, the British trials by court-martial of inhabitants and other civilians in New York during the War of American Independence.

There have been found the names of 156 persons unconnected with the Army (including Captain Lippincott, whose case and claim of civilian status are discussed at length below), all of whom faced general courts-martial of the British Army in New York and its environs during the war.[119] In one of these, jurisdiction was declined,[120] while in seventy-nine instances, or almost 51 per cent of the remainder, the accused was acquitted. The high percentage of acquittals reflects the circumstance that, at this time, a charge once made was required to be brought to trial, barring only a retraction by the accuser. There is no suggestion, either in textbooks or in the consistent practice, then and for some time to come, that the convening authority had any discretion whatever in respect of dismissing charges before trial for groundlessness or for triviality. The court-martial in finding the person on trial not guilty could thus

---

[116] New York, 1930 (vol. VI of *A History of the United States*).

[117] Gipson C.R. 223. And see *id*. 233–234, noting "the anomaly that in our own day the fundamental positions taken by Great Britain and America in the year 1775 are reversed." Subject only to a reservation in respect of a guaranty of fundamental liberties at the moment of separation—which is all that the Rhodesian case can possibly mean in the light of the Nkrumah regime in Ghana—modern Britain recognizes the right of secession from Commonwealth and Empire. But modern America does not, and moreover has maintained territories and possessions whose inhabitants have only such rights in respect of taxation and representation as Congress from time to time sees fit to allow them. Cf. W. T. Perkins, *Denial of Empire: The United States and Its Dependencies* (Leyden, 1962).

[118] DAB.

[119] See Appendix II, *infra*. Followers and retainers to the army, soldiers' wives, and civil officers or employees have been excluded; mariners and members of the Royal Navy have been included as being unconnected with the army. The special verdicts (*infra*, pp. 126–127) are counted as convictions because of the action taken thereon.

[120] No. 106; see *infra*, pp. 112–113.

characterize the accusations made; the Commander in Chief was apparently not free to do so on his own.[121]

Many of the accused were specifically described as inhabitants, not infrequently as being of other provinces. In all of the calculations herein, there have been included as inhabitants all who were described by their trade, or described as Negroes not alleged (as many were) to be followers of the army, or not described as having any military rank or connection. This group included fourteen women.[122] In addition, one member of the military government, an employee of the Magistrates of Police, was tried by court-martial.[123]

Seafaring persons tried included, from the merchant marine, the master of a sloop, a mate, a ship's surgeon, a supercargo, many mariners, three carpenters, a cooper, a gunner, and a steward.[124] The privateer fleet furnished as grist for the court-martial mill an owner, a master, and a lieutenant.[125] Members of the Royal Navy were also tried—one midshipman, three mates, and two mariners.[126] One of the mates was tried by Army court-martial for murdering another member of the Royal Navy.[127] But since the offense was committed on shore, and since the victim died there, the accused, notwithstanding his naval status, would not have been within the jurisdiction of a naval court-martial.[128]

The offenses charged constitute a catalogue of the criminal law: murder, rape, arson, assault, plundering, burglary, robbery, theft, embezzlement, receiving stolen goods, obtaining property by false pretenses, forgery, and counterfeiting, among the civil crimes; corresponding with or aiding the enemy, assisting or advising desertion of soldiers, enticing Royal Navy sailors to desert, forcing a safeguard,[129] and violating military government regulations[130]

---

[121] Nos. 50 and 164 (complaint frivolous); No. 80 (prosecution vexatious, malicious, and groundless); cf. No. 108 (groundless and malicious; but see the text *infra*, pp. 129–133, for the special circumstances of this last trial, that of Cornelius Hetfield.) Compare the case of Capt. Campbell, *infra*, pp. 147–148, the charges in which Gen. Howe requested the accuser to retract, but which on her refusal were required to be tried.

[122] Nos. 11, 64, 68, 86, 97, 114, 141, 146, 163, 169, 182, 185, 213, 216.

[123] No. 227.

[124] Nos. 6–8, 44, 49, 50, 58, 59, 84, 91, 100, 118, 120, 130, 149, 152, 157, 179, 187, 196, 200, 203, 228.

[125] Nos. 106, 123, 147.

[126] Nos. 14, 48, 90, 92, 161, 191.

[127] No. 161.

[128] 1 McArthur 179–183, 326–329.

[129] Nos. 6, 196.

[130] Nos. 15, 106.

among the military offenses, including—inevitably—insulting officers.[131]

The sentences imposed reflect the views of criminal law enforcement that were prevalent at the time: death; flogging from fifty lashes up to one thousand, frequently combined with imprisonment, or with drumming out of camp, or with service in the Navy; confinement for stated periods of one to twelve months, in one instance for the duration of the Rebellion; [132] fines; penalties where directed by Act of Parliament, as in the case of enticing desertion or purchasing soldiers' effects; [133] and turning out of the camp or lines, sometimes with a halter around the accused's neck. Many were directed to find security for future good behavior. Some were turned out of the lines after an acquittal,[134] four were pardoned on condition that they transport themselves to the West Indies or elsewhere.[135] One laborer convicted of robbery was sent to the West Indies after a flogging,[136] while several Negro followers of the army were also sent there following their acquittal on a joint charge of murder; [137] doubtless this meant return to slavery for the latter group.

Convicted merchant mariners were sentenced to serve in the Royal Navy, generally following corporal punishment, as a species of impressment enforced by the Army; [138] one convicted officer's servant was also dealt with in that manner.[139] Offenders against property were frequently required, in addition to other punishment, to make restitution,[140] while two fines imposed were ordered paid to the victims.[141] There was one sentence to transportation,[142] one to an hour in the stocks (later pardoned), [143] and two, where inhabitants charged with murder were convicted only of

---

[131] Nos. 53A, 54, 80 (charge 3).

[132] No. 201.

[133] Nos. 47, 130, 147, 150, 180, 193. Penalty for purchasing soldiers' effects, recurring clause in Mutiny Act; penalty for enticing soldiers to desert, 1 Geo. I stat. 2 c. 47; penalty for enticing sailors to desert, 6 Anne c. 37, §10.

[134] Nos. 135, 141.

[135] Nos. 74, 208. 218, 227.

[136] No. 222.

[137] Nos. 10, 60, 93, 186.

[138] Nos. 7, 44, 49, 149, 157.

[139] No. 26. Cf. No. 121, "to be sent on board ship"; the notorious prison ship was doubtless meant.

[140] Nos. 15, 61, 86, 212.

[141] No. 51 (assault); No. 127 (manslaughter, fine to be paid to widow).

[142] No. 95.

[143] No. 70.

manslaughter, to burning in the hand.[144] Sentences passed on the few women who were convicted—there were only four of these in all, three inhabitants and one soldier's wife—were perhaps somewhat milder, though they reflected a climate of opinion that had not yet outlawed burning at the stake for petty treason, though it had just abolished the *peine forte et dure*.[145]

Two inhabitants, convicted by general court-martial of insulting an officer, were sentenced to make public apology.[146] One of these cases is duly recorded by Judge Jones,[147] who instances another where the outcome was more painful; there the insult, which led to blows on both sides, was expunged by three hundred lashes adjudged by garrison court-martial.[148] And in May 1782, a ferryman who quarreled with a serjeant was, two days after trial, "brought out to be whipp'd 200 lashes & fainting under 106 was dismissed."[149]

A number of the trials that have been instanced raised legal and jurisdictional questions warranting more extensive comments, but perhaps the most interesting preliminary to be noted is that Charles Gould, who had become Judge Advocate General in 1769 on the death of his father-in-law, considerably muted his strictures by comparison with those loosed earlier in consequence of the trials of inhabitants in occupied Canada, of the Royal Navy boatswain in occupied Martinique, and of civilian dependents and employees in reacquired Minorca.[150]

He did not change his opinion; writing Sir William Howe in 1777, he submitted "whether Courts Martial are well founded in the Jurisdiction exercised by them in the Trial of persons, who are in no sort belonging to the Army." But, recognizing that "These

---

[144] Nos. 74, 127.

[145] No. 68 (receiving stolen goods; 1 month confinement); No. 86 (stealing; 300 lashes at three different times and confinement until 2 guineas stolen are repaid); No. 146 (burglary; death); No. 221 (soldier's wife; receiving and secreting stolen goods; "to be Drumm'd out of the lines with a Rope about her Neck"). The *peine forte et dure* was abolished in 1772 (12 Geo. III c. 20), burning at the stake for petty treason in 1790 (30 Geo. III c. 48).

[146] Nos. 53A, 54.

[147] 2 Jones 82–83.

[148] 2 Jones 83–84. And see 2 *id.* 84–85, for the case of an inhabitant who, to avoid trial by court-martial for kicking a Negro driver, was obliged to ask pardon of the driver, his conductor, and the driver's commanding officer.

On 26 May 1778 (1 Kemble 620), the Commandant in New York ordered that "A Surgeon's Mate from the Hospital is to attend the Corporal Punishment of the Garrison Courts Martial, who is to receive his Orders from the Commandant. He is to be appointed weekly to this Duty."

[149] William Smith Diary, 4 June 1782, quoted in 5 I.N.P. Stokes 1146–1147.

[150] *Supra*, pp. 55–59, 69–70, 75–76.

are delicate Subjects," he contented himself with suggesting that where "Courts Martial have been induced to exceed the limits of their ordinary Jurisdiction," it would be well "not to call the attention to any of the Articles of War in the penning of their Sentence." [151]

The mildness of this suggestion represented a substantial retreat from the somewhat peremptory corrective measures he had earlier pressed upon Governor Murray, General Gage, and Governor Townshend; [152] doubtless the necessities of the war then under way induced a more temperate criticism. Just how much effect Gould's suggestion had on the actual practice of the British Army in America during the balance of the war admits of doubt; in the Lippincott trial in 1782 (treated in detail below), the court-martial overruled the accused's plea to the jurisdiction by invoking Article 2 of Section XX, the familiar "no Form of Our Civil Judicature" provision. No reply from General Howe appears in the JAG correspondence, and it may therefore, at the very least, be plausibly inferred that Gould's letter found a resting place in the drawer marked, whether visibly or otherwise does not at all alter the position, "File and forget."

One tell-tale mark of the civil law origin of the law military made its appearance at about this time. The civil law did not recognize manslaughter as a lesser included offense within murder, and in cases falling in the admiralty's criminal jurisdiction that were tried on shore, where the Act of 11 & 12 Will. III c. 7 provided that they should proceed "according to the civil law," sailors charged with murder who if tried at common law would be found guilty only of manslaughter were simply acquitted.[153] The same doctrine made its appearance in contemporary trials by court-martial.

Thus, in one case tried in New York, an officer charged with murder was convicted only of manslaughter, and in consequence was sentenced to be suspended from rank and pay for three months. Sir William Howe returned the proceedings for revision,

---

[151] Gould, JAG, to Sir William Howe, C. in C., 20 June 1777, WO 72/8; Appendix IG1, *infra*, pp. 265–266.

[152] *Supra*, pp. 55–59, 75–76.

[153] See the very fully documented discussion in "Admiralty—Criminal Jurisdiction," 2 Adams *Leg. Pap.* 275 *et seq.*, especially the civil law authorities collected and cited by John Adams in his argument in *Rex* v. *Corbet* at pp. 326–330, 334–335.

For the same result under the law of Scotland, a civil law jurisdiction, see Appendix IA, *infra*, at p. 246.

whereupon the court then sentenced the accused to be cashiered. When that revised sentence reached London for confirmation, the action noted thereon was that "The King considers the Decision of the Court as a complete Acquittal to the Prisoner for the Crime of Murder and His Majesty is pleased to confirm the said Acquittal which seems to be warranted by the Evidences, but His Majesty does not think fit, to ratify the Opinion of the Court by which the Prisoner is found Guilty of Manslaughter (a Distinction peculiar to the Common Law of England)." Accordingly, all of the revised sentence was remitted.[154]

In a letter to Captain Adye, DJA to General Gage and successor commanders in America, Gould himself was less positive: "With regard to the Species of Crime, technically denominated Manslaughter, I don't know, that a *Court Martial*, the question before whom turns upon a fact committed in *America*, is bound to notice that distinction, peculiar to the Common Law of England." [155] Three years earlier, advising the DJA at Minorca, where a court-martial had similarly found an accused charged with murder guilty only of manslaughter, Gould had written that although this distinction "seems perfectly right according to the Common Law of England," still, even "where the Question arises upon an Act committed in Minorca, I conceive the Court is not holden to that distinction, but would be well warranted, where the Crime does not amount to Murther, in acquitting the Prisoner generally." [156]

Thereafter, in 1779 and again in 1783, two civilians in New York, charged with murder, were convicted by the court-martial of manslaughter only; with Adye still officiating as DJA, the proceedings were approved in both instances.[157]

Five final cases, from the last three years of the occupation, deserve particular treatment.

Hayes the Privateer Owner

On 17 July 1781, James Hayes, an owner of the *True Blue* Privateer, faced a general court-martial in New York on three charges: (1) Fitting out the vessel without a register, in violation

---

[154] WO 71/54/155, 176; Clinton OB, 11 Sept. 1778.
[155] Gould, JAG, to Capt. Adye, DJA at New York, 1 Aug. 1778, WO 81/13/218.
[156] Gould, JAG, to Joseph Collins, Esq., DJA at Minorca, 19 Dec. 1775, WO 81/13/71, 72.
[157] Nos. 74 and 127. Sullivan 75 reflects complete unawareness both of the views of the King and of the doubts expressed by Gould.

of the Navigation Act. (2) Sending out a vessel without any pass or protection from the officer of the port. (3) Stirring up rebellion by exercising unlawful authority in the said vessel. The proceedings had not been long under way before "The Court was of opinion from many circumstances on which the Charges were founded, that they could not come under their Jurisdiction. They therefore declined proceeding on the Trial," and requested their President and the DJA to report the matter to the Commander in Chief, Sir Henry Clinton.

This being done, General Clinton entirely approved, but requested the court's reasons in writing, "in order that they might be communicated to the Admiral of the Fleet, at whose request, the Prisoner James Hayes had been brought before the Court." And the court then reported "that from the nature of the Crimes alledged against James Hayes, and the place and situation in which they are said to have been committed, that they cannot come in their opinion within their Cognizance and Jurisdiction." [158]

General Clinton's ready acquiescence suggests that the naval commander in question was Vice-Admiral Marriot Arbuthnot, the aged incompetent with whom he had been hopelessly at odds for two years and who sailed for home on 4 July 1781, rather than the latter's successor, Rear-Admiral Thomas Graves. Certainly any request to bring before an Army court-martial the purely bluewater charges against Hayes would have been entirely in character for the former, who was far too advanced in years for useful active service in an obviously critical area, who was called "the old woman" by Clinton, and who is characterized by Clinton's definitive biographer as "a pompous weathercock." [159]

Captain Lippincott of the Associated Loyalists

As the war dragged on, it became more virulent, especially on the part of Loyalist refugees. Over General Clinton's objection, but with the approval of Lord George Germain, an independent group of Loyalists was recognized as the Board of Directors of the Associated Loyalists and authorized to enroll refugees into duly officered companies and battalions in order to make raids on neighboring shores. Actually, they were simply

---

[158] No. 106; the quotations are from WO 71/94/251–253.

[159] For Arbuthnot in detail, see index entries in Willcox. Date of departure, Willcox 400, 402; "pompous weathercock," id. 285; "the old woman," id. 344; cf. Gov. Robertson's comment on Clinton and Arbuthnot, made in 1780 (id. 325), that it was "hard to tell which was the greatest fool."

armed bands, whose objective was retaliation; predictably enough, a savage guerrilla struggle ensued.[160] At the head of these organized marauders stood William Franklin, natural son of Dr. Benjamin Franklin and a barrister at law of the Middle Temple, who was nominally the Royal Governor of the Province of New Jersey, but who in actual fact was himself a refugee in New York.[161] The evidence recited below makes it virtually certain that William Franklin was the moving spirit in the tragedy about to be recounted.[162]

Captain Richard Lippincott, a company commander, received permission from the Board to take three prisoners from the provost in New York to be "exchanged" for others in Monmouth County, New Jersey. Lippincott executed this permission by taking to New Jersey one of the prisoners, Joshua Huddy, and hanging him there, in "exchange" for an Associator said to have been executed by the Americans; a placard on the victim's body proclaimed, "Up goes Huddy for Philip White." [163]

General Washington, once the news reached him, asked his senior officers whether retaliation would be appropriate; [164] when they answered in the affirmative, he reported the matter to the Congress, which authorized him to proceed accordingly.[165] Thus fortified by the civil authority, Washington warned Clinton that, unless the murderer were delivered to him for punishment, he would retaliate

---

[160] H. Clinton, 192 and n. 9, 237–238, 352–353; 2 HMC Am. MSS. 237; 2 Jones 227–234, 481–483; Barck 203–206; Van Doren S.H. 236–237, 405–406; Wertenbaker 229–231.

[161] DAB; W. A. Whitehead, *A Biographical Sketch of William Franklin, Governor from 1763 to 1776* (NJHS, 1848); 2 *Register of Admissions to . . . the Middle Temple* (London, 1949) 343 (William Franklin, son and heir of Benjamin Franklin of Philadelphia, America, admitted 11 Feb. 1751, called 10 Nov. 1758).

[162] *Infra*, pp. 115, 116, 121, 129.

[163] K. Mayo, *General Washington's Dilemma* (New York, 1938); H. Clinton 359–361; 5 Freeman 412–414, 419–420, 425; 4 *The Papers of James Madison* (Chicago, 1965) 199–200, nn. 17 and 18; Van Doren S.H. 430–431; 2 Sabine 17–21; Wertenbaker 231–232; J. W. Barber and H. Howe, *Historical Collections of the State of New Jersey* (New York, 1846) 364–368; R. J. Koke, *Washington and Captain Joshua Huddy*, 41 NYHS Q. 335.

Judge Jones's account of the case (2 Jones 227–234) is quite incomplete, because he makes no mention whatever of Lippincott's trial by court-martial. A. G. Bradley, *Lord Dorchester* (London and Toronto, 1926) 198, where it is said that "Lippincott was tried by the highest jurists in New York, who found themselves powerless to convict him for sufficient but technical reasons irrelevant here," is of course wholly mistaken—except only if the general court-martial in question is equated with "the highest jurists in New York."

[164] 24 Washington 136.

[165] 22 J. Cont. Cong. 217.

by hanging a British captain.[166] While Clinton hesitated, Washington directed the selection by lot of a British captain in American hands who was an unconditional prisoner.[167] The victim thus selected was Lieutenant Asgill of the Guards, who through that circumstance ranked as a Captain in the Army. One part of Washington's direction was thus complied with, but since Asgill had been surrendered at Yorktown he was not an unconditional prisoner but, to the contrary, was protected against reprisals. This was the circumstance that put in train a series of developments which, in their entirety, placed Washington in a most unfortunate dilemma—particularly after Lippincott, who was in due course tried by court-martial, had been acquitted by that tribunal.

Asgill's mother wrote to the Comte de Vergennes at Versailles, seeking the aid of the French King and Queen; the French Minister to the United States accordingly interceded with Washington on the footing that young Asgill was in part a prisoner of the French by reason of their contribution at Yorktown; this provided a rationalized loophole through which Washington, once more sustained by a new resolution of the Continental Congress, was more than happy to escape; and in the event Asgill was released, to the great relief of all concerned in the unhappy affair.[108] Here, however, the only item of interest concerns Lippincott's trial by court-martial.

Once the matter had been brought to his attention by Washington, General Clinton ordered a report from Governor Franklin, a demand that was slow in being met.[169] Shortly thereafter, Clinton put the problem before a formidable board whose membership comprised no less than fourteen general officers; they unanimously recommended that Captain Lippincott be tried by general court-martial,[170] and next day advised "that a General Courtmartial, is the only legal mode, when Civil Government does not act," the court-martial to be composed "Of Officers of the most Respectable

[166] 24 Washington 146.

[167] 24 Washington 217.

[168] References in n. 163, *supra;* 2 Jones 483–487; entries in 24 and 25 Washington relating to Asgill. The second resolution of Congress is at 23 J. Cont. Cong. 715. Asgill himself stayed in the Army, inherited a baronetcy, and died a full General. DNB.

[169] Gen. Clinton to Gov. Franklin, 20 Apr. 1782, PRO 30/55 No. 4438; same to same, 25 Apr. 1782, *id.,* No. 4470, both listed at 2 HMC Am. MSS. 460 and 466, respectively.

[170] Board proceedings, 25 Apr. 1782, 2 HMC Am. MSS. 466, PRO 30/55 No. 4469.

Rank from the British Regular & Provincial Corps in the usual Proportions." [171] Such a tribunal duly convened on 3 May 1782, with Major-General Paterson presiding and Captain Adye appearing as DJA, to try Lippincott on a charge of murdering Joshua Huddy. [172]

Governor Franklin had meanwhile on behalf of the Board of Directors protested that the court-martial had no authority. If such authority is derived from the Mutiny Act, then what clause confers it? "If it is urged that the Articles of War contain Authority competent to the purpose, we must take the Liberty to assert that any Article not authorised by the Mutiny Act is a mere Nullity, and will prove no justification *in Law* for any Man who acts under it." Lippincott himself was neither a soldier nor an officer in pay or with rank, and the Articles of Association he had subscribed expressly stipulated that the Associators should not be regarded as enlisted soldiers. If the trial is sought to be justified in reliance on the "no Form of Our Civil Judicature" provision, Article 2 of Section XX, then "This Article appears to be unauthorised by the Mutiny Act, unless by the words (*all persons*) be meant *only* all such Persons as are *Soldiers*, none other than such being in fact the objects of the operation of that Act." The proof of this construction is to be found in 15 Geo. III c. 15, the re-enactment of the old Mutiny Act for North America of 1765, which expressly provided for offenders to be turned over by the military commander to the civil authorities in the nearest province. [173] And if courts-martial affected inhabitants, why are the Articles of War directed to be published to the soldiers and obeyed only by officers and soldiers? [174]

It was an argument not only thoroughly lawyer-like but most effective as well, and all of it except only the construction of

---

[171] Minutes of a meeting at Headquarters, 26 Apr. 1782, 2 HMC Am. MSS. 467, PRO 30/55 No. 4476.

[172] No. 131; WO 71/95/321–408.

[173] *Supra*, p. 68.

[174] Gov. Franklin (for Board of Directors) to Gen. Clinton, 2 HMC Am. MSS. 479, PRO 30/55 No. 4540. The arrogant attitude of the Board sufficiently appears from its Minutes for 3 May 1782 (listed at 2 HMC Am. MSS. 508, PRO 30/55 No. 4707), which note that "the Board . . . being of Opinion that the attempting to punish Captain Lippincott by a Court Martial for the Execution of Joshua Huddy was illegal and extremely improper in a political view, they remonstrated in a Letter of this day to his Excellency the Commander in Chief against this Attempt as neither warranted by the Mutiny Act nor the Articles of War, but altogether illegal unjustifiable and impolitic."

Article 2 of Section XX was repeated in Lippincott's plea to the jurisdiction, interposed on 6 May—and overruled by the court-martial in reliance on that precise provision.[175]

Around this time, Chief Justice Smith of the Supreme Court of the Province of New York advised General Clinton "That the Death of Huddy was not Murder and that Lippincott who caused him to be executed was not triable by a Court Martial." [176] (Smith, in commission since 1779 and thus drawing pay, never officiated as a judge; his court had been and remained closed for the duration; instead, he advised Generals Clinton and Carleton to the end, keeping a gossipy diary that illuminates the occupation in general and the Lippincott case in particular for anyone able to decipher his difficult hand; after the war he became Chief Justice of Canada.) [177]

General Clinton's reference of the case for trial, pursuant to the advice of his generals rather than that of the Chief Justice, was assuredly a course calculated to quiet General Washington and to preserve the life of the latter's prospective victim; and, perhaps more to the point, the Lippincott case was one of many burdens cheerfully to be turned over to his own successor, Sir Guy Carleton.

The latter arrived on 5 May 1782,[178] the day before Lippincott's plea to the jurisdiction had been tendered; assumed command on 8 May; [179] and soon afterwards directed suspension of the court-martial proceedings until the objections to its jurisdiction could be considered.[180]

He invoked the advice of Chief Justice William Smith of New York; of Chief Justice Frederick Smyth of New Jersey, another jurist lacking a judicature; and of John Tabor Kempe, the nominal Attorney General of the Province of New York. (Smyth, C.J., of New Jersey ultimately declined to give any opinion.) [181] General Carleton told Smith, C.J., of New York that the matter was too important to be decided by "Sash & Gorget," by which he meant

---

[175] WO 71/95/324–326; Appendix IG3, *infra*, at pp. 271–273.
[176] William Smith Diary, 5 May 1782.
[177] Barck 64 (Smith appointed Chief Justice 4 May 1779); L. F. S. Upton, ed., *The Diary . . . of Chief Justice William Smith, 1784–1793* (Toronto, 1963) xxiii (same); *id.* 2 (Smith left with Sir Guy Carleton and "sailed with the Troops"), and *passim* (Smith's later career in Canada); and see DAB.
[178] WO 1/12/277; *N.-Y. Royal Gazette*, 8 May 1782.
[179] Clinton OB and Carleton OB, 8 May 1782.
[180] WO 71/95/327–328; Appendix IG3, *infra*, at pp. 273–274.
[181] William Smith Diary, 29 May and 9 June 1782.

the opinion of an *ad hoc* court-martial.[182] But when the latter jurist, who was obsessed with the desirability of restoring civil government in New York, never once faced up to the difficulty that a restored civil judicature in that province would be quite incompetent to try Lippincott (or anyone else) for an offense committed in New Jersey, virtually all of which was firmly in American hands, General Carleton on 5 June cut the Gordian knot by publishing the following in General Orders:

> The Proceedings of the General Court-Martial of which Major General Paterson is President having been suspended in consequence of the Prisoner Captain Richard Lippincott pleading against the legality of the Court; the Commander in Chief after the most mature consultation and deliberation, finding that there is no other Method of obtaining Justice, has thought proper to Order that the said Court shall assemble on Thursday the 13th. Instant at 10 o'clock in the Morning at the City Hall in New York and proceed in the Trial of the said Captain Richard Lippincott.[183]

It now remained to find some proper legal rationalization to support this conclusion, and after much discussion and soul-searching—to say nothing of more than a little trimming and shilly-shallying, all of which the New York Smith recorded at length [184]—the Smith-Kempe opinion was delivered on 9 June, a hedging, mealy-mouthed production: If the civil courts of New York were open, they could not try the case, for the murder alleged had been committed in New Jersey; the course of the common law—trial by a jury of the vicinage—must be followed in the absence of an Act of Parliament or a colonial law to the contrary; the Petition of Right [185] prohibits military trials except in time of war, rebellion, or invasion; it would be a question of fact whether there exists sufficient necessity to authorize the present

---

[182] William Smith Diary, 27 May 1782, quoted in 5 I.N.P. Stokes 1147: "Before Dinner at Headquarters Sir Guy Carleton took me aside and talked of Courts to decide by Grand Juries & Petty Juries exclaiming ag^t referring Decisions to Courts Martial or as he expressed it to the Sash & Gorget &ca. . . ."

[183] WO 71/95/328; Appendix IG3, *infra*, at p. 274; Carleton OB, 5 June 1782.

[184] His entries on this subject cover some 22 closely written folio pages. To have set them forth in Appendix IG following the jurisdictional excerpts from the Lippincott trial would have resulted in wholly disproportionate space given to that proceeding. Moreover, the present author's cryptographic talents proved insufficient to effect a complete transcription even if it had seemed desirable to include one.

[185] 3 Car. I c. 1.

trial; "and unacquainted as we must be supposed to be, with all those great and profound Considerations of Policy upon which it turns, it becomes us to be silent." [186] A poor performance, true enough, but it sufficed to support General Carleton's direction to the court-martial that it proceed with the trial, without interference either by way of the civil prohibition that Lippincott's counsel sought from Governor Robertson in that official's capacity as Chancellor of the Province of New York,[187] or through the habeas corpus that Smith, C.J., considered the appropriate remedy.[188] For, after all, law officers' opinions, over the centuries and in all lands, exemplify the motto, "We Strive to Please."

But the real mystery is why there should have been any jurisdictional doubt whatever in the premises. Even in the seventeenth century, Grotius and the English civilian Zouche were in agreement over the complete absence of justification for killing prisoners of war.[189] Vattel concurred in 1758,[190] and indeed his work was translated into English as early as 1760.[191] Far from being esoteric doctrine, this was a principle axiomatically accepted by both sides throughout the war. Lippincott had, quite simply, committed an offense against the law and usage of war by killing a prisoner taken from the enemy; for this he was amenable to trial by military tribunal, any kind of military tribunal. After all, Major André

---

[186] WO 71/95/330–332; Appendix IG3, *infra*, at pp. 275–276. This opinion is only listed at 2 HMC Am. MSS. 517; its text is in PRO 30/55 No. 4758, with a copy in WO 72/9. The opinion itself was written by Chief Justice Smith, "& Mr. Kempe approved with the Alteration of a few Words." William Smith Diary, 9 June 1782.

[187] Gov. Robertson to Gen. Carleton, 18 June 1782, 2 HMC Am. MSS. 528, PRO 30/55 No. 4804; William Smith Diary, 14 June 1782; M. Morgann (Secretary to Gen. Carleton) to Gov. Robertson, 18 June 1782, 2 HMC Am. MSS. 528.

A prayer for a writ of prohibition dated 13 June 1782, by one William Courlies as relator, and directed to the President and DJA of the Lippincott court-martial, as well as a 14-page written suggestion in support of the petition, both signed by Lippincott's two counsel, are in WO 72/9.

[188] William Smith Diary, 14 June 1782: "Lippincott's Counsel should proceed by Hab Corpus vid Yelv. Rep 134." The reference is to *Scadding's Case*, s.c., Noy 131, a decision of the Court of King's Bench in Michaelmas Term, 6 Jac. I, which, though it supports the Chief Justice regarding the remedy, is quite inapposite on the merits.

[189] H. Grotius, *De Jure Belli ac Pacis* (1646) Bk. III, Ch. XIV, §III (F. W. Kelsey, tr., Oxford, 1925, p. 763); R. Zouche, *Law between Nations* (1650) §X, ¶12 (J. L. Brierly, tr., Washington, 1911, p. 178).

[190] E. de Vattel, *The Law of Nations* (1758) Bk. III, Ch. VIII, §§140, 149 (C. G. Fenwick, tr., Washington, 1916, pp. 280, 284).

[191] London, 1760, printed for J. Newbery *et al*. The suggestion at 12 Holdsworth 638, that the first English translation appeared in 1797, must be considered an inadvertence.

suffered death as a spy, not pursuant to findings and sentence of a court-martial, but by reason of the opinion of a court of inquiry;[192] and while the circumstances of his end aroused much emotion on both sides—for wholly different reasons—no objective military lawyer has ever come forward to assert either that he was not a spy or that he had met his fate illegally.

Yet, in connection with Lippincott's trial, it seems never to have occurred to anyone on the British side to support the military jurisdiction on the footing of the accused's obvious violation of the law of war, and this although Sir Henry Clinton in a contemporaneous letter to Washington listed "Offenders against the Laws of War" as one out of four kinds of prisoners;[193] although Chief Justice Smith quoted Grotius to General Carleton;[194] and although Adye noted specifically that "the irregular, 'though casually necessary operations of War, have occasioned causes to be brought to tryal before Courts Martial, which not only call for a knowledge of the laws of the land, civil as well as military, but also require some acquaintance with those of Nations."[195]

Writing to Sir Charles Gould during the pendency of the Lippincott trial, Adye expressed the hope that Parliament "will take pains to give Courts Martial a surer and more substantial ground to tread on, in cases similar to the one, now in Agitation"; after calling attention to "the awkward situation I stand in," exposed "to the Attacks of every smatterer in the law, who is conscientious enough, to give his Client, What he deems a penny-worth for his penny," he assured the Judge Advocate General that "I take every pains in my power to proceed according to the Laws and Constitution of Great Britain, which I highly venerate, and hope never to be driven to the despicable Refuge expressed in the Adage of *inter Arma silent Leges*."[196]

In the event, as has been indicated, Lippincott was acquitted, the court-martial specifically finding that he obeyed orders.[197] Not

---

[192] Winthrop *798–799.

[193] Gen. Clinton to Gen. Washington, 22 Apr. 1782, 2 HMC Am. MSS. 462, PRO 30/55 No. 4447, p. 3. The three other kinds of prisoners listed were military, naval, and citizens.

[194] William Smith Diary, 19 June 1783.

[195] Major Adye, DJA, to Sir Charles Gould, JAG, 31 Aug. 1783, WO 72/11.

[196] Capt. Adye, DJA, to Sir Charles Gould, JAG, 15 June 1782, WO 72/9, a letter of four folio pages explaining the Lippincott case in detail.

[197] WO 71/95/395. For modern views of this perennial problem, see A. N. Sack, *Punishment of War Criminals and the Defence of Superior Order*, 60 L.Q.R. 63; M. Greenspan, *The Modern Law of Land Warfare* (Berkeley and Los Angeles, 1959) 490–496; cf. G.I.A.D. Draper, *The Red Cross Conventions* (London and New York, 1958) 21–22, 103–104.

unnaturally, General Carleton did not publish this embarrassing result officially, although Governor Franklin importuned him to do so.[198]

This seems as appropriate a place as any to call attention to William Franklin's conduct before and during the trial. His legal opinion and the minutes of the Board of Directors of the Associated Loyalists have already been mentioned.[199] Later, when Captain Adye as DJA requested the attendance of members of the Board as witnesses at the trial, Franklin wrote, "I can venture to assure You that the Board do not mean, by any Act of theirs, to give the least countenance to the proposed Trial, as being in their Opinion, for the Reasons they have given, altogether illegal." [200] Perhaps the most telling mark of his complicity is contained in his reply to Sir Henry Clinton's demand for information: "By the inclosed deposition your Excellency will be enabled to judge whether the Execution of Huddy was not as just as it was necessary." [201] In the light of the quoted letter, which undertook a long and detailed justification of Lippincott's act, Franklin's subsequent effort at personal exculpation following conclusion of the trial remains peculiarly unpersuasive.[202]

Thereafter, all in due course, Franklin sailed for home; [203] Asgill, as has been seen, was released; General Carleton took effectual steps to lock the stable door against any recurrences of the Lippincott affair; [204] Adye advised "my not having been able to gather any further information relative to this transaction that could give me hopes of prosecuting any other person with effect"; [205] General

---

[198] Gov. Franklin to Gen. Carleton, 15 July 1782, 3 HMC Am. MSS. 20.

[199] *Supra*, p. 116, and n. 174.

[200] Capt. Adye, DJA, to Gov. Franklin, 2 May 1782; same to same, 3 May 1782; two letters, Gov. Franklin to Capt. Adye, 3 May 1782; all in WO 72/9.

[201] Gov. Franklin to Gen. Clinton, 27 Apr. 1782, 2 HMC Am. MSS. 469, PRO 30/55 No. 4485; copy in WO 72/9.

[202] Gov. Franklin to Gov. Robertson, 12 Aug. 1782, 3 HMC Am. MSS. 66, PRO 30/55 No. 5274.

[203] Gov. Franklin to Gen. Carleton, 9 Aug. 1782, 3 HMC Am. MSS. 61.

[204] Following the trial, Gen. Robertson came forward with suggestions regarding the steps necessary to prevent like murders being committed in the future. Gov. Robertson to Gen. Carleton and Adm. Digby, 22 July 1782 (3 HMC Am. MSS. 34, PRO 30/55 No. 5128). On 1 Aug. it was accordingly ordered (Carleton OB) that "In future all Persons taken from the Enemy by any denomination of people are to be put under the charge of Joshua Loring, Esqr Commissary General of Prisoners who is the only person that is Properly authorised to treat for their Exchange."

[205] Adye, DJA, to M. Morgann, Esq., 30 Nov. 1782, 3 HMC Am. MSS. 241, PRO 30/55 No. 6286; noted in 25 Washington 437, n. 50.

Carleton at long last dissolved the Associated Loyalists; [206] and Sir Charles Gould declined comment: "As the business is finally disposed of by the Commander in Chief having ratified the Sentence of the Court, and as it is not probable the like case should again present itself, you will excuse me from entering a Volunteer into the discussion of a matter of so delicate a nature." [207]

Duryee, Todd, and Fighliman

However unpalatable the fact has now become, slavery was universal in colonial America, and Lord Mansfield's judgment in *Sommersett's Case* [208] did not extend there. Therefore Negro slaves were not only property, but both the preliminary as well as the definitive articles of peace specifically provided for the British to withdraw "without causing any Destruction or carrying away any Negroes, or other Property of the American Inhabitants." [209] And, to insure that no slaves taken from their American owners in the course of the war should be removed on the evacuation, Generals Washington and Carleton agreed early in 1783 that a joint board composed of three representatives from each side should inspect all ships leaving New York.[210] This background must be kept in mind to understand the case of Jacob Duryee, inhabitant, who was tried by general court-martial in New York on 11 July 1783 for "Having by force and violence carried off Francis Griffin a Negro under the protection of the British Government, without

[206] Sir Guy Carleton to Gen. Washington, 11 Dec. 1782, 25 Washington 437, n. 50; Wertenbaker 232.

[207] Sir Charles Gould, JAG, to Capt. Adye, DJA, 2 Oct. 1782, WO 81/15/167.

[208] 20 How. St. Tr. 1; s.c., *sub nom. Somerset* v. *Stewart*, Lofft 1.

For slavery cases in Massachusetts during John Adams' time at the bar, see the copious documentation in 2 Adams *Leg. Pap.* 48–67. It was not until 1783 at the earliest that slavery ended in that commonwealth. See, e.g., J. D. Cushing, *The Cushing Court and the Abolition of Slavery in Massachusetts: More Notes on the Quock Walker Case*, 5 Am. J. Leg. Hist. 118. And in New York slavery was not finally ended until 1827. See ch. IX, "Abolition," in E. J. McManus, *A History of Negro Slavery in New York* (Syracuse, 1966).

[209] Art. VII of the preliminary articles of 30 Nov. 1782, 8 Stat. 54, 57; 2 H. Miller 96, 99–100. Art. VII of the definitive Treaty of Paris of 3 Sept. 1783 was virtually a verbatim copy. 10 Eng. Hist. Doc. 943, 945–946; 8 Stat. 80, 83; 2 H. Miller 151, 155.

The words quoted in the text were suggested by Henry Laurens of South Carolina, who had just put in his appearance after release from confinement in the Tower of London; they were "inserted almost at the moment of signature" of the preliminary articles, and were in fact interlined in the fair copy of that instrument. 2 H. Miller 100, 104; 3 Adams D. & A. 80–83.

[210] See 26 Washington 370, 402, 410, 412, 499; Carleton OB, 18 Apr. 1783; Dawson 141–147; 2 Hartley Papers (WLCL) 79, 87.

permission or authority." [211] Tried jointly with Duryee as aiders and abettors were Adam Todd, a mariner, and Frederick Fighliman, another inhabitant.

Duryee pleaded that the court-martial lacked jurisdiction:

> I am a Citizen of the United States of North America, whose Freedom and Independence have been solemnly recognized by the King of Great Britain and therefore I cant admit the present mode of trial to be such as either the Laws of England or the United States appear to authorise. . . .
>
> I must beg leave also to mention that as the present is not an Offence, within any clause of the Mutiny Act, the Proceedings and Determinations of the Court will I flatter myself, be regulated by the Rules of the Municipal Law, and that they will not attach Criminality to any Action in a greater degree than what that law would, under all the circumstances, ascribe to it.

This plea was overruled, and both Duryee and Fighliman were convicted. The former was sentenced to pay a fine of 50 guineas, "to be expelled the Kings Lines, and not be suffered to return, whilst the British Troops remain and hold Command there; and the Court is further of Opinion that the Fine thus adjudged to be paid by Mr. Duryee should be appropriated to the use, comfort, and relief of the Poor and Sick Negroes, who have taken protection under the British Government." Fighliman was sentenced "to be set in the Stocks, and there to be exhibited to Public view, for the space of one hour, in some one of the most conspicuous places within the City of New York."

General Carleton approved the proceedings. But "in consideration of the new state of things" he remitted both portions of Duryee's sentence on condition that the latter "find reasonable bail for his good and peaceable behaviour" during the time he remained within the British lines, and gave Fighliman an unconditional pardon. [212]

Trial of the Counterfeiters

Duryee and his counsel, for presumably he had professional assistance in formulating his plea to the jurisdiction, would assuredly have been amazed to learn that, shortly after his trial, the

---

[211] Nos. 63, 70, and 203; WO 71/97/320–351.

[212] Carleton OB, 22 July 1783; record sent home under cover of Major Adye, DJA, to Sir Charles Gould, JAG, 1 Aug. 1783, WO 72/11.

Continental Congress in effect requested the British commander to try American citizens by court-martial.

The background of this request appears in a letter from Adye, by then a Major, to Sir Charles Gould: "It has been a common custom during the War, to counterfeit the paper money issued by Congress, in order to depreciate its value, and some certain persons have continued in the practise thereof, since the notification of the Provisional Articles of Peace having been signed." [213]

When complaint was made by individuals to whom these counterfeit bills had been passed, some of those suspected were confined in the provost, and threatened with irons to make them confess; this incident took place on 15 July 1783.[214] Thereafter, on the twenty-third, the two Chief Justices, Smith of New York and Smyth of New Jersey, took the examinations of a number of persons, in which "It comes out from one John Powers a Copper plate Printer that he has counterfeited Millions during the War at the Instance of Persons on the other Side of the Lines and chiefly in their Commissary Departments." The first-named Chief Justice then prepared a letter, which he considered a ten-strike, for General Carleton to send to the President of the American Congress: "If Congress sends Persons to attend the further Examinations or declines that Proposition Advantages will flow from it. In the first Case the credit of the Notes will be blown up. In the latter Impeachments will fall upon the Congress as in the Plott to avoid the payment of these Bills which they have issued to the Soldiers & which are now in general Circulation." [215] Poor William Smith! He was still living in a dream world, prattling hopefully that "there is little Reason to apprehend an Evacuation this Winter." [216] For General Carleton had declared that "not a Soldier should stir till he

---

[213] Major Adye, DJA, to Sir Charles Gould, JAG, 31 Aug. 1783, WO 72/11.

Warfare in this respect has changed but little; in World War II, when the Japanese circulated occupation currency in the Philippines, Gen. MacArthur similarly introduced forged counterparts "to support United States intelligence agents and the Filipino resistance movement as well as to sabotage and dislocate the economy of the islands during Japanese occupation." See *Japanese War Notes Claimants Assn.* v. *United States,* 373 F. 2d 356 (C. Cls.).

[214] Complaints concerning passing of counterfeit bills; Fisher affidavit, 13 July 1783, 4 HMC Am. MSS. 226; and see *id.* 362 (case of counterfeit money); *id.* 391 (minutes of Commissioners for Settling Debts regarding claim to recover value of counterfeit money).

Threat to use irons on May: Statement of Fisher, 25 Aug. 1783, 4 HMC Am. MSS. 307, PRO 30/55 No. 8865; affidavit of Provost Marshal Cunningham, 26 Aug. 1783, 4 HMC Am. MSS. 311, PRO 30/55 No. 8883.

[215] William Smith Diary, 24 July 1783.

[216] *Id.,* 2 July 1783.

had taken care of the Loyalists," [217] an event that the Chief Justice did not envisage taking place until the following spring.[218]

Sir Guy sent to President Elias Boudinot of the Continental Congress the letter Smith, C.J., had drafted, which expressed willingness to deal with the offenders.[219] Congress thereupon requested that any American citizens in custody on charges of making or passing counterfeit notes "be delivered up, together with the proofs which shall be collected against them, to be tried under the jurisdiction to whom the cognizance of the crimes belongs . . . and that with regard . . . to criminals who are not amenable to any of these United States, Congress has entire confidence that justice will be done, and such atrocious offenders brought to condign punishment." [220]

On 13 August 1783, accordingly, there was commenced the trial by general court-martial of six individuals, charged with "having combined and confederated together with some other persons . . . to counterfeit divers Bills or Notes used or circulated by order of the Congress, or the respective Legislative States of America, and having uttered and passed them as good and genuine Bills & Notes, altho' they knew them to be Counterfeits." [221]

Adye considered that their case "united the seriousness" of the Lippincott trial with "the intricacy" of Duryee's, and advised Sir Charles Gould that "The matter was of so delicate and serious a nature, that it was judged we could not tread on too safe ground." Accordingly, "by the consent and desire of Sir Guy Carleton," he had not only consulted Chief Justice Smith—who did not deign to mention the consultation in his diary—but "employed Mr. Aplin, a Councillor at Law, to assist in carrying on the prosecution on the part of the crown. This Gentleman, besides being one of those, who had fled from his native home, and forfeited his property, by his attachment to the Royal cause, is eminent in his profession, and had at times been employed as King's Attorney in the Province of Rhode Island." [222] (Aplin next appears in history as Attorney General of Prince Edward Island; he had been counsel for Lippincott

---

[217] *Id.*, 4 June 1783.

[218] *Id.*, 18 Aug. and 13 Sept. 1783.

[219] Gen. Carleton to President of Congress, 24 July 1783, 4 HMC Am. MSS. 240, PRO 30/55 No. 8510; same to same, 13 Aug. 1783, 4 HMC Am. MSS. 274, 24 J. Cont. Cong. 509, note.

[220] 24 J. Cont. Cong. 485 (1 Aug. 1783).

[221] Nos. 72, 132, 138, 158, 159, and 175; WO 71/97/386; WO 71/155. This trial is not mentioned in K. Scott, *Counterfeiting in New York during the Revolution*, 42 NYHS Q. 221.

[222] Major Adye, DJA, to Sir Charles Gould, JAG, 31 Aug. 1783, WO 72/11.

together with one Richard Harison; the latter thereafter sufficiently accommodated himself to the new dispensation that he became United States Attorney in New York in 1789 and Recorder of the City thereafter.) [223]

After a trial that extended over a ten-day period, four of the accused were acquitted, because "they have not been parties to the conspiracy," and this was duly announced in orders.[224] With respect to the other two, the court-martial "has given a *special Verdict* . . . which," Adye reported, "I am well aware, is a practice rather uncommon, if not unprecedented, at Courts Martial; but where uncommon and unprecedented causes arise, effects of the same nature will consequently ensue." [225]

The court had found that the prisoner John Power,

> a British subject, has been so far a Partner in the Combination and Confederacy . . . as that the said Power has, between the month of June last, and the present Month of August, printed blank Notes or Bills, similar to those, called Morris's Notes or Bills,[226] within the City of New York, and delivered one or more of them to the Prisoner William May, to be by him passed, but with this restriction or limitation, that the same should not be passed to any person or persons, resident in New York, and under the protection of His Majesty's Garrison—But whether such agency in the said Combination and Confederacy is criminal and punishable, by any or either of the laws referred to, or specified in the said charge, they doubt, and therefore beg leave to report the matter to His

---

[223] Counsel for Lippincott: Gov. Franklin to Gen. Carleton, 12 Aug. 1782, 3 HMC Am. MSS. 66, PRO 30/55 No. 5274; documents in connection with proposed writ of prohibition cited in n. 187, *supra.*

For Harison's career, see 1 Goebel 311 n. 76; there are many other references to him in that volume, indexed under "Lawyers."

The Aplin in question was Joseph Aplin, who sought assistance in going to Nova Scotia (4 HMC Am. MSS. 264) and became Attorney General of Prince Edward Island (2 C. W. Bowen, *The History of Woodstock Connecticut* [Norwood, Mass., 1930] 214), not his father, John Aplin, also a Rhode Island lawyer; the latter had been run out of Rhode Island in the late 1760's for malpractice, and died in Connecticut in 1772. W. Updike, *Memoirs of the Rhode Island Bar* (Boston, 1842) 73–74; W. R. Staples, *Annals of Providence* (Providence, 1843) 603; 2 Sabine 472; "Something about Providence Lawyers in Colony Times," 7 S. S. Rider, ed., *Book Notes* (Providence, 1890) 133, 134–136.

I owe the Woodstock Connecticut reference to the kindness of Mrs. L. E. Tilley of the Rhode Island Historical Society.

[224] Carleton OB, 26 Aug. 1783.

[225] Major Adye, DJA, to Sir Charles Gould, JAG, 31 Aug. 1783, WO 72/11.

[226] Robert Morris was the American Superintendent of Finance, and, in a very real sense, "the financier of the American Revolution." DAB.

Excellency the Commander in Chief, without further determination.[227]

And the same reference was made, and for the same reason, in respect of the prisoner William May, the court finding that he

> appears to have to have been so far a partner in the Combination, and Confederacy, . . . that the said May, did between the month of June last, and the present month of August, receive numbers of printed blank notes, similar to those, called Morris's Notes or bills, of the Prisoner John Power, and that after having signed the same, with the words, "Robert Morris," he passed several of them in New York.[228]

Here were nice points of law, but they were never publicly resolved; the announcement of the result of trial makes absolutely no mention of Power and May,[229] neither of whom for aught that appears in the headquarters order book ever even existed. But General Carleton took action respecting both of them. Chief Justice Smith noted that Power was to be released upon giving security for future good behavior, while "Sir Guy Carleton was for sending May to the Congress. I opposed it as an explicit acknowledgement of Independency of the Colonies prior to a Definitive Treaty. He consented to a Banishment of May." [230]

General Carleton reported the results of the trial of the counterfeiters to President Boudinot in a letter so amusing in its indirections and insinuations as to deserve quotation:

> I have directed as to May, that he be banished as an infamous Cheat; and he shall be turned out of our lines by King's bridge. It is a great aggravation of this man's Offences, that by his own account, he had an education and the Degrees of Bachelor and Master of arts at one of your Colleges; and a much greater, if it is true, as I am informed, that he is in Orders, and has served some time as Chaplain in the American Army.
>
> Power being a British subject, I must treat him in a different manner, but he shall not be released without security for his good behaviour in future, and particularly his abstaining from the reproachful practices, which, as it would seem, were consistent with the loose principles he had adopted and openly avowed. The instruments of fraud and such Counterfeit notes

---

[227] WO 71/155.
[228] *Ibid.*
[229] Carleton OB, 26 Aug. 1783.
[230] William Smith Diary, 30 Aug. 1783.

as were found in his possession, I send herewith, and they will
be delivered to your Excellency by the Bearer.[231]

Thus the Congress received, not May himself, but some at least
of the counterfeit notes that the court-martial found he had signed.
Inasmuch as even genuine American currency was by then griev-
ously depreciated—hence the familiar expression, "Not worth a
Continental," which dates from this period—it cannot be concluded that President Boudinot was much the gainer by the exchange.

But May was dealt with as indicated, despite at least two petitions imploring that he be not banished beyond the lines, which
according to him would mean instant death;[232] he was duly deposited within the American lines on 15 October by Cornet Tucker of
the 17th Dragoons, who told him not to return.[233]

When May thereafter did return, he was promptly clapped into
the provost, where in the 1 November list of prisoners the reason
noted for his detention was, "Turned out of the Lines, and returned again to the Garrison without leave." [234] May protested
lamely that he did not know that he was forbidden to return,
contending that the officer sending him out had only said he must
report himself, which he had done.[235] He is last mentioned in a
peremptory demand made on Major Adye on 8 November, that
quotes His Excellency as saying that he *must*—there is underscor-
ing in the original—have a copy of the record of trial in May's
case.[236] Perhaps therefore General Carleton was even then considering May's wish to go to Nova Scotia before New York was handed
back to the Americans. But whether May was ultimately granted
the boon he so urgently sought does not appear.[237]

---

[231] Gen. Carleton to the President of Congress, 1 Sept. 1783, noted at 4 HMC
Am. MSS. 324, PRO 30/55 No. 8954.

[232] Petitions dated 11 and 30 Sept. 1783, 4 HMC Am. MSS. 347, 382, PRO 30/55
Nos. 10169 and 9234.

[233] Lt.-Col. Delancey, AG, to Cornet Tucker, 14 Oct. 1783, together with the
latter's certificate, 4 HMC Am. MSS. 413, PRO 30/55 No. 9370.

[234] *N.-Y. Royal Gazette*, 5 Nov. 1783.

[235] May to Gen. Carleton, [?] Nov. 1783, 4 HMC Am. MSS. 471, PRO 30/55 No.
9688.

[236] Two letters, Major Adye, DJA, to Major Mackenzie, DAG, both 8 Nov.
1783, 4 HMC Am. MSS. 447, PRO 30/55 Nos. 9562 and 9563.

[237] May is not mentioned in Sabine, which lists most of the Loyalists who
emigrated.

A curious point in connection with the counterfeiters' trial is that, when the
proceedings in the case reached the JAG Office in London, only the first part of
the testimony was transcribed into the court-martial books; the record of the case
in those volumes stops abruptly in mid-trial. See WO 71/97/435.

Cornelius Hetfield

The trial of the counterfeiters in August 1783 was followed by that of Cornelius Hetfield in September, the latter case demonstrating all but conclusively that, when put to the test, Chief Justice William Smith of New York was even more partisan than doctrinaire.

Hetfield,[238] like Lippincott, was a refugee; like Lippincott, he committed an offense in New Jersey outside the British lines, namely, breaking into a house in Elizabeth-Town and robbing its inmates; like Lippincott, he fled to New York; unlike Lippincott, he was a civilian pure and simple, without pretension either to military rank or even military title; and, again unlike Lippincott, his offense did not in even the faintest aspect involve any violation of the law of war. (By way of background, however, it should be noted that Cornelius Hetfield was mentioned in Governor Franklin's incriminating letter the previous year as one who "likewise had a prisoner hung in the same manner, and it was attended with the desired effect."[239] This circumstance may serve to explain the rather rigid positions taken in the jurisdictional argument about to be recited.)

Yet, despite the similarity between Hetfield's case in 1783 and Lippincott's in 1782, Chief Justice Smith (without once adverting to Hetfield's earlier guerrilla activities) advised General Carleton to try Hetfield by court-martial in New York in preference to delivering him to Governor Livingston of the State of New Jersey, on the ground that the other course might be thought to involve a premature recognition of American Independence before signature of the definitive treaty of peace; nothing whatever was said about the beatitude of the civil power.[240]

(It should be noted that the basic reason assigned by Chief Justice Smith was quite untenable. The American negotiators at Paris in 1782 insisted, over British objection and French indifference, that the independence of the United States must be recog-

---

[238] Sometimes spelled "Hatfield" (e.g., 1 Sabine 525), and probably related to but wholly distinct from John Smith Hatfield (1 Sabine 524).

At the time of the controversy over Lippincott, J. S. Hatfield was the subject of complaint on the part of the British; the latter contended that he had been apprehended while under the sanction of a flag of truce; Washington disclaimed responsibility, as Hatfield was not held by the military but only by the civil power. 24 Washington 220–221, 227, 240–241, 324–325, 372.

[239] *Supra*, n. 201.

[240] William Smith Diary, 19 June 1783.

nized at the outset, even in the British commissioner's credentials. In consequence of this insistence, the latter was supplied with a new commission that impliedly acknowledged the existence of the United States. Thereafter the preliminary treaty of 30 November 1782 specifically recognized the United States "to be free Sovereign and independent States," and that agreement became effective on 30 January 1783 when Britain made its preliminary peace with France. Accordingly, on 14 February 1783, King George III proclaimed the end of hostilities with "the United States of *America*," a proclamation that was publicly announced in New York on 8 April 1783. Later, with the fall of the Earl of Shelburne's administration, no further concessions were forthcoming from Britain. Consequently the final treaty, signed 3 September 1783, differed from the earlier one only in the omission of the conditional separate article, which had been included to cover the possibility of the British retaining the Floridas, and in the addition of a time limitation on ratification—which could not be met, and which both sides were quite willing to ignore.) [241]

Nonetheless, the correspondence concerning Hetfield casts a revealing light on jurisdictional questions and attitudes, and hence warrants detailed examination.

On 25 August 1783, Hetfield having been apprehended in New York following an earlier unsuccessful search made at the request of Governor Livingston,[242] General Carleton asked the Governor that the witnesses against the prisoner be sent to New York:

> On a Consideration of the violent spirit which prevails against the Refugees, I am persuaded you will be of Opinion

---

[241] Text of treaties: Preliminary Treaty, 8 Stat. 54 and 2 H. Miller 96; separate article at 8 Stat. 57 and 2 H. Miller 101 n. 1. Armistice agreement putting preliminary articles into effect: 8 Stat. 58 and 2 H. Miller 108. Definitive Treaty: 8 Stat. 80 and 2 H. Miller 151.

Insistence of American negotiators on recognition of independence of United States at the outset: R. B. Morris, *The Peacemakers* (New York, 1965) *passim;* new commission for British negotiator, *id.* at 335–342. This book is now the most complete study of the diplomatic exchanges that ended the conflict, though it supplements more than it supersedes the earlier and still standard work, S. F. Bemis, *The Diplomacy of the American Revolution* (4th ed., Bloomington, Ind., 1957), the last three chapters of which are relevant here.

Proclamation of end of hostilities on 8 Apr.: Carleton OB, 7 Apr. 1783; *N.-Y. Royal Gazette*, 9 Apr. 1783, giving the text of the proclamation. A legible facsimile thereof as printed in New York appears facing Abbott 284.

No further concessions in definitive treaty: R. B. Morris, *supra*, at 425–437.

Delay in ratification of definitive treaty: R. B. Morris, *supra*, at 447–448.

[242] Gen. Carleton to Gov. Livingston, 20 June 1783, 4 HMC Am. MSS. 168, PRO 30/55 No. 8094.

with me, that the most impartial Justice will be obtained in a trial of the Prisoner by a General Court Martial at New York, where if your Excellency will direct all the Evidences within your Jurisdiction to attend, a Court Martial shall be Appointed immediately for the purpose.[243]

When Governor Livingston reiterated his demand for Hetfield's surrender,[244] General Carleton, deleting substantially from a draft prepared by his adviser, the Chief Justice, asserted that

upon the maturest consideration, I cannot reconcile myself to the surrender of the Prisoner, as the measure most likely to satisfy what substantial Justice requires.

I certainly am not disposed to controvert the general right of Nations at amity, to make reciprocal requisitions for the delivery up of great, dangerous and atrocious Criminals; or that Justice be executed in the place to which the fugitive resorts; it is, Sir, because there is so much reason, to lament the slow abatement of that hostile spirit, which it was the intention of the articles of peace to subdue, that I prefer the trial of the prisoner at this place. . . .[245]

Your Excellency may dismiss all apprehension of the prisoner's escaping by the exception to our authority, in a course not conforming exactly to the common law, since our Courts here for the trial of offences against that law stand upon the ground of absolute necessity to avoid all the miseries of a wanton and perilous licentiousness.

And General Carleton went on to say that the court-martial would sit from 8 to 13 September, that the witnesses would find the amplest protection, and that if they did not come "it tends not a little to confirm the preference I have made of the trial here, to surrendering the Prisoner to one on your side of the lines." [246]

---

[243] Gen. Carleton to Gov. Livingston, 25 Aug. 1783, 4 HMC Am. MSS. 306, PRO 30/55 Nos. 8859 and 10130.

[244] Gov. Livingston to Gen. Carleton, 26 Aug. 1783, 4 HMC Am. MSS. 313, PRO 30/55 No. 10155.

[245] At this point the following paragraph in the draft was deleted: "The Sovereignty usurped, and in daily exercise by Committees in defiance of the acknowledged Governments, in the Country, and not controled by them, furnished no good ground for the confidence you repose in the common Jurisdiction; and which is due only to a state of composure under an Established System for regularity and order." Yet Chief Justice Smith, who had drafted the whole, noted that "My object was to be safe & yet not exasperate and to prevent him from Appeals ad Populam." William Smith Diary, 30 Aug. 1783.

[246] Gen. Carleton to Gov. Livingston, 31 Aug. 1783, 4 HMC Am. MSS. 319, PRO 30/55 No. 8927.

The American Governor could not agree, particularly since the offense alleged had taken place in May 1783, well after the effective date of the preliminary articles. And there were further objections to the proposed military proceeding:

> As such a trial, Sir, from the illegality of it, even according to the British Constitution, can by no means be decisive, as being altogether unauthoritative and as the Lawyers term it, *coram non Judice*, it follows that his Acquittal by such Court, it will not be pleadable in bar of our future Proceedings against him for the same Offence, whenever either his indiscretion, or his incurable passion for robbery shall induce him to repeat his Visits to New Jersey.

Moreover, added Livingston, what Hetfield did could not be legalized under the pretext of resorting to hostilities.[247]

Nonetheless, the trial took place on General Carleton's terms; he after all had the prisoner. The court-martial convened in New York on 8 September 1783, "at Roubalet's Tavern, in the Broad-Way"; although Major Adye advertised for witnesses to appear, none did; the court-martial sat for six days; but because no *viva voce* evidence was produced, Hetfield was honorably acquitted. The court-martial, not unnaturally, aligned itself with the Commander in Chief, announcing that it was "of Opinion from the said Exhibits and the Non Appearance of Witnesses, on the part of the Prosecution, although they were offered Protection, as appears from some of these exhibits, that the Prosecution is not only groundless but invidious and Malicious in the utmost extreme." [248] Or, more succinctly if less elegantly stated, the absent are always wrong.

Hetfield himself exhibited an amazing degree of gall. While still in confinement awaiting trial, he asked General Carleton's aide to omit his name from the monthly return of prisoners in the provost,

---

[247] Gov. Livingston, to Gen. Carleton, 1 Sept. 1783, 4 HMC Am. MSS. 324, PRO 30/55 No. 10173. The paragraph merely summarized in the text was as follows:

"But how, Sir, can it be expected that the present spirit of the People will ever abate, while the Refugees continue their depredations and robberies, at a time when they have not that flimsey and transparent cloak to veil their predatory incursions Amongst us, in which they were wont to wrap themselves, as long as they could make use of the pretext of resorting from the Sheer principle of Loyalty to the British Standard, when they only meant to legalize their plunders, as hostilities agreeable to the Laws of War."

[248] No. 108; the record of trial is noted at 4 HMC Am. MSS. 376–377, and contained in PRO 30/55 No. 10173. No action by Gen. Carleton appears, and the result was not announced in the Carleton OB. The advertisements by Major Adye, DJA, are in the *N.-Y. Royal Gazette* for 6, 10, and 13 Sept. 1783.

lest his character be thereby injured;[249] after acquittal, he thanked the General for preserving his life, at the same time requesting a copy of the papers to publish in vindication.[250] According to tradition, he did in fact indulge in the indiscretion that even Governor Livingston did not seriously anticipate; he returned to New Jersey nearly a quarter of a century later, in 1807—and was promptly arrested.[251]

It is difficult, comparing the cases of Lippincott and Hetfield in retrospect, nor to agree with Judge Jones that "Sir Guy was not over-burdened with legal knowledge."[252] But then, the latter's own legal adviser was far from objective; refusing either to accept or to reconcile himself to the unpleasant fact of an unsuccessful war, Chief Justice Smith was amazed and shocked to learn, early in October, that the evacuation would take place in November;[253] and, as late as 18 October 1783, he was still of opinion that "the Provisional Articles were nothing without a Definitive Treaty & every Subject clearly under his old Bonds of Allegiance."[254] This last was more than wishful thinking; it was euphoric self-delusion.

Nearly two months remained after Hetfield's acquittal before the British left New York. Apparently, however, their courts-martial sat, tried, and sentenced offenders nearly up to the end. Indeed, a number of death sentences adjudged in the closing months of occupation appear to have been executed,[255] all except one, that of inhabitant George Johnston, whose execution had been ordered for 2 September.[256] Just three days earlier, he was respited

---

[249] Hetfield to Major Beckwith, ADC, 1 Sept. 1783, 4 HMC Am. MSS. 324, PRO 30/55 No. 8955.

[250] Hetfield to Gen. Carleton, 18 Oct. 1783, 4 HMC Am. MSS. 417, PRO 30/55 No. 9391.

[251] 1 Sabine 525.

[252] 2 Jones 126.

[253] William Smith Diary, 6 Oct. 1783.

[254] William Smith Diary, 18 Oct. 1783. The last diary entry made by Smith, C.J., in New York is dated 12 Nov.

Actually the definitive treaty had been signed on 3 Sept., but news of the fact did not reach America until 1 Nov. See Washington to Rochambeau, 1 Nov. 1783, 27 Washington 218, 219.

[255] Mary McNeal, inhabitant (Carleton OB, 8 July 1783); Solomon Chandler, inhabitant, and Cornelius Donnaly, mariner (id., 21 Aug. 1783); Nathaniel Parker and Isaac Alger, refugees (ibid.); Chandler and Donnaly respited to 29 Oct. (id., 30 Aug. 1783). These are, respectively, Nos. 146, 34, 59, 166, and 5.

Trials in September and October are reflected in the provost marshal's returns for 1 Oct. and 1 Nov. 1783, infra, nn. 258 and 280. But the last action on a record of trial in Gen. Carleton's orders is dated 17 Oct. 1783.

[256] Carleton OB, 16 Aug. 1783; No. 119.

until 29 October.[257] He seems in the end to have escaped the noose, because General Carleton's orders contain no further direction for his execution, and the provost marshal's monthly return of prisoners dated 1 November reflects Johnston's continued detention.[258]

The Jurisdictional Enigma of the Evacuation

That final return of British prisoners in North America lists fifty-seven civil prisoners, thirty-eight of whom had been convicted by court-martial of civil offenses (no less than thirty-two of them for various robberies, a revealing commentary on the state of law and order during the final months of occupation), plus two additional prisoners convicted of essentially military crimes.[259]

What happened to these persons after New York City was reoccupied by General Washington and Governor George Clinton of New York State? The answer, were it known, would throw a revealing light on the jurisdictional thinking of the time. If the view of Judge Jones and of Governor Livingston of New Jersey that every trial of an inhabitant by court-martial was illegal had been shared by the returning New York State government, then all of these prisoners should have been retried, at least to the extent that the availability of witnesses permitted, on the footing that the military proceedings had been fatally defective *ab initio*. Contrariwise, if those who constituted that government agreed with the apparent opinion of the Continental Congress that General Carleton could properly proceed in his own way against counterfeiters whose activities had been limited to the area within the British lines,[260] then those whose military sentences had been confirmed should serve out their time, on the basis that the British commander could lawfully exercise military jurisdiction over all who were still present there while he still commanded.

Alexander Hamilton in 1798 rendered an opinion to a client expressing the view that the law in force at a particular place at any given time depended on the fact of what sovereign was in actual control, not on whether the territory in question should as a matter

---

[257] *Id.*, 30 Aug. 1783.

[258] *N.-Y. Royal Gazette*, 5 Nov. 1783.

[259] Eight prisoners were not listed as having been tried; 2 more had been convicted in the Courts of Police established under the military government; 6 were imprisoned for debt; while the final civilian inmate was an insane man awaiting passage home to Scotland.

[260] *Supra*, p. 125.

of treaty have been transferred to another sovereign.[261] Some nine years later an American court in Michigan duly held that slavery existed at Detroit by virtue of British occupancy of that place in fact until July 1796, even though Detroit should have been surrendered in 1782–1783 and even though the Northwest Ordinance adopted by the Continental Congress in 1787 had in terms rendered slavery illegal throughout the area.[262] But these were views expressed in calmer days and cannot be taken to reflect the sentiments prevailing in the full flush of enthusiasm over the evacuation of New York City, which marked in such overt and tangible fashion the victorious culmination on the American side of the long and arduous war for independence. Similarly, any distinction between confirmed and unconfirmed sentences, to the effect that prisoners whose sentences following trial by court-martial had not been confirmed by the Commander in Chief were to be treated as not convicted but as under accusation only, and moreover under the accusation of a sovereignty that had packed up and sailed away, so that they were entitled to their release, was doubtless too refined a differentiation for the thinking of the weeks immediately after evacuation.[263]

Unhappily, however, the final disposition made of the prisoners who were in the provost on Evacuation Day remains tantalizingly obscure. It was not mentioned in any of the numerous accounts of the evacuation, private or official; it was not noticed in the newspapers; extended and indeed intensive search in manuscript and

---

[261] See "Opinion for Alexander Macomb Respecting Acts of British Courts in Districts Comprising Western Posts," in 1 Goebel 527–531. The problem arose because, although all British posts within the territory of the newly recognized United States were required to be surrendered by the terms of both the preliminary and definitive articles of peace in 1782 and 1783, in fact they were retained by way of security for the recognition of debts due the Loyalists, and were not actually surrendered until July 1796, in consequence of a new treaty made in 1794. See generally S. F. Bemis, *Jay's Treaty* (rev. ed., New Haven, 1962).

[262] *Denison* v. *Tucker*, Sup. Ct. of Michigan Terr., 26 Sept. 1807, in 1 W. W. Blume, ed., *Transactions of the Supreme Court of the Territory of Michigan, 1805–1814* (Ann Arbor, 1935) 86–88, 385–395.

[263] According to Simmons 294, the rule that "The sentences of military courts-martial, unlike the sentences of courts of ordinary criminal jurisdiction, are inoperative until the directions of the Queen or of the confirming officer have been signified thereon," dates from 1691. It is still the rule today; Sec. 107(2) of both the Army Act 1955 and the Air Force Act 1955 provides that "A finding of guilty or sentence of a court-martial shall not be treated as a finding or sentence of the court until confirmed."

In the United States, also, the sentence of a court-martial is "interlocutory and inchoate only" until approved. *Runkle* v. *United States*, 122 U.S. 543, 555; Winthrop *683; Art. 64 UCMJ; *Manual for Courts-Martial*, U.S. 1951, par. 86a.

printed sources alike has failed to turn up a single syllable to permit answering with assurance the jurisdictional query posed above. All that can be ventured is a plausible inference, which rests on the few, the very few, facts actually uncovered.[264]

1. Eyewitness accounts establish that these prisoners were not immediately released, that as the British provost serjeant and his guards left the provost to march to the Battery for embarkation, the former simply threw his keys on the floor of the prison, after which the American provost guard took over.[265] This was on Evacuation Day, 25 November 1783. The transfer of government was in consequence wholly peaceable.[266] The prisoners' continued custody in the hands of the American military—General Knox and his handful of soldiers [267]—had been authorized by an ordinance of the executive council that the New York legislature had created four years earlier in hopeful anticipation of ultimate evacuation.[268] And,

---

[264] As the text that follows indicates, positive proof to support the tentative conclusion here ventured, even by a preponderance of evidence, has not been found. To search even farther afield in hope of eventually reaching an unassailable conclusion was a strong temptation, ultimately resisted because such a course would have involved too disproportionate an expenditure of both time and effort on what despite its fascination is still a collateral detail of the present work as a whole.

[265] J. Pintard, "The Old Jail," 9 *The New-York Mirror* 73–74 (Sept. 10, 1831); Onderdonk 210–211, quoting one Gen. Johnson, an eyewitness. Pintard, also an eyewitness, was a nephew of Lewis Pintard, Deputy Commissary-General of Prisoners of the American Army; his Reminiscences (MS, NYHS) were copied in part by the historian Bancroft (Bancroft Transcripts, New York and Misc., MS, NYPL).

J. Riker, *"Evacuation Day," 1783* (New York, 1883) 13 simply quotes J. Pintard.

See also H. Onderdonk, Jr., "A Brief Sketch of the British Prisons in New-York during the Revolutionary War," in *Manual of the Common Council of the City of New York* (1849) 372, 374.

[266] Washington to the President of Congress, 3 Dec. 1783, 27 Washington 255; *The Independent New-York Gazette*, 29 Nov. 1783; *Pennsylvania Packet*, 2 Dec. 1783, quoting a New York letter dated 26 Nov.; *Rivington's New-York Gazette*, 26 Nov. 1783; Maria Chrystie to her husband, Capt. James Chrystie of the 2d Pa. Line, New York, 28 Nov. 1783 (MS, NYHS): "The disaffected party, I believe were much mortified to see the good order & moderation of our People; there were no mobs, plunders or abuse as they expected."

[267] See the resolution of thanks by the Council, 18 Dec. 1783, to "Major General Knox & the officers & privates of the detachment under his command, . . . for their aid in preserving the Peace and Good Order of the Southern District, since the evacuation thereof by the forces of his Britanic Majesty" (8 G. Clinton 323; *New-York Independent Journal*, 1 Jan. 1784; *The Independent Gazette; or, the New-York Journal Revived*, 27 Dec. 1783).

[268] The enabling legislation was the Act of 23 Oct. 1779, "to provide for the temporary Government of the Southern Parts of this State, whenever the Enemy shall abandon or be dispossessed of the same, and until the Legislature can be convened," c. 39 of the Third Session, *Laws of the State of New-York* (Pough-

on 2 December, the council adopted another ordinance declaring that, by reason of the unsafe condition of the gaols in the other counties "all Persons now in actual Custody, or who shall hereafter be apprehended, charged with Felony, Breach of the Peace, or other Offences, within the Southern District of this State, may be committed to the Gaol of the City and County of New-York." [269]

2. The prisoners in question were contemporarily referred to as "a few British criminals," [270] even though all but one were inhabitants of the United States.

3. The state courts resumed early in 1784; the Court of Oyer and Terminer and General Gaol Delivery first sat in New York on 15 March 1784, and thereafter grand juries met and returned indictments quarterly, generally in February, May, August, and November.[271] In 1784, there were returned 105 indictments, in 1785 only 55, and in 1786 the number rose to 75, though at least 17 in the latter year involved only the rather nominal offense of keeping a billiard table.[272] The wartime crime wave, therefore, abated after the first year of restored American government.

Those indictments, returned in New York County during the first two years of American reoccupation, do not disclose any rec-

---

keepsie, 1782) 96. The Council order authorizing further detention of "all persons now in actual Custody," 2 Dec. 1783, appears in *The Independent New-York Gazette*, 6 Dec. 1783, and *Rivington's New-York Gazette*, 3 Dec. 1783; it was specifically ratified by the Act of 19 Feb. 1784, "to revive and continue in Force certain Ordinances therein mentioned," c. 3 of the Seventh Session, *Laws of the State of New-York* (N.Y., 1784) 5. The earlier Council order authorizing the military to confine prisoners, dated Haerlem, 21 Nov. 1783, appears in *The New-York Packet*, 24 Nov. 1783; *New-York Independent Journal*, 24 Nov. 1783; and *Rivington's New-York Gazette*, 26 Nov. 1783.

A good many of these items can also be found in "Papers Relating to the Evacuation of New York, in the Year 1783," in *Manual of the Common Council of the City of New York* (1870) 772–844.

[269] *The Independent New-York Gazette*, 6 Dec. 1783.

[270] So characterized by Gen. Johnson, *supra* n. 265. Pintard noted (9 *The New-York Mirror* at 74) that "a few British subjects remained, for various crimes, in [the provost serjeant's] custody." Of the 42 individuals held on 1 Nov. 1783 who had been convicted either by court-martial or by the Courts of Police, all but one were American inhabitants, and of these 15 were born either in the United States or in non-British foreign countries. Of the 8 held awaiting trial, 5 were native-born.

[271] See the Minute Book of the Court of Oyer and Terminer and General Gaol Delivery, 1784–1796, in the Office of the Clerk of the Criminal Division of the Supreme Court of the State of New York for New York County, 100 Centre Street, New York City. For the benefit of English lawyers it should be noted here that in New York State the Supreme Court is the court of general jurisdiction.

[272] All of these indictments, as well as those cited in the four notes following, are contained in a metal box, marked "Indictments, 1784–1786," kept in the same office as the Minute Book cited in the preceding note.

ognition that Evacuation Day imposed a jurisdictional barrier blocking inquiry into all that had gone before. In 1784, two indictments were returned for offenses alleged to have been committed on 18 November 1783, a week before the evacuation, one for assault and battery, the second for larceny,[273] while two other 1784 indictments recalled the war: one charged misprision of treason, alleging a going over to the enemy on 9 July 1776,[274] the other high treason in fitting out a privateer on 1 October 1782.[275] Of the 1785 indictments, one charged a larceny occurring in February 1783,[276] another a larceny taking place in July 1781.[277] None of the 1786 indictments alleged offenses occurring during the British occupation.

4. The final provost marshal return lists 44 prisoners as tried and sentenced by general court-martial, and 9 more as simply tried. Only 9 of the former group, and none of the latter, appear in General Carleton's order book. It would seem, therefore, that in respect of 44 prisoners duly tried no final action was in fact taken by the Commander in Chief.

5. In June 1783, an individual named Patrick Halfpenny was tried by general court-martial for "Forging the name of William Fowler, Esq., Naval Storekeeper at this Port to Bills of Exchange drawn on the Treasurer of the Royal Navy"; his acquittal was announced on 22 June.[278] On 15 July, he was again confined, the charge against him being listed in the provost marshal's reports for 1 August and 1 September as "Forgery (in the Name of Mr. Fowler, Naval-Storekeeper)."[279] He appears to have been again tried, in respect of this presumably new and separate offense; this time he was convicted, for in the list of prisoners for 1 October and 1 November the entry opposite his name is, "Forgery,—tried, and under Sentence of a General Court-Martial."[280] No action on this second trial appears in General Carleton's orders.

Some time after Evacuation Day, Patrick turned up again, like the bad Halfpenny that he was: On 20 March 1784 he was tried before a jury empaneled in the New York Court of Oyer and

---

[273] *People* v. *Martin McEvoy* (assault and battery), *People* v. *Martin McEvoy* (larceny), both returned in September 1784.
[274] *People* v. *Gilbert Livingston*, returned in May 1784.
[275] *People* v. *John Haley*, returned in March 1784.
[276] *People* v. *Joseph Tipcony*, returned in May 1785.
[277] *People* v. *Peter Risberg*, returned in June 1785.
[278] No. 100; Carleton OB, 22 June 1783.
[279] *N.-Y Royal Gazette*, 6 Aug. and 3 Sept. 1783.
[280] *N.-Y. Royal Gazette*, 1 Oct. and 5 Nov. 1783.

Terminer, etc., on an indictment charging him with uttering, to one John Delafield on 3 January 1784—over five weeks after the evacuation—three forged bills of exchange purportedly drawn by William Fowler, Naval Storekeeper, on the Commissioners of the Navy, each dated 15 November 1783, and each in the sum of £50; the forged bills were set out in full in the indictment.[281] He was convicted, after which it was adjudged that he "Stand in the Pillory for one hour on the 19th [April 1784] between the hours of ten and two of the Clock of the same day, and that he stand Committed for three months then to be discharged on payment of Costs." [282]

6. The file of court-martial proceedings had in the year 1783 that is preserved in the Public Record Office contains only three records of trial from New York: one officer's case, the trial of Duryee *et al.*, and the case of the counterfeiters.[283] No other records of any trial either noted in General Carleton's orders for 1783 or reflected in his provost marshal's returns of prisoners in New York are preserved, either as proceedings or as copied into the War Office court-martial books. Some may, of course, have miscarried; but it seems at least equally possible that the original records of trial were left behind with the prisoners confined in the New York provost, by way of commitment papers.

7. A good many prisoners listed on the provost marshal's November 1783 return had fairly common names, frequently encountered: James Brown, William Douglas, Robert Field, John Holmes, George Johnston, Charles Jones, George Miller, Patrick Murphy, William Read, John Smith, James Stewart, John Wilson. But even in a city as large and as cosmopolitan as New York, it seems unlikely that there could have been found in November 1783 more than one individual with the distinctive name of Patrick Halfpenny, and well-nigh mathematically impossible that separate persons bearing that same name should on three distinct occasions have endeavored to pass bills of exchange purporting to have been drawn by an identical maker on an identical drawee.

8. Two other factors, not susceptible of precise measurement, must also be considered. One of these is the climate of opinion following the occupation, which doubtless regarded these prisoners

---

[281] *People* v. *Patrick Halfpenny*, returned in March 1784; Minute Book, Court of Oyer & Terminer, &c., 1784–1796, p. 7.

[282] Minute Book, p. 43 (5 Apr. 1784). The conviction was noted in *New-York Independent Journal*, 24 Mar. 1784.

[283] PRO, WO 71/155.

more as victims of British tyranny than as potential threats to American security. Another factor, less weighty but still not to be ignored, is that the pattern of every successful revolution over the years has included, in greater or less degree, the concomitant incident of a general jail delivery.

9. The conclusion therefore reached, and, as has been said, it rests on probabilities more than on positive proof, is that all who were in the provost on Evacuation Day by reason of commitment under British authority were released before the end of the year, in all probability before Christmas, free to breathe once more the unpolluted air of liberty, free to sin again some other day.

CHAPTER VI

THE WAR OF AMERICAN INDEPENDENCE —PART TWO

SIX OCCUPIED CITIES (CONTINUED)

In the four other cities to be discussed, only Philadelphia witnessed any sizable number of civilians tried by general court-martial, and only Savannah saw the restoration of civil government under the Crown. Accordingly, the emphasis below shifts from trials to the other incidents of military rule. As in the preceding chapter, the several cities are considered in the chronological sequence of their initial occupation. Finally, to complete the recital, the military-civilian relationships incident to the Burgoyne expedition will be dealt with briefly.

NEWPORT

Newport in the Colony of Rhode Island and Providence Plantations [1] was occupied by the British Army from 8 December 1776 until 26 October 1779.[2] The justification for trying its inhabitants by court-martial was contemporaneously articulated by Captain Mackenzie of the 23d Foot, later Major and DAG to Generals Clinton and Carleton in New York,[3] in these terms: "As no Civil

---

[1] Rhode Island and Connecticut were colonies and, under separate charters granted by King Charles II, elected their own governors; the other eleven were provinces with governors appointed by the Crown. The official designation of the first named, even today, is "State of Rhode Island and Providence Plantations."

[2] H. Clinton 57, 146–147, 427; 2 Gaine 69. 1 Stedman 220 considered the occupation of Newport "an unlucky measure, as it had no use but to keep a great body of troops unemployed during three years." Clinton had been opposed to it (Willcox 115–116, 120, 291), but then compounded the error by withdrawing after the French entered the war, thus enabling them to occupy Rhode Island in July 1780. Ch. VIII, "Triumph and Frustration, December 1779–November 1780," in Willcox.

[3] Army List of the British Forces in North America, New York, 16 Oct. 1781 (WLCL); *A List of the Officers of the Army, serving in North-America, Under the Command of his Excellency General Sir Guy Carleton, K.B.* (New York, 1783). A copy of the latter compilation, printed by James Rivington, is in the New-York Historical Society, while the Carleton Order Book in the Clements Library forms part of the Mackenzie Papers there.

Government exists in any of the places occupied by The King's Troops in the Rebel Colonies, offences of a trifling nature, wherein Inhabitants have been concerned, have generally been tried by a Garrison Court Martial. When Inhabitants have been accused of Capital crimes, they have been tried by a General Court Martial." [4] His diary records two trials of inhabitants by garrison court-martial, one a merchant fined for insulting an officer, one of a man fined for buying a soldier's necessaries.[5] No record of the trial of any Rhode Island inhabitant by general court-martial has been found;[6] the only civilian to face such a tribunal during the occupation was Mr. Lewis Latham Clarke, Clerk of H.M.'s Provision Stores, who was charged with embezzling the King's stores and defrauding the troops of their due. He obtained findings in the nature of a Scotch verdict: "They are of opinion he has mixed water with the Rum, but for want of Sufficient Evidence as the Act of Parliament directs, the Court acquit him." [7]

The military government on Rhode Island appears to have been reasonably mild in its impact. As in New York, there was a Superintendent of Police, in this instance Joseph Wanton, Jr., a former Deputy Governor (and son of the last Loyalist Governor of the same name, who had been deposed by the General Assembly in 1775, after Lexington and Concord).[8] A number of unexceptionable police regulations were issued—liquor dealers to register on pain of forfeiture,[9] inhabitants to keep the streets clean,[10] small arms not to be fired,[11] no depredations to be committed in the barracks,[12] no fences to be destroyed.[13] A captain of the port was appointed,

---

[4] 1 Mackenzie 309.

[5] *Ibid.* The trial of the merchant for insulting the officer took place on 13 July 1778, that of the man fined £5 sterling for buying the soldier's necessaries in November 1777. *Newport Gazette*, 27 Nov. and 11 Dec. 1777.

[6] See the order book for the Rhode Island command, WO 36/2, with entries covering the entire period of British occupation.

[7] No. 37.

[8] *Newport Gazette*, 15 July 1779 (Wanton as Superintendent-General); DAB *s.v.* Joseph Wanton, Sr.; 80 NEHGR 252–254 (Joseph Wanton, Jr.); J. R. Bartlett, *History of the Wanton Family of Newport, R.I.* (Providence, 1878) 78–114 (Joseph Wanton, Sr.); 2 Sabine 397–399 (both); D. S. Lovejoy, *Rhode Island Politics and the American Revolution, 1760–1776* (Providence, 1958) 182–184 (removal from office of Gov. Joseph Wanton, Sr.).

[9] *Newport Gazette*, 6 Mar. 1777. This and many of the later notices mentioned were repeated, but only the first publication of each will be cited. More than one citation indicates a different notice thereafter.

[10] *Newport Gazette*, 13 Mar. 1777.

[11] *Newport Gazette*, 1 July 1779.

[12] *Newport Gazette*, 22 July 1779.

[13] *Newport Gazette*, 9 Apr. 1778, 25 Mar. 1779.

with whom arrivals and departures were to be entered.[14] Vessels were forbidden to move at night.[15] A nightly watch was established in the town.[16]

Food was a problem.[17] Inhabitants were exhorted to cultivate vacant lands and not to trespass on crops or rob gardens.[18] No oxen were to be slaughtered without permission,[19] and inhabitants were warned against frightening or shooting the King's cattle [20] and against purchasing stolen vegetables.[21] Farmers threshing grain on Conanicut Island (the Town of Jamestown) were required to bring the straw to the King's wharf.[22] A guard was directed to attend at the market, with orders to confine anyone found guilty of committing disorders.[23] A series of orders fixed the prices at which fish, meat, and bread might be sold, on penalty of forfeiture if those prices were exceeded.[24]

Inhabitants were warned against going to or returning from the mainland clandestinely. "All persons hereafter convicted of such iniquitous Proceedings, as well as their Aiders and Abettors, will be deemed SPIES, and treated with the utmost Rigour of Martial Law." [25] Major Mackenzie urged that the first person so convicted be "hanged immediately," noting that "The first example would probably put a stop to the practice." [26] Another notice threatened punishment and confiscation of property for anyone supplying the rebels with rum and salt.[27] These threats may have sufficed; more likely, however, is the conclusion that no offender was caught. Nor was there any indication that there were claimants for the $2,000 reward offered "for the author of the treasonable Paper posted up at the Corner of the Grand Parade under one of the Proclamations

---

[14] *Newport Gazette,* 25 Sept. 1777, 22 Oct. 1778.

[15] *Newport Gazette,* 29 Oct. 1778.

[16] *Newport Gazette,* 1 and 8 Jan. 1778.

[17] This was also the case in those portions of Rhode Island that were not in British hands. "During the winter of 1778–79, the food situation in Rhode Island became desperate." J. B. Hedges, *The Browns of Providence Plantations* (Cambridge, Mass., 1952) 263.

[18] *Newport Gazette,* 3 Apr., 8 May 1777.

[19] *Newport Gazette,* 12 Mar. 1778.

[20] *Newport Gazette,* 19 Aug. 1779.

[21] *Newport Gazette,* 26 Aug. 1779.

[22] *Newport Gazette,* 29 July 1779.

[23] *Newport Gazette,* 26 Dec. 1777.

[24] *Newport Gazette,* 24 Apr., 12 and 26 June 1777, 16 Apr. 1778, 15 and 22 July 1779.

[25] *Newport Gazette,* 29 May 1777.

[26] 1 Mackenzie 173, 185 (4 and 23 Sept. 1777).

[27] *Newport Gazette,* 4 Sept. 1777.

affixed here." [28] Over the centuries, military occupiers have never been remarkable for a sense of humor; severity is more in their line.

Thus, on one occasion, the inhabitants of the Town of Portsmouth (north of Newport on the same island) were ordered during the occupation to work on the fortifications. But only seventeen appeared; the rest, Quakers, who said it was contrary to their principles to assist in any manner in matters of war, and refused even to construct barracks,[29] appear to have been suffered to continue in their refusal. Later, in October 1777, "About 70 of the most disaffected Inhabitants of Newport, were taken up yesterday and this day, and sent on board the Prison ship." [30]

When the British evacuated Newport in October 1779, the Loyalists sailed to New York with them; among them was Superintendent Joseph Wanton, Jr., with "a small box containing the proceedings of the police." When he died in 1780, the box passed to his brother William, who still had it in August 1782.[31] But those papers have disappeared, and with them were lost the day-by-day details of occupation of a city that, however much it later became the social capital of American wealth, has never recovered, even to the present day, its position as a thriving commercial community. In 1775 it was the fifth largest city in America.[32]

PHILADELPHIA

On 26 September 1777, Howe took Philadelphia,[33] after which, so Benjamin Franklin is reported to have said in Paris at the time, Philadelphia took Howe.[34] The venerable philosopher's remark was not at all facetious, for ultimately the snug winter quarters that the British Army had acquired there inclined its officers to a winter of outstanding gaiety,[35] and disinclined them and their commander

---

[28] *Newport Gazette*, 29 May 1777.

[29] 1 Mackenzie 177, 178.

[30] 1 Mackenzie 197, 200. And see the extract from a contemporary diary, immediately after the first British landing on Newport. "The town remained peaceful for a few days. A woman was committed to the military jail for wishing the provincials to come to the Island." E. B. Lyman, *A Reminiscence of Newport before and during the Revolutionary War* (Newport, R.I., 1906) 25.

[31] 3 HMC Am. MSS. 85. And see the reference to Isaac Touro of Newport coming to New York with the troops, 2 *id.* 102.

[32] Bridenbaugh, *passim*.

[33] 4 Freeman 498; 1 C. Ward 361; cf. 3 Fortescue 219.

[34] Van Doren *Franklin* 585; cf. Alden A.R. ch. 8, "Philadelphia Takes Howe."

[35] *Diary of James Allen*, 9 PMHB at 436; *Extracts from the Letter-Book of Capt. Heinrichs*, 22 *id.* at 139; Fisher 462 ("Very bad accounts of the licentiousness of

from any offensive action against Washington's ragged and starving troops, freezing at Valley Forge, not more than twenty miles away. In actual fact, Sir William's heart had never been in the business.[36] Then, in November, shortly before he received news of Burgoyne's surrender at Saratoga, he resigned,[37] and in May 1778 he turned over the command to Sir Henry Clinton.[38] Very soon thereafter, on 18 June 1778, Clinton marched the British Army out of the city.[39]

The occupation pattern in Philadelphia followed the New York precedent. Howe appointed Joseph Galloway Superintendent-General, assisted by three Magistrates of Police, and simultaneously made him "Superintendent of all Imports and Exports." [40]

Galloway had been a member of the First Continental Congress in the fall of 1774; that body rejected as too conservative his plan for American autonomy. For his part, he could not accept independence and left his home for the British camp near New Bruns-

---

the English officers in deluding young girls"); 1 Stedman 309. For the elaborate Mischianza fete in May 1778, reputed to have cost over 3,000 guineas, see Baurmeister 65–66; Drinker 306; 1 Jones 241–251, 716–720.

[36] If proof were still needed that the two Howes, Adm. Lord Howe and Gen. Sir William Howe, were less than completely dedicated to the cause whose sea and land forces they respectively commanded, the several "olive branch" proclamations with which they sought to reclaim the colonists' allegiance should be examined. A set of these is in Mackenzie Papers—D (WCLC).

See, generally, T. S. Anderson, *The Command of the Howe Brothers* (New York, 1936). Probably B. Partridge, *Sir Billy Howe* (New York, 1932) does not rise above historical journalism, but it includes Clinton's masked message (pp. 193–195; see Willcox 175 n. 5), and it contains (pp. 261–289) *The Narrative of Lieut. Gen. Sir William Howe, &c.* (London, 1780), the commander's defense before a committee of the House of Commons in April 1779. The first, where a message apparently to one effect conveys an entirely different meaning when covered with a peculiarly shaped mask, has not been published anywhere else, while the second is hard to come by.

[37] Alden A.R. 126; 2 C. Ward 567.

[38] Clinton OB, 24 May 1778; 1 Kemble 585–586; Montrésor 492.

[39] 5 Freeman 10; 3 Fortescue 255.

On the day before the Army left, Capt. Montrésor, CRE, wrote: "We are, it seems, to evacuate this city, which I should think too great a present to make to the Rebels as a preparation. In short, the whole has been a Comedy of Errors, or all in the wrong, and now comes on the Farce." 1 Porter 203.

For the ministry's orders to Gen. Clinton to evacuate Philadelphia as a measure of retrenchment in view of France's entry into the war, see H. Clinton 86; Willcox 223–226; Valentine 333–334. Characteristically, neither the Earl of Carlisle nor any of his fellow commissioners were advised of these evacuation orders. Willcox 229–230; Valentine 318, 320–321; Alden A.R. 197.

For the effect of the evacuation of Philadelphia on the mission of the Carlisle Commission, see n. 77 of ch. V, *supra*, pp. 98–99.

[40] Proclamations by Sir William Howe, 4 Dec. 1777, in *The Pennsylvania Ledger or the Weekly Advertiser*, 6 Dec. 1777. These appointments were duly noted by Judge Jones. 1 Jones 237, 239; 2 Jones 109 n.

wick, New Jersey, in December 1776. When the British evacuated Philadelphia, he retired with them to New York, from whence he left for London in October 1778. There he became a leading spokesman for American Loyalists, as well as a most voluble—and virulent—critic of General Howe.[41]

The proclamations issued by General Howe and his Superintendent-General during the occupation covered a wide range indeed. The acts required of the population included observing a curfew "between Tattoo and Revellie," keeping the streets and chimneys clean, entering vessels coming to the port, suppressing vice and immorality, and growing vegetables; the acts prohibited included purchases from soldiers, unlicensed sale of liquor, setting up of new ferries, cutting of wood required by H.M.'s troops, unlicensed auction sales, unrestricted sale of beef, acting as drayman or porter without registration, depredations, trampling hay in the fields, taking provisions from loyal subjects, and importing goods without a permit.[42] On various occasions the inhabitants were called on to make return of the horses, waggons, teams, carts, naval stores, oil, and forage in their possession.[43] The penalties involved were fines, "to be recovered in a summary way before any one magistrate of police,"[44] or else imprisonment;[45] some of the fines were to be applied toward the support of the poor,[46] some of the license fees toward the maintenance of the nightly watch and lamps.[47] Violation of the proclamation restricting sales of beef resulted in forfeiture, one-half to the poor, the other half to the informer, while claims to the forfeited articles were to be summarily determined by any one magistrate of police, "and the burthen of proof shall be on the claimant."[48]

---

[41] See E. H. Baldwin, *Joseph Galloway, the Loyalist Politician*, 26 PMHB 161, 289, 417; J. P. Boyd, *Anglo-American Union: Joseph Galloway's Plan to Preserve the British Empire, 1774–1788* (Philadelphia, 1941); O. C. Kuntzleman, *Joseph Galloway, Loyalist* (Philadelphia, 1941).

The three Magistrates of Police were Samuel Shoemaker, Daniel Coxe, and John Potts (1 HMC Am. MSS. 364; cf. E. H. Tatum, ed., *The American Journal of Ambrose Serle* [San Marino, Calif., 1940] 295), while Galloway's deputies as Superintendent of Exports and Imports were Enoch Story and one Smith (1 HMC Am. MSS. 160).

[42] *Pennsylvania Ledger*, 12 and 26 Nov., 10, 17, and 20 Dec. 1777, 10, 14, 17, 21, and 24 Jan., 21 Feb., 2 and 25 Mar., 15 Apr. 1778; 1 HMC Am. MSS. 201.

[43] *Pennsylvania Ledger*, 19 Nov. 1777, 14 Jan., 4, 14, and 28 Feb. 1778.

[44] *Pennsylvania Ledger*, 17 Jan., 21 Feb., 25 Mar. 1778.

[45] *Pennsylvania Ledger*, 17 and 21 Jan. 1778.

[46] *Pennsylvania Ledger*, 21 Feb. 1778.

[47] *Pennsylvania Ledger*, 21 Jan. 1778.

[48] *Pennsylvania Ledger*, 24 Jan. 1778. In this instance, the forfeitures were to be

One of the outstanding hardships of the occupation flowed from the requisitioning of private residences to serve as quarters for the troops,[49] a process that moved a British officer to note in his diary, "Finished Quartering the Troops which has been a very disagreeable Fatiguing piece of Business."[50] Another and more severe burden was the arrest and imprisonment of selected individuals without trial,[51] on one occasion resulting in deportation to New York.[52] Early in the occupation, also, forced labor had been required of the inhabitants.[53]

Apparently the only civil courts functioning were those of the Magistrates of Police under Superintendent-General Galloway; he certified to the probate of a deceased British officer's will on 8 March 1778, whether before those magistrates or otherwise is unclear.[54] But they were plainly the ones before whom, according to the record of two trials by general court-martial, an oath was subscribed.[55]

Captain Alexander Campbell, *Fourier de la Cour* of the Army,[56] was tried for holding correspondence with and giving intelligence to the enemy, the principal witness against him being a girl less than seventeen years of age, one Mary Fygis. She swore before Messrs. Coxe and Potts, two of the three magistrates, apparently under considerable pressure from Galloway himself, that she had brought

---

equally divided between the informer and the poor of the city. See generally, W. O. Mishoff, *Business in Philadelphia during the British Occupation, 1777–1778*, 61 PMHB 165, an excellent study based on the proclamations, newspaper advertisements, and contemporary letters.

[49] Drinker 298 (29 Sept. 1777), 302 (18 Dec.), 303 (29 Dec.); Popp 30 (13 Dec. 1777; "We were quartered in old empty houses of Front Street"); Fisher 460 (30 Dec. 1777), 461 (28 Jan. 1778); 1 Stedman 309; 1 André 131 (16 Dec. 1777; "The Quarter Majors were employed in distributing quarters to the Troops in Philadelphia").

[50] H. M. Lydenberg, ed., *Archibald Robertson, Lieutenant-General Royal Engineers: His Diaries and Sketches in America, 1762–1780* (New York, 1930) 162 (entry for 26 Dec. 1777).

[51] Drinker 298–299 (29 Sept. 1777); *Diary of Christiana Leach*, 35 PMHB 343, 345 (18 and 28 Mar. 1778); Baurmeister 25–26; see also *Pennsylvania Ledger*, 18 Feb. 1778 (one John Benner, charged with robbery, imprisoned in a dungeon).

[52] Drinker 300 (23 Oct. 1777); Fisher 455 (24 Oct. 1777). Both entries refer to the removal of Richard Waln.

[53] Montrésor 129.

[54] Evelyn 94; compare n. 19 of ch. V, *supra* p. 90.

[55] WO 71/85/304 and 442.

[56] The *Fourier de la Cour* was the officer responsible for taking up quarters for the army commander and his staff (S. G. P. Ward 135–136), i.e., in modern terminology, the Headquarters Commandant. See also Maclachlan 70 (reference in 1745 to *Fouriers* as billet masters).

Captain Campbell a letter from the American side, which she concealed on her person. Her story did not hold water, and even though Sir William Howe in a personal interview suggested for that reason a retraction of her accusation, she refused; here was one woman who would not change her mind. Captain Campbell was acquitted, General Howe proclaimed in orders his own conviction of Campbell's innocence,[57] and young Miss Fygis was thereupon tried for having committed perjury at the earlier proceeding. She was duly convicted, "but in consideration of her youth, and voluntary Confession, the Court only adjudge her to be turned out of the Lines, and in case of her returning to be put in the Pillory for half an hour and to be imprisoned for six Months." [58]

The other Philadelphia trials of civilians by general court-martial reflect the same elements as those in New York—mariners and other seafarers, waggoners and conductors, Negroes, followers of the army, inhabitants, with women included in the last two groups; attempted murder, assault, arson, plundering, robbery, burglary, stealing, embezzlement, and receiving stolen goods among the civil offenses; advising desertion and enticing sailors to desert among the military ones. The sentences imposed ranged from death and flogging from a hundred to a thousand lashes to payment of statutory penalties and expulsion. In Philadelphia the acquittals of civilians ran particularly high, being 62 per cent of those tried.[59]

Only one of the foregoing cases appears to present a point of substantive law. Thomas Lamb, an inhabitant from the testimony though not specifically designated as such in the proceedings, was tried with another civilian for breaking open the house of one John Reynolds "& feloniously taking thereout a box Containing Sundry Plate, Cash and other Articles, the property of the said Jnº Reynolds." Lamb was acquitted, so was the woman charged with receiving the stolen goods, while the other civilian principal was convicted and sentenced to death.[60] Then, four days later, Lamb was

[57] Howe OB, 30 Mar. 1778. Captain and *Fourier de la Cour* Campbell appears once more in the records; on 28 Sept. 1778 he was tried by general court-martial at New York for murder, and acquitted. WO 71/87/265–298.

For the reason why Gen. Howe permitted this obviously groundless accusation to go to trial, see pp. 107–108, *supra*.

[58] No. 82.

[59] First number gives the total number of trials in each category, the second one, in parentheses, the number of acquittals: inhabitants, 5(2); no status indicated, 8(5); mariners, 9(6); followers of the army, 8(5); civilian employees, 7(5). One woman inhabitant was convicted; two women with no status indicated were acquitted; one woman follower was convicted, one acquitted.

[60] No. 128(1), tried together with Nos. 41 and 42. Richard Collins, the convicted civilian, was duly executed. 1 Kemble 571; Howe OB, 24 Apr. 1778.

put on trial again, "accused of having been accessory before and after to the Breaking open & feloniously taking out of the House of Mr. John Reynolds of the City of Philadelphia, sundry Plate, Cash, and other Articles, the Property of the said Mr. John Reynolds." [61] This time he was convicted and sentenced to death, to the modern reader an obvious instance of being put twice in jeopardy for the same offense. The court-martial books show that Adye prosecuted both cases as DJA.

What makes the case the more surprising is the circumstance that the prohibition against double jeopardy was not only specifically repeated in a recurring provision of every annual Mutiny Act, but was particularly noted in Adye's own treatise.[62] Contemporary texts on criminal law moreover stated that, while acquittal as principal did not bar a subsequent indictment as accessory after the fact, it very plainly precluded a later charge of being accessory before the fact in respect of the same offense—texts that Adye himself cited.[63]

The explanation of Lamb's second trial must accordingly be looked for in the very precise charge there made against him, "accessory before and after," and in a final sentence in Adye's discussion, "yet in some books it is holden that one who has been acquitted as a principal, may be tried again as an accessary before, as well as after." [64] Actually, the authorities Adye had cited in support of the quoted statement were even then without vitality,[65] a circumstance Adye may well have recognized by the time his probable disagreement with the original acquittal had, in all likelihood, somewhat subsided. Because, when the death sentence imposed at the second trial came before General Howe for confirmation, the latter respited Lamb's punishment and recommended him for a pardon; and in the end the prisoner was pardoned by the King

---

[61] No. 128(2).

[62] Adye (1st ed. 1769) 63–65.

[63] M. Hale, *Pleas of the Crown* (7th ed., London, 1773) *244; 2 W. Hawkins, *A Summary of Crown Law* (London, 1770) 359.

[64] Adye (1st ed. 1769) 65.

[65] Adye cited "Kielwood's Rep. 107. Daliston's Rep. 114." The first is a citation to a case in law French of uncertain date, in Kielway's Reports—which end with the year 1531. J. W. Wallace, *The Reporters* (Heard's 4th ed., Boston, 1882) 119–121. The second reference is to Dalison, another volume of reports in law French not extending beyond 1580 (Wallace, *supra,* 114–118)—and is moreover a complete mis-citation: Dalison 114 starts in the middle of a case on chantries decided in 16 Eliz. I (1574–1575). It is therefore entirely plain that Adye did not make any independent examination of the authorities he cited to support his text. He was not the first text-writer, and assuredly not the last, to demonstrate that citations merely lifted are generally wrong.

"in Consideration of some peculiar circumstances." [66] So, ultimately, Lamb received the benefit of the prohibition against double jeopardy that has always been so fundamental in every area of English law.

Apart from particular cases, the principal variant between the position in Philadelphia and that in New York arises by reason of the happenstance that the manuscript copy of the Howe Order Book in the Clements Library is not restricted to general courts-martial but also announces the results of trials of civilians by garrison court-martial from January through April 1778. It is accordingly possible to evaluate the incidence of lesser offenses in that city during a part of the occupation. [67]

On the day of his departure from Philadelphia, General Clinton directed that "The women of the Army are constantly to march upon the Flanks of the Baggage of their respective Corps and the Provost Martial has received positive orders to drum out any Woman who shall dare to disobey this Order." [68] But the march had not been long under way before two female followers of the army, Mary Colethrate and Elizabeth Clarke, were tried for plundering by a general court-martial; the first was acquitted, the second convicted; sentence, "to receive *an hundred* Lashes on her bare Back in the most public Manner possible." [69] The record of trial suggests that the plundering for which she was punished was in the nature of a holocaust. One of the witnesses testified that "there were about twenty or thirty women in the house." The wonder is, not that some plundering ensued in those circumstances, but that the house itself was left standing.

---

[66] Charles Gould, JAG, to Gen. Sir William Howe, 12 June 1778, WO 71/86/82–83. A marginal note in the court-martial book, initialed "C. G.," states that Lamb was pardoned by the King that same day.

[67] Of the 8 trials of civilians recorded, 6 resulted in convictions, 1 in acquittal, and the last, where no sentence appears, probably in another acquittal. Kemble records the appointment of garrison courts-martial in Philadelphia for the trial of disorderly patients at the Pennsylvania Hospital, whether military or civilian does not appear. 1 Kemble 547–548, 554 (27 Feb. and 12 Mar. 1778).

Older accounts of the British occupation of Philadelphia appear in 2 J. F. Watson, *Annals of Philadelphia and Pennsylvania* (Philadelphia, 1870) 282–302, and in J. T. Scharf and T. Westcott, *History of Philadelphia, 1609–1884* (Philadelphia, 1884) 350–385. These add little but discursive gossip to the primary sources already cited, and, as was customary at the time of publication, are undocumented.

[68] Clinton OB, 18 June 1778.

[69] Nos. 36 and 39. It is noted in 2 André 8 that on 24 June 1778 "A good deal of attention was paid to enforcing the Orders respecting plunder and also the Battalion horses and followers of the Army not mixing in the line of march."

SAVANNAH

Savannah is in Georgia, the southernmost, the youngest, and then the poorest of the Thirteen Colonies; [70] the city was in British hands from 29 December 1778 until 11 July 1782,[71] and Georgia became the only one of the thirteen in which, during the War of Independence, a Loyalist legislature and the normal complement of H.M.'s judges functioned. Indeed, from the end of May 1780 until July 1781 both the whereabouts and existence of the Georgia state government remain unknown.

The date of the re-establishment of the royal civil government was 4 March 1779; in July the former royal officials—Governor, Lieutenant-Governor, and Chief Justice—all of whom had been driven out early in 1776, returned from England; and, after the Franco-American effort to recapture the city in September 1779 had been repulsed,[72] all of the restored civilian regime began to function throughout the province. The Assembly was elected, met regularly, and enacted much legislation; the courts (including the Court of Vice-Admiralty) were reopened, the grand jury reconvened, and justices of the peace were appointed. Almost immediately thereafter, the conflicts between military and civil authority that Generals Howe and Clinton had anticipated and largely prevented elsewhere made their appearance. These involved basic differences in policy between the restored Governor, who wanted all of the province recovered, and the local military commander,[73] who was painfully aware of other and more pressing military requirements, while, on a lower level, there were disputes between the judges and the military over quarters for the courts and in connection with the service of writs upon military officers.

All this was reported to Sir Henry Clinton, who in consequence was determined that civil government in the next province to be recovered—South Carolina, which as will be seen was captured under his immediate command in May 1780—be restored as slowly as possible. " 'Tis too great a blessing to bestow upon them at once;

---

[70] French F.Y. 139.

[71] Alden A.R. 228; 2 C. Ward 679–681, 839–840; 3 Fortescue 276–279.

[72] Alden A.R. 230; 2 C. Ward 688–694; 3 Fortescue 283–286; A. A. Lawrence, *Storm over Savannah* (Athens, Ga., 1951).

[73] Maj.-Gen. Augustin Prevost until May 1780, and then Lt.-Col., later Brig.-Gen., Alured Clarke (2 HMC Am. MSS. 3, 120, 125, 128, 510).

it will intoxicate, as it has done in Georgia." [74] But it was not too long before the difficulties encountered in Georgia disappeared in the flood tide of larger events. For, shortly after the middle of 1781, British withdrawals from the interior began, and by the time Savannah was evacuated in July 1782, the revived state government was waiting at the gates to move into the city with the American army. [75] But, with incurable if wholly unrealistic optimism, the royal Governor maintained to the end that with four or five hundred additional soldiers the entire province could have been reconquered for the King. [76]

No record has been found of any inhabitant of Savannah tried by British court-martial after its capture and before the restoration of civil government. [77]

CHARLESTON, SOUTH CAROLINA

Clinton had failed to capture Charleston in June 1776, but he succeeded in doing so four years later; [78] the city was in consequence occupied from 12 May 1780 to 14 December 1782. [79] The

---

[74] Gen. Clinton to W. Eden, Under SS, 30 May 1780, quoted in Willcox 313. Smith L. & R. 104–106 notes the British inability to restore civil government completely in Georgia.

[75] The foregoing text is drawn primarily from two sources, K. Coleman, *The American Revolution in Georgia, 1763–1789* (Athens, Ga., 1958), a thorough study based on the records; and *A Narrative of the Official Conduct of Anthony Stokes* (London, 1784), the account written by the Chief Justice of the Province of Georgia after his second eviction therefrom with a view to his receiving proper compensation for "the Dangers and Distresses He Underwent in the Cause of Government."

The recital of Stokes, C.J., fully corroborates what Judge Jones wrote at about the same time regarding the position in Georgia. 1 Jones 354; 2 Jones 175 n.

[76] Gov. Sir James Wright to Gen. Carleton, 6 July 1782, 3 HMC Am. MSS. 11.

[77] A regimental order book, kept during the siege of Savannah from 2 July to 2 Oct. 1779 (MS., LC), contains no entries reflecting the results of trials by court-martial.

[78] Unsuccessful 1776 attack: H. Clinton 23–28; Willcox 66–96; 2 C. Ward 669–678; 3 Fortescue 182–183. Siege and capture in 1780: H. Clinton 157–172; Willcox 292–322; 2 C. Ward 695–703; 3 Fortescue 313–316.

The English reader will perhaps need to be reminded that there is also a Charleston in West Virginia, the capital of that state; a Charlestown in Massachusetts near Boston, which was largely burned during the Battle of Bunker Hill (see the reference in Evelyn 71 to "stacks of chimneys like Charlestown here"); also a Charles Town in West Virginia, where John Brown was tried for and convicted of treason in 1859 after his raid on Harper's Ferry; and that, having mastered the foregoing geographical learning, he must also remember an additional complication: during the period here in question, Charleston, South Carolina, was known, and appears in contemporary newspapers, as "Charlestown"!

[79] 2 C. Ward 842; J. W. Barnwell, *The Evacuation of Charleston by the British in 1782*, 11 SCHGM 1. And see the letter dated 15 July 1782 from Gen. Carleton at

capture of Charleston was Clinton's major military success during the war. "At the moment when he stood watching the Americans marching out to pile their arms, their drums beating and flags cased, he stood on the pinnacle of his career." [80] But, unhappily for the British cause, this expedition divided the small army he commanded, and thus it led inevitably and inexorably to the ultimate disaster at Yorktown.

After taking Charleston, Clinton returned to New York, leaving Lord Cornwallis in command in the former city. In the Commander in Chief's words,

> as it was universally agreed that no good could possibly be expected (but, on the contrary, much inconvenience and obstruction might arise to the King's service) from the revival of civil government in South Carolina in its present state, I left directions with Lord Cornwallis for the establishing a board of police at Charleston on much the same footing with that at New York, the extent of whose powers I knew, and which had now stood the test of some years. This simple and approved mode of administering justice was, however, soon after entirely changed and another adopted by Lord Cornwallis— which, being a sort of mixed jurisdiction (built partly on the system I recommended and partly on the laws and practices of the civil courts under the old government, many of whose former officers were taken into the administration), His Lordship perhaps thought might give more satisfaction to the people, as more nearly resembling what they had been before accustomed to.[81]

And, added Clinton, the new system's "decisions on cases of private property were more unlimited than I would willingly have given my sanction to." [82]

In actual fact, although the restoration of civil government had early been recommended by the Superintendent of Police, James Simpson,[83] who had been the last Attorney General of the province under the Crown,[84] that government was never restored in any

---

New York to Lt.-Gen. Leslie, the commander at Charleston after Cornwallis had surrendered at Yorktown: "The evacuation is not a matter of choice but of deplorable necessity in consequence of an unsuccessful war." 3 HMC Am. MSS. 19.

[80] Willcox 309.

[81] H. Clinton 182; Willcox 312–313.

[82] H. Clinton 183.

[83] Simpson to Clinton, 16 July 1780, 2 HMC Am. MSS. 158. His successor appears to have been William Bull; see the latter's communication to Gen. Carleton, 25 May 1782, 2 HMC Am. MSS. 498, PRO 30/55 No. 4654.

[84] 1 McCrady 713; 2 McCrady 365.

form. General Clinton, as has been seen, was opposed to restoration, which, he feared, would bring on friction between the civil government and the military commander. In this respect, his instinct had been confirmed by the earlier experience: "it will intoxicate, as it has done in Georgia." [85] Contrariwise, and it must be recognized that Clinton faced a dilemma, failure to restore civil government hardened local feeling against the British. [86]

The only substantive innovations introduced by the occupation regime in South Carolina differing from what had been done in New York and Philadelphia were that in Charleston the Board of Police took jurisdiction over debts contracted before the occupation, without allowing the defendant any counterclaim or set-off, and that it undertook to deal with "the Property of Rebels, lying within the British lines." [87] Both extensions were strongly disapproved by successive Commanders in Chief in New York, apparently without avail. [88]

Some of the occupation proceedings followed the by now familiar pattern. Inhabitants were directed to make return of the rice and corn and surplus salt in their possession and to deliver up all gunpowder, [89] to get passes for their Negroes, [90] and to report all persons arriving from without the city. [91] Proclamations or less formal orders regulated the markets, declared which ferries should be open, and required all householders to have fire buckets in their possession; [92] fines were threatened for not keeping such buckets and for not sweeping out chimneys. [93] Prohibited acts included permitting cattle to go on the lines, keeping gaming tables in taverns, exporting rice without a license, galloping one's horses in the streets, driving wagons, carts, or drays for hire without a license,

---

[85] *Supra*, n. 74.

[86] 1 McCrady 533–560; A. Nevins, *The American States during and after the Revolution, 1775–1789* (New York, 1924) 376. This fact was duly noted by Judge Jones. 1 Jones 354.

[87] Gen. Clinton to Gen. Leslie, 17 Mar. 1782, 2 HMC Am. MSS. 423; Gen. Carleton to Gen. Leslie, 15 Aug. 1782, 3 *id.* 71. See also the petition of the Charleston merchants, 30 Aug. 1781, 2 *id.* 325, and the application of the Charleston inhabitant for redress from a decree of the Board of Police that placed him in danger of imprisonment from debt although denied the right to recover money owing to himself. 2 *id.* 395.

[88] Letters from Gens. Clinton and Carleton to Gen. Leslie cited in the preceding note.

[89] *S.C. Royal Gazette*, 31 Mar.–4 Apr., 5–8 Sept. 1781.

[90] *S.C. Royal Gazette*, 2–5 Jan., 17–20 Apr. 1782.

[91] *S.C. Royal Gazette*, 26–30 Jan. 1782.

[92] *S.C. Royal Gazette*, 3–7 and 28–31 Mar., 23–27 June, 1–5 Sept. 1781.

[93] *S.C. Royal Gazette*, 2–5 Jan. 1782.

keeping taverns or dram shops on the wharves, shooting firearms,[94] and serving in any capacity under "the second Usurpation"—by which was of course meant the state government.[95] One inhabitant was imprisoned for two months, and had over £200 worth of property confiscated, for forestalling cattle in violation of a Tudor statute that, unbeknownst to all concerned, had been repealed some nine years earlier.[96] The price of bread was regulated, with suitable penalties,[97] while, affirmatively, the Board of Police encouraged fishermen to increase their catch.[98]

Other orders reflect the virulence of the conflict in the South. Just as "Perhaps the bitterest fighting in the Revolution was between neighbors in the southern colonies," [99] so the tone of the occupation in Charleston was without question the most bitter of all. In part this was a consequence of Sir Henry Clinton's ill-fated proclamation, which, by declaring that all who refused to take the oath of allegiance would be treated as being in rebellion, rendered neutral obedience impossible.[100] In considerable measure, however, the tenor of military rule must be taken as reflecting the exacerbating personality of the officer who was there longest as Comman-

---

[94] *S.C. Royal Gazette*, 21–25 Apr., 16–20 June, 4–7 and 25–28 July, 10–13 and 24–27 Oct. 1781; 2–5 Jan. 1782. Most of the foregoing orders were many times repeated; the citations in all instances are to the first appearance of each.

[95] *S.C. Royal Gazette*, 2–5 Jan. 1782.

[96] "The Commissioners of the Markets having posted a very publick spirited Memorial to the Board of Police complaining against *Richard Ellis*, tavern-keeper, at the Quarter-House, for forestalling cattle driving to the Charlestown market, the Board appointed a day for an inquiry into his conduct; when it appeared that he had forestalled the market, by buying cattle at a very reasonable price, which he sold the same day at an exorbitant advance for his own private advantage; whereupon being duly convicted, the Board of Police adjudged him to suffer two months imprisonment, and to forfeit the balance of the cattle, amounting to *one hundred and ninety-six Guineas*, according to the statute of the 5th and 6th of Edward the 6th against forestalling.—It is hoped that this example will deter others from such oppressive and illegal practices, whereby the inhabitants of this town have been greatly distressed." *S.C. Royal Gazette*, 9–12 May 1781.

The statute cited was 5 & 6 Edw. VI c. 14, "An Acte againste Regratours Forestallers and Engrossers," 4 Stat. Realm 148. It had been repealed in 1772 by 12 Geo. III c. 71.

[97] *S.C. Royal Gazette*, 20–23 and 23–27 Mar., 22–25 May, 10–13 July 1782.

[98] *S.C. Royal Gazette*, 3–6 Apr. 1782.

[99] French F.Y. 460.

[100] Smith L. & R. 131–133; Willcox 321: "Many men who had given their parole, and retired into a state of neutrality, suddenly found themselves forced to choose between open rebellion and active collaboration. They complained that their status had been arbitrarily changed. Some fled to join the rebels; some took an oath that they considered forced upon them and did not intend to keep. The loyalists also complained that notorious firebrands reacquired, by a mere gesture of allegiance, all the privileges of British subjects."

dant, Lieutenant-Colonel Nisbet Balfour.[101] "This gentleman displayed in the exercise of this new office all the frivolous self-importance, and all the disgusting insolence, which are natural to little minds when puffed up by sudden elevation." [102] True, this was a description written by a member of the state legislature whom the Commandant banished to St. Augustine in East Florida; even so, the portrait is that of a recurring military type, and the orders actually issued by Lieutenant-Colonel Balfour strongly suggest that it was not overly exaggerated.

Thus, persons who were prisoners or on parole, and this included every adult free man of the city who had refused after its capture to take the oath of allegiance under the Clinton proclamation,[103] were forbidden "to exercise any Profession, Trade, Mechanick Art, Business or Occupation," and H.M.'s subjects were forbidden to employ any such persons.[104] All wives and children of exchanged prisoners of war were directed to leave the city.[105] No persons living under the rebel (i.e., state) government were permitted to give powers of attorney to lease houses within the city, and no persons whatever were allowed to sell any real property without written permission from the Board of Police.[106] Enforcement of the several directions and prohibitions was correspondingly harsh: to be sent on board the prison ships and expelled the province,[107] to lose their licenses and be dismissed the garrison,[108] and, in the case of any inhabitant violating the order against keeping taverns or

---

[101] The first Commandant was Maj.-Gen. Leslie, designated as such on 12 May 1780, shortly after the surrender. B. A. Uhlendorf, ed., *The Siege of Charleston* (Ann Arbor, 1938) 291. After Lord Cornwallis took the field, Leslie succeeded to the command in Charleston and was promoted to Lieutenant-General.

Balfour appears to have become Commandant some time in the summer of 1780. He was an officer of the 4th Regiment (The King's Own) who had fought at Bunker Hill. Then he became Gen. Howe's ADC, who for carrying home the news of the taking of New York was brevetted Major. Thereafter he was a messenger between the Ministry at home and Gen. Howe. Balfour served as Commandant of Charleston until late in July 1782, and died a full General in 1823. 1 Cowper 245, 247, 256; Valentine 148, 179–180, 236; *S.C. Royal Gazette*, 20–24 and 27–31 July 1782; DNB.

The last Commandant was Lt.-Col. Isaac Allen of the New Jersey Volunteers, an American Loyalist. E. A. Jones, ed., *The Journal of Alexander Chesney* (Columbus, Ohio, 1921) 10 n. 69, 21 n. 145.

[102] 1 Ramsay HSC 443, a passage plainly plagiarized in Simms 246.
[103] 1 Ramsay HSC 329.
[104] *S.C. Royal Gazette*, 31 Mar.–4 Apr. 1781.
[105] *S.C. Royal Gazette*, 25–27 June 1781.
[106] *S.C. Royal Gazette*, 7–11 July 1781.
[107] *S.C. Royal Gazette*, 3–7 Mar. 1781.
[108] *S.C. Royal Gazette*, 16–20 June 1781.

dram shops on the wharves, "will have his Liquor seized for the Benefit of the Poor, and himself lodged in the Provost, till tried by a Court-Martial for Disobedience of Orders." [109] Imprisonment in the provost without trial for other offenses was commonplace.[110] And, in August and again in November 1780, many citizens of Charleston who had been active in the state government between the Declaration of Independence and the fall of the city were deported to St. Augustine in the then British Province of East Florida and kept there until July 1781.[111]

Dr. Ramsay's estimate of Lieutenant-Colonel Balfour was accordingly but little overdrawn if at all. Nor was there in Charleston any suggestion, as in New York, that the events enumerated above were simply a consequence of the Prohibitory Act. Here again, Dr. Ramsay diagnosed the position accurately while his memory was still fresh: "The reduction of Charleston in May 1780, was followed by the establishment of a military government.[112] . . . The British conceived themselves in possession of the rights of sovereignty over a conquered country." [113]

The ordinary civil jurisdiction of the Board of Police has already been discussed; it also acted as a court of probate.[114] On occasion it warned civil defendants to plead or suffer default; [115] it administered the law for the relief of insolvent debtors; [116] and it directed the sale of property seized on execution.[117] Some juries apparently sat, since jurors were warned of fines if they were in default without a proper excuse.[118] Parish assessments appear to have been

---

[109] *S.C. Royal Gazette*, 24–27 Oct. 1781.

[110] 1 Ramsay HSC 444, only slightly paraphrased in Simms 246; 2 McCrady 368–370; 3 R. W. Gibbes, *Documentary History of the American Revolution . . . in 1781 and 1782* (Columbia, S.C., 1853) 287 (letter from a secret correspondent, 1 Apr. 1782, "Judge Pendleton is in the Provost"). Shortly thereafter, the newspaper remarked on the alleged "cruelty and tyrannical disposition of Mr. Pendleton in his judicial capacity," noting that he was "the Rebel Chief Justice of the Province." *S.C. Royal Gazette*, 3–6 Apr. 1782.

[111] 1 Ramsay HSC 370–373; 1 McCrady 716–726; *Josiah Smith's Diary, 1780–1781*, 33 SCHGM 1, 79, 197, 281; 34 *id.* 31, 67, 138, 194; A. R. Stoesen, *The British Occupation of Charleston, 1780–1782*, 63 S.C. Hist. Mag. 63, 77–78.

[112] 1 Ramsay HSC 441 (published in 1809).

[113] 2 D. Ramsay, *The History of the American Revolution* (London, 1793) 170; 1 Ramsay HSC 367.

[114] *S.C. Royal Gazette*, 7–10 Mar., 12–15 Dec. 1781.

[115] *S.C. Royal Gazette*, 2–5 Jan. 1782.

[116] *S.C. Royal Gazette*, 4–8 Aug., 8–12 Dec. 1781; 2–5 Jan., 2–6 Mar. 1782 (and many others).

[117] *S.C. Royal Gazette*, 9–13 Mar., 20–24 Apr. 1782. For notice of an attachment, *id.*, 29 Dec. 1781–2 Jan. 1782.

[118] *S.C. Royal Gazette*, 22–25 May 1782.

regularly made and collected.[119] In October 1781, a newly appointed judge held the Court of Vice-Admiralty "for the first time since the reduction of this town." [120]

For the rest, inhabitants were regularly tried by court-martial. An orderly book kept in Charleston during the first ten months of the occupation by Mr. Commissary Wray of the Royal Artillery lists the trials of twenty civilians, all but two tried by garrison court-martial.[121] Here again, there was no novelty—inhabitants, sailors, a refugee, and "Catherine Bryon, a Woman belonging to the British Legion" were included among the several accused, while the offenses covered attempting to pass the lines without leave, theft, robbery, "Insolent and Turbulent behaviour," plundering, "Suspicion of Embezzling Rum the Property of Government," "Inticing three Hessian Soldiers to Desert," and defacing the King's brand on the Quarter Master General's horses.

Needless to add, the endemic liquor problem made its presence felt. An early order read, "It having been represented to Major Traille [CRA] [122] that the Married men who are indulged with laying out of their Barracks, make a practice of selling Liquor— He takes this opportunity of declaring that the first who shall be discovered, will be immediately confined & punished for disobedience of Orders, and the women sent to the Provost." [123] A violation shortly thereafter was punished in somewhat different fashion: "Mrs. Faulknor confin'd for disobedience of orders in selling Liquor. Major Traille orders her to be struck off the provision list of the Corps, and if ever guilty again to be turn'd out of the Artillery district. Faulknor is no longer to have the indulgence of laying out of his Barracks." [124] This separation *a mensa et thoro* appears to

---

[119] *S.C. Royal Gazette*, 23–26 Jan. 1782.

[120] *S.C. Royal Gazette*, 17–20 and 27–31 Oct. 1781.

[121] MS, WLCL. The entries extend from 16 May 1780 through 3 Mar. 1781. Mr. Wray was "the first Civil Officer" as well as acting Paymaster of the Royal Artillery in Charleston. Pattison 169. The trials by general court-martial are Nos. 103 and 133. Of the 18 civilians tried by garrison court-martial, 8 were acquitted, 5 of these being sailors tried jointly.

[122] Gen. Clinton conferred the provincial rank of Major on Traille, "in Consideration of his long Services, and of his being one of the oldest Captains in the Army." Pattison 157, 162, 169. He was "a man with a grievance" (1 Duncan 337), doubtless a consequence of promotion deferred, and the rebuke he received at Gen. Clinton's hands for bombarding Charleston and starting fires there (Willcox 306) was probably not calculated to ease his spirit. But by the time New York was preparing for evacuation, he was a Lieutenant-Colonel (*N.-Y. Royal Gazette*, 2 Aug. 1783), and he died in 1795 a Major-General (1 Duncan 361).

[123] Wray OB, 8 June 1780.

[124] Wray OB, 15 July 1780.

have been effective, for no further liquor offenses were recorded in the remaining six and a half months of the Wray Orderly Book.

BURGOYNE'S CAMPAIGN

In 1777—briefly to recall the event to mind—Burgoyne marched south from Canada with a mixed British and German force, his object being to meet Howe coming north from New York, and by this junction to sever New England from the other colonies.[125] But the cognizant Secretary of State failed to advise Howe of Burgoyne's objective and never disapproved the former's announced intention of moving south.[126] (This Secretary of State was Lord George Germain, who *sub nomine* Lord George Sackville had been cashiered for disobedience at the Battle of Minden;[127] and, however much lay revisionist sentiment may now seek to characterize that punishment as a purely political act, the underlying conduct that called it forth is still as strongly condemned by British soldiers today as it was by the commander concerned two centuries ago.)[128]

In consequence of Germain's incredible negligence, Howe not

---

[125] Alden A.R., ch. 9; 1 C. Ward, chs. 36 and 37; 2 *id.*, chs. 40, 42, and 43; 3 Fortescue 225–244. Burgoyne's own account is *A State of the Expedition from Canada* (two eds., both London, 1780); the citations below are to the 1st (quarto) edition. Willcox, chs. IV and V, is, pre-eminently, required reading for any serious student of the campaign. Two other modern accounts are H. Nickerson, *The Turning Point of the Revolution* (Boston and New York, 1928), and H. Bird, *March to Saratoga* (New York, 1963).

[126] Willcox 144–146; Valentine 174–178. The old legend that Lord George Germain neglected to sign the instructions to Howe because he would not delay his weekend to await the completion of a fair copy has now been disproved (Alden A.R. 117 n. 6 and authorities there cited). Even so, the comment in 3 Fortescue 210—"Never was there a finer example of the art of organising disaster"—still applies in full measure. Indeed, Willcox entitles his Chapter IV, covering the period from January to July 1777, "The Planning of Disaster."

[127] *Supra*, pp. 32, 33.
The private Act of Parliament authorizing his change of name from Sackville to Germain is 10 Geo. III c. i. But when he was created a peer in his own right in 1782, after the surrender at Yorktown resulted in the fall of Lord North's government, in which he had played such a prominent part and to whose downfall he had so greatly contributed, he chose the title of Viscount Sackville. For the reaction of the House of Lords to its new member, see Valentine 456–459.

[128] The view expressed at length in G. S. Brown, *The Court-Martial of Lord George Sackville, Whipping Boy of the Revolutionary War*, Wm. & Mary Q., 3:9:317, and repeated, though in less detail, by the same author in *The American Secretary: The Colonial Policy of Lord George Germain, 1775–1778* (Ann Arbor, 1963), that because Lord G. Sackville's disobedience on the field of battle probably did not exceed 8 or 10 minutes, his cashiering therefore stands as a purely political act, not only ignores the realities of cavalry action on an eighteenth-century

only went to Philadelphia when he should have been going in the opposite direction to Albany, but he went there by sea, the long way around, which—by actual test—took just three times the interval required for marching overland.[129]

Burgoyne, who had started his own advance auspiciously by retaking Fort Ticonderoga, lost a substantial part of his force in a sideshow at Bennington, and then, bogged down with the remainder in the wilderness, failed to get help from any of the other commanders on whom he had counted, and whose assistance was indeed indispensable to the success of his own mission. There were three of these: St. Leger, who, coming from Lake Ontario, had been repulsed, first at Oriskany and then at Fort Schuyler; Howe, who was in Philadelphia, and not only had his hands full there but was quite without information that he was under any obligation whatever to move in conjunction with Burgoyne; and Clinton, who was in New York and did what he could by capturing the Hudson River forts. That last was Clinton at his best,[130] but it was not enough to save the expedition from Canada. So, surrounded and outnumbered at Saratoga, Burgoyne surrendered his entire

---

battlefield, but runs directly counter to the judgment of both contemporary and modern military men.

1. The commander of the allied forces at Minden, Prince Ferdinand of Brunswick and Lüneburg, requested King George II, within a fortnight after the battle, to recall Lord G. Sackville; see text of the request at Savory 474.

2. Brigadier R. Whitworth, author of the standard life of Field Marshal Lord Ligonier, Commander in Chief of the British Army at the time of Minden, wrote in 1958: "But the charge was disobedience and try as he would Sackville could not explain to a court of soldiers how Granby had reached the battlefield and he had not." Whitworth 322.

3. Lt.-Gen. Sir R. Savory, whose account of the British Army in Germany in the Seven Years War supplants everything hitherto written on that subject in English, wrote in 1966:
"Sackville had refused to advance despite repeated orders from Prince Ferdinand. Seldom, if ever, has there been in battle such disgraceful disobedience. Those magnificent regiments [of British and Hanoverian cavalry], burning for their opportunity, stayed near Hartum, within close distance of the desperate fighting of their fellow countrymen; and when Lord Granby (during Sackville's temporary absence to receive Ferdinand's personal orders) led them forward on his own responsibility, they were halted by Sackville on his return. When at length they did move, they were too late. The battle was over; and one of the greatest opportunities for cavalry in the whole of military history was lost for ever." Savory 171.

[129] Willcox 172–173, esp. 173: "It took thirty-five days to get into position for assaulting Philadelphia, whereas eleven months later Clinton, with a heavily encumbered army that fought a battle on the way, took only twelve days to march overland from Philadelphia to Sandy Hook."

[130] Willcox 176–197, and comments at 496, 523.

force on 17 October 1777. France thereupon entered the lists against Britain, with the result that the United States ultimately made good the independence they had declared.[131] Sir Edward Creasy was thus fully justified in listing Saratoga as one of his Fifteen Decisive Battles.

All of the foregoing is, of course, tolerably well known; here we are concerned only with whatever jurisdiction Burgoyne may have exercised over civilians.

His order book reflects the customary infiltration and proliferation of civilians—a Waggon Master, a Paymaster, servants, sutlers, artificers, drivers, conductors, "Dependents upon and followers of the Army." [132] Such persons when offending he ordered brought before "Camp Courts Martial . . . in the nature of Garrison Courts Martial, consisting of one Captain and four Subalterns from the Line, who will try such offenders according to the Clause of the Mutiny Act. All followers of the Army are subject to Military Law." [133]

Actually, of course, neither the Mutiny Act at home nor that specifically enacted for America so much as mentioned followers of the army.[134] Their subjection to military law was provided for in terms in the camp follower article,[135] and, on the reading preferred in the field (however much it was regularly rejected in Whitehall), in the "no Form of Our Civil Judicature" article.[136] In the next century, as will be seen in Chapter VIII, the wartime jurisdiction over civilians accompanying the army was more accurately rested on the common law of war until the enactment of particular statutes governing specific offenses by such persons.[137] But this and similar jurisdictional niceties could scarcely be tested in the course of the campaign, if indeed any had been minded to do so; and in actual fact no trials of civilians are recorded, either in the surviving order books or in the numerous published journals and letters of members of the expedition.[138]

---

[131] The late Dr. D. S. Freeman realistically subtitled vol. 5 of his *George Washington*, "Victory with the Help of France."

[132] Burgoyne OB; Hadden.

[133] Burgoyne OB, 27 Aug. 1777; Stanley's OB, same date.

[134] 16 Geo. III c. 2 (Mutiny Act for 1776); 17 Geo. III c. 3 (same for 1777); 15 Geo. III c. 15 (American Mutiny Act to March 1777); 16 Geo. III c. 11 (same to March 1778).

[135] Art. 23 of §14, AW's for 1776 and 1777.

[136] *Supra*, pp. 14–15, 23–24, 55–59, 69–70, 75–77.

[137] *Infra*, pp. 203–204.

[138] Anburey, Digby, DuRoi, Hadden, Pausch, Riedesel, Baroness Riedesel.

Only the usual threats make their appearance—drumming out of camp, striking from the provision lists, and return to Canada for women selling spirits to Indians; [139] destruction of improper quantities of liquor found in the women's possession. [140] A board of officers fixed a sutler's prices at such "that the Officers and Soldiers situated as the Advanced Corps now is, can with propriety afford to give for his Goods and Liquors." Then "it may be left in Mr White's option, to sell them at that price or not remain any longer with the Corps." [141]

Inhabitants stealing horses were threatened with punishment, [142] but none appears to have been tried. One journal mentions a Board of Commissioners to examine non-military prisoners in the provost guard, presided over by Governor Philip Skene. [143] This was the lord of Skenesborough, appointed by the Crown Lieutenant-Governor of Ticonderoga and Crown Point, detained and confined by the colonists after his arrival from England, exchanged and then named by Burgoyne "Commissioner to administer the Oath of Allegiance and to grant Certificates of Protection to Loyalists," who after the surrender signed a parole simply as "Philip Skene, a poor follower of the British Army." [144] None of the non-military prisoners whom he examined appears to have been tried by any of that Army's military tribunals.

The number of women who accompanied General Burgoyne's expedition has never been clearly determined. They included the Baroness von Riedesel, wife of the Brunswick general who was Burgoyne's second-in-command, their three small daughters, and a number of her maidservants; [145] some officers' wives, among whom was the heroic Lady Harriett Acland, who crossed the lines *flagrante bello* to nurse her wounded husband in captivity; [146] and in addition, as reported by both von Riedesels, who assuredly had ample opportunity for observation, Burgoyne "liked having a jolly

---

[139] Grenadier Bn. OB, 20 June and 2 July 1777; Stanley's OB 119–120.

[140] Grenadier Bn. OB, 2 July 1777.

[141] *Id.*, 15 June 1777. The entry for the next day gives the prices to which White agreed, which include 10s. per gallon of West India rum, and 8s. for the same amount of "Second Rum."

[142] Burgoyne OB, 30 Aug. 1777.

[143] Hadden 142 (7 Sept. 1777).

[144] D. B. Morton, *Philip Skene of Skenesborough* (Granville, N.Y., 1959); Van Doren S.H. 49–52; Burgoyne OB, 179; Stanley's OB 113.

[145] Baroness Riedesel 33, 52–55, 58–60, 62–63.

[146] Burgoyne 127–129; Baroness Riedesel 52–55, 59–60; 1 Riedesel 168; 1 Anbury 176–177, 206–207, 376, 426–428, 445–457; Digby 298; Pettengill 107.

time and spending half the night singing and drinking and amusing himself in the company of the wife of a commissary, who was his mistress and, like him, loved champagne." [147]

Women less prepossessing were present also, and though formal orders at the outset of the campaign limited these to three per company,[148] the impression that this limitation was not rigidly enforced is confirmed by the obvious evasiveness of Burgoyne's DAG, Lieutenant-Colonel Kingston, during that officer's later examination on the point before a House of Commons committee:

> Q. Can you say, in a general way, how many women attended the army?
> A. I had really so much to do that I had not much leisure to pay much attention to the ladies; and I know very little of their beauty or their numbers.[149]

Indubitably a whole swarm of women marched with the surrendered Convention Army from Saratoga across the Berkshire Mountains to Cambridge, Massachusetts, this in bitter November weather, with "men cursing, women shrieking, and children squalling"; [150] a child was born on the march; [151] here is how the bedraggled survivors appeared on arrival:

> I never had the least idea that the Creation producd such a sordid set of creatures in human Figure—poor, dirty, emaciated men, great numbers of women, who seemd to be the beasts of burthen, having a bushel basket on their back, by which they were bent double, the contents seemd to be Pots and Kettles, various sorts of Furniture, children peeping thro' gridirons and other utensils, some very young Infants who were born on the road, the women bare feet, cloathd in dirty raggs, such effluvia filld the air while they were passing, had they not been smoking all the time, I should have been apprehensive of being contaminated by them.[152]

---

[147] Baroness Riedesel 55–56; 1 Riedesel 211. A recent effort to identify the commander's inamorata as a Mrs. Higgins (L. H. Tharp, *The Baroness and the General* [Boston, 1962] 176) fails to convince; no civil official by that name appears either in Hadden or in the Burgoyne OB or in the list of the other commissaries who were paroled with the rest of the officers (Burgoyne OB 176, 179).

[148] Burgoyne 89; Burgoyne OB 192. See also Baroness Riedesel 33, 162; Hadden 297; DuRoi 169.

[149] Burgoyne 87. Kingston became a Major-General in 1793. Stanley's OB 100 n. 48.

[150] 2 Anburey 39.

[151] 2 Anburey 39–40.

[152] Hannah Winthrop to Mercy Warren, Cambridge, Mass., 11 Nov. 1777, 2 *Warren-Adams Letters* (73 MHS Coll., 1925) 451.

There are further sad chapters in the long hegira of the Convention forces.[153] But it may well be doubted whether any of those individuals sank lower in the scale of human misery than on this so graphically described occasion.

---

[153] A. J. Wall, *The Story of the Convention Army*, 11 NYHS Q. Bull. 67; W. M. Dabney, *After Saratoga: The Story of the Convention Army* (Albuquerque, 1954); 2 C. Ward 540–542; 2 Anburey, 2 Riedesel, and DuRoi, all *passim;* Pettengill 146–152; "Burgoyne and his Officers in Cambridge," in S. F. Batchelder, *Bits of Cambridge History* (Cambridge, Mass., 1930) 3–113.

CHAPTER VII

JUDGE ADVOCATES GENERAL AND THEIR DEPUTIES IN AMERICA

The boundaries of British military jurisdiction having now been traced through the first century of its constitutional existence, it seems appropriate to pause, and to call attention to the men who drew those boundaries: the several Judge Advocates General of H.M.'s Land Forces at home, and the three who served as Deputy Judge Advocates on the staff of successive Commanders in Chief in North America.

The first phase of this biographical exercise has been difficult in the extreme, because of the obscurity of the individuals involved. Of the seven Judge Advocates General listed in Haydn's *Book of Dignities* [1] as holding the office from the Restoration through the end of the eighteenth century, only two have notices of their own in the *Dictionary of National Biography*, and both accounts are inaccurate in significant respects. Indeed, two dates in Haydn are certainly incorrect, and a third is probably wrong. What follows is accordingly offered, not in any sense as the last word on these little-known officials, but rather as the first, for below is collected more concerning them than could up to now be found anywhere in one place.

By way of preliminary, it should be noted that the Court of the Constable and the Marshal and its still extant survival, the High Court of Chivalry, were part of the domain of the civilians.[2] The

---

[1] (London, 1890) 937. M. Powicke *et al.*, eds., *Handbook of British Chronology* (2d ed., R. Hist. Soc., 1961) does not list Judge Advocates General.

[2] See 1 Holdsworth 573–580 for the older learning. The decision recognizing the continued existence of the High Court of Chivalry after it had not sat for over 200 years is *Manchester Corporation* v. *Manchester Palace of Varieties Ltd.*, [1955] P. 133. See generally G. D. Squibb, *The High Court of Chivalry* (Oxford, 1959), subtitled "A Study of the Civil Law in England," and note particularly Mr. Squibb's demonstration that the court-martial of today has an ancestry quite distinct from that of the Court of Chivalry. E.g., during the Commonwealth, there functioned a Parliamentary Heraldic Tribunal wholly independent of the courts-martial that administered military justice. This is a suggestion that cries out for re-examination of all the old legends that still trace the pedigree of the court-martial in direct line from the Court of the Constable and the Marshal.

It is perhaps appropriate to note here that the first mention of English military

laws of war and of nations remained in the civilians' sphere for centuries.[3] One military judge with the Earl of Leicester in the Low Countries in 1587 and 1588 was Dr. Matthew Sutcliffe, a clergyman who thereafter became an active pluralist and a member of Doctors' Commons.[4] In 1593 he wrote what is undoubtedly one of the earliest texts in English on the functions of the "iudge Marshall," the substance of which makes it abundantly clear that his ecclesiastical character never tempered for a moment his resolution to ferret out offenders, "by racke or other paine" if necessary.[5]

Similarly, in the Civil War members of Doctors' Commons served as judge advocates both in the Parliamentary Army and in the King's.[6] With the Restoration, however, the civilians were driven from the field; the application for the office then made by a member of the College of Advocates was unsuccessful.[7] But,

---

law in action is found in the record of an eyre held at York in 1218–1219: ". . . and he denies definitely that Thomas was ever maimed through him, on the contrary he lost his hand in the war by judgment of the marshal of the army for a cow which he stole in a churchyard. . . ." D. M. Stenton, ed., *Rolls of the Justices in Eyre for Yorkshire 1218–19* (Selden Soc., vol. 56) 310–311, No. 851.

[3] 4 Holdsworth 235–238, 272–273; 5 *id.* 4–8.

[4] DNB; H. J. Webb, *Elizabethan Military Science* (Madison, 1965); Coote 54; *Cal. S. P. Foreign 1587*, p. 427 (Mr. Dr. Sutcliffe, Judge Martial, paid £40); *Cal. S.P. Foreign Jan.-Jun. 1588*, p. 2 ("The Judge marshal, *nuper* Dr. Mathew Sutcliffe, *olim* Dr. William Clarke"). Sutcliffe was Archdeacon of Taunton, Dean of Exeter, held four prebends in the church of Bath and Wells, and became provost of King James the First's "College at Chelsey."

[5] M. Sutcliffe, *The Practice, Proceedings, and Lawes of Armes* (London, 1593) 339–342 (ch. XXI, Part 9). The full passage referred to in the text reads (p. 340):

". . . lawe is nothing without execution. But because iustice cannot be executed vnlesse offenders be detected, therefore the first care of those that purpose to proceede orderly, is to find out the authours of offences, and persons culpable. This is by examination and othe both of the parties principall, as farre as they are bound by lawe to answere, and of witnesses also: further where presumptions are sufficient, and the matter heinous: by racke or other paine."

[6] For parliamentary judge advocates, see Coote 82 (Isaac Dorislaus), 83 (John Mylles). For Dorislaus, see also 5 Holdsworth 8, and C. Firth, *Cromwell's Army* (4th ed., London, 1962) 282; the second reference also mentions "John Mills."

For royalist judge advocates, see Coote 83 (Dr., afterwards Sir Justinian, Lewyn, judge-martial in the expedition to Scotland in 1639); cf. *Cal. S.P. Dom. 1660–1661*, p. 11 (petition of Wm. Lewin, D.C.L.—"Was Judge Marshall of the late King's northern expedition"). Another royalist judge advocate was Sir Edmond Peirce, D.C.L., who is noted at Coote 85, but without any identification; his services as judge advocate are recited by himself at *Cal. S.P. Dom. 1660–1661*, pp. 11–12 and 494–495. Coote's list is copied, though with less biographical detail, in E. Nys, *Le Droit Romain, le Droit des Gens et le Collège des Docteurs en Droit Civil* (Brussels, 1910) 139 *et seq.*

[7] Sir Edmond Peirce, noted just above, successively petitioned for the place of Master of Requests, Master of Requests Extraordinary, and Advocate General for the Forces, annexing to the last of these petitions the form of the warrant

though not a single Judge Advocate General listed by Haydn was a civilian lawyer, the common lawyers were hardly more successful, for not until eighty years after the first Mutiny Act was the office conferred upon a duly called member of the bar. Early English military law, accordingly, was law administered by laymen.

THE EARLIEST JUDGE ADVOCATES GENERAL

The first post-Restoration name on the list is Dr. Samuel Barrow. We encountered him earlier as the recipient of a warrant from the Duke of York, 11 May 1666, directing him to convene a court-martial for the earliest such trial now preserved in the Public Record Office.[8]

Barrow had neither D.C.L. nor connection with the law, common or civil; his doctorate was in medicine.[9] But he had, what was far more important, the friendship and confidence of General Monck, the architect of the Restoration, later Duke of Albemarle. Dr. Barrow had been physician-general of that commander's army in Scotland; he had counseled Monck in the critical winter of 1659–1660; and in August 1660 he became one of the King's Physicians in Ordinary with an annuity of £100 a year. His appointment as Judge Advocate followed in the succeeding winter, probably in February 1661 at the time of the permanent establishment of the Guards regiments; the pay of this other office was for many years 12s. 6d. a day. Lawyers today quite regularly practice applied psychology—they must—and by inversion if not precisely by parity of reasoning, medical experience in a military environment appears to have been preparation entirely adequate prior to the first Mutiny Act for discharging the office of Advocate-General and Judge Martial of all H.M.'s Land Forces.

Dr. Barrow had other talents as well. He was a friend of John Milton, and his encomium on *Paradise Lost*, in Latin verse, was prefixed to the poet's second edition of that work. In the late 1660's he married Lady Clarke, impoverished relict of Sir William Clarke; the latter, secretary to General Monck for twelve years or

---

requested (*Cal. S.P. Dom. 1660–1661*, pp. 11–12, 106, 494–495). He seems in the end to have been appointed a Master in Chancery. Cf. *Cal. S.P. Dom. 1667*, p. 449.

[8] *Supra*, n. 6 of Ch. I, at pp. 7–8.

[9] In this as in all other instances in the present chapter, the sources examined have been: Gray's Inn, *Register of Admissions* and *Pension Books;* Inner Temple, *Calendar of Inner Temple Records;* Lincoln's Inn, *Admissions* and *Black Books;* Middle Temple, *Admissions Register; Alumni Oxonienses; Alumni Cantabrigienses.*

so prior to 1661, had then been knighted and named Secretary at War, after which, in 1666, he died of wounds suffered in the naval action against the Dutch in the Downs.[10]

The good doctor's stepson, George Clarke, went to Oxford in 1676 with a legal career in mind, and in fact was duly admitted to the Inner Temple in the same year.[11] But, instead of becoming a lawyer, he was elected a Fellow of All Souls; here is how he later explained the matter in his engaging autobiography:

> My coming into this college diverted me from going to the Temple, and my father-in-law, the year after, finding his health and strength very sensibly decline, endeavoured to get me joined with him in his commission of Judge Advocate, which the King did not care to do, but was pleased to say he would give me the employment if Dr. Barrow would resign it. . . .[12]

On 10 February 1682, accordingly, the office was granted to young George Clarke, then some months short of attaining his majority, "in consideration of his skill and ability and of the services of his late father Sir William Clarke, secretary at war, who was

----

[10] Career generally: 5 D. Masson, *The Life of John Milton* (London, 1877) 476, 499, 500, 528, 534; 6 *id.* 714–715; 2 D. Lysons, *The Environs of London* (2d ed. London, 1810) 243; DNB *s.v.* William Clarke; 4 C. H. Firth, ed., *The Clarke Papers* (London, 1901; Camden Soc., vol. 62) 83, 274–276; J. D. Griffith Davies, *Honest George Monck* (London, 1936) 176. Appointment as King's physician, *Cal. S.P. Dom. 1660–1661*, p. 207, warrant to pay annuity as such, *Cal. Treas. Books 1660–1667*, p. 195. No warrant or commission for Dr. Barrow as JAG has been found. It is said (Walton 824 n.) that "There is also a Commission of Judge Advocate General in W.O. Com. Bks., Vol. I," but no such commission is listed in the first volume of C. Dalton, *English Army Lists and Commission Registers, 1661–1714* (London, 1892). This apparent discrepancy may be explained by the fact that the earliest War Office Commission Book in the Public Record Office (WO 25/1) now lacks the first two pages and begins at page 3. In any event, Dr. Barrow's successor in office later asserted that the office of judge advocate was provided for in the first establishment of the Guards with pay at 12s. 6d. a day plus 2s. 6d. a day for a clerk (*Cal. Treas. Books 1685–1689*, p. 289), and other sources indicate that this establishment was erected in January and February 1661. 1 F. W. Hamilton, *The Origin and History of the First or Grenadier Guards* (London, 1874) 45–46; Davies, C. G. 111–112.

Lady Clarke's plight, see *Cal. S.P. Dom. 1666–1667*, p. 53, corroborated by her son's Autobiography, *infra* n. 12, at 259. There is no support for Masson's statement (*op. cit.*, vol. 6 at 714) that she was "a wealthy widow."

[11] 3 *Calendar of Inner Temple Records* 107 (29 Oct. 1676).

[12] This and all other quotations not otherwise specifically identified are from the "Autobiography of Dr. George Clarke," in HMC, *Report on the Manuscripts of F.W. Leyborne-Popham, Esq.* (Norwich, 1899) 259–289. The DNB notice of George Clarke, which appeared much earlier, is in consequence quite unreliable.

slain in the King's service." [13] Six weeks later, on 21 March, Dr. Barrow died.

The reference to young Clarke's skill and ability may well have been something more than formal recital. Soon after his appointment, a struggle ensued with the Secretary at War, William Blathwayt,[14] and, although the latter was a veteran administrator with all of the professional civil servant's aptitude for bureaucratic infighting, Clarke emerged the victor:

> There being hardly any land forces in England but the Horse and Foot Guards there were not very frequent occasions for Courts Martial. The first after I came in was upon a complaint of false musters against Sir Robert Holmes, Governor of the Isle of Wight, who made himself so well with Mr. Blathwayt, Secretary at War, that all endeavours were used to avoid the bringing it to that sort of trial, and whether to favour Sir Robert or to engross all business to himself or that he was ignorant of the methods of the army, Mr. Blathwayt did all he could to keep off a Court Martial, and would have had the matter heard at his Office, by what he called a council of war, where the Secretary at War was to be, and not the Judge Advocate. Upon getting an intimation of this design, I immediately went down to Windsor and visited upon the King, whom I acquainted with it, and had the pleasure, as Mr. Blathwayt had the mortification, to hear his Majesty disapprove Mr. Blathwayt's project in pretty harsh terms and order a Court Martial to examine into the false musters that were laid to Sir Robert's charge. This put a stop to the attempts that were on foot to render the Judge-Advocate's place useless, and which, if they had succeeded, would of course have put a stop to the employment.

Not for nothing is George Clarke characterized in the *Dictionary of National Biography* as "politician and virtuoso." On King Charles II's death, "his successor, King James, renewed my patent and increased my salary." [15] The new reign brought more contests and difficult positions. At Oxford, where he had received the B.C.L. degree in 1686, Clarke managed to avoid direct conflict with the new monarch in the latter's efforts to place Roman Catholics in the colleges. In the military area, Clarke was judge advocate

---

[13] *Cal. S.P. Dom. 1682*, p. 69. Haydn and Walton say 1684; the DNB has 1681.
[14] See G. A. Jacobsen, *William Blathwayt* (New Haven, 1932); Scouller 13–18.
[15] Renewal of patent, *Cal. S.P. Dom. Feb.–Dec. 1685*, p. 36. Increased pay, *Cal. Treas. Books 1685–1689*, pp. 186–187, 289; see also Walton 649.

of the permanent general court-martial at the Horse Guards. "The intention of establishing this court was to withdraw the soldiery from the civil power, and all matters, as well civil as military, relating to the army were to be brought before them." But Clarke successfully evaded the efforts of one Beddingfield, K.C., a Catholic who had been appointed to attend the court-martial, to direct or counsel its proceedings.

Clarke was with the Army when Prince William landed, and witnessed the disappearance of its several leaders as they left King James II to fend for himself as best he could. Then, following the Glorious Revolution, "Immediately I went to London, and after the Prince and Princess of Orange were declared King and Queen, had my commission of Judge Advocate renewed,[16] and a deputy allowed me for the forces which were to go to Flanders under the command of the now Duke of Marlborough"; this Deputy was Mr. Whitfield, Marlborough's secretary.

Accordingly George Clarke stands not only as the first Judge Advocate General following the original Mutiny Act of 1689, but as a man gifted with unusual talent for survival.

A little later, in 1690, he accompanied King William III to Ireland, where he was Secretary at War as well as Chief Secretary to that government.[17] Thereafter, for the remainder of the reign, he was Secretary at War in England—but only during the King's absence; William Blathwayt, his old adversary, continued as Secretary at War (and functioned as a Secretary of State) while attending King William III abroad.

"Before King William's death I was desirous to retire from public business, and had bargained with a gentleman to sell him my place of Judge Advocate, but his Majesty died and the bargain was never completed, and upon Queen Anne's coming in to the Crown I could not get leave to part with it, but was pressed very much to be Secretary to the Prince of Denmark"—the Queen's Consort— "who was declared Lord High Admiral."

Clarke was first elected to the Parliament of James II's reign. He was again elected in 1705, but in consequence of his having voted against the Court's candidate for Speaker, he was dismissed as the Prince's secretary. Meanwhile Clarke had been building a house at

---

[16] Clarke's commission granted by King William III has not been found. But on 1 Aug. 1689, Clarke as judge advocate of the army petitioned "that as the forces are increased, he may have an addition to his pay." *Cal. S.P. Dom. 1689–1690*, p. 206.

[17] *Cal. S.P. Dom. 1690–1691*, pp. 20, 21.

All Souls. "This house was almost finished at the time I was dismissed by the Prince, and having disposed of my patent of Judge Advocate to Mr. Byde of Ware Park about half a year before, I was now entirely my own master." A few years later, in 1710, Clarke became one of the Commissioners of the Admiralty [18] and remained such until the accession of George I; he was re-elected to the next four Parliaments; and he died in 1736, in his seventy-sixth year. His autobiography, commenced in 1720 and periodically revised up to shortly before his death, expresses the inevitable lament of those who have outlived their early friends: "I think there are few so good men left behind."

The individual to whom Clarke had sold the office of Judge Advocate General in 1705, Thomas Byde of Ware Park, Herts, was the grandson of a Sir Thomas Byde who had been M.P. for Hertfordshire from 1661 through the first Parliament of William and Mary, and sheriff of the county in 1669. Young Thomas entered Lincoln's Inn as a boy of sixteen, but evidently thought better of a legal career, because he was never called. Once become Judge Advocate General, he was the one who ruled in 1706 that the cashiered officer committing murder while accompanying the troops in Portugal could be dealt with only by the courts of that country.[19] He appears from time to time in the *Calendar of Treasury Books,* on one occasion soliciting an extra allowance for allegedly extraordinary attendance, successfully, because his successor thereafter requested the same allowance on the basis of the precedent then made. Byde's landed property was sufficiently substantial—and complicated—to require passage of a private relief Act.

Although Byde's tenure as Judge Advocate General for ten years after 1705 spans the greater part of the Duke of Marlborough's campaigns, he is noticed only once in that commander's dispatches, and then only before he assumed office. Whether his exit from public service in 1715 was voluntary or otherwise does not appear; in any event, he survived the loss of his place by a number of years, living until 1732. Byde remains the most obscure figure in the succession; today, two centuries and a half later, he is hardly more than a name on the roster.[20]

---

[18] 6 Luttrell 633, 666.

[19] *Supra,* p. 13.

[20] Genealogy: 3 *Victoria County History, Hertford,* 388; 4 *id.* 38; W. Berry, *Pedigrees of Hertfordshire Families* (London, 1842) viii, 11. Lincoln's Inn: 1 *Admissions* 351 (12 Dec. 1695). Private Act: HMC, *Manuscripts of the House of*

Following Byde came Edward Hughes, in office from 19 September 1715 until his death on 13 January 1734, who seems to have owed the appointment to his friendship with Lord Chancellor Cowper.[21] Hughes was a Fellow of the Royal Society, M.P. for Saltash from 1727 until his death, and father of Admiral Sir Edward Hughes. Yet he is himself so little known that the *Dictionary of National Biography* article on the Admiral states that "His father is said by his biographer to have been alderman and several times mayor of Hertford, but the local histories fail to corroborate the statement." This last should not be too surprising, since it was not the fact.

Edward Hughes quarreled with Henry Fox, Secretary at War, in 1729;[22] as has been seen, he held the Royal Artillery subject to the Mutiny Act even in the absence of any clause in that measure subjecting them thereto;[23] but he introduced some degree of continuity into the work of the office by appointing King Gould in 1723 to be his Deputy. He remembered the latter in his will, naming him as his "beloved and much valued friend," and evidencing his friendship in tangible form by a half share in the ultimate reversion of his estate. Hughes does not appear to have been admitted to or called by any Inn of Court.

King Gould continued as Deputy through the tenure of Sir Henry Hoghton, Bt., who served as Judge Advocate General from 1734 until 1741, and whose qualifications were pragmatic rather than professional: Although admitted to the Middle Temple as a lad of seventeen, he never went on to become a barrister; more

---

Lords 1712–1714, pp. 59–60; 12 Anne c. xxvii. Request for extra allowances: *Cal. Treas. Books 1708*, p. 223; repeated by successor on basis of earlier precedent, *id. 1716*, p. 387. Mention by Duke of Marlborough, 1 G. Murray, ed., *The Letters and Dispatches of the Duke of Marlborough from 1702–1712* (London, 1845) 294–295 (letter to Mr. Clarke, 4 June 1704: ". . . if you have obtained his Royal Highness's consent, I shall not make any objection to Mr. Byde's succeeding you in your place of judge advocate").

It is said in 4 Luttrell 443 (19 May 1709) that "A patent is past the great seal for Thomas Byde, esq, to be judge advocate of Great Brittain." This must have been a new instrument, cf. Scouller 59 n. 1, because Byde had already rendered an opinion as JAG in 1706 (*supra*, p. 13), and there are many references to him in the *Cal. Treas. Books 1708* (pp. 46, 201, 360, 399).

[21] I have drawn freely on an unpublished memorandum, solidly based on the Hertford County Records and on the files of the Judge Advocate General's Office, that was made available to me through the kindness of Oliver C. Barnett, Esq., Q.C., C.B.E., presently Judge Advocate General of the Forces. Date of entry on duty, letters patent cited in foregoing memorandum; date of death, 4 *Gentleman's Magazine* (May 1734) 50.

[22] *Supra*, n. 23 of Ch. I.

[23] *Supra*, p. 11; *infra*, Appendix IB, p. 247.

significant, however, were the circumstances that in 1710 he succeeded his father as 5th baronet of what in point of precedence was—and still is—the second baronetcy in England; that in 1715 he commanded the local militia and assisted the regular forces in dispersing the rebels at Preston; and that from 1710 to 1741 he was an M.P., for Preston and for East Looe. The former was a family borough, where for fifty-three years between 1710 and 1802 the Hoghtons held one seat.

During the seven or so years that Sir Henry Hoghton served as Judge Advocate General, the letter books show only a very few letters signed by him, almost all of them during his first year or so in office, when it may be supposed that his enthusiasm for the problems of administering military justice still waxed high. Thereafter correspondence—and everything else—were left to his faithful Deputy. Sir Henry's departure from the House of Commons occurred in 1741, when the Tories captured what until then had been a safe Whig seat. Indeed, he ran an abysmally poor fourth in the poll at Preston, obtaining only 14 votes against the winners' 394 and 391 and the other loser's 231.

This being the general election that substantially cut Sir Robert Walpole's majority in Commons, Sir Henry Hoghton was thereafter, all too obviously, of no further use to Government. The office of Judge Advocate, "a patent place, though only held during pleasure," was in consequence conferred on another, whose appointment was noted in the same number of the *Gentleman's Magazine* that recorded the electoral debacle at Preston. But Sir Henry Hoghton, now completely freed of official duties, lived on until 1768, aged eighty-nine and survived by his third wife.[24]

The new Judge Advocate General was Thomas Morgan, re-

---

[24] Career generally: 1 G.E.C., *Complete Baronetage* (Exeter, 1900) 11; Burke's *Peerage* (current editions) *s.v.* De Hoghton; 2 Hist. Parl. H.C. 628–629; H. W. Clemensha, *A History of Preston in Amounderness* (Manchester, 1912) 188, 191, 199, 200; W. Dobson, *History of the Parliamentary Representation of Preston* (2d ed., Preston, 1868) 29, 95; 4 *Gentleman's Magazine* (Apr. 1734) 219 (appointment as "Judge Martial").

Admission to Middle Temple: 1 *Register of Admissions* 237 (3 Aug. 1695). His elder brother John, who predeceased their father, was admitted on the same day.

Correspondence as JAG: WO 81/2 and 81/3 (JAG letter books from 1 Jan. 1734 through 31 Dec. 1741); WO 71/36/288; WO 26/19/161.

1741 election: 11 *Gentleman's Magazine* (May 1741) 230 (Sir H. Hoghton's defeat); *id.* 230 (re-election of T. Morgan); *id.* 278 (T. Morgan appointed "Advocate-General of all His Majesty's Forces").

"A patent place": Dr. George Clarke's "Autobiography," *supra* n. 12, at 262.

Pay: J. Chamberlayne, *General List . . . of all the Offices and Officers* (London, 1736) 101: "Sir Hen. Hoghton, Bart., Judge Advocate General, and for his Clerk and Deputy at Jersey and Guernsey, £1 per day."

elected member for Monmouthshire without opposition at the same election. Like Hoghton, the new appointee rarely troubled to sign the mail; like Hoghton, he was no lawyer. Indeed, Thomas Morgan had never even been admitted to any Inn of Court. But he had other qualifications for office that were infinitely more impressive:

> The Morgans of Tredegar, probably the leading political family in South Wales, commanded three seats in the House of Commons during this period. Five members of the family sat in Parliament between 1754 and 1790 for a combined total of 85 years. Only two of them are known to have spoken in the House: John Morgan [son of the JAG] in 1772, to ask why there had been a delay in issuing a writ for Monmouthshire; and Charles Morgan [another son] in 1780, when he presented the Breconshire petition for economical reform.[25]

Thomas Morgan the Judge Advocate General had been Lord Lieutenant of both Monmouthshire and Breconshire since 1731—and would continue in all three capacities until his death. In addition, he "was a supporter successively of Walpole, Pelham and Newcastle." Consequently, having the good sense to continue King Gould as Deputy to manage the business of his office, there was no need for him to travel to London to deal with letters; he had the office, he had the honor, he had the pay—and he commanded three seats in Commons. What better qualifications could the eighteenth century show—or need? [26]

King Gould lived until 1756, and was agent for the Province of Nova Scotia for some time before then.[27] But he seems to have retired as Deputy Judge Advocate General in 1749.[28] By then his son Charles, who has figured so prominently in four of the preceding six chapters, was already in the Judge Advocate General's

---

[25] 1 Hist. Parl. H.C. 53; Morgan of Tredegar, 3 *id.* 164–165; and biographies of the several Morgans, 3 *id.* 165–166.

[26] 3 Hist. Parl. H.C. 165; examination of JAG Letter Books (WO 81 series) during his tenure. See also Ogborn 144, though the attribution on the chart there of a baronetcy to Morgan from 1763 lacks support in the records; see n. 34, *infra*. If Morgan had actually been a baronet at the time of his death in 1769, Charles Gould would hardly have referred to him shortly thereafter simply as "Mr.," nor would an official document emanating from Morgan's own office have addressed him at that same period as "Esq."

[27] Death: Died at Little Ealing, Middlesex, on 23 July 1756 (26 *Gentleman's Magazine* 361), and buried at St. Mary's Church, Ealing, on 29 July (Parish records, communicated by Mr. Barnett). Agent for Nova Scotia: K. Gould to the Rt. Hon. Lords Commissioners for Trade & Plantations, 14 June 1751 (A. Shortt *et al.*, eds., *Documents Relating to Currency, Exchange and Finance in Nova Scotia, 1675–1758* (Ottawa, 1933) 343 (No. 367).

[28] The last letter signed by King Gould is dated 30 Mar. 1749. WO 81/4/79.

Office, prepared to take over and perform its work. The latter's career deserves—and requires—extended treatment.

CHARLES GOULD, DJAG AND JAG

Charles Gould, born in 1726, was educated at Westminster and at Christ Church, Oxford.[29] He was admitted to Lincoln's Inn on 11 January 1743, being listed as "son and heir apparent of King Gould, of Whitehall, Middlesex, Esq.," and was called on 20 November 1750;[30] the statement that he was called by the Middle Temple, originally made in the *Dictionary of National Biography*, and from thence assiduously copied elsewhere, is quite without foundation.[31]

At first Charles was jointly Deputy JAG with his father, probably by 1747.[32] After King Gould's retirement in 1749, Charles became Judge Advocate General in fact, carrying on all the duties of the office, and officiating at every important trial by court-martial held at the Horse Guards during the period. In 1758 he took a most important step, marrying Jane Morgan, daughter of his nominal chief.[33] Accordingly, when Thomas Morgan died on 11 April 1769, Gould was his obvious successor on two grounds, and in fact was appointed to his father-in-law's place from 13 April. He was thus the first lawyer Judge Advocate General of the British Army. Here also other books of reference, which give the date of succession variously as 1768 and 1771, demonstrate primarily that *communis error fecit historiam* as well as *jus*.[34]

---

[29] Here the principal sources relied on are Ogborn; 2 Hist. Parl. H.C. 522–523; the JAG memorandum on Hughes; and another unpublished memorandum on Charles Gould likewise prepared in the Office of the Judge Advocate General and similarly made available by Mr. Barnett.

[30] 1 *Admissions* 425–426; 3 *Black Books* 346.

[31] The first correction of this theretofore universal error appears at Ogborn 138.

[32] The first letter signed by Charles Gould as Deputy (WO 81/4/26) is dated 14 Aug. 1747.

[33] For some amusing if unflattering gossip on this point, see 5 H. B. Wheatley, ed., *The Historical and the Posthumous Memoirs of Sir N. W. Wraxall* (London, 1884) 328–330.

[34] Haydn and his successors say 1768, the DNB and its followers give 1771; both are wrong. In a letter dated 8 June 1769 to Col. O'Hara, Governor of Senegambia (WO 72/6), Gould mentions "His Majesty having been graciously pleased to confer upon me the office of Judge Advocate General, lately vacant by the death of M.ʳ Morgan." The year 1769 is further supported by the circumstance that while a warrant dated 23 Mar. 1769 (WO 71/27/210) is directed to Thomas Morgan, Esq., JAG, the one next following (*id.* at 212), dated 23 June 1769, is addressed to Charles Gould as JAG. The actual date of Gould's appointment, from the JAG memorandum already cited, is based on a pay warrant in Vol. A

Legal income being a matter of eternal fascination to lawyers everywhere, it may be noted that Gould's pay upon succession to his father-in-law's office was 15s. a day, plus an additional allowance of 20s. a day for services as Secretary to the Board of General Officers. When the latter duty lapsed in 1793 and Gould became legal adviser to the Commander in Chief, the additional fee continued, so that his net salary after poundage deductions was £557 3s. 1d. per annum over this period. Moreover, Gould received sums for clerk hire and, after 1778, for a deputy.[35]

In 1756 and again in 1759, Thomas Morgan made unsuccessful applications to the Duke of Newcastle for a parliamentary seat for Charles Gould. Not until 1778, however, did the latter become a Member of Parliament; in that year he was returned for Brecon, "a pocket borough of the Morgans of Tredegar, . . . used by them to provide seats for junior members of the family who could not yet aspire to the honour of a county seat." [36] Gould, though no oratorical virtuoso, was not quite so taciturn as the Morgans: "His few speeches in the House all dealt with the business of his office." [37]

Gould attained the seat for Breconshire in 1787, on the death of his brother-in-law Charles Morgan, at which time his own son Charles became M.P. for Brecon,[38] and remained member for Breconshire until his death in 1806. Meanwhile he had been the recipient of many honors—K.C. in 1754, an Oxford D.C.L. in 1773, a knighthood in 1779, a baronetcy in 1792, and a Privy Councillorship in 1802. Only a peerage was denied him. But in 1792 there had ensued a great change in his fortunes; the last of his brothers-in-law died without issue, his wife inherited the family estates of Ruperra and Tredegar, and he took the name of Morgan by Royal Licence. Thereafter he signed himself "Charles Morgan."

For some years before that significant event, Charles Gould had become interested in The Society for Equitable Assurances on Lives and Survivorships, now known as The Equitable Life Assur-

---

(1769–1793) of "Letters of Estimates, Official Alterations, Patents, etc.," now in the JAG Office.

See also Gen. Gage to Gould, 9 Sept. 1769 (2 Gage *Corr.* 523), acknowledging Gould's letter of 6 June and congratulating him on his new appointment.

As a matter of interest, the DNB article rested on and simply perpetuated the original error made in R. Beatson, *A Political Index,* . . . *or, A Complete Register* (3d ed., London, 1806).

[35] Figures for pay are drawn from the JAG memorandum on Gould. As from 3 Dec. 1778, James Hume became Deputy JAG, at £200 per annum. WO 26/30/38.
[36] 1 Hist. Parl. H.C. 460.
[37] 2 Hist. Parl. H.C. 523.
[38] 2 Hist. Parl. H.C. 523.

ance Society, and from 1773 until his death served as its president. In the latter position he was succeeded first by his son, Sir Charles Morgan, and then by his grandson, Sir Charles Morgan Robinson Morgan (later first Baron Tredegar). The son, an officer in the 2d Foot Guards, had been captured at Yorktown in 1781, and the draft of Charles Gould's obviously distraught inquiry concerning his fate breathes a paternal concern not less heartfelt for having become a sentiment all too commonplace over the last fifty years.[39]

So successful was the Equitable under the first Sir Charles Gould's direction that in 1782 its General Court commissioned Thomas Gainsborough to paint his portrait. The picture, a magnificent full-length painting, today "still adorns the Board Room of the Society and is one of its most proud possessions." A fine reproduction in color appears, through the kindness of The Equitable Life Assurance Society, as the frontispiece of the present book.

It is placed there because Charles Gould, pre-eminently, is the father of modern military law. The first lawyer Judge Advocate General, his was the first professional mind that undertook to shape what Blackstone still denigrated: "For martial law,"—by which of course the author of the *Commentaries* meant military law— "which is built upon no settled principles, but is entirely arbitrary in its decisions, is, as Sir Matthew Hale observes, in truth and reality no law, but something indulged rather than allowed as a law."[40] Gould did much to dispel such reproaches; he imparted regularity to proceedings at military law, both substantively and procedurally. Even to enumerate the major instances wherein he shaped that law for future generations would constitute a wholly unjustifiable digression from the theme of the present volume; his labors in the larger field fully warrant independent treatment.[41] Yet it is proper to note here that, on one occasion, Gould was persuasive enough to induce the law officers to change their opinions, as in the case of the soldiers offending against the Mutiny Act in one province overseas and then sought to be tried by court-martial in another.[42] In that instance it was Gould who demonstrated why the military jurisdiction continued.

But, where non-military persons were concerned, Gould was

[39] Draft of letter, Gould to Adye, 2 Jan. 1782, WO 72/9.

[40] 1 Bl. Comm. *413.

[41] It seems appropriate to emphasize that the history of English military law has yet to be written. Clode's works, indispensable as they are, fall far short of providing such an account, even to the date when he wrote, now nearly a century ago.

[42] 1 Clode M.F. 538–541.

most solicitous, as has been seen, to insure that courts-martial should try only those individuals who were in terms subjected to the Mutiny Act. True, the Gibraltar-Minorca Article of War literally embraced "all Persons." But since the Articles of War could rise no higher than their source, which Gould quite properly took to be the Mutiny Act, the reference in what over many years appeared as Article 2 of Section XX was necessarily in his opinion to be read as restricted to "all Persons subject to the Mutiny Act." In this reading he anticipated what the Supreme Court of the United States was to rule two centuries later, and it is only fair to say that if that tribunal had been advised of Gould's rulings by counsel contending before it, judicial determination of the issue in the United States would undoubtedly have been both easier and speedier.[43] Gould failed by modern standards only in respect of the scope of military government jurisdiction—but, as has been pointed out at length above, that jurisdiction was not articulated until after his own death.[44]

It is eminently proper, therefore, to commemorate Charles Gould, and to make generally available to the profession his strong features, so perceptively preserved by a master of English portraiture. For up to now Gould has in truth been largely a forgotten man despite his very real accomplishments. Indeed, except for the citation and discussion of the case of *Grant* v. *Gould*,[45] the application for a writ of prohibition against him that called forth what until 1952 remained the classic determination regarding the scope of judicial review of military proceedings,[46] Gould is not so much as mentioned anywhere in the sixteen solidly packed volumes of Sir William Holdsworth's immortal *History of English Law.*

It is now time to turn to the three gentlemen who served as Deputy Judge Advocate in North America from 1756 through 1783.

JOHN APPY, DJA

John Appy, born in Amsterdam in 1725 of a French Huguenot family, was brought to England as a boy.[47] In February 1756, he

---

[43] See the present author's paper, *History Vindicates the Supreme Court's Rulings on Military Jurisdiction*, 51 Am. Bar Assn. J. 1127, and pp. 3–5, *supra.*

[44] *Supra*, pp. 59–62.

[45] 2 H. Bl. 69.

[46] 10 Holdsworth 382–383, 709; 12 *id.* 575. The Courts-Martial (Appeals) Act 1951 (14 & 15 Geo. VI c. 46) became effective on 1 May 1952.

[47] The account that follows is drawn primarily from O'Conor.

was engaged as Secretary by Lord Loudoun, then about to leave for his ill-fated American command, who noted that "the great recommendation of him given to me was that he was a Drudge that could work for ever." Following arrival in New York early that summer, Lord Loudoun appointed Appy to additional duty as Judge Advocate. Appy originally received as Secretary 10s. a day plus emoluments; his new office carried with it a tidy increase; and at the end his aggregate compensation for both was 12s. a day for pay, plus an additional per diem for rations and provision money.[48]

Appy officiated at a few trials by court-martial, at New York and Halifax;[49] for trials in the field, however, he deputized a Lieutenant Burton and paid him for that duty,[50] a form of generosity not paralleled at home. (The correspondence of the Judge Advocate General at the Horse Guards during this period is full of requests by subalterns who acted as DJA, asking reimbursement for clerk hire and other out-of-pocket expenses. Invariably, the JAG replied that he had no funds for that purpose, though on occasion payments were made from contingent funds, or suggested to the commander concerned as proper to be made from similar sources.)

Appy continued in the same double capacity after Lord Loudoun's recall, serving successively the even less competent General Abercromby—dubbed "Mrs. Nabbycromby" by the colonials after his repulse at Fort Ticonderoga in 1758—and then General Amherst, whom Appy accompanied on the campaign of 1760 that culminated in the surrender of Canada. When Amherst moved his headquarters to New York, Appy went with him, dying in that city on 14 October 1761.[51]

Appy flits through the journal of the elder Montrésor (the Colonel who was Chief Engineer in America beginning in 1754) as a correspondent and dinner companion;[52] on the affirmative side, he disallowed many accounts submitted by Major Robert Rogers of the Rangers;[53] and he is himself memorialized after a fashion in a

---

[48] O'Conor 227.

[49] WO 71/65/388 (Halifax, July 1757); WO 71/66/97 (New York, Sept. 1757); WO 71/66/108 (same, Oct. 1757).

[50] O'Conor 210, 214; see *Commissary Wilson's Orderly Book* (Albany, 1857) *s.v.* Burton.

[51] Gen. Amherst to Gov. Murray, 22 Oct. 1761, WO 34/3/122; same to Gen. Gage, WO 34/7/69; same to Col. Burton, WO 34/7/255. Appy had complained of illness much earlier. Appy to Gould, DJAG, 4 Jan. 1760, WO 72/4.

[52] Montrésor 11–111.

[53] Cuneo 118–119, 144–147.

biography that is notable principally for transcriptions of his account books. "Poor Appy," as Lord Amherst referred to him at the end,[54] accordingly remains but a shadowy figure, nor is he mentioned in the *Dictionary of National Biography*.

HECTOR THEOPHILUS CRAMAHÉ, DJA

Appy's successor as Judge Advocate, effective 15 October 1761, was Captain Hector Theophilus Cramahé of the 15th Foot.[55] Cramahé, variously described as a Huguenot and as a Swiss by birth, had been named by General Wolfe to be Deputy Judge Advocate of the expedition that took Quebec in 1759. After Wolfe's death, Cramahé became Secretary to General James Murray at Quebec, and, when civil government was instituted in Canada in 1764, he was named first a senior Councillor and then Lieutenant-Governor.[56]

Shortly after his appointment as Judge Advocate, Cramahé resigned his military commission; he does not appear in the 1762 Army List, or in the list of officers on half-pay. But, notwithstanding his other civil offices, he retained his appointment as Judge Advocate, drawing pay at 10s. per day in respect of the latter office.[57] He prosecuted at the trials of Joseph Corriveaux and of the latter's daughter in 1763,[58] and at that of Major Rogers of the Rangers in 1768.[59] Thereafter, though he performed few if any services as Judge Advocate, what with his being Lieutenant-Governor at Quebec while the Commander in Chief maintained headquarters at New York until 1773 and then at Boston after 1774,[60] he continued to serve—and draw pay—as "Judge Advocate upon the American staff" as long as such a staff existed.[61]

[54] Gen. Amherst to Gen. Gage, 13 Oct. 1761, WO 34/7/66.
[55] Amherst letters cited *supra*, n. 51; Gen. Amherst to Gen. Gage, 24 Oct. 1761, WO 34/7/70; WO 34/74/88.
[56] Birth: Burt 14; 1 Knox 346 n. 1; 5 Kingsford 219–220. Trials showing Cramahé officiating as DJA: WO 71/65/32 (Isle of Wight, Aug. 1757); WO 71/66/356 (Louisbourg, Aug. 1758). Subsequent career: 1 Knox 346 (Maj.-Gen. Wolfe's Orders, Louisbourg, 17 May 1759); Doughty, Appendix B to Part 2, pp. 2–3, and Appendix C to Part 2, p. 20; references to Cramahé in Burt.
[57] See List of General and Staff Officers in Viscount Barrington, SW, to Gen. Gage, 12 Dec. 1767, Gage Papers, WLCL, vol. 10, English Series.
[58] *Supra*, pp. 53–55.
[59] Cuneo 231–242; the trial is at WO 71/51/256–345; the King's comment on Rogers' acquittal was that "at the same time it appears to His Majesty that there was great reason to suspect the said Major Rogers entertains an improper and dangerous Correspondence, which Suspicion the Account afterwards given of his meditating an Escape tended to confirm."
[60] *Supra*, pp. 52, 78.
[61] *Infra*, pp. 181, 182.

During the time that he was Lieutenant-Governor of Quebec, Cramahé played a significant and indeed critical part in repulsing the American attack on Quebec in December 1775.[62] Before the start of the Burgoyne campaign, Brunswick officers noted that he was "liked by all as an honest, unselfish man," "whose venerable appearance called forth as much respect as his righteousness." [63]

Thereafter Cramahé's exploits were civil rather than military. Later, however, he lost the confidence of General Haldimand, who in 1778 had succeeded General Carleton as Governor of Canada, and Lord George Germain became hostile. "That province," the latter wrote in August 1780, "will never be properly govern'd until Mr. Cramahé is recalled." [64] Cramahé himself, who began to show the effects of declining health and advancing years, left Canada in October 1781.[65] In April of the following year, Lord Shelburne advised the King that Cramahé "appears totally unfit to be continued" as Lieutenant-Governor of Quebec.[66] Four months later, in August 1782, Cramahé wrote from England to General Carleton, then in command at New York, asking leave of absence as Judge Advocate, "the Pay attending that Employment being the only subsistence left me," since ceasing to be Lieutenant-Governor. "In such a Situation to request your Leave as above, will appear, I hope, not an unreasonable Boon, as well as to be continued on the Returns, in Order that I may get the Pay." [67] This was granted by the compassionate Carleton, who had personally observed Cramahé's exertions during the successful defense of Quebec in 1775. Accordingly, Cramahé is still listed as the DJA serving in Canada on 24 June 1783, drawing his 10s. per day.[68] Ultimately, by way of pension against the day when there would no longer be any American staff, Cramahé was appointed Lieutenant-Governor of Detroit, a sinecure. He died at Exeter in Devon in 1788, at an advanced age.[69]

---

[62] 1 C. Ward 183–184; references to Cramahé in French F.Y.

[63] Pettengill 8; DuRoi 67.

[64] Lord G. Germain, SS, to W. Knox, 7 Aug. 1780, 6 HMC *Var. Coll.* 169.

[65] Loss of Haldimand's confidence: Burt 308–311, 409–410. Departure: Lt.-Col. Lacorne St. Luc to Gen. Carleton, 30 Oct. 1781, 2 HMC Am. MSS. 344–345; *S.C. Royal Gazette* 23–26, Jan. 1782, publishing dispatch from Quebec dated 28 Oct. 1781.

[66] Earl of Shelburne, SS, to the King, 22 Apr. 1782, 5 Geo. III *Corr.* 483 (No. 3678).

[67] Cramahé to Gen. Carleton, 1 Aug. 1782; 3 HMC Am. MSS. 49, PRO 30/55 No. 5194.

[68] List of staff officers in Canada, 24 June 1783, WO 28/6/199; pay of 10s. per day in 1782, WO 4/275/207.

[69] Burt 525 n. 8a.

Cramahé accordingly had a career that left a distinct mark on Canadian history. Yet the vast card index catalogues in the Library of Congress do not list a single book or pamphlet concerning him, and the *Dictionary of National Biography* knows him not.[70]

STEPHEN PAYNE ADYE, DJA

It was surely characteristic of eighteenth-century administration in England that while the office of Judge Advocate on the North American establishment and the pay thereunto appertaining were enjoyed by an elderly gentleman who held other offices and drew other pay, the actual work was done by another who enjoyed neither. This was Captain Stephen Payne Adye of the Royal Artillery, who for eight long years, from 1775 through 1783, aspired to Cramahé's position but without avail; Cramahé outlived both the war and the establishment, while Adye died a Major in 1794 in command of an invalid battery on the Island of Jersey.[71] But though deprived of his due here on earth, Adye assuredly was rewarded thereafter; alone of the three American DJA's, he is commemorated in the *Dictionary of National Biography*, and moreover his mention in the pages of Holdsworth's *History of English Law* constitutes a distinction that was denied his chief, Judge Advocate General Sir Charles Gould.

While still a Lieutenant and stationed in New York, Adye in 1766 or so was appointed by General Gage, then Commander in Chief in North America, to act as Judge Advocate.[72] After officiating in that capacity on numerous occasions,[73] he seems to have become sufficiently fascinated by the law to study it seriously, and in 1769 he published in New York, "under the protection of my General, though totally unassisted by any Gentleman versed in the law," *A Treatise on Courts-Martial*.[74] This was not only the first

---

[70] He is mentioned, very briefly, in L. J. Burpee & A. G. Doughty, eds., *Index and Dictionary of Canadian History* (Toronto, 1911) 92. In his lifetime, he achieved a measure of immortality in reverse, by the perverse misspelling of his name in official records. The Army Lists consistently refer to him as Cramaké, while Fortescue's editing (n. 66, *supra*) distorts even that, transforming him into Cromake.

[71] DNB; Army Lists for 1794 and 1795.

[72] Adye (1st ed.) ii; and see his letter of 4 Oct. 1775 to Gould: "My appointment to this office [DJA to the Troops in Boston], I attribute more to the General's Goodness than to any merit of my own (although I might perhaps found some pretensions to it, upon having done the duty, almost uninterruptedly, for nine years past). . . ." WO 72/7.

[73] Gould to Adye, 29 May 1767, acknowledging receipt of records of trial by general courts-martial held at New York, 25–28 Feb. 1767 (WO 81/11/200).

[74] Adye to Gould, 1 Aug. 1769, WO 72/6.

English book written on military law since the passage of the first Mutiny Act,[75] it was in addition one of the earliest law books of any kind ever printed in America.[76] Adye's work went through many editions, a second published in London in 1778, a third at Philadelphia in 1779, and an eighth in London in 1810.[77] Finally, in 1825, more than thirty years after the author's death, *Adye on Courts-Martial* was one of the authorities that President John Quincy Adams consulted before confirming the court-martial proceedings in the case of Captain David Porter of the United States Navy.[78]

But this was posthumous fame; during the eight years of Adye's service in the War of American Independence, he never attained his principal desire, appointment as Judge Advocate on the establishment in succession to Cramahé. On 7 August 1775, during the siege of Boston, he was appointed "Deputy Judge Advocate to the Troops in Boston," [79] who then numbered twenty-two battalions. Not only that, but "by Martial law being proclaimed throughout the province of Massachusetts Bay, General Courts Martial became possessed of greater power and authority, and consequently would be more frequently held." [80] Even so, he wrote Gould, that appointment carried only 5s. per day—"as much, I may presume to suppose, as [General Gage] could venture on his own authority, to assign me, yet when I consider what a vast field of business is before me, and what an absolute necessity I am under of hiring one Clerk at least, and of establishing a regular Office, I cannot help solliciting your good offices with Lord Barrington, (and which I have every reason to think General Gage will rather join in than oppose) that I may have the same allowance of pay, as is usually given to Judge Advocates of the army, and which M.'

---

[75] 12 Holdsworth 347. The last previous book in English on military law was *An Abridgment of the English Military Discipline,* published in 1682. 6 Holdsworth 612, 699.

[76] E. R. James, "A List of Legal Treatises Printed in the British Colonies and the American States before 1801," in *Harvard Legal Essays* (Cambridge, Mass., 1934) 159, 170; 1 Gaine 49, 120–121.

[77] E. R. James, *supra,* at 180. The 8th edition is incorrectly dated at 12 Holdsworth 347, and n. 5 on the same page gives Adye's rank as that is listed on the title page of the 8th edition; in the 1st edition it is simply "First Lieut. in the Royal Regiment of Artillery."

[78] 7 C. F. Adams, ed., *Memoirs of John Quincy Adams* (Boston, 1874) 46. The record of the Porter trial (*Minutes of Proceedings of the Courts of Inquiry and Court Martial, in Relation to Captain David Porter* [Washington, 1825]), is reprinted in 2 *Am. State Pap., Naval Affairs* (Washington, 1860) 132–440.

[79] Gage OB, 7 Aug. 1775.

[80] For the doctrine of martial law in England at this period, see 10 Holdsworth 705–713.

Cramahé, who has not put pen to paper as a Judge Advocate for many years, enjoys." [81]

Two months later Adye recurred to the matter of the appointment; he himself had three commissions, one a deputation only, one from General Gage, one from General Howe—but what if there were a new commander? Adye wanted a commission from home, like that held by Cramahé, "who has much the smaller army of the two." [82] In June 1777, Adye reported happily that Sir William Howe had increased his pay as Judge Advocate to 10s. per day [83]—but in May of the next year he was still asking for the broader commission. [84]

Meanwhile, from May 1779 through August 1780, while General Pattison was simultaneously CRA and Commandant in New York, [85] Adye performed additional duty as his ADC, and in substance functioned as Assistant Commandant, dealing on occasion with so mundane a matter as providing for the removal of an insane female inhabitant to the almshouse. [86]

After General Pattison returned to England, he had good news for Adye, which the latter immediately forwarded to Sir Charles Gould:

> In a late letter from M. Genl Pattison, he tells me that by the last Accounts from Canada, Mr Cramahé, who is D. Judge Advocate upon the Establishment, for America, was said to be on his death bed, and that in consequence thereof, he had made his application to You in my favor, and that You had been so good as to assure him of all your good Offices to serve me, in case that event should happen. . . . I cannot but hope for a Continuance of [your assurances], particularly on this occasion, should it be Mr Cramahé's fate, to quit this transitory World. [87]

---

[81] Adye to Gould, 4 Oct. 1775, WO 72/7. Viscount Barrington was then Secretary at War. The quotation in the text preceding this one is from the same letter.

[82] Adye to Gould, 12 Dec. 1775, WO 72/7.

[83] Adye to Gould, 5 June 1777, WO 72/8.

[84] Adye to Gould, 20 May 1778, WO 72/8.

[85] 1 Duncan, ch. XXVIII and p. 326; Clinton OB, 2 May 1779.

[86] Pattison 414, 416. Many of the letters dealing with Gen. Pattison's duties as Commandant (Pattison 221–430) went out over Adye's signature. The suggestion in C. I. A. Ritchie, ed., *A New York Diary of the Revolutionary War*, 50 NYHS Q. 221, 222–224, that the diary there transcribed may have been written by Adye, is, so Dr. Ritchie advises, confirmed by comparison of its handwriting with that of Adye's letters in the WO 72 series in the PRO.

[87] Adye to Gould, 2 July 1781, WO 72/9.

Again in December 1781, Adye wrote Sir Charles Gould that "I am very sensible of the Honor You do me, in the favorable opinion you entertained of my being the most proper person to succeed to Mr. Cramahé's appointment, in case of his Death. . . . I have had some conversation respecting it, with Sir Henry Clinton, who most readily acquiesced in throwing his Interest into the Scale in my favor, and, as he informs me, wrote home accordingly." [88] A very similar letter went to Sir Charles Gould in March 1782, this time with a suggestion designed to overcome the stumbling block of Cramahé's perverse longevity: there might be two American DJA's—one in Canada, and another "in the middle and southern Colonies." [89]

But this was desperately wishful thinking, because, although Adye could not yet know it, the shooting war was over; the House of Commons had already declared against further military operations in North America.[90] The result was that, nine days after Adye's suggestion for expanding the establishment, the Cabinet at home was determining instead that the British garrisons remaining in the colonies must be withdrawn.[91] So Adye simply continued as Judge Advocate to Clinton's successor, Sir Guy Carleton, the fourth Commander in Chief whom he had served since the war began, trying cases and working on records of trial to the very end [92]—and drawing 10s. per day.[93] But the decrepit Cramahé proved amazingly—disappointingly, one is almost tempted to say—viable, and when General Carleton, as already noted, gave the latter leave of absence in August 1782,[94] that was action wholly consistent with the eighteenth-century view—indeed it was the clearly recognized law of the time—that an office was property.[95]

---

[88] Adye to Gould, 8 Dec. 1781, WO 72/9.

[89] Adye to Gould, 21 Mar. 1782, WO 72/10.

[90] *Supra,* p. 101.

[91] *Supra,* pp. 95–96 n. 53.

[92] Trial of Hetfield in Sept. 1783, *supra,* pp. 129–133; work on May record of trial in Nov. 1783, *supra,* p. 128; late trials listed in final provost marshal's returns but not noted in the Carleton OB, *supra* pp. 134–135.

[93] Abstract of pay due, 1 Apr.–30 June 1783, claiming 10s. per day for Adye as DJA and 5s. per day for Lt. Richard Porter, Asst. DJA, 4 HMC Am. MSS. 190, PRO 30/55 No. 8249; warrant for payment of those sums, 4 HMC Am. MSS. 196. The total came to £68 5s.

[94] *Supra,* p. 181; 3 HMC Am. MSS. 49; reference to "the decrepit Cramahé," Burt 409.

[95] "Offices, which are a right to exercise a public or private employment, and to take the fees and emoluments thereunto belonging, are also incorporeal hereditaments; whether public, as those of magistrates, or private, as of bailiffs, receivers, and the like." 2 Bl. Comm. *36.

Consequently an office was not to be taken away from its holder for the benefit of the person who did the work of that office, any more than the great country estates of England were to be distributed to the rustics who tilled them. [95a]

More significant here than Major Adye's disappointment—he had been promoted in the Army early in 1783, though he never rose higher than Captain in the Royal Artillery—is the statement in his *Treatise* that construes the Gibraltar-Minorca-no-form-of-civil-judicature article of war.

In 1769, Adye had written that "In some Parts of his Majesty's Dominions, *viz. Gibraltar, Minorca, &c.* where there is no Form of Civil Judicature, all Persons guilty of any capital Crime or other Offences, are to be tried by Courts Martial," citing Article 2 of Section XX as authority.[96] The same statement was repeated in his second and third editions, published, respectively, in London in 1778 and in Philadelphia in 1779,[97] and was continued through the eighth and last edition, published in London in 1810.[98] Meanwhile, in 1784, the same thought had been included in Sullivan's *Thoughts on Martial Law:* "And in those places abroad (such as Gibraltar) where there is no other than the Law Martial for English subjects, and where Courts Martial are therefore held for other

---

[95a] Historical completeness requires notation here of the only Hessian legal officer whose name appears in the British records (Carleton OB, 28 May 1783):

"Description of Charles Broeske, Quarter Master Major, Paymaster and Judge Advocate to Colonel Linsings Battalion of Hessian Grenadiers, who absconded the 26th Instant in the Afternoon and took with him the sum of £340 Subsistence Money belonging to the above Battalion. He is about 40 Years old under the middle size, rather fat, a round full and pale face, short neck, his head bending forwards, not much hair, which he used to tye in a Queue, had on before he went away a blue Coat with lappels, the button holes trimmed with a small silver lace, white under cloth, and boots, he had a connection with a Young Woman, Name Sally Bunn at Perth Amboy, who may now perhaps be with him, she went to the Jerseys on Saturday 24th Instant, is a good looking Woman of the middle size, about 22 Years old, her face and features rather large, dark hair and black eyes, had on a yellow Silk Gown when she went away. All Persons Civil and Military are desired to assist in apprehending the above Deserter."

This was nearly two months after the proclamation of the end of hostilities that followed the effective date of the preliminary treaty of peace; see notes 55 and 241 of Ch. V. Two weeks after the order book entry quoted above, Gen. Lossberg, the senior Hessian officer, requested Sir Guy Carleton to invoke the aid of the American Governor of New Jersey in recovering the fugitives—and the missing funds. 4 HMC Am. MSS. 142. But there is no indication that Sir Guy did so, and so Broeske, Judge Advocate, etc., etc., does not figure further either in the Carleton papers—or in any other pages of history.

[96] Adye (1st ed.) 7, n.†
[97] Adye (2d ed.) 15; *id.* (3d ed.) 18.
[98] Adye (8th ed.) 57.

offences, . . . the English inhabitants are subject to military discipline." [99]

Adye's third Philadelphia edition in 1779 doubtless was pirated, from a copy abandoned after the British occupation; that city had been entirely in American hands after Sir Henry Clinton's departure in June 1778.[100] All subsequent editions were posthumous, beginning with the fourth in 1797, although the last in 1810 included substantial additions knowledgeably made. Thus the later editions of Adye may properly be taken to reflect the informed professional opinion of the time.

Therein lies the mystery: How was it that neither Adye, nor Sullivan, nor Adye's revisers, ever so much as hinted that, in respect of the passage in question, the settled doctrine of the Judge Advocate General's Office was quite the other way? For there, as has been seen, it had long been the rule that "all Persons" in the Gibraltar-Minorca Article meant only "all Persons subject to the Mutiny Act."

That was a principle first laid down by Attorney General Sir J. Willes in 1734,[101] and then frequently reaffirmed by Gould: in respect of the Clerk of the Works at Gibraltar in 1755,[102] in 1763 in connection with the Royal Navy boatswain on Martinique[103] and the trials of inhabitants in Canada,[104] and again in 1765 and 1770 in respect of soldiers' wives on Minorca.[105] Yet it appears to have remained a doctrine that was hidden even from judge advocates of long service. Indeed, no publication of the restrictive interpretation of the Gibraltar-Minorca Article appears to have been made until the appearance of Clode's first work in 1869.[106]

This is not to say that Gould was ultimately correct in his views of the laws of war. Generals Howe, Clinton, and Carleton in New York and the other American cities, no less than Generals Gage and Murray in Canada, were facing a condition rather than a theory; they could properly assert, with full factual accuracy, that "our Courts here for the trial of offences against [the common] law stand upon the ground of absolute necessity to avoid all the

---

[99] Pp. 63–64. This book is briefly mentioned at 12 Holdsworth 630.
[100] *Supra*, p. 145.
[101] *Supra*, pp. 14–15.
[102] *Supra*, p. 124.
[103] *Supra*, pp. 69–70.
[104] *Supra*, pp. 55–59.
[105] *Supra*, pp. 75–77.
[106] 1 Clode M.F. 532–533.

miseries of a wanton and perilous licentiousness." [107] Their legal instinct was actually sounder than Gould's; the subsequent development of the law of belligerent occupation that did not come to full flowering until the second American civil war in the following century [108] sustained their approach rather than that of Gould or of Judge Jones.[109]

Nor is it surprising that Adye acceded to the views of the general officers whom he was serving; a judge advocate's loyalty, after all, properly runs to his own commander rather than to the Judge Advocate General, even if as a lawyer he is in agreement with the views of the second when they differ from those held by the first. But what is and remains mysterious, strange, even amazing—nothing turns on the precise adjective selected—is that the Judge Advocate General's rulings regarding the scope of military jurisdiction in domestic territory in time of piping peace should have remained for so long so very well concealed even from official view. Here, pre-eminently, was an official secret closely and effectively guarded without the slightest help from—or need for—legislative sanction.

---

[107] Gen. Carleton to Gov. Livingston of N.J., 31 Aug. 1783, 4 HMC Am. MSS. 319, PRO 30/55 No. 8927; *supra*, p. 131.

[108] *Supra*, pp. 105–107.

[109] The contemporary justification for the military trials of inhabitants in occupied New York and other American cities, that these communities were garrisons identical to Gibraltar, was vehemently rejected by Judge Jones. 2 Jones 134–142.

CHAPTER VIII

WELLINGTON'S ARMY

The British armies that the Duke of Wellington commanded during the Peninsular campaign and later at Waterloo differed organizationally but little from the British army with which Sir Guy Carleton sailed from New York in December 1783.[1]

The division of authority under which the British land forces operated during the more than two decades of war that followed the French Revolution—it would be an impermissible exaggeration in this connection to speak either of a system or of a pattern—was quite as diffused and as complicated as it had been in the earlier conflict. The ghosts of Cromwell's Major-Generals, and the deep-seated fear of a revived military dictatorship that their memory engendered, still stalked the land, with the consequence that, to prevent the recurrence of this ultimate horrible, administrative supervision of the Army was splintered among the Treasury, the Secretary of State, the Secretary at War, the Commander in Chief, and the Board of Ordnance. The cavalry and infantry were under the Commander in Chief, the artillery and the engineers fell within the domain of the Board of Ordnance, and the medical services were subject to a divided control: the Commander in Chief through the Medical Board superintended the Physician-General, the Surgeon-General, and the Inspector-General of Hospitals, leaving the Purveyor-General and the Apothecary-General to be dealt with directly by the Secretary at War.[2]

Successful administration, true, is not necessarily a matter of logic, but, all too plainly, the arrangements briefly outlined above imposed heavy handicaps on statesmen and field commanders alike. Wellington emerged victorious, not because of the manner in which military administration was carried on at home, but in spite

---

[1] The last entry in Gen. Carleton's order book in the Clements Library is dated 2 Dec. 1783, on board H.M.S. *Ceres*, off Staten Island. That vessel was a frigate, Captain Hawkins commanding; she reached Falmouth on 10 Jan. 1784, and Gen. Carleton arrived in London on the 14th. *N.-Y. Independent Journal*, 4–8 Dec. 1783, 27 Mar. 1784; 54 *Gentleman's Magazine* 69. See also 5 Freeman 468 n. 54.

[2] See ch. I, "The Administration of the Army in Peace and War," in S. G. P. Ward, and note particularly at p. 7 the chart—one is almost tempted to say "wiring diagram"—illustrating the text.

of it, because—and only because—he was an authentic genius. Generals less gifted simply bogged down, as the Crimean War was unhappily to demonstrate in the decades ahead. Not until Mr. Haldane's time was the military structure in Whitehall made adequate and appropriate to Britain's military potential.

Internally, at the period now in question, there had been a few changes in the direction of militarizing civilians of the supporting services. Thus, "the works at Gibraltar were mainly executed by civilian mechanics . . . , who were not engaged for any term of years, but were hired like ordinary artificers, and could leave the Rock whenever they felt disposed. Not being amenable to military discipline, they were indolent and disorderly, and wholly regardless of authority. The only means of punishing them was by reprimand, suspension, or dismissal, and these means were quite ineffectual to check irregularities." [3] Accordingly, by Royal Warrant dated 6 March 1772, there was organized at Gibraltar the Soldier-Artificer Company.[4]

The experiment proved so successful that, on 10 October 1787, a new Royal Warrant provided for the organization of the Corps of Royal Military Artificers,[5] who in 1788 were specifically made subject to the Mutiny Act, over the protests of numerous voluble and articulate libertarians, including Charles James Fox and the dramatist Richard Brinsley Sheridan, all of whom deprecated the very idea of subjecting artificers to military law.[6] In 1812, this corps was redesignated the "Royal Military Artificers or Sappers and Miners." [7] They were officered by Engineers, who had been constituted the Corps of Royal Engineers in 1787, but who remained wholly separate from the soldiers they commanded for years still to come.[8]

The other branch under the Board of Ordnance developed in similar fashion; the Royal Corps of Artillery Drivers was created in 1794, to be reconstituted in 1802 as the Corps of Gunner-Drivers.[9] The same trend toward militarization affected those who worked

---

[3] 1 Connolly 1.

[4] 1 Connolly 2–3; 2 *id.* 291–292.

[5] 1 Connolly 61; Glover 38.

[6] 1 Connolly 57–60; 1 Clode M.F. 88, 181, citing 27 Parl. Hist. 163–167 and 28 Geo. III c. 12, §75; Clode M.L. 31–32; 3 Fortescue 517, 547; testimony of C. M. Clode, Esq., Solicitor to the War Office, in *First and Second Reports of the Courts-Martial Commission, 1869* (H.M.S.O., 1869) 252, ¶24.

[7] 1 Connolly 183.

[8] 1 Connolly v; Glover 103.

[9] Glover 86–87; 2 Duncan 30, 58, 136.

for the Commissariat Department and the Quarter Master General. The Royal Waggoners existed from 1794 to 1795, to be followed in 1799 by the Royal Waggon Corps and Train; the latter were continued until 1833.[10] The year 1799 also saw the creation of the Royal Staff Corps, the year 1805 the organization of the Barrack Artificers Corps.[11]

The several civil departments of the Army remained just that during the war. It was necessary, wrote Lieutenant-General Viscount Wellington in December 1810, "that the Commissariat should be formed, in respect to promotion, on the principle of a civil rather than a military establishment," viz., pay to be increased "in proportion to the number of years of their service; and that none should be promoted who are not recommended for promotion by the officers in command of the troops." No room there for aristocratic notions of purchase; these were still civilians, taken from drawers several layers below the top. ". . . officers of the army have rank and other objects to look to, to which not only a Commissary cannot aspire, but from which he is precluded; and indeed I might add that the prejudices of society against a Commissary almost prevent him from receiving the common respect due to the character of a gentleman." [12] The only concession made was that a series of orders conferred relative rank on the several members of the civil departments—doctors, apothecaries, commissaries, judge advocates—so that they could be more conveniently integrated into the hierarchical military community of which, in fact, they were an indispensable part.[13]

All of them, however, were regarded as non-combatants, and in September 1813 the Marquess of Wellington deplored the current fashion that required them when captured to be exchanged, so that a French commissary needed to be given up as *quid pro quo* for the return of his own judge advocate, taken by Napoleon's forces in utter disregard of the respect normally due a man of law. "In former wars, a person in your situation," he wrote Mr. Larpent, his

---

[10] 1 J. W. Fortescue, *The Royal Army Service Corps* (Cambridge, 1930) 48–50, 268–272; C. H. Massé, *The Predecessors of the Royal Army Service Corps* (Aldershot, 1948) chs. 1–2; Glover 24, 256–258, 273–275.

[11] Glover 38, 104–105.

[12] Lt.-Gen. Visc. Wellington to Col. Gordon, Commissary in Chief, 19 Dec. 1810, 4 Well. *Disp.* 465, 466.

[13] 3 Well. G.O. 137 (8 July 1811; officers of the medical staff); 7 Well. G.O. 293 (22 Dec. 1815; officers of the Commissariat Dept.); 8 Well. G.O. 46 (11 Feb. 1816; relative rank of judge advocates and chaplains). For similar orders fixing relative rank in the Seven Years War, see 2 HMC Rutland 252, 267

captured DJA, "would have been considered a non-combatant, and would have been immediately released; but in this war, which, on account of the violence of enmity with which it is conducted, it is to be hoped will be the last, for some time at least, every body is considered a prisoner of war, and none are released without exchange." [14]

Finally, during the Waterloo campaign, what was actually an old civil department rejoined the Army. The Accounts Branch of the Commissariat, sometimes called the Accountant-General's Department, now took the field as the Comptrollers of Army Accounts. Two gentlemen thus entitled were dispatched from home to the Army, and were themselves accompanied by Inspectors, Examiners, Clerks Superior and Inferior, private secretaries, and an Office-Keeper, all of whom were duly ranked with the several grades of Commissaries.[15] At first blush it might seem that this horde of bookkeepers and auditors was a plague to the troops, constituting a force potentially even more fearful than the hosts of the Emperor-escaped-from-Elban-exile, so that these accountants, harrying the British Army from the rear, in the end contributed quite as much to the final victory as did the far more renowned playing fields of Eton. In fact, however, Wellington had himself recommended just this step while still in the Peninsula. In April 1813 he had written the Secretary of State "that the Commissary Gen. of an army should be relieved from all responsibility for the accounts of the army. . . . With these views it is desirable that an Auditor General of Accounts should be attached to the army." [16]

The only groups to escape both militarization as well as relative rank were the followers and the women. In respect of the latter it will suffice to quote from Sir Charles Oman's comprehensive summary, *Wellington's Army*, a work based on that author's monumental study of the Peninsular War:

---

[14] F. M. Marquess of Wellington to F. S. Larpent, Esq., DJA, 4 Sept. 1813, 6 Well. *Disp.* 737; Larpent 258. The Treaty and Conventions of Écluse (in Flanders), signed by the British and French commanders on 9 Feb. 1759 during the Seven Years War, exempted from being made prisoners of war the Provost-General and his officers and constables, the Auditor-General and his staff, the Director and staffs of chancelleries of war, all secretaries, almoners, chaplains, postmasters, doctors, surgeons, apothecaries, officers serving in the hospitals, and all servants. Such individuals if captured were to be returned to their own forces. Savory 462–464. For other references to this convention, known also as the Cartel of Sluys, see 2 HMC Rutland 230, 238, 251.

[15] 7 Well. G.O. 100 (24 May 1815); 8 Well. *Disp.* 107.

[16] Gen. Marquess of Wellington to Earl Bathurst, SS, 13 Apr. 1813, 6 Well. *Disp.* 420, 421.

One of the worst impediments to the free movement of the host came from the unhappy practice that then prevailed of allowing corps on foreign service to take with them a proportion of soldiers' wives—four or six per company. Forty or sixty of these women, mostly mounted on donkeys, formed the most unmanageable portion of every regimental train. They were always straggling or being left behind, because they could not keep up with the long marches that the army had often to take. Wayside tragedies of this sort are to be found recorded in almost every Peninsular memoir—often of the most harrowing sort. In especial we may mention the number of these poor women who dropped in the Corunna retreat, and died in the snow, or fell into the hands of the French. The interesting little book of a married sergeant of the 42nd, who took his wife about with him during the last three years of the war, is full of curious little shifts and anxieties that they went through. The best description of this curious stratum of the Peninsular Army that I know is in the autobiography of Bell of the 34th.

. . . .

The soldiers' wives were indeed an extraordinary community—as hard as nails, expert plunderers, furious partisans of the supreme excellence of their own battalion, much given to fighting. Many of them were widows twice and even thrice over—for when a married man was shot, and his wife was a capable and desirable person, she would receive half a dozen proposals before her husband was forty-eight hours in his grave. And since the alternative was a hazardous voyage back to relatives in England or Ireland, who had probably broken off with the "girl who ran away with a soldier," most of the widows concluded to stop with the battalion, with a new spouse and a new name. As the war dragged on many of the men picked up Portuguese and Spanish helpmates, who joined the regimental drove, and made it strangely polyglot. At the end of the struggle in 1814 there was a most harrowing scene at Bordeaux, when the general order was issued that all these foreigners who could not prove that they had been legitimately married to soldiers, with the colonel's leave, were to be refused transport to the British Isles. There were hundreds of them, and only in a few cases could the men find money to get them taken home in private merchantmen. The bulk marched back to the Peninsula in charge of a brigade of homeward bound Portuguese—a most melancholy and distressful assembly.

It is extraordinary to find that a sprinkling of the officers of the Peninsular Army were unwise enough to take their wives with them to the front—thereby securing a life of wearing anxiety for both, and of dire hardship for the poor ladies. One of the best known cases was that of Hill's senior aide-de-camp, Captain Currie, whose wife I have found mentioned half a dozen times as making tea for the second division staff, and holding a little reception whenever the division was settled down for a few days. Another was Mrs. Dalbiac, wife of the colonel of the 4th Dragoons, whose adventures on the field of Salamanca are mentioned by Napier. But the best chronicle of the ups and downs of a young married couple may be found in the breezy autobiography of Sir Harry Smith, then a subaltern in the 95th Rifles. His tale is well known—he rescued a young Spanish lady among the horrors of the sack of Badajoz, married her two days later, and had her with him for the remaining three years of the war. The story of their Odyssey, as related by him, is one of the most touching narratives of loyal love, and hardship cheerfully borne, that any man can read. They lived together for forty years in storm and sunshine, and she survived to christen the town of Ladysmith by her name, while her husband was commanding the forces in South Africa. He gave his name to the sister town of Harrismith, less well remembered now than the long-besieged place with which the memory of Juana Smith is linked.[17]

The task of portraying Wellington's Army as it actually was differs markedly from, because so very much easier than, the effort to picture the British forces that were engaged in the War of American Independence. That is because there are so many more detailed accounts by eyewitnesses of the later struggle, a circumstance that appears to have resulted from three distinct factors.

First, the Peninsular and other campaigns against Napoleon

---

[17] Pp. 274, 275–277 (footnotes omitted). It seems worthwhile to quote the paragraph next following (pp. 277–278):

"There is a sketch in Paris by the well-known artist, Colonel Lejeune, who, when a prisoner at Elvas, made a drawing of an English military family which passed him. As he describes it in his diary, 'The captain rode first on a very fine horse, warding off the sun with a parasol: then came his wife very prettily dressed, with a small straw hat, riding on a mule and carrying not only a parasol, but a little black and tan dog on her knee, while she led by a cord a she-goat, to supply her with milk. Beside madame walked her Irish nurse, carrying in a green silk wrapper a baby, the hope of the family. A grenadier, the captain's servant, came behind and occasionally poked up the long-eared steed of his mistress with a staff. Last in the procession came a donkey loaded with much miscellaneous baggage, which included a tea-kettle and a cage of canaries; it was guarded by an English servant in livery, mounted on a sturdy cob and carrying a long posting-whip, with which he occasionally made the donkey mend its pace.' If this picture is not exaggerated, it certainly helps us to understand the strong objection which Wellington had for ladies at the front, and all forms of impedimenta."

added up to a victorious war, hence the hardships and early set-backs only enhanced the sweetness of ultimate victory. Second, the level of national literacy had been steadily rising over the years, and even though an amazingly high percentage of private soldiers in the British Army could neither read nor write as late as the Crimean War,[18] many enlisted men who fought in Wellington's ranks added their memoirs to the rest, while all that was written at every social and military level found an ever widening audience avid for personal reminiscences of the incidents of what was obviously the most satisfactory series of campaigns on land in many years of British history.[19] Third, by 1808 the type of man who had enlisted in the ranks prior to the Napoleonic Wars had been pretty well killed off, and thereafter, under the pressure of wartime legislation designed to fill up the Army, men of much better education joined first the militia and then the regular forces. A very considerable proportion of the memoir-writers from the ranks were ex-militiamen.[20]

Even the Field Marshal's judge advocate, F. Seymour Larpent, Esq., whom we saw briefly above as a reluctant guest of the French, was among those who broke into print. His letters, posthumously published, provide a particularly revealing account of daily Army life, because, written by a civilian wholly unacquainted with military matters, they describe in detail much routine that professional soldiers simply took for granted and hence never troubled to record.[21]

Larpent's letters reflect a distinctly non-humanitarian attitude;

---

[18] De Fonblanque *Admin.* 239, note (written in 1858): "Out of 73,000 men in the infantry of the line, including non-commissioned officers, 20,000 can neither read nor write; 13,000 can read only; 38,000 can read and write with more or less proficiency, and 2,000 are of 'superior education;' by which should be understood that degree of education which would fit them for the lower branches of mercantile or other civil employment, and for regimental clerkships."

[19] Appendix III, "Peninsular Autobiographies, Journals, Letters, Etc.," in Oman (published in 1913). No effort has been made to supplement this listing with even the more significant works in the same category published in the more than fifty years following.

[20] I owe this information to the kindness of Mr. S. G. P. Ward. For the scope and effect of the legislation in question, see 1 Clode M.F. 283–305.

[21] All references herein are to the 3d edition, London 1854. For Larpent's career, see DNB; Larpent iii–xiv. Wellington asked for a judge advocate in July 1812 (F.M. Earl of Wellington to Earl Bathurst, SS, 25 July 1812, 5 Well. *Disp.* 761); Larpent joined in November (Larpent 23; 4 Well. G.O. 219, 221, "with the allowances of a Colonel"); but when Wellington asked for him again during the Waterloo campaign he was not available (F.M. Duke of Wellington to Earl Bathurst, SS, Brussels, 25 June 1815, 8 Well. *Disp.* 119). After Waterloo, John Greathead Harris, Esq., a barrister of the Middle Temple called on 28 Jan. 1800 (2 *Register of Admissions,* 415), was appointed DJA (7 Well. G.O. 175, 1 Aug. 1815).

to lapse anachronistically into modern idiom, he was anything but a bleeding heart. He could write periodically without any apparent emotion of busy days of hanging and flogging,[22] and after fourteen months with the Army he reported in all calmness that "I am only aware of forty-one having been shot or hung since my arrival in the country."[23] And, surely most characteristic because completely unconscious, when he rode over the battlefield of Vitoria in June 1813, and was appealed to for succor by wounded soldiers who thought him a surgeon because of his black plume, Larpent simply removed the plume and rode on.[24]

But this is a study of jurisdictional limitations. Accordingly, it is necessary to forgo digressions, however tempting and attractive, into prevailing attitudes toward crime and punishment, or into the light that Wellington's *Dispatches* cast on his disciplinary views. But one legal change affecting British forces abroad must be noted, which took effect a few years before Lieutenant-General Sir Arthur Wellesley was appointed to command the Army in the Peninsula.

By 1802, while the Mutiny Act and the Articles of War promulgated pursuant thereto were operative at home and in the dominions abroad, troops on active service in foreign countries were governed by the prerogative Articles of War. After 1746 or 1747, as has been seen,[25] a single set applied both on British soil as well as in foreign parts, but the legal position was different; this appears from the case of *Barwis* v. *Keppel*,[26] an action by a serjeant against a major for an allegedly wrongful reduction to the ranks while serving in Germany, in which the Court of King's Bench in 1761 held that neither the Mutiny Act nor the Articles of War made thereunder applied to the Army when engaged in war abroad. The Court held that it had no jurisdiction whatever:

> By the Act of Parliament to punish mutiny and desertion the King's power to make articles of war is confined to his own dominions; when his army is out of his dominions, he acts by virtue of his prerogative, and without the statute or articles of war; and therefore you cannot argue upon either of them, for they are both to be laid out of this case, and flagrante bello, the common law has never interfered with the

---

[22] Larpent 69, 74, 78, 239, 244.
[23] Larpent 345.
[24] Larpent 159.
[25] *Supra*, pp. 21–22.
[26] 2 Wils. K.B. 314.

army: inter arma silent leges. We think (as at present advised) we have no jurisdiction at all in this case; . . .[27]

Then, in 1803, consequent upon the Peace of Amiens, in order to provide for the government of the troops who had not yet been brought home, and who following the peace could no longer be governed by prerogative articles, that power having been suspended on the conclusion of the peace, the Mutiny Act and the statutory Articles of War were extended to the Army whether within or without the dominions of the Crown.[28] Later, after the resumption of hostilities, the same principle was applied in 1813 to the troops wherever stationed.[29] Thereafter all the forces were governed by Articles of War that rested on explicit statutory authority.[30]

It is now appropriate to look to the trials of civilians by general court-martial that are set out in Lord Wellington's general orders, and then to consider the legal bases underlying those trials.

During the Peninsular War, more civilian officials and employees were tried by general court-martial than camp followers, twenty-two of the former (eight of whom were officers of the medical services) as against only twelve camp followers. Of the latter group two alone were women, one of them a soldier's wife.[31] In respect of the civil officers tried, the punishments adjudged ranged from cashiering and dismissal (combined with confinement where their offenses involved embezzlement), down to mere reprimands. On one occasion, when a hospital mate was sentenced to be put at the bottom of the list of hospital mates in the Peninsula, the Commander of the Forces returned the proceedings for revision on the ground that this was no punishment at all and hence no deterrent: "These gentlemen, as far as I know, assume no command over each other, nor do they rise by seniority." [32]

During the Waterloo campaign, no trials of civilians by general

---

[27] 2 Wils. K.B. at 318.

[28] 43 Geo. III c. 20, preamble.

[29] 53 Geo. III c. 17, §146.

[30] The foregoing paragraphs are drawn from the discussion in MML 1914, pp. 13–14; MML 1929, pp. 13–14; and MML, Part II, Sec. I, pp. 9–10, pars. 29–32 (1958).

[31] Nos. 12 and 15 in Appendix III, where all the trials of civilians by general court-martial appearing in Wellington's General Orders are enumerated in detail. As in Chs. V and VI, it has seemed more convenient thus to avoid a great repetition of references.

[32] Gen. Marquess of Wellington to Maj.-Gen. Baron Bock, 20 Mar. 1813, 6 Well. Disp. 371, 372.

court-martial are recorded. Two Deputy Assistant Commissaries General were summarily dismissed without trial for having left their units during the battle itself.[33]

The three years of the Army of Occupation yielded up only nine trials of civilians by general court-martial, five of them civil officers, the other four followers (including one soldier's wife who was acquitted).[34]

These distinctly low figures are not to be taken as establishing that the civilians who accompanied the forces of the commander who in 1814 took his seat in the House of Lords simultaneously as a member of all five ranks in the peerage were better behaved than those who had followed or served with the British Army in earlier conflicts. All that the later figures show is that the general court-martial was resorted to by Wellington only for capital offenses committed by followers, and for offenses that appeared to warrant dismissal or cashiering of the civil officers in the event that they were convicted. Most of the lesser crimes of which the accompanying civilian followers, male and female, were guilty, were dealt with by two other means, neither of which left (or was likely to leave) much residue by way of records.

Many, many cases were relegated to the tender mercies of regimental courts-martial, tribunals whose punishing power was limited by the Mutiny Act to sentences not exceeding three hundred lashes. The reason for not sending every charge of crime to a general court-martial was articulated in one of Larpent's letters. After describing a scheme to plunder, "I said that they could only be flogged for this," meaning that the offense was not capital. "Lord Wellington therefore said they might as well be tried in their regiment, for three hundred lashes was as good as a thousand, and that to publish these things was only to put similar ideas into other people's heads." [35] In this connection it is well to note another of Larpent's remarks, which cautions against taking too literally the more severe of the corporal sentences adjudged: "I have presented four Courts-martial to Lord Wellington, . . . and confirmed three, two against one man—together, two thousand lashes. This is absurd, he will bear six or seven hundred, and there it will end." [36]

[33] 7 Well. G.O. 135 (23 June 1815); 7 *id.* 138 (24 June 1815); F.M. Duke of Wellington to Earl Bathurst, SS, 23 June 1815, 8 Well. *Disp.* 163.

[34] No. 33; see the discussion *infra*, pp. 204–205.

[35] Larpent 198.

[36] Larpent 80.

The other essentially unreported instrumentality for enforcing discipline was the Provost Marshal, who had authority to punish summarily any member of the Army actually observed in the commission of a crime, usually plundering.[37] This authority on occasion included orders to execute offenders without trial.[38]

Larpent notes an instance of the latter form of enforcement in March 1814 where the order of execution was given by the Commander of the Forces himself: "Lord Wellington had him shot in the most impressive manner this morning, before all the corps, after a solemn admonition and much parade. The man, it is said, appeared absolutely dead from fear before a musquet was fired."[39] Three other warrants for the execution of plunderers without trial were recorded in November 1813, the last one with this macabre touch, that the accomplice of the plundering soldier "did the office of executioner, and afterwards received 36 lashes, under the direction of the Assistant Provost Marshal, at the head quarters of the army."[40]

There were few jurisdictional problems, certainly none that was recognized as such. The whole of the Peninsular campaign was waged in Spain and Portugal, both of which were friendly countries, except for the last few months in France, where the government of the Bourbon monarchy was restored just as soon as Wellington's troops beat back the forces of Napoleon.

The rule universally applied by Lord Wellington was that, for offenses committed by members of his forces in Portugal, they were amenable to the courts of that country, and would be turned

---

[37] General Orders, 1 Nov. 1811, 3 Well. G.O. 225–227; 5 Well. *Disp.* 347 n.

[38] 5 Well. *Disp.* 577 n. (Bajadoz, 7 Apr. 1812); 7 *id.* 142 (St. Pé, 15 Nov. 1813). Twenty years earlier, during the Duke of York's campaign in the Low Countries, two soldiers had been executed without trial for the murder of a woman and her child. H.R.H. the Duke of York to King George III, St. Amand, 11 Apr. 1794; 2 Aspinall 194–195 (No. 1045).

[39] Larpent 459.

[40] 7 Well. *Disp.* 129, 130, 131.

The reason for the form of punishment visited on the accomplice appears more clearly from a letter of King George III to the Duke of Portland, then Home Secretary, dated 14 June 1795 (2 Aspinall 355, No. 1259):

"I am now fully master as to the question of the sentence of death by a Military Court Martial. There being no military man to perform the ignominious office of hangman, the sentence of course, if confirmed, is executed by shooting the prisoner. Even when our troops are on the Continent, if found guilty of maroding, which is looked on as a civil offence, it is executed by obtaining one of the hangmen attending the German troops to execute the sentence, we having no one of that description with the British troops, and no soldier of any nation would lend himself to such an employment."

over to the Portuguese government on request,[41] notwithstanding the circumstance that in fact they would be held there for many months without trial, and this in perfectly abominable prisons.[42] Nowhere in Wellington's dispatches is there the slightest trace of any doctrine, of international law or otherwise, that friendly foreign forces enjoy immunity from domestic criminal jurisdiction.[43] If the Portuguese made no demand for delivery of the offenders, they would be tried by court-martial, even though this involved the countervailing difficulty that such tribunals were not recognized by Portuguese law, with the result that it was impossible to compel the attendance of the very inhabitants who were so often the victims of those on trial.[44] And, of course, there were certain charges which in practice could not usefully be sent to a court-martial: "Excepting in cases in which it appears that there has been some gross and flagrant departure from the laws of hospitality, or violence has been used, or gross fraud practised, it does not answer to bring cases of seduction under the cognizance of the military tribunals." [45]

The same general approach characterized the Waterloo cam-

---

[41] See the following letters, most of them to Sir C. Stuart, H.B.M. Minister at Lisbon: 4 Well. *Disp.* 31 (24 Apr. 1810); 4 *id*. 502 (5 Jan. 1811); 6 *id*. 381 (25 Mar. 1813); 6 *id*. 494 (18 May 1813); 6 *id*. 515 (6 June 1813). And see Larpent 97 (24 Apr. 1813): "The Portuguese Government have got bolder, and have tried some of our people by their laws, when caught in the act, and have sent two or three of them to the coast of Africa. If this were generally known, it would do more good, I believe, than our flogging."

[42] More letters to Minister Stuart: 4 Well. *Disp.* 611 (20 Feb. 1811); 5 *id*. 306 (4 Oct. 1811); 6 *id*. 616 (20 July 1813).

[43] This is a vexed question, currently at rest under the compromise effected by NATO Status of Forces arrangements and similar agreements, which is far too complicated for treatment here. See, e.g., *The Schooner Exchange* v. *M'Faddon*, 7 Cranch 116; *Chung Chi Cheung* v. *The King*, [1939] A.C. 160; *Reference re Exemption of U.S. Forces from Canadian Criminal Law*, [1943] 4 Dom. L.R. 11; cf. *Wilson* v. *Girard*, 354 U.S. 524. On a realistic view, the friendly nation today can obtain complete immunity primarily when its assistance is very urgently required by the receiving state in time of actual war. Compare the Visiting Forces (British Commonwealth) Act, 1933 (23 Geo. V c. 6) and the Allied Forces Act, 1940 (3 & 4 Geo. VI c. 51) with the United States of America (Visiting Forces) Act, 1942 (5 & 6 Geo. VI c. 31), and all three in turn with the Visiting Forces Act, 1952 (15 & 16 Geo. VI & 1 Eliz. II c. 67). In this connection it is illuminating to consider the position of the British forces in France during the First World War, who were never subjected to French law. See, generally, G. P. Barton, *Foreign Armed Forces: Immunity from Supervisory Jurisdiction*, 26 Br. Y. B. Int. L. 380; G. P. Barton, *Foreign Armed Forces: Immunity from Criminal Jurisdiction*, 27 *id*. 186; G.I.A.D. Draper, *Civilians and the NATO Status of Forces Agreements* (Leyden, 1966).

[44] Letter to Minister Stuart, 5 Well. *Disp.* 306 (4 Oct. 1811); 6 *id*. 312 (22 Feb. 1813); 6 *id*. 353 (15 Mar. 1813).

[45] Letter to Minister Stuart, 4 Well. *Disp.* 730 (8 Apr. 1811).

paign. On 14 June 1815 it was announced in orders that "As the Army is about to enter the French Territory, The Field Marshal desires it may be understood by the Troops of the several Nations composing the Army which he has the honor to Command, that their Sovereigns are in alliance with the King of France; and that France therefore must be considered as a friendly Country." [46] Earlier, while the forces were still in the Netherlands, and at this time Belgium and Holland were a single country under a single monarch, the Duke of Wellington indicated that members of his forces committing offenses, whether soldier or soldier's wife, would be delivered over to the Netherlands government at the request of their King.[47] Indeed, in one instance where two soldiers had been acquitted by court-martial of murdering a local civilian, the Duke would not confirm the acquittal until the proceedings had been submitted to the King of the Netherlands and the latter "should be satisfied that the matter has been sufficiently investigated." [48]

The amenability of camp followers to military law was broadly asserted throughout the period considered in the present chapter. Here was Larpent's letter home from St. Jean de Luz early in 1814:

> A party of our suttling merchants here behaved ill the other night, by insulting a sick officer; the worst among them escaped. One is now in confinement, and I have sent in his charge. They are all in a terrible fright of military law. Most probably he will not be tried if he makes an apology; but it has answered Lord Wellington's intention by convincing these men that there is law here, and that they are followers of the army and liable to that law.[49]

A little later, the Adjutant General wrote to the chief of the merchant party, in reply to the representation the latter seems to have made on behalf of his incarcerated associate; unhappily for history, Colonel Gurwood in editing the Duke's dispatches invariably deleted the names of all malefactors named therein:

> In reply I am to observe, that Mr. ——, as a follower of the army, made himself subject to the provisions of the Mutiny Act and Articles of War.

---

[46] 7 Well. G.O. 130.
[47] F.M. Duke of Wellington to Sir C. Stuart, H.B.M. Minister at Brussels, 11 May 1815, 8 Well. *Disp.* 77; same to same, 19 May 1815, 8 *id.* 95.
[48] Same to same, 9 June 1815, 8 *id.* 131.
[49] Larpent 353.

Mr. —— committed a gross and unprovoked insult against Capt. Streeruwitz, of the York chasseurs, for which he was desired to make atonement, as well as to satisfy the inkeeper of the "Cerf," whom he had forced to leave his house at night, for safety. Mr. —— delayed complying with those injunctions, and absconded to avoid the consequence of disobedience of orders: his Excellency, under these circumstances, is under the necessity of deciding, that Mr. ——'s property is to be detained, as a security for his submitting himself to the law, when it will be immediately restored.[50]

No record of any trial appears in general orders, from which it may be concluded that the anonymous brawler on reflection made due apology. What is of greater interest is the assertion that, as a follower, he was subject to the Mutiny Act. (Sutlers, of course, had been specifically mentioned in the Articles of War for many years.) [51]

In actual fact, followers at this time were not so much as mentioned in the Mutiny Act. In 1809, true, commissaries and storekeepers had been expressly made subject to military law for embezzlement while serving with the Army.[52] But it was only in July 1813, in response to Wellington's repeated requests for means less cumbersome than the Mutiny Act's thirteen-member general court-martial to deal with marauders at isolated stations,[53] that Parliament authorized detachment courts-martial of three officers, to deal with offenses "done or committed against the Property or Person of any Inhabitant of or Resident in" places beyond the seas out of H.M.'s dominions, "by any Non Commissioned Officer, Soldier or other Person serving with or belonging to H.M.'s Armies in the Field." [54]

---

[50] AG to Mr. O'Connell, merchant, 20 Jan. 1814, 7 Well. *Disp.* 277. Mr. S. G. P. Ward advises that Col. Gurwood, the editor of the Duke's *Dispatches*, "always calls this officer 'Strenuwitz' but correctly spelled he is really 'Streeruwitz.'"

[51] *Supra*, pp. 13, 16, 22.

[52] 49 Geo. III c. 12, §101; see 1 Clode M.F. 181–182; testimony of Mr. Clode, *supra*, n. 6, at 252, ¶25.

[53] Viscount Wellington to Lt.-Col. Torrens, Mil. Sec., 4 Aug. 1811, 5 Well. *Disp.* 200; same to Earl of Liverpool, SS, 10 June 1812, 5 *id.* 704; Marquess of Wellington to Earl Bathurst, SS, 10 Feb. 1813, 6 *id.* 295; same to same, 13 Apr. 1813, 6 *id.* 422–423.

[54] 53 Geo. III c. 99, §1. Wellington also repeatedly urged legislation to authorize courts-martial to consider written evidence for essentially the same reasons. Marquess of Wellington to the AG of the Forces, 3 Feb. 1813, 6 Well. *Disp.* 277, 278; same to Earl Bathurst, SS, 10 Feb. 1813, 6 *id.* 295, 296; same to same, 16 Mar. 1813, 6 *id.* 359–360. But that power was never granted and is still unavailable, except in certain limited instances in connection with the modern court-martial appeal. See MML 1965, pp. 742, 778, 787. Contrariwise, American courts-martial

Here was the first statutory mention of camp followers—but one strictly limited as to places and class of offenses. These same detachment court-martial provisions were, effective in March 1814, introduced into the Mutiny Act, where they remained for many years.[55] But neither the jurisdiction of general courts-martial as to persons nor that of detachment courts-martial as to offenses seems ever to have been enlarged by Parliament.

Military amenability of such civilians as failed to fall within the narrow terms of the detachment court-martial provision had a different—and wholly non-statutory—basis, a circumstance frankly disclosed in a work published in London in 1816. One E. Samuel, in *An Historical Account of the British Army, and of the Law Military*, after quoting the camp follower Article of War, then Article 3 of Section 24, wrote:

> The second description of persons, to which the Article refers, namely, "*sutlers*, and *retainers* to the *camp*, and persons serving with the *King's* armies in the field," though they should not be enlisted soldiers, are subject to military orders, not by the letter of the Mutiny Act, but by the usage and customs of war.
>
> . . . .
>
> Every one of the persons specified are subject, by the second branch of this Article, to military command, and as a necessary resulting consequence to military law; so that the proof of their submission to the one, would seem decisive of their subjection to the other.
>
> . . . .
>
> This Article, so far as it respects sutlers and retainers, and persons serving the armies in actual service and in the field, does not attach to the same persons, in cantonments, or in barracks at home, or in similar establishments, which are of a permanent and domestic nature abroad, where the ordinary laws have their force, and are administered through the medium of the civil courts.[56]

Here was a rationalization of the jurisdiction over civilian camp followers, one that should have been obvious to everyone who had

---

have been able to receive depositions in non-capital cases since 1779, and since 1916 deposition evidence has also been available to the accused in capital cases. Res. of 16 Nov. 1779, 15 J. Cont. Cong. 1277, 1278; AW 10 of 1786; AW 74 of 1806; AW 91 of 1874; AW 25 and AW 26 of 1916, 1920, and 1948; Art. 49 UCMJ.

[55] They were incorporated in 54 Geo. III c. 25 as §21, and remained in the Mutiny Act without change through 1859. See *infra*, pp. 211–212.

[56] Pp. 691, 694, 695.

ever examined the provisions of successive Mutiny Acts over more than a hundred and twenty-five years. In fact, however, the true basis of such jurisdiction had been pretty consistently blurred, first by a series of lay Judge Advocates General, who assumed without more that the Articles of War supplied an independent basis of jurisdiction wholly apart from whatever the current Mutiny Act may have provided; and, second, by commanders in the field, whose concern did not extend beyond the indispensable necessity of disciplining the substantial number of undisciplined followers who accompanied, and mingled with, their troops.

One does not expect a commander, even a Commander in Chief, to differentiate between a jurisdiction conferred by the Mutiny Act and one resting on the common law of war. But it seems strange in retrospect that the recognized power to hale before courts-martial civilian followers who misbehaved on active service should not have been placed on a defensible legal basis prior to 1816.

Whether the distinction meant much in actual practice may well be doubted; a case arising in that very year, in the British Army of Occupation in France, affords an intriguing test.

In February 1816, three privates of the Grenadier Guards, together with Jane Richards, wife of another soldier in the same regiment, were tried in France on charges of entering a church, stealing from it, and damaging articles contained therein.[57] This was an offense, and Jane Richards was an individual, falling squarely within the terms of the detachment court-martial provision of the 1813 legislation as that had been continued in force in every subsequent Mutiny Act enacted up to the time of trial.[58] Contrariwise, Jane Richards had never been subjected by Parliament to trial by any other form of military tribunal.

Hence the question here is, was this group of four alleged offenders tried by a detachment court-martial of three officers, which had statutory jurisdiction to deal not only with the soldiers but with Jane Richards also, or by a Mutiny Act general court-martial of thirteen officers, whose powers were limited to officers and soldiers?

Unhappily for the preoccupations of those who, a century and a

---

[57] No. 33.

[58] See §21 of each of the following: 55 Geo. III c. 20; 55 Geo. III c. 108; 56 Geo. III c. 10.

half later, are concerned with military jurisdiction, no answer is available: The record of Jane Richards' trial, though looked for in a number of likely and indeed logical places, has not been found.[59]

---

[59] Jane Richards' co-accused were Privates James Lees, Thomas Roberts, and George Hill. Search under all four names in WO 71/244 and 245 (court-martial proceedings for 1816) and in WO 92/1 (index to court-martial proceedings) has proved unavailing.

CHAPTER IX

JURISDICTIONAL LAW AND PRACTICE FROM WATERLOO TO SUEZ

More than 140 years in time separate Waterloo in June 1815 from Suez in October 1956, and the chasm in ways of military life is even wider. Two revolutions over that period, the industrial first and then the scientific, effected an ever increasing tempo of change whose accelerating emanations have literally transformed almost every phase of human activity.

The epoch now under consideration began with the musket, the sailing ship, and the semaphore, and ended with radar, the nuclear submarine, and the rocket-launcher. In 1815 the issue turned on the outcome of cavalry charges against hollow squares of infantry; in 1956 it was determined by the threat of ballistic missiles with atomic warheads.

Due proportion makes it necessary sternly to resist every temptation to press these comparisons or to weigh even briefly the pervasive consequences of burgeoning technological advances. The scheme of the present work requires that all such digressions be avoided, and that the narrow line of jurisdiction, which is to say, the lawful power of military tribunals to deal with persons lacking military status, be pursued with singleness of purpose. Accordingly, even basic institutional changes must be dealt with in briefest fashion.

The disclosures of the Crimean War, even while that conflict was in progress, resulted in the passing of the Board of Ordnance, the demise of the Secretary at War, and the consolidation of all authority over the forces in the War Office.[1] Clode deplored the result, at great and learned length;[2] Fortescue, reviewing the posi-

---

[1] Abolition of Board of Ordnance, 18 & 19 Vict. c. 117; Commissariat officials and Paymaster-General placed under supervision of the Secretary of State, 18 & 19 Vict. cc. 10, 11; abolition of office of Secretary at War, 26 & 27 Vict. c. 12; 2 Clode M.F., chs. XX ("The late Board of Ordnance"), XXI ("The Office of Secretary at War"), XXIX ("The Consolidated War Office"); The War Office Act, 1870 (33 & 34 Vict. c. 17); MML 1914, pp. 161–163; MML 1929, 180–185; 13 Fortescue 169–173; De Fonblanque *Admin.* 77–86; 14 Holdsworth 114–116; H. Gordon, *The War Office* (London, 1935) *passim.*

[2] 1 Clode M.F. 384–389; 2 *id.* 197–203, 249–252, 390–430.

tion many years later, wrote scathingly of "civilian sticklers for constitutional control of military expenditure," and made the observation, obvious today—a century after Clode—that "it was a great gain to have placed the whole of the military forces under one head instead of under four different departments." [3] Consequently, under strong Secretaries of State, men of the caliber of Cardwell (who put an end to the purchase of commissions) and of Haldane (who created the Territorial Army), genuine reform was not only possible but inevitable.

Abolition of the office of Commander in Chief, creation of the Army Council and the General Staff, constitution of the Royal Air Force as a separate service, and the gradual growth of a Ministry of Defence to harness the country's war potential are all, preeminently, matters extraneous to the present study. But it is entirely appropriate to note here the change in the status of the Judge Advocate General.

After Sir Charles Morgan's death, the office became a political one; its incumbent was not only regularly a Privy Councillor, charged with advising the Sovereign on the proceedings of courts-martial, but a member of Parliament as well and one of the subordinate members of the government of the day. Thus there was always a new Judge Advocate General as successive ministries rose and fell.[4] In 1871 and 1872—shades of the pre-Restoration civilians!—the office of Judge Advocate General was temporarily held by Sir Robert Phillimore while he was simultaneously Judge of the High Court of Admiralty and Dean of the Arches.[5] Then, in 1892, the Judge Advocate General became non-political, and from that year until 1905, a period that included the whole of the South African War, the office was, apparently on the basis of the Phillimore precedent, entrusted to Sir Francis Jeune, the President of the Probate, Divorce and Admiralty Division of the High Court of Justice.[6] On the latter's retirement, the Judge Advocate General once more became a permanent official, this time under the orders of and acting as legal adviser to the Secretary of State, and no longer advising the Crown directly.[7] Finally, toward the end of the

[3] 13 Fortescue 171, 172.

[4] 2 Clode M.F. 360, 363, 365, 747–750.

[5] DNB s.v. R. J. Phillimore; 16 Holdsworth 146–147.

[6] DNB s.v. F. H. Jeune, and MML citations in the note following.

[7] MML 1914, p. 161; MML 1929, p. 181; 8 *Halsbury's Laws of England* (Lord Hailsham's 2d ed., London, 1933) 640, s.v. *Courts*, §1395. It is not possible to give later MML references to this matter, inasmuch as Section II of Part II of the current MML, entitled "The history and constitution of the forces," has not yet been printed. See MML 1965, p. 4, par. 8.

present period, he and his assistants were placed under the Lord Chancellor, so that currently the Judge Advocate General is appointed on the recommendation of, and his assistants are appointed by, the Lord Chancellor; this last change was effected by the Courts-Martial (Appeals) Act 1951,[8] which also introduced the far more revolutionary change of making the judgments of courts-martial subject to direct review in the civil courts.

Now it is time to resume the narrative of military amenability, the single facet of military life that has continued to be governed by identical considerations over the centuries: From the first Mutiny Act of 1689 down to the enactments to be considered in this chapter and the one to follow, lawful subjection of any individual or any class of persons to the jurisdiction of military tribunals has required either express statutory provision or the existence of a rule that, regardless of its source, has found recognition in the common law.[9]

THE POST-WATERLOO MUTINY ACTS

Beginning in 1809, as has already been noted, storekeepers, commissaries, their deputies and assistants "or other persons employed in the Commissariat Department" were authorized to be tried by court-martial for embezzling stores.[10] In 1818 civil officers acting under the Treasury and War Office were made similarly amenable to military law, extended in 1819 in respect of "persons hired to be employed in the Corps of Royal Engineers" and of storekeepers or other civil officers acting under the Board of Ordnance at foreign stations.[11]

Then, commencing with the Mutiny Act for 1829, there were always enumerated in one of the sections of that measure the classes of persons to whom it was applicable, i.e., who were subject to military law; here is the provision then enacted:

> That all the Provisions of this Act shall apply to all Persons employed on the Recruiting Service, receiving Pay in respect

---

[8] 14 & 15 Geo. VI c. 46, §§29–35 (appointment, qualifications, tenure, salaries, and pensions of JAG and assistants).

[9] I.e., military jurisdiction in military government situations, a rule of international law which is a part of the common law; and military jurisdiction in martial law situations, which is part of the common law of public self-defense, and is further considered below, *infra* pp. 219–226.

[10] *Supra*, p. 202.

[11] 58 Geo. III c. 11, §136; 59 Geo. III c. 9, §138; 6 Geo. IV c. 5, §§130, 138, 140; testimony of C. M. Clode, Esq., Solicitor to the War Office, in *First and Second Reports of the Court-Martial Commission, 1869* (H.M.S.O., 1869) 252, ¶¶26 and 27.

of such Service, and to the Officers and Persons now or hereafter serving and hired to be employed in the Royal Artillery and Field Train, and Master Gunner and Gunners, and Conductors of Stores, and in the Regiment of Royal Engineers, and in the Corps of Royal Sappers and Miners, and in the Corps of Royal Military Surveyors and Draftsmen, in the Ordnance and in the Commissariat Departments, and who are or shall be serving with any Part of His Majesty's Forces, at Home or Abroad, under the Command of any Officer having Commission from His Majesty, and all Storekeepers and other Civil Officers who are or shall be employed by or act under the Ordnance at any of His Majesty's Ordnance Establishments at Foreign Stations.[12]

Thereafter, in every Mutiny Act until the end, the legislative draftsman eschewed generalization in favor of particularized mention, so that it is possible to trace the organizational development of the British Army over the next fifty years simply by examining the listing of those to whom the Act applied.[13]

Thus, in 1856, there were added the Land Transport Corps and the Army Works Corps, while the abolition of the Board of Ordnance was reflected in the reference to "Persons in the War Department, who are or shall be serving with any Part of Her Majesty's Forces at home or abroad," etc.[14] In the following year the Field Train or Medical Staff Corps and Army Schoolmasters were included,[15] while in 1858 the Land Transport Corps and the Army Works Corps were dropped, and the Field Train, the Medical Staff Corps, the Hospital Corps, the Military Train, and Armourer Serjeants were added.[16] In 1859 Probationary Armourers were added, and the earlier commissaries and the like were redesignated as "all Officers and Persons who are or shall be serving on the Commissariat Staff and in the Commissariat Corps."[17]

Almost every year saw some change as the Crimean lessons were

---

[12] 10 Geo. IV c. 6, §28.

Beginning with the Mutiny Act for 1847, 10 & 11 Vict. c. 12, this enumeration appeared in Sec. 2; and it remained in Sec. 2 as long as the Mutiny Act was annually enacted.

[13] The Mutiny Act for 1830 (11 Geo. IV & 1 Will. IV c. 7, §29) added the troops of the East India Company while present in any part of the United Kingdom.

[14] 19 & 20 Vict. c. 10, §2; 1 Clode M.F. 277; 13 Fortescue 224–226.

[15] 20 Vict. c. 13, §2; 1 Clode M.F. 277; 13 Fortescue 552–554.

[16] 21 & 22 Vict. c. 9, §2; 1 Clode M.F. 278.

[17] 22 Vict. c. 4, §2; 1 Clode M.F. 276–277; 13 Fortescue 554.

taken to heart. In 1860, the former "Royal Artillery and Field Train" was changed to "Royal Artillery and Military Store Department," [18] while in 1862 the long overdue consolidation of Engineer officers with their troops was reflected in the reference to "Royal Engineers." [19] (Mention of Indian forces in the Mutiny Act of the United Kingdom, first appearing in 1863, is a matter more conveniently deferred to the section following.)

Warrant officers were first specifically mentioned in 1865,[20] the Military Store Staff Corps in 1866,[21] and the Commissariat Staff Corps in 1867.[22] The first appearance of the Army Service Corps is in the Mutiny Act for 1869[23] of the Control Department in that for 1871,[24] and of the Army Hospital Corps in the measure for 1872.[25] With the Mutiny Act for 1876, which included the Commissariat and Ordnance Store Departments,[26] the statutory recital was not further altered.

Clode, reviewing most of the foregoing changes in 1869, complained that "The military element has extinguished the Civil element, and the Mutiny Act, like Aaron's rod, has swallowed up all other principles of governing men in any degree connected with the Army." [27]

If indeed the Mutiny Act had reached its tentacles into Whitehall, there might have been substance to the foregoing lament. In fact, however, the statutory provisions for military amenability of civil officers accompanying the forces reflected the essential artificiality of continuing them in a civilian status, and thus it anticipated, as it may well have hastened, their ultimate militarization—which surely was long overdue. The paymaster, the doctor, the member of the Royal Army Service Corps, may lack the glam-

---

[18] 23 Vict. c. 9, §2; 1 Clode M.F. 276–277. This Act also added out-pensioners at Chelsea Hospital while engaged in suppressing civil disturbances.

[19] 25 Vict. c. 5, §2.

[20] 28 Vict. c. 11, §2.

[21] 29 & 30 Vict. c. 9, §2.

[22] 30 & 31 Vict. c. 13, §2. The corresponding provision of the Mutiny Act for 1868 may be found at 1 Clode M.F. 528–529.

[23] 32 Vict. c. 4, §2. But the Army Service Corps was not placed on its present footing until 1888. 13 Fortescue 565–566.

[24] 34 Vict. c. 9, §2.

[25] 35 Vict. c. 3, §2.

[26] 39 Vict. c. 8, §2. The amenability provision of the Mutiny Act for 1875 is set forth in Simmons §59.

[27] 1 Clode M.F. 183. He had testified before the Courts-Martial Commission in 1868 to the same effect; *supra*, n. 11, at 250.

our of the foot soldier or the gunner, but all are equally part of the Army, and it is therefore imperative to the discipline and effectiveness of the forces in the field that all be subject to the same law.

Yet the scope of the painfully detailed enumerations in the annual Mutiny Acts seems to have been subject to misunderstanding, as the case of *Wolton* v. *Gavin*,[28] decided by the Court of Queen's Bench late in 1850, plainly shows. This was an action for false imprisonment that raised two issues, first whether the plaintiff had been duly enlisted, second whether the terms of AW 20, an old provision forbidding any commanding officer to refuse to receive prisoners delivered by an officer with an account in writing, served to exculpate the defendant, a Major, Royal Artillery. But the members of the Court, while upholding a judgment in the defendant's favor, made observations that are difficult to reconcile with the plain language of the amenability provisions of the statute. Lord Campbell, C.J., said, "I think . . . that none are bound by the Mutiny Act or the Articles of War except Her Majesty's forces; and I am most anxious as a constitutional Judge, that this should be fully understood to be my opinion." And Erle, J., though dissenting on another point, noted that "It is conceded that the Mutiny Act and the Articles of War apply only to military men." [29]

What was said elsewhere in the several judgments quite sufficed to decide the case at bar, plainly enough; but, equally plainly, the quoted expression did not take into account the subjection of numerous civilians to military law by the clear terms of the statute. Clode indeed indicated as much,[30] though perhaps with more diffidence than does the present text.

Mention must also be made of the detachment court-martial, already noted in the preceding chapter, on which had been conferred jurisdiction over "Persons serving with or belonging to His Majesty's Armies," limited first as to place, beyond H.M.'s dominions, and second as to offenses, which were only those committed against the property or persons of inhabitants or residents of such places. First enacted in 1813, those provisions were carried into the Mutiny Act for 1814,[31] and were continued thereafter without change through 1859. In 1860 the locale in which jurisdiction was

---

[28] 16 Q.B. 48.
[29] 16 Q.B. at 61, 70.
[30] Clode M.L. 94: "The expression of Lord Campbell's opinion, as given in Wolton *v.* Gavin . . . should be received with some caution."
[31] *Supra*, pp. 202–203; Clode M.L. 99–100.

granted was changed to "any Place beyond Seas"; jurisdiction as to persons and offenses remained limited as before;[32] and in that new form the provision for detachment courts-martial continued as long as an annual Mutiny Act was passed by Parliament.

It hardly needs to be repeated that the detachment court-martial had a very limited scope. There never was any doubt about the amenability to military law of followers on active service, whatever may have been the case concerning its supporting articulation. All the detachment court-martial did in such situations was to provide a less cumbersome tribunal to try this class of offenders. Thereafter, it remained available to deal with misbehaving followers on foreign soil even in time of peace, but, after the Army of Occupation in France was dissolved in 1818, there were few if any instances of British troops so stationed.[33]

But the position in respect of subjecting followers on active service to military law remained unchanged, particularly in substance. Here is what Assistant Commissary General de Fonblanque wrote shortly after the close of the Crimean War:

> Not only the officers and soldiers of the army, but all persons attached to it or in immediate connexion with it, become amenable to martial law for the infraction of established regulations. Thus sutlers and other camp followers are liable to be tried and punished by courts-martial, although they are not and never were soldiers; and in like manner persons attached to the departments of the army in civil capacities are subject to military jurisdiction while so employed.[34]

And, he added in a footnote,

> This is not as generally known as it should be. Of the tribes of civilians sent out to join the army in various capacities during the late war, the majority objected to submit to military discipline, and refused to acknowledge their liability to

---

[32] 23 Vict. c. 9, §12; Simmons §§278–279.

[33] See Carey 85, ¶95: "Again, in reference to detachment general courts-martial, they may be held at any place beyond seas for the trial of any person under the immediate command of an officer and for one special class of offence there named, provided that there is not any civil judicature in force competent to deal with the matter.

"96. It is a fixed rule that these special military courts are not to be assembled at any place abroad *within* H.M.'s dominions where there is, under H.M.'s authority, a competent civil judicature in force. This does not apply to places without H.M.'s dominions. . . ."

[34] De Fonblanque *Admin.* 215.

military law, with a pertinacity which it frequently required the practical arguments of the provost-marshal to bend.

JURISDICTION OVER FOLLOWERS OF THE INDIAN ARMY

Two Acts of Parliament in the eighteenth century subjected the officers and soldiers in the service of the Honourable East India Company to military law, but neither so much as mentioned followers.[35] Nor did the Act authorizing the Company to hold courts-martial on native troops mention any but officers and soldiers.[36] Then, effective 1 February 1824, there was adopted a new Mutiny Act for India, in which it was specifically provided that "licensed Sutlers and Followers, shall be at all times subject to all the Penalties and Punishments mentioned in this Act, and shall in all respects whatsoever be holden to be within the Intent and Meaning of every Part of this Act." [37]

A number of soldiers' wives were actually tried under this provision, as Lieutenant-Colonel Hough, for many years a Deputy Judge Advocate General in the East India Company's Service, duly recorded in his interesting if painfully discursive collection of precedents.[38] Much later, in fact after World War II, when the wife of an American airman in occupied Germany had been convicted by a civilian American military government court of killing her husband, she invoked those Indian trials in seeking to obtain release by habeas corpus; Mrs. Madsen accordingly stands as the only civilian woman in legal history who asked to be tried by court-martial. Her arguments proved unavailing, as the Supreme Court of the United States sustained her trial on familiar military government principles.[39] On that occasion, the law officers of the United States minimized the weight to be accorded the old Indian camp follower cases. Thereafter, when a number of other American women similarly sought release after having been convicted by the only tribunals that Mrs. Madsen had deemed competent, namely, courts-martial, these same Indian trials became transformed, in the view of successor Solicitors General of the United States, into instances of overwhelming and indeed transcendent significance. It

---

[35] 27 Geo. II c. 9; 1 Geo. III c. 14.

[36] 53 Geo. III c. 155, §§96 and 97.

[37] 4 Geo. IV c. 81, §45. Again, the next Act authorizing the discipline of native troops did not make mention of followers. 3 & 4 Will. IV c. 85, §73.

[38] W. Hough, *Precedents in Military Law* (London, 1855) 401, 402, 629–630. One of these cases is mentioned in Simmons §71 n. 6.

[39] *Madsen v. Kinsella,* 343 U.S. 341.

is a pity that the several law officers' differing versions of the trials of Martha Stevens and Hannah Fitchet in 1825, and of the trial of a Mrs. R—— that was "considered" in 1831, are not conveniently available in their entirety for the professional amusement of legal readers.[40]

During the reign of Queen Victoria, three more Indian Mutiny Acts were adopted, each of which continued to render licensed sutlers and followers subject to military law.[41] These, as Simmons pointed out, were European sutlers and followers, not natives of India.[42] For, as each of the three Acts specifically provided, "on the Trial of all Offences committed by any Native Officer or Soldier or Follower, Reference shall be had to the Articles of War framed by the Government of *India* for such Native Officers, Soldiers, or Followers, and to the established Usages of the Service." [43]

Following the Indian Mutiny, the forces of John Company were legislatively transferred to the Crown,[44] and a few years later, in 1863, the Indian Mutiny Act was expressly repealed.[45] Thereafter, the amenability of H.M.'s Indian Forces to military law was specifically set forth in §2 of each annual Mutiny Act, following the enumeration of the British forces in the same section that has already been discussed. From 1863 through 1878, which is to say, as long as there was a Mutiny Act, all sutlers and followers of the Army in India thus remained subject to military law.

---

[40] The Government's brief (i.e., written argument) in *Madsen* v. *Kinsella* asserted (U.S. Br., No. 411, Oct. T. 1951, pp. 44–45) that "the status of the wife or alleged wife of an English soldier in India in 1825 has little bearing as to whether the wife of an American soldier was regarded as subject to court-martial jurisdiction then or later." Later, in *Reid* v. *Covert*, 351 U.S. 487, the Government mentioned the Indian trials as quoted by Winthrop *133.

Then, after rehearing was granted in the case last cited, the Government argued, citing the trials from Hough (Reply Br. on Rehearing, Nos. 701 and 713, Oct. T. 1955, p. 47): "But the clearest demonstration of exercising court martial jurisdiction over women camp-followers in peace time are these in which the British tried soldiers' wives for murder." When the case was then decided in favor of the relator (*Reid* v. *Covert*, 354 U.S. 1), and the issue once more arose in respect of a soldier's wife tried by court-martial for a non-capital offense (*Kinsella* v. *Singleton*, 361 U.S. 234), the Government's argument based on the same Indian precedents was (Appellant's Br., No. 22, Oct. T. 1959, p. 27): "British records for the period following the American Revolution likewise show the exercise of jurisdiction in the colonies (i.e., 'in the field')."

[41] 3 & 4 Vict. c. 37; 12 & 13 Vict. c. 43; 20 & 21 Vict. c. 66.

[42] Sec. 59, n. 4; see also *id.*, §§71 and 72.

[43] 3 & 4 Vict. c. 37, §8; 12 & 13 Vict. c. 43, §1 (last proviso); 20 & 21 Vict. c. 66, §1 (last proviso).

[44] 21 & 22 Vict. c. 106.

[45] 26 & 27 Vict. c. 48.

The only difference concerned the native Indian troops under the Government of India; they were never included either in the Mutiny Acts or in the later legislation enacted by the Parliament of the United Kingdom, but were governed, until the end, by Indian law.[45a]

CONSOLIDATION OF THE MILITARY CODE

The need for simplification of the elaborate and essentially repetitious provisions that had governed the land forces for so long was obvious. In 1869 a Courts-Martial Commission had surveyed the field and made recommendations,[46] but no action was taken for another decade, after the House of Commons had in 1878 constituted a Select Committee on the Mutiny and Marine Mutiny Acts.

By this time, the Mutiny Act contained no less than 110 sections [47]—far less, be it noted, than had been included in a number of earlier versions [48]—while the Articles of War promulgated in implementation of the statute numbered 187.[49] This cumbersome structure involved considerable duplication, and offered, if indeed it did not affirmatively invite, broad opportunities for inconsistencies. Yet every company commander was under a solemn duty to familiarize himself with the details of both Act and Articles.

Sir Henry Thring, later Lord Thring, was the Parliamentary Counsel who hit upon a scheme that, without in any sense impinging on the constitutional principle of Parliamentary control of the Army, placed the military code upon a sound, simple, and stable basis. First, the provisions of the Mutiny Act and Articles of War were consolidated into a single statute, the Army Discipline and Regulation Act 1879,[50] which two years later was repealed and re-enacted with some amendments as the Army Act 1881.[51] Nei-

---

[45a] Sec. 5 of 26 & 27 Vict. c. 48; Simmons 24 n.7; MML 1914, p. 194; MML 1929, pp. 238–239. The Indian Army Act 1911 mentioned in both of the references last cited was not an act of the Parliament at Westminster, it was legislation enacted in India.

[46] *Supra*, n. 11.

[47] 41 Vict. c. 10. This, the last Mutiny Act, was continued by the Mutiny Act (Temporary) Continuance Act, 1879 (42 Vict. c. 4), until the new legislation could take effect.

[48] Thus, the Mutiny Act for 1824 (5 Geo. IV c. 13), contained 159 sections, while that enacted three years later (7 & 8 Geo. IV c. 4) contained 163, plus some 14 Schedules.

[49] The numbers ran consecutively to 192, but Arts. 28, 45, 48, 144, and 187 were omitted without renumbering the remainder.

[50] 42 & 43 Vict. c. 33, hereinafter simply "ADRA."

[51] 44 & 45 Vict. c. 58. hereinafter simply "AA."

ther statute had any force of itself.[52] Therefore, second, each was required to be brought into operation annually by another Act of Parliament, first the Army Discipline and Regulation (Annual) Act, then the Army (Annual) Act, and in the last thirty years or so of the present period, the Army and Air Force (Annual) Act. Thus constitutional principle and effective regulation were both satisfied; thus, as Lord Thring wrote, "was accomplished, after the lapse of more than a century, a wish expressed by Mr. Justice Blackstone in his Commentaries, that 'it may be thought worthy the wisdom of parliament to ascertain the limits of military subjection, and to enact express articles for the government of the army, as is done for the government of the navy.' "[53]

Four substantive features of the new legislative scheme need to be mentioned.

First, although the new legislation continued the authority of the Crown to promulgate Articles of War,[54] a provision retained at the insistence of that bastion of military conservatism, Field Marshal H.R.H. the Duke of Cambridge, the Commander in Chief,[55] no further Articles of War were in fact ever promulgated; their essential and proper function of implementing the basic statute was thereafter performed by Rules of Procedure.

Second, the provost marshal article, that has been seen in operation in Europe and America during the eighteenth century[56] and in the Iberian and Crimean peninsulas in the nineteenth,[57] was legislatively abrogated.

In 1829, in an apparent effort at legitimization, the long-standing custom of the service in this area had been specifically included in the Articles of War;[58] here are the essential portions of the final version, AW 164 of 1878, respecting the provost marshal and his assistants:

> . . . their powers shall be regulated according to the established usages of war and the rules of our service, being limited to the punishment of offenders whom they detect in the actual commission of any crime. . . .

---

[52] ADRA §2; AA §2.
[53] MML, 1914, p. 14, citing 1 Bl. Comm. *416.
[54] ADRA §68; AA §69.
[55] *Report of the Select Committee on Mutiny and Marine Mutiny Acts* (H.C. 316 of 1878), Minutes of Ev., p. 10.
[56] *Supra*, pp. 17–19, 90–91.
[57] *Supra*, pp. 199, 212–213.
[58] Clode M.L. 182–183.

> . . . their duties are . . . to prevent breaches of both [good order and discipline], by soldiers and followers of the army, and to punish on the spot, on the same day, those whom they may find in the imminent act of committing breaches of good order and military discipline;—provided that the punishment be limited to the necessity of the case, and shall accord with the orders which the provost may from time to time receive from our commander of the forces in the field, and that whatever may be the crime, the provost marshal or his assistants shall see the offender commit the act for which summary punishment may be inflicted, or if the provost martial or his assistants should not actually see the offender actually commit the crime, but that sufficient proof can be established of the offender's guilt, the report shall be made to the commander of our army in the field, who is hereby empowered to deal with the case as he may deem most conducive to the maintenance of good order and military discipline.

These were strong, not to say violent, sanctions for the enlightened age of the late 1870's, as the Duke of Cambridge recognized when the new legislation proposed a change; here is what he noted in his diary on 25 June 1879:

> To the Office for a Meeting on the Army Discipline Bill, where the Provost Marshal Clause was fully discussed. It would be impossible, I fear, to pass this Clause, as we would wish to do so, and as it has been at present administered on Service, as to modern notions it is too arbitrary, but in practice it is deemed essential. The problem to solve is a very difficult one.[59]

As H.R.H. correctly recognized, the Army was fighting a rear-guard action; mid-Victorian England recoiled from the notion of summary punishment without trial. Accordingly, both the 1879 and the 1881 Acts provided:

> A provost-marshal or his assistants may at any time arrest and detain for trial persons subject to military law committing offences, and may also carry into execution any punishments to be inflicted in pursuance of a court-martial, but shall not inflict any punishment of his or their own authority.[60]

---

[59] 2 E. Sheppard, *H.R.H. George Duke of Cambridge* (London, 1906) 76. Cf. Maj.-Gen. R. Carey, formerly DJA, in H.C. 316 of 1878, Minutes of Ev. at p. 26: "I look upon this Provost Marshal article principally in reference to camp followers, and people who go about plundering a camp, or anything of that sort."

[60] ADRA §72; AA §74(2); see MML 1914, pp. 33–34; MML 1929, p. 41. It is an

Third, the detachment court-martial was abolished. The new field general court-martial of three members [61] continued the summary features of the older institution, while, fourth, the new definitions covering civilian amenability to military law sufficed to replace most of the remainder of the powers of the detachment court-martial.

There are indications that the drafters of the Army Discipline and Regulation Act contemplated that all camp followers should, like those of the Indian Army, be subject to military law.[62] In the event, equality of treatment was in fact secured, but only in more limited fashion, namely, that such subjection should take place only when the civilians concerned were on active service,[63] which was defined as "whenever [a person subject to military law] is attached to or forms a part of a force which is engaged in operations against an enemy or is engaged in military operations in a country or place wholly or partly occupied by an enemy, or is in military occupation of any foreign country." [64] That provision remained unchanged from its enactment in the Army Discipline and Regulation Act in 1879 until 1952. In that year Parliament slightly widened the scope of "active service" to reflect the facts of military life in an unsettled world, substituting for the former clause, "engaged in military operations in a country or place wholly or partly occupied by the enemy," the broader words, "engaged in a foreign country in operations for the protection of life or property." [65] And, with these definitions of "active service," the Army Act of 1881 was annually brought into force through the end of the year 1956.[66]

Interestingly enough, the amenability to military law of camp followers that was thus enacted by Parliament in 1879 was almost exactly paralleled by the contemporary state of the law in the

---

interesting reflection of the change of climate in military thinking since 1879 that Parliament did not deem it necessary to repeat in the Army Act 1955 the last clause quoted in the text, and that there has been no comment on the problem in any edition of the MML since that measure became effective.

[61] ADRA §49; AA §49.

[62] H.C. 316 of 1878, Report, p. vi, and Minutes of Ev. at pp. 48, 50, 117, 119, 129.

[63] ADRA §§168(7) and (8), 169(9) and (10); AA §§175(7) and (8), 176(9) and (10).

[64] ADRA §181; AA §189(1). It was recognized that military occupation did not necessarily mean hostile occupation. See 248 H.C. Deb. (3d ser.) 814–815.

[65] Sec. 3(1) of the Army and Air Force (Annual) Act 1952, 15 & 16 Geo. VI & 1 Eliz. II c. 24.

[66] It has not seemed necessary to consider the amenability to military law of any auxiliary forces, such as militia, volunteers, yeomanry, territorials, or any other reserve components of the Army.

United States. At this time, AW 63 of §1342 of the Revised Statutes of the United States (enacted in 1874 and revised as positive law in 1878) still continued the old camp follower article first promulgated by the Crown in 1746 or 1747, then adopted by the Continental Congress in 1775 and 1776,[67] which a century thereafter read as follows:

> All retainers to the camp, and all persons serving with the armies of the United States in the field, though not enlisted soldiers, are to be subject to orders, according to the rules and discipline of war.

The significant words here were "in the field," which the Attorney General and the Judge Advocate General and Colonel Winthrop defined as meaning "in time of war and in the theatre of war," [68] "confined both to the period and pendency of war and to acts committed on the theatre of the war." [69] These, obviously, are definitions identical in substance with the original scope of "active service" in the English legislation of 1879 and 1881.

JURISDICTION UNDER MARTIAL LAW

By "martial law" under the present heading is meant neither the law governing the armed forces, the sense in which the term was used by Blackstone and before him by Hale; [70] nor military government (or the law of belligerent occupation), the sense in which the words were used by Viscount Wellington when he wrote that "Martial law . . . is neither more or less than the will of the General of the army"; [71] but rather the public law of self-defense, the right to use military means to preserve the peace against public enemies within the jurisdiction.[72]

For many decades, of course, it was uncompromisingly laid down that martial law is unknown to the law of England; expressions to this effect appear in *Grant* v. *Gould*,[73] Mr. Curran argued

---

[67] *Supra*, pp. 22–23.

[68] 14 Op. Atty. Gen. 22; 16 *id.* 13; 16 *id.* 48; *Digest of Opinions of the Judge Advocates General of the Army* (Washington, 1880) 48–49; *id.*, 1895, pp. 75–77; *id.*, 1901, pp. 56–58; *id.*, 1912, pp. 151–152.

[69] Winthrop *136.

[70] 1 Bl. Comm. *413; M. Hale, *The History of the Common Law of England* (6th ed.; London, 1820) 42.

[71] Lt.-Gen. Visc. Wellington to Minister Stuart, 19 Apr. 1810, 4 Well. *Disp.* 23, 24; see 8 Op. Atty. Gen. 365, 366–368, *per* Cushing, A.G.

[72] 10 Holdsworth 705–713.

[73] 2 H. Bl. 69, 99: "Therefore it is totally inaccurate, to state martial law, as having any place whatever within the realm of *Great Britain*."

the same proposition eloquently in *Wolf Tone's Case*,[74] and Professor Dicey popularized and indeed broadcast the concept: " 'Martial law,' in the proper sense of that term, in which it means the suspension of ordinary law and the temporary government of a country or parts of it by military tribunals, is unknown to the law of England." [75] At home, of course, the Petition of Right [76] had ended martial law in the sense of a roving power to suspend the reign of law and to punish at will.

It was different in many British colonies, where endemic indigenous revolts engendered excesses by way of repression. Numerous early incidents of true martial law in Crown Colonies are listed in Clode; [77] the instance that most disturbed opinion at home, to the point where it resulted in a number of private criminal prosecutions, was Governor Eyre's sanguinary suppression of the revolt in Jamaica in 1865.[78] The prosecutions failed, and a civil action for damages foundered on an insurmountable obstacle, an act of indemnity passed by the Jamaica legislature.[79] The radicals of the day, persons whose outlook would today be called "liberal"—small "l"—or left wing, depending on the attitude of the person formulating the characterization, were shocked. But they would have been more shocked had they known to what extent the defense of Governor Eyre had burned into the very fiber of his counsel, Mr. Hardinge Giffard, Q.C., the view that the executive authority on the ground is to be supported, not only during crisis, but at all times thereafter.[80]

The English public generally were thereafter content, if indeed they ever again dwelled on the outcome of the Jamaica case, to read and to repeat Dicey's rounded periods—until *Ex parte Marais* [81] in 1902 once more, in even sharper fashion, focused attention on the problem. For in that decision the Judicial Committee of the Privy Council abandoned the ancient test that martial law is

---

[74] Curran, *arguendo*, 27 How. St. Tr. 613, 625: "I stand upon this sacred and immutable principle of the constitution—*that martial law and civil law are incompatible*."

[75] A. V. Dicey, *The Law of the Constitution* (8th ed., London, 1915) 283, and see ch. VIII, "Martial Law," *passim*.

[76] 3 Car. I c. 1.

[77] 2 Clode M.F. 481–511, 666–667, 360 n. 5.

[78] 10 Holdsworth 712–713; 2 Clode M.F. 490–497; and see now, for a recent discussion that collects the extensive literature on the incident, B. Semmel, *The Governor Eyre Controversy* (London, 1962).

[79] *Phillips* v. *Eyre*, L.R. 4 Q.B. 225, affirmed L.R. 6 Q.B. 1.

[80] Heuston 15–16; Semmel, *op. cit.*, *supra* n. 78, 148–150.

[81] [1902] A.C. 109.

justifiable only when the disorder it is seeking to repress has closed the courts, a test theretofore only jettisoned by legislation of very limited impact,[82] and held that the circumstance of the civil courts being open did not in and of itself bar a trial of civilians by military tribunals, even where the legislature had not spoken.[83] Their Lordships' judgment on this occasion was delivered by Governor Eyre's erstwhile counsel, then and for some years past the Earl of Halsbury, L.C.

This decision really shook the thinking of English lawyers, as a spate of articles in the *Law Quarterly Review* immediately thereafter clearly showed.[84] Unquestionably the doctrine of public self-defense implicit in the *Marais* case is now law. What is far less well known, however, is how its principle has since been applied in a series of cases arising in British colonies and in Ireland after *Marais* and until the "trouble" in the latter country subsided,[85] cases that underscore the accuracy of an American comment written a generation ago, "In the British Empire 'martial law' followed by an act of indemnity has been a device whereby servile and native uprisings have been stamped out, often with more celerity than decorum." [86]

The first of these instances involved an application by a Zulu named Mgomini, and by certain of his companions, for leave to appeal to the Judicial Committee of the Privy Council against the sentence of a military court condemning them to death. There had been discontent among the natives of Natal over the imposition of a

---

[82] See the Irish and Canadian enactments cited in Simmons §35, n. 6.

[83] In some of the Irish cases during "the trouble," the courts were hardly open in any fair sense. See *King (Childers)* v. *Adjutant General*, [1923] 1 Ir. R. 5, 15, where the court was sitting in a temporary makeshift, the courthouse itself being a crumbling ruin: "Can the Court be said to be freely functioning when it requires the protection of a military guard, when the circuits of the Judges are interfered with, and when some of the County Court Judges dare not enter their districts?"

The Supreme Court of the former independent Republic of Hawaii had anticipated the Privy Council on the point of open courts, and for much the same reason, viz., a native uprising. *In re Kalanianaole*, 10 Haw. 29. Whether that decision is now authority in the State of Hawaii may well be questioned, in view of the United States Supreme Court's decision in the World War II Hawaiian martial law cases, *Duncan* v. *Kahanamoku*, 327 U.S. 304.

[84] W. S. Holdsworth, *Martial Law Historically Considered*, 18 L.Q.R. 117; H. E. Richards, *Martial Law*, 18 L.Q.R. 133; C. Dodd, *The Case of Marais*, 18 L.Q.R. 143; F. Pollock, *What Is Martial Law?* 18 L.Q.R. 152.

[85] In the paragraphs that follow, I have drawn freely on one of my earlier books, *A Practical Manual of Martial Law* (Harrisburg, 1940).

[86] C. Fairman, *The Law of Martial Rule* (Chicago, 1930) 27–28. This first edition is to be preferred over the second, published in 1943.

poll tax, and the local police, who had made some arrests, were obstructed and resisted. In the resultant melee, some persons were killed. On the next day martial law was declared by the Natal government, the proclamation expressly providing that the local civil courts should sit. Yet the prisoners were tried by a military court for the murder of the policemen in question.

The Governor of the colony had suggested that this charge be withdrawn and the prisoners left to the processes of the ordinary courts. The ministers, however, voicing the traditional attitude, opposed. For their part they were of opinion "that any interference with the Court-martial now sitting would have disastrous effects on the natives generally. Further, that such interference would probably conduce to outbreak in the near future, as any sign of weakness or indecision on the part of the Government would immediately be observed by the natives, who for the most part are adopting a waiting attitude."

Accordingly, the prisoners were tried by a military court under martial law—for an act committed prior to the declaration of martial law. The trial took place at a great military demonstration of Cameron Highlanders, Carabineers, and Natal Field Artillery, who surrounded the court on three sides while native witnesses were testifying. It is therefore hardly necessary to repeat that the prosecution was successful in the instance now in question.

Notwithstanding all these facts, however, the Judicial Committee of the Privy Council denied leave to appeal against the judgments.[87] In part, certainly, the decision was based on the circumstance that no application for habeas corpus or for other relief had been made to the courts in Natal,[88] but the Judicial Committee were not wholly unmindful of the imperial considerations involved. As Lord Loreburn, L.C., said:

> Their Lordships are unable to advise his Majesty to grant this petition. It is not an appeal from a Court, but in substance from the act of the Executive. Evidently the responsible Government of the colony consider that a serious situation exists, for martial law has been proclaimed. The Courts of justice in the colony have not been asked to interpose, and, apart from any question of jurisdiction, any interposition of a judicial character directed with most imperfect knowledge both of

---

[87] *Mgomini* v. *Governor and Attorney General of Natal*, 22 T.L.R. 413.
[88] "Lord Davey asked how it was that, if no application had been made to the Court in Natal, the present petition came before the Board." 22 T.L.R. at 415.

the danger that has threatened, and may threaten, Natal and of the facts which came before the tribunal of war, would be inconsistent with their Lordships' duties.[89]

Doubtless the last days of Mgomini *et al.* were greatly eased by the assurances of constitutional commentators that martial law was unknown to the law of England.

Another similar case soon arose.[90] Tilonko, a Zulu chief, had been brought before the Natal military court for acts of sedition and for causing a large assembly of natives to collect and to go about the colony armed with guns, assegais, and other weapons. Upon conviction, he was sentenced to ten years' imprisonment at hard labor, and to pay a fine of 500 head of cattle. His counsel, the same who had represented the hapless Mgomini, asked for leave to appeal from this judgment, arguing that the military court was a court-martial in substance, and hence a court of justice under English law. Here also the Judicial Committee refused leave to appeal, Lord Halsbury delivering their judgment in language that was frank to the point of cynicism:

> The foundation upon which counsel for the petitioner has proceeded is a totally inaccurate analogy between the proceedings of a military court sitting under what is called the Mutiny Act, and proceedings which are not constituted according to any system of law at all. It is by this time a very familiar observation that what is called "martial law" is no law at all. The notion that "martial law" exists by reason of the proclamation—an expression which the learned counsel has more than once used—is an entire delusion. The right to administer force against force in actual war does not depend upon the proclamation of martial law at all. It depends upon the question whether there is war or not. If there is war, there is the right to repel force by force, but it is found convenient and decorous, from time to time, to authorize what are called "courts" to administer punishments, and to restrain by acts of repression the violence that is committed in time of war, instead of leaving such punishment and repression to the casual action of persons acting without sufficient consultation, or without sufficient order or regularity in the procedure in which things alleged to have been done are proved. But to attempt to make these proceedings of "courts-martial," ad-

---

[89] 22 T.L.R. at 416.
[90] *Tilonko* v. *Attorney General of Natal*, [1907] A.C. 93; s.c., 95 L.T.R. 853, 23 T.L.R. 21.

ministering summary justice under the supervision of a military commander, analogous to the regular proceedings of Courts of justice, is quite illusory. Such acts of justice are justified by necessity, by the fact of actual war; and that they are so justified under the circumstances is a fact that it is no longer necessary to insist upon, because it has been over and over again so decided by Courts as to whose authority there can be no doubt.[91]

After this second setback at the hands of the Judicial Committee, Tilonko's counsel showed himself more knowledgeable concerning the nature of martial law tribunals under English law. He then proceeded to make application to the courts of Natal for a writ of habeas corpus, and, this being refused, once more applied to the Privy Council for leave to appeal from that denial of habeas corpus. But by this time the Natal legislature had passed an act of indemnity legalizing everything done during the disturbances; this was a legislative measure that bound not only the courts of the colony but also the Privy Council. In the event, therefore, leave to appeal was denied—and Tilonko remained in jail.[92]

It may be helpful briefly to summarize the present doctrines of martial law as they appear in English decisions. As has been indicated, the ancient test of open courts as a touchstone of the legality of trials of civilians by military tribunals was abandoned in the case of *Marais*.[93] Since then the only judicial inquiry open is whether war exists, and "the test that I apply to determine whether war exists or no is this: Is the forcible resistance to authority so widespread, so continuous, so formidable, of such duration that the help of an army must be invoked, not merely in one or two instances, but habitually or constantly, lest the State shall perish?" [94]

Judicial intervention is available only on a finding that no state of war exists.[95] If a court finds that a state of war does exist, it will not interfere with the military commander in any respect during the time that the state of war continues,[96] whether the relief sought is a habeas corpus to prevent the execution of a death sentence or

---

[91] [1907] A.C. at 94–95.

[92] *Tilonko* v. *Attorney General of Natal*, 23 T.L.R. 668.

[93] *Accord, King* v. *Allen*, [1921] 2 Ir. R. 241; *King (Garde)* v. *Strickland*, [1921] 2 Ir. R. 317; *King (Ronayne & Mulcahy)* v. *Strickland*, [1921] 2 Ir. R. 333.

[94] *King (Johnstone)* v. *O'Sullivan*, [1923] 2 Ir. R. 13, 25.

[95] *King (O'Brien)* v. *Military Governor*, [1924] 1 Ir. R. 32.

[96] *Ex parte Marais*, [1902] A.C. 109; *King (Childers)* v. *Adjutant General*, [1923] 1 Ir. R. 5; cases cited in nn. 93 and 94.

shades off into merely an action for damages against the military commander because of destruction of property. Habeas corpus will be denied [97] and the civil action stayed.[98] Judicial intervention can be had only after termination of the state of war—by which time an act of indemnity will have legalized all that was done.[99]

As has been seen, under these decisions the military court for martial law situations is sharply differentiated from the court-martial established pursuant to the Army Act.[100] The former is neither a court nor a tribunal; [101] a proceeding before it, however penal, is not a criminal case; [102] it neither has nor requires any record of its proceedings; [103] and its jurisdiction cannot be restrained by writ of prohibition.[104] Its action may be *ex post facto*.[105] Its sentences normally expire with the end of the state of war,[106] though they may be legislatively extended.[107] Indeed, where any form of detention is in issue, even without a trial or a proceeding

---

[97] *King* v. *Allen*, [1921] 2 Ir. R. 241.

[98] *Higgins* v. *Willis*, [1921] 2 Ir. R. 386.

[99] Cf. *King (Ronayne & Mulcahy)* v. *Strickland*, [1921] 2 Ir. R. 333, 334.

[100] *Tilonko* v. *Attorney General of Natal*, [1907] A.C. 93; *Clifford & O'Sullivan*, [1921] 2 A.C. 570, 581: "It was not a Court Martial, that is to say, a tribunal regularly constituted under military law, but a body of military officers entrusted by the commanding officer with the duty of inquiring into certain alleged breaches of his commands contained in the proclamation, and of advising him as to the manner in which he should deal with the offenses; and its 'sentences,' if confirmed, will derive their force not from the decision of the military Court, but from the authority of the officer commanding His Majesty's forces in the field." *Per* Viscount Cave.

[101] *Mgomini* v. *Governor and Attorney General of Natal*, 22 T.L.R. 413; *Tilonko* v. *Attorney General of Natal*, [1907] A.C. 93; *Clifford & O'Sullivan*, [1921] 2 A.C. 570.

[102] *Clifford & O'Sullivan*, [1921] 2 A.C. 570.

[103] "The truth is that the whole matter rests upon the initial mistake of calling the memorandum a 'record' and treating it as if it were a record of a Court of justice. There would be no necessity, certainly in point of law, and probably not in practice, to have a written memorandum of each sentence or judgment of the Martial Law Court; certainly no such principle applies as is known to the Courts of ordinary criminal jurisdiction in respect of records, the record being itself the official and operative order which the judgment demands." *Attorney General for the Cape of Good Hope* v. *Van Reenen*, [1904] A.C. 114, 119. Is it necessary to add that this judgment was delivered by Lord Chancellor Halsbury? His style and sentiments are by this time so familiar as to render resort to the report quite superfluous.

[104] *Clifford & O'Sullivan*, [1921] 2 A.C. 570.

[105] *King* v. *Allen*, [1921] 2 Ir. R. 241 (death sentence for an offense not capitally punishable under the ordinary criminal law).

[106] *King* v. *Allen*, [1921] 2 Ir. R. 241, 273.

[107] *King (O'Connell)* v. *Military Governor*, [1935] Ir. R. 247; *King (Cooney)* v. *Clinton*, [1935] Ir. R. 245.

resembling a trial, the only question for judicial determination is whether the particular detention has statutory warrant.[108]

The proposition that martial law is unknown to the law of England assuredly makes an admirable constitutional law slogan. But, thanks in large measure to the rugged authoritarianism of the first Earl of Halsbury, who had successfully defended Governor Eyre of Jamaica while still at the bar, it is a slogan that quite fails to add up to an accurate statement of current English constitutional law.[109]

---

[108] *Liversidge* v. *Anderson,* [1942] A.C. 206; *Greene* v. *Secretary of State,* [1942] A.C. 284; *Rex* v. *Halliday,* [1917] A.C. 260; cases cited in n. 107.

[109] Search of *The Law Reports Digest* for the years 1931–1965 fails to reveal the *Marais, Mgomini,* or *Tilonko* decisions as cases judicially considered during that period.

CHAPTER X

THE ARMY AND AIR FORCE ACTS 1955

For nearly forty years after the effective date of the Army Discipline and Regulation Act 1879, military jurisdiction over civilians accompanying both British and American forces remained parallel, and extended only to such civilians as were actually with the forces "on active service" (the British term) or "in the field" (the American expression).

Then, once the American Articles of War of 1916 became effective, the military jurisdiction of the United States was expanded to cover all accompanying civilians overseas, even when not in the field, and this jurisdiction, which was exercised through the two World Wars and thereafter, was advisedly copied by the British legislation to be dealt with in this chapter. Later, the expanded American jurisdiction on which Parliament had drawn in 1955 was held unconstitutional, a result that was foreshadowed just two months before the British legislation went into effect. Here, certainly, is grist for the mill of those who insist that history is primarily a series of paradoxes and ironies.

The new American jurisdiction must now be briefly considered, because it is an indispensable predicate to an understanding of the Parliamentary measures of 1955. But to avoid intruding discussions that are essentially extraneous to the British practice—the subject matter of the present book—the details of the rise and fall of the expanded American jurisdiction, including the bulk of the citations relevant thereto, have been relegated to Appendix IV. That story is there fully set forth, not only for the information of the American reader, but also to satisfy the curiosity of any English lawyer who might be tempted to examine the course and impact of American constitutional litigation in a particularly interesting instance.

EXTENSION OF AMERICAN MILITARY JURISDICTION OVER CIVILIANS ACCOMPANYING THE ARMY ABROAD

AW 2(d) of the American Articles of War of 1916, which became effective on 1 March 1917, and which remained the same through the legislative revisions of 1920 and of 1948, provided as follows:

ART. 2. PERSONS SUBJECT TO MILITARY LAW.—The following persons are subject to these articles and shall be understood as included in the term "any person subject to military law," or "persons subject to military law," whenever used in these articles:

. . . .

(d) All retainers to the camp and all persons accompanying or serving with the armies of the United States without the territorial jurisdiction of the United States, and in time of war all such retainers and persons accompanying or serving with the armies of the United States in the field, both within and without the territorial jurisdiction of the United States, though not otherwise subject to these articles; . . .

This provision was drafted by General E. H. Crowder, Judge Advocate General of the United States Army, one of the ablest lawyers ever to hold that office, who had been occupied for more than a decade in preparing a revision of the American Articles of War, which by 1900 had become notoriously outdated.[1] He had presented such a revision to Congress in 1912, at which time draft AW 2(d) simply continued the traditional active service jurisdiction over accompanying civilians in these terms:

(d) In time of war all retainers to the camp and all persons accompanying or serving with the Armies of the United States in the field though not otherwise subject to these articles; . . .

As he then testified, "It is a jurisdiction which has always been exercised," [2] because, as has been seen, the American "in the field" was the precise equivalent of the British "on active service." [3]

---

[1] Actually, the American Articles of War had never been comprehensively recast since 1806, having been subjected only to piecemeal amendment and then renumbered and rearranged in the Revised Statutes of 1874. See General Crowder's testimony, *passim*, in *Revision of the Articles of War*, Hearings before the House Committee on Military Affairs, 62d Cong., 2d sess., on H.R. 23628, and in Sen. Rep. No. 130, 64th Cong., 1st sess., pp. 27–28. The substance of the foregoing, in shorter compass, will also be found in the U.S. Army *Manual for Courts-Martial*, 1917 ed., pp. ix–x.

[2] *Revision of the Articles of War*, just cited, at p. 61.

But H.R. 23628, the 1912 draft, purported in its proposed AW 2(f) to subject to military law:

"(f) All persons now or hereafter declared by Congress to constitute a part of or belonging to the Armies of the United States or to be subject to the Articles of War or to trial by courts-martial."

The latter provision, which even on its face bristles with constitutional questions, was not discussed at all during the cited hearing.

[3] *Supra*, pp. 218–219.

Congress did not act on General Crowder's revision until 1916, at which time his jurisdictional proposals had been perceptibly broadened, extending, as the first quotation has shown, to all civilians accompanying the forces in time of peace outside the territorial jurisdiction of the United States. As Appendix IV shows in detail, General Crowder rested his expanded proposal on two assumptions respecting constitutional doctrine, both of which in 1916 had ample support in case law. But what is still strange fifty years later is that, although General Crowder regarded Colonel Winthrop highly, with an esteem that bordered on veneration, and later spoke of him publicly as "the Blackstone of military law, a man of superb reasoning power," [4] he never once referred at any of the hearings to the view expressed in the older man's standard text, that (italics in the original) *a statute cannot be framed by which a civilian can lawfully be made amenable to the military jurisdiction in time of peace.*" [5] Nor did General Crowder ever make mention of the 1912 edition of the *Digest of Opinions of the Judge Advocates General of the Army*, which had just been published under the supervision of his own office, and which faithfully echoed Colonel Winthrop's views.[6]

Congress accepted General Crowder's proposal, and the expanded military jurisdiction thus conferred was widely exercised during both World Wars,[7] although the judicial tests of AW 2 (d) until well after V-J Day in 1945 concerned only the scope of the wartime "in the field" provision.[8] Thereafter, the jurisdiction over

---

[4] *Establishment of Military Justice*, Hearings before a Subcommittee of the Senate Committee on Military Affairs, 66th Cong., 1st sess., on S. 64, p. 1171.

[5] P. *146.

[6] Pp. 151–152. Gen. Crowder's essentially inadequate biography throws no light on the present problem. D. A. Lockmiller, *Enoch H. Crowder: Soldier, Lawyer, Statesman* (Columbia, Mo., 1955) 137–142.

[7] See 4 *Bull. of the JAG of the Army* (Washington, June 1945) 223–229; M. Maurer, *The Court-Martialing of Camp Followers, World War I*, 9 Am. J. Leg. Hist. 203.

[8] Military jurisdiction sustained: *Ex parte Gerlach*, 247 Fed. 616 (S.D. N.Y.) (Army transport on high seas, World War I); *Ex parte Falls*, 251 Fed. 415 (D. N.J.) (cook leaving Army transport at Brooklyn, N.Y., World War I); *Ex parte Jochen*, 257 Fed. 200 (S.D. Tex.) (quartermaster employee on Mexican border, World War I); *Hines v. Mikell*, 259 Fed. 28 (C.A. 4), certiorari denied, 250 U.S. 645 (quartermaster's stenographer at Camp Jackson, S.C., World War I); *In re Di Bartolo*, 50 F. Supp. 929 (S.D. N.Y.) (Eritrea, World War II); *McCune v. Kilpatrick*, 53 F. Supp. 80 (E.D. Va.) (cook leaving Army transport at Norfolk, Va., World War II); *In re Berue*, 54 F. Supp. 252 (S.D. Ohio) (Army vessel on high seas, World War II); *Shilman v. United States*, 73 F. Supp. 648 (S.D. N.Y.), reversed in part, 164 F. 2d 649 (C.A. 2), certiorari denied, 333 U.S. 837 (Tunisia, World War II); *Perlstein v. United States*, 151 F.2d 167 (C.A. 3), certiorari

civilians with the forces overseas was not only continued but was actually further extended by the Uniform Code of Military Justice that went into effect on 31 May 1951.[9] Indeed, it was on this

granted, 327 U.S. 777, then dismissed because moot, 328 U.S. 822 (Eritrea, World War II); *Grewe* v. *France*, 75 F. Supp. 433 (E.D. Wis.) (occupied Germany, 1946); *United States* v. *Handy*, 176 F.2d 491 (C.A. 5), certiorari denied, 338 U.S. 904 (occupied Germany, 1949). Military jurisdiction not sustained: *Ex parte Weitz*, 256 Fed. 58 (D. Mass.) (contractor's employee, Camp Devens, Mass., World War I); *Walker* v. *Chief Quarantine Officer*, 69 F. Supp. 980 (D. C.Z.) (engineer employee, Canal Zone, World War II); *Hammond* v. *Squier*, 51 F. Supp. 227 (W.D. Wash.) ("special military commission" appointed by admiral commanding South Pacific Area, World War II).

No case reached the Supreme Court on the merits. But one, involving a suspected spy and hence resting on different considerations that were not articulated until 20 years later (in *Ex parte Quirin*, 317 U.S. 1), was deliberately rendered moot, doubtless to preclude an appeal. *U.S. ex rel. Wessels* v. *McDonald*, 265 Fed. 754 (S.D. N.Y.), appeal dismissed, 256 U.S. 705, pursuant to a stipulation "that, court-martial proceedings against this appellant having been dismissed by the Secretary of the Navy at the instance of the Department of Justice, this appeal may be dismissed."

This stipulation was filed on 21 April 1921, after the Joint Resolution of March 3, 1921, 41 Stat. 1359, that ended the state of war with Germany, and that rendered at least arguably applicable the Civil War decision holding that military courts have no jurisdiction to try a spy once the war ends. *Matter of Martin*, 45 Barb. 142, 31 How. Pr. 228 (N.Y.).

[9] As originally enacted in 1950, Arts. 2(11) and 2(12) UCMJ, provided as follows:

"Art. 2. Persons subject to the code.
"The following persons are subject to this code:

. . . .

"(11) Subject to the provisions of any treaty or agreement to which the United States is or may be a party or to any accepted rule of international law, all persons serving with, employed by, or accompanying the armed forces without the continental limits of the United States and without the following territories: That part of Alaska east of longitude one hundred and seventy-two degrees west, the Canal Zone, the main group of the Hawaiian Islands, Puerto Rico, and the Virgin Islands;

"(12) Subject to the provisions of any treaty or agreement to which the United States is or may be a party or to any accepted rule of international law, all persons within an area leased by or otherwise reserved or acquired for the use of the United States which is under the control of the Secretary of a Department and which is without the continental limits of the United States and without the following Territories: That part of Alaska east of longitude one hundred and seventy-two degrees west, the Canal Zone, the main group of the Hawaiian Islands, Puerto Rico, and the Virgin Islands."

Following revision and re-enactment of Title 10, United States Code, and amendments to reflect the adoption of an organic act for Guam and the admission of Alaska and Hawaii as States of the Union, these provisions now read as follows:

. . . .

"§802. Art. 2. Persons subject to this chapter
"The following persons are subject to this chapter:

"(11) Subject to any treaty or agreement to which the United States is or may be a party or to any accepted rule of international law, persons serving with,

jurisdiction that the NATO Status of Forces Agreements, as well the Administrative Agreement with Japan that was adopted following the end of the Allied occupation of that country, in fact rested, for both arrangements proceeded on the assumption that each visiting military force had full power to deal with any civilians who accompanied it.[10]

SIMILAR BRITISH EXTENSION PATTERNED ON AMERICAN EXAMPLE

Meanwhile, in Britain, the Army Act 1881 was about to be rewritten. Despite constant amendment in detail, many of its sections had never been touched, and its basic fabric still stood much as it had been fashioned by Lord Thring. But the winds of change and the climate of opinion after the Second World War coincided in making thorough recasting necessary.

First, on 1 October 1948, all functions of pretrial advice and prosecution had been transferred from the Judge Advocate General of the Forces to the new Directorates of Legal Services in the War Office and in the Air Ministry.[11] Second, effective on 1 May 1952, the Courts-Martial (Appeals) Act 1951 [12] had, by providing for direct review of court-martial judgments in the civil courts, gone far toward assimilating the processes of military law to the more familiar and hence more readily acceptable forms of the common law. (As a matter of completeness, though both steps followed the new legislation about to be discussed, the Administra-

---

employed by, or accompanying the armed forces outside the United States and outside the following: the Canal Zone, Puerto Rico, Guam, and the Virgin Islands.

"(12) Subject to any treaty or agreement to which the United States is or may be a party or to any accepted rule of international law, persons within an area leased by or otherwise reserved or acquired for the use of the United States which is under the control of the Secretary concerned and which is outside the United States and outside the following: the Canal Zone, Puerto Rico, Guam, and the Virgin Islands."

[10] NATO Status of Forces Agreement 1953, 4 U.S. Treaties 1792, esp. Arts. I(1) (b) and (c), and VII(3) (a) and (b); Administrative Agreement with Japan, 3 U.S. Treaties 3342, esp. Arts. I(c) (1), XVII(2), and XVII(4).

[11] Such a transfer had been recommended by the Army and Air Force Courts-Martial Committee 1946; see its Report (Cmd. 7608), dated 13 April 1948, at pars. 105–113 (pp. 23–25, 55, 66–68). Following a question in Parliament on 21 Sept. 1948 (456 H.C. Deb. [5th Series] 691–692), the Government adopted the recommendation, which was implemented as of the date mentioned in the text by Army Council Instruction 880 of 1948 and Air Ministry Order A798 of the same year. I am indebted to Oliver C. Barnett, Esq., C.B.E., Q.C., the present Judge Advocate General, for all of the foregoing references.

[12] 14 & 15 Geo. VI c. 46.

tion of Justice Act 1960 [13] permitted court-martial cases to be taken to the House of Lords on the same footing as other criminal cases, while the Criminal Appeal Act 1964 [14] authorized retrials of criminal cases, by courts-martial as well as by the civil courts, in cases of fresh evidence. And, under the Criminal Appeal Act 1966, [15] the scope of appellate review in military cases has been even further enlarged.)

The provision for direct review of courts-martial in the civil courts was in no sense a development peculiar to Britain. Indeed, every other large English-speaking country similarly and almost simultaneously adopted a scheme providing for appeals of the judgments of courts-martial directly to civilian tribunals—the United States in 1950, effective 1951; Canada in 1952; New Zealand in 1953; and finally Australia in 1955. [16] With surprising unanimity, the common law world concluded virtually at the same moment in time that, just as war is too important to be left to the generals, so military justice is too vital to be entrusted only to judge advocates.

Changes were also required in the British law in respect of jurisdiction over accompanying civilians, which as already indicated had long been limited to those on active service. In the past, civilians with forces not on active service in Egypt or Iraq could be dealt with by the British Consular Courts sitting in those countries; now, however, the capitulatory system with its scheme of extraterritoriality (increasingly and indeed inevitably regarded in the countries where it still applied as involving a stigma) was nearing abandonment. And, in the immediate past, civilians with the British Army on the Rhine, the force that occupied the British Zone of Germany, were on active service under the plain terms of the Army Act 1881. [17] But the German occupation was about to be

---

[13] 8 & 9 Eliz. II c. 65. The portions particularly applicable to courts-martial are set out and annotated at MML 1965, pp. 756–765.

[14] 1964 c. 43. Here again, the provisions with military relevance appear at MML 1965, pp. 767–770.

Retrials in American military law following appellate review, which are termed "rehearings," were first authorized by AW 50½ of 1920, continued by AW 52 of 1948, and are now governed by Art. 63 UCMJ. New trials for matters *dehors* the record, the only "new trial" proper, were first introduced by AW 53 of 1948 and then continued by Art. 73 UCMJ.

[15] 1966 c. 31.

[16] *United States:* UCMJ, Art. 67, enacted 5 May 1950, effective 31 May 1951. *Canada:* National Defence Act of 1952, c. 184, §§186, 190. *New Zealand:* The Courts Martial Appeals Act 1953 (1953, No. 104). *Australia:* Courts-Martial Appeals Act 1955 (No. 16 of 1955).

[17] AA, §189(1).

terminated, and the several Bonn Conventions of 1955 substituted in its stead. Moreover, and pre-eminently, those Conventions as well as the NATO Status of Forces Agreements presupposed that every military force serving abroad on the soil of an associated power had plenary military jurisdiction to deal with its own accompanying civilians.[18]

True, the thought of trying civilians by court-martial, particularly dependent female civilians, was difficult to accept; public opinion had come a long way since the eighteenth century, when misbehaving soldiers' wives and women followers were flogged at the cart's tail.[19] Nonetheless, even with corporal punishment outlawed and confinement substituted, the very idea of turning over British subjects to German, or Japanese, or Turkish courts, for unfamiliar proceedings in a foreign tongue taking place in what might well be a hostile atmosphere, and with at least a strong possibility of confinement in a foreign prison, was a very real probability that was even more difficult to accept.

The choice was not an easy one, but in the end trial of these persons by courts-martial of their own country loomed as distinctly the lesser of the two evils,[20] particularly since, as the testimony before the Select Committee disclosed, this was precisely what both the American and the French forces did with their accompanying civilians.[21]

Accordingly, the Army Act 1955[22] and the Air Force Act 1955[23] provided for the exercise of military and air force jurisdiction over accompanying civilians who, though abroad, are not on active service.

Section 209(1) of the Army Act 1955 makes Part II thereof (the sections relating to discipline and trial and punishment of military offenses) applicable "where any body of the regular forces is on active service . . . to any person who is employed in the service of that body of the forces or any part or member thereof," and is not otherwise subject to military law, air-force law, or the Naval Disci-

---

[18] *Supra*, n. 10; Convention on the Rights and Obligations of Foreign Forces and their Members in the Federal Republic of Germany, 6 U.S. Treaties 4278; Convention on the Presence of Foreign Forces in the Federal Republic of Germany, 6 U.S. Treaties 5689.

[19] *Supra*, pp. 84–85, 93.

[20] *Report from the Select Committee on the Army Act and the Air Force Act,* H.C. 223 of 1954, pp. xxvi–xxvii, xxxiv–xxxv, 147–148, 150, 156–161.

[21] *Id.*, pp. 147, 155–156.

[22] 3 & 4 Eliz. II c. 18.

[23] 3 & 4 Eliz. II c. 19.

pline Act, subject to certain modifications. Except for those modifications, this is of course a continuation in substance of the former amenability, because §224 defines "active service" substantially in the terms of §189 of the Army Act 1881 after its amendment in 1952.[24] But the former fighting words, "subject to military law," appear to have been advisedly deleted in all references to civilians who are made subject to the new legislation by its terms.

Then §209(2) goes on to make Part II of the 1955 Act applicable, subject to the like modifications, "to a person of any description specified in the Fifth Schedule to this Act who is within the limits of the command of any officer commanding a body of the regular forces outside the United Kingdom"—i.e., who is abroad but not on active service, and who is not otherwise subject to military law, air-force law, or the Naval Discipline Act, except for military offenses.[25]

The principal modifications, set out in detail in §209(3), are that the court-martial may impose fines, but shall not impose any punishment less than imprisonment (i.e., reprimands, stoppages, dismissal, cashiering, reduction, forfeiture of service); that if the accused is found guilty in summary proceedings, the finding shall not be recorded until after the accused has been afforded an opportunity of electing to be tried by court-martial; that for purposes of investigation of offenses, the commanding officer shall be as determined by the Army Summary Jurisdiction Regulations, which means (see Rule 10 thereof) no one of a grade lower than lieutenant-colonel;[26] and that any fines imposed, whether by court-martial or summarily, shall be recoverable as a debt due the Crown.

The Fifth Schedule of the Army Act 1955 lists the civilians outside the United Kingdom who are subject to Part II when not on active service. These include (1) specified persons serving the Crown or employed in capacities connected with H.M.'s military, naval, or air forces; (2) persons employed by treaty organizations to which H.M.'s Government in the United Kingdom is a party,

---

[24] *Supra*, p. 218.

[25] The proviso to §209(2) excludes all military offenses except offenses against sentries, obstruction of provost officers, disobedience of standing orders, resisting arrest, escaping from confinement, offenses relating to courts-martial, giving false evidence, and attempting to commit military offenses. But the accompanying civilians remain subject to §70, which provides that the commission of a civil offense, whether in the United Kingdom or elsewhere, constitutes a violation of that section.

[26] The Army Summary Jurisdiction Regulations 1966 are set forth in MML 1965, Amdt. 2, pp. 559–570.

such as NATO; (3) and persons in the service of affiliated organizations, such as NAAFI and the Red Cross; all these several classes are enumerated in detail in implementing regulations.[27] Also included are (4) persons attached to or accompanying the forces, such as press correspondents and members of the JAG staff; (5) and (6) families of members of the forces and families of persons falling within the above-enumerated categories "and residing with them or about to reside or departing after residing with them"; (7) persons employed by members of the forces, such as governesses and nurses; (8) persons employed by persons in categories (1) through (6); and, finally, (9), families of persons in categories (7) and (8) "and residing with them or about to reside or departing after residing with them." [28]

In short, every conceivable class of camp follower is included. The same is true of the corresponding provisions of the Air Force Act 1955, which are identical.

Both measures also effected, not only an innovation in respect of jurisdiction over accompanying civilians not on active service, but also a substantial deflection in what up to then had been established constitutional doctrine.

As has been seen in the preceding chapter, the residual remnant of the principle that there must be a new Mutiny Act annually could be found after the First World War in the Army and Air Force (Annual) Act, a measure that was necessary each year to put into force the Army Act as well as its counterpart, the Air Force Act, so-called. (The latter was actually synthetic legislation, a collection of the applicable provisions of the Army Act given a new title.) [29] Under that scheme, in Maitland's words, "the principle is still preserved that the army shall be legalized only from year to year." [30]

---

[27] See Civilians (Application of Part II of the Army Act, 1955) Regulations 1956, as amended, set forth in MML 1965, pp. 730–731.

[28] See notes to Fifth Schedule in MML 1965, p. 519.

[29] "For this purpose the Army Act, as it stood in 1917, was taken as a model. The amendments required to adapt its provisions to the needs of the new service were made by the Air Force (Constitution) Act, 1917 [7 & 8 Geo. V c. 51, § 12(1)], and statutory effect was given to the code thus evolved under the title of the 'Air Force Act.' This Act forms the foundation of 'air force law.' Like the Army Act, it has in itself no continuous operative force, being merely a collection of provisions approved by Parliament as suitable for the government of an Air Force, and capable of being easily applied to such a force from year to year." MAFL 1933, p. 14.

[30] F. W. Maitland, *The Constitutional History of England* (Cambridge, 1908) 448.

The Royal Navy, as is well known, had been governed on a different principle, as a series of permanent Naval Discipline Acts from 1661 bore witness.[31] But in 1955 it might well be asked, and not only by outsiders, whether it still made either good sense or good constitutional law to continue to treat the standing Army as a menace to the rights of Englishmen and as a potential subverter of the constitution, while the standing Navy, drawn from the same classes of society and officered on identical principles, was plainly neither. In Professor Hanbury's words, "The maintenance of phrases indicative of dislike of a standing army had for some time been regarded as merely a concession to a historical sentiment which had ceased to correspond with realities." [32]

Of course there had been unpleasant experiences with the Army under Cromwell; Pride's Purge rankled in the hearts of all who read of it, even three centuries after the event; throughout the eighteenth century "the Debates on the Army are redolent with Political Strife"; and the Navy had never been called upon to aid or to restore civil authority.[33] But, in one of Mr. Justice Holmes's oft-quoted (if even more frequently disregarded) apothegms, "continuity with the past is only a necessity and not a duty." [34] Just as, in his words, "It is revolting to have no better reason for a rule of law than that so it was laid down in the time of Henry IV," [35] so also it hardly seemed a valid constitutional reason in the Britain of 1955 still to treat the Army differently from the Navy simply because "Every person may visit the Field of Waterloo, but no one can discover the arena of Trafalgar." Yet Clode penned that very sentence to underscore what he deemed basic constitutional divergences between the two services.[36]

In 1955, Parliament at long last embarked on a somewhat altered course in respect of the Army—and of the Air Force as well. (No doubt the skies wherein was fought the Battle of Britain were also visible to all.) It did not legalize these fighting services permanently, as two years later it was once again to do in respect of the Navy by the Naval Discipline Act 1957.[37] So sudden and abrupt a

---

[31] The first two were 13 Car. II c. 9, and 16 Car. II c. 5.

[32] MML, Part II, Sec. I ¶36 (1958); see MAFL 1964, p. 23.

[33] 2 Clode M.F. 179–180.

[34] "Law in Science—Science in Law," in O. W. Holmes, *Collected Legal Papers* (New York, 1921) 210, 211.

[35] "The Path of the Law," in *id*. 167, 187.

[36] 2 Clode M.F. 180.

[37] 5 & 6 Eliz. II c. 53.

divergence would have been worse than unconstitutional, it might indeed have been regarded as un-English. But Parliament did extend the statutory authorization for the Army and Air Force from one year to five, and then provided that within the five-year term the necessary bringing into force could be effected by Orders in Council.

Accordingly, the Army and Air Force (Annual) Act 1954,[38] is the last of that series. The underlying pre-1955 Army and Air Force Acts were continued in force through the end of the year 1956 by a companion measure to the new 1955 Acts (which received the royal assent on the same day), the Revision of the Army and Air Force Acts (Transitional Provisions) Act 1955.[39]

Unlike their statutory predecessors of 1879 and 1881, which specifically declared that they had no force of their own [40] and thus required additional legislation to put them into effect, both of the new measures did have force of their own, and could become effective by simple Order in Council. Both in fact went into effect in that manner on 1 January 1957.[41] Under the terms of each Act, both could be similarly extended by Order in Council for five years,[42] and were; later, by the Army and Air Force Act 1961,[43] both were further extended in the same manner through the end of the year 1966; and now similar extensions can be made pursuant to the Armed Forces Act 1966.[44]

FALL OF THE AMERICAN MILITARY JURISDICTION OVER ACCOMPANYING CIVILIANS

But, between the time that the 1955 legislation received the royal assent and the time that it came into force, two proceedings were wending their way through the courts of the United States which would eventually undermine the American jurisdiction that had provided the persuasive precedent for the expanded British scope of military law.

On 17 November 1955, just ten days after the announcement of the Supreme Court's decision in the *Toth* case [45]—which as Appen-

---

[38] 2 & 3 Eliz. II c. 35.

[39] 3 & 4 Eliz. II c. 20.

[40] *Supra*, pp. 215–216.

[41] Pursuant to the Army Act 1955 (Commencement) Order and the Air Force Act 1955 (Commencement) Order, S.I. 1955 Nos. 1805 and 1806, respectively.

[42] Army Act 1955, §226; Air Force Act 1955, §224.

[43] 9 & 10 Eliz. II c. 52.

[44] 1966 c. 45.

[45] *Toth* v. *Quarles*, 350 U.S. 11.

dix IV shows, was interpreted as destroying the primary constitutional assumptions on which General Crowder had rested the extension of military jurisdiction over accompanying civilians—Mrs. Clarice B. Covert filed a petition for habeas corpus in the District of Columbia. She had been convicted and sentenced to life imprisonment for the premeditated murder of her husband, an Air Force sergeant, by a United States Air Force court-martial sitting in England. Inasmuch as the United States of America (Visiting Forces) Act 1942 was still in force, she was exempt from trial in the English courts once the requisite certificate was filed pursuant to its provisions.[46] Following her conviction, she had been returned to the United States to serve her sentence pending appellate proceedings within the military judicial system. The United States Courts of Military Appeals reversed her conviction for errors in the treatment of her defense of temporary insanity—actually the only issue in the case [47]—after which she was brought to the District of Columbia to be retried on the original charge at Bolling Air Force Base. Following a hearing on her petition for habeas corpus—which was brought shortly before that retrial was scheduled to commence—she was released from Air Force custody by the district court, on the view that "a civilian is entitled to a civilian trial." [48]

Encouraged by this ruling, an identical petition was filed by General Walter Krueger on behalf of his daughter, Mrs. Dorothy Krueger Smith, in West Virginia, where she was serving a similar life sentence following her conviction for the premeditated murder of *her* husband, an Army colonel, by a United States Army court-martial, sitting in Japan following the close of the Allied occupation. Under the terms of the Administrative Agreement with Japan then in force, she was not subject to trial in the Japanese courts.[49] But the United States District Judge in the Southern

---

[46] 5 & 6 Geo. VI c. 31; see particularly §2(2), providing that "a certificate issued by or on behalf of such authority as may be appointed for the purpose by the Government of the United States of America stating that a person of the name and description specified in the certificate is, or was at a time so specified, subject to the military or naval law of the United States of America, shall be conclusive evidence of that fact."

[47] *United States* v. *Covert*, 6 USCMA 48, 19 CMR 174.

[48] *U.S. ex rel. Covert* v. *Reid*, H.C. No. 87–55, D.D.C., unreported, *per* Tamm, D.J., Nov. 22, 1955; R. 131–132, No. 701, Oct. T. 1955.

[49] Art. XVII of the Administrative Agreement with Japan, TIAS 2492, 3 U.S. Treaties 3342, 3353.

District of West Virginia declined to follow the ruling of his colleague in the District of Columbia, and denied the petition.[50]

Both cases then came to the Supreme Court; they were argued together; and on 11 June 1956, the Court sustained the military jurisdiction in both cases—but without examining the scope of the constitutional provision that empowers Congress to govern the armed forces.[51] The details of the holding are discussed in Appendix IV; it suffices to note here that three of the nine Justices dissented and that another reserved decision.

The vote was thus 5 to 4 against the two ladies, a familiar score in American constitutional cases involving difficult questions. The losers thereupon requested reconsideration, though more as an act of faith than of hope; the percentage of successful petitions for rehearing in the Supreme Court is literally infinitesimal, primarily because, as its Rule 58 spells out, no such petition will be granted "except at the instance of a justice who concurred in the judgment or decision and with the concurrence of a majority of the court." Otherwise stated, rehearing will be denied in every 5 to 4 case unless some member of the original majority has changed his mind or at the least is beset by controlling doubts. It is scarcely necessary to remind lawyer readers that appellate judges rarely suffer such qualms once they have publicly concurred in a decision.

In this instance, the petition for rehearing was granted on 5 November 1956; the order announcing that rare event disclosed that Mr. Justice Harlan, who had been with the majority in June, five months later voted to rehear the case.[52] Consequently the fact that the rehearing had been granted at all indicated rather strongly that, after additional briefs, a second argument, and further consideration, a different result would follow. And that was precisely what did happen on 10 June 1957, just 364 days after the first decisions; on that day the earlier opinions were withdrawn, and new ones were announced.[53]

The two women were accordingly released, and although the differences in opinion among the members of the new majority narrowed the holding to apply only to military trials in time of

---

[50] *United States* v. *Kinsella*, 137 F. Supp. 806 (S.D. W.Va.). The military proceedings, all *sub nom. United States* v. *Smith*, are reported at 10 CMR 350; 13 CMR 307; and 5 USCMA 314, 17 CMR 314.

[51] *Kinsella* v. *Krueger*, 351 U.S. 470; *Reid* v. *Covert*, 351 U.S. 487.

[52] 352 U.S. 901.

[53] *Reid* v. *Covert* and *Kinsella* v. *Krueger*, 354 U.S. 1.

peace of civilian dependents for capital offenses, a few years later, in January 1960, the prohibition against military trials of civilians in time of peace was extended to employees as well as dependents, and to non-capital offenses equally with capital crimes.[54]

ACTUAL EXERCISE OF BRITISH MILITARY JURISDICTION OVER CIVILIANS WITH THE FORCES ABROAD

In the light of the events set forth in the preceding section, it is the fact that the British military jurisdiction over accompanying civilians not on active service went into effect just two months after the Supreme Court's grant of rehearing in the *Covert* and *Krueger* cases presaged the end of the very American military jurisdiction on which Parliament drew and which it imitated when it enacted the Army and Air Force Acts 1955. For that rehearing was granted on 5 November 1956, while the new Acts of Parliament became effective on 1 January 1957.

The British die, however, was cast, without fear of overturn by judicial decision; unwritten constitutions have their advantages also.

In actual fact, the British military jurisdiction over accompanying civilians has not been an oppressive one. Statistics kept in the office of the Judge Advocate General of the Forces, who of course reviews Royal Air Force as well as Army cases, show that through the end of July 1966, which is to say, over a period of nine and a half years, there had been only ninety-six trials of civilians by court-martial. This comes to about ten such trials a year.[55]

Sixteen of these civilians, including four women, were tried by general court-martial. All four women were charged with and convicted of serious offenses: two for murder, the third for cruelty to a child, the last for infanticide. The two women convicted of murder were severally sentenced to life imprisonment, which in the

---

[54] *Kinsella* v. *Singleton*, 361 U.S. 234 (civilian dependent, non-capital offense); *Grisham* v. *Hagan*, 361 U.S. 278 (civilian employee, capital offense); *McElroy* v. *Guagliardo* and *Wilson* v. *Bohlender*, 361 U.S. 281 (civilian employees, non-capital offenses).

Accordingly, Arts. 2(11) and 2(12) UCMJ, even though twice amended since, see note 9, *supra*, have no legal validity, except in time of war, which is covered by Art. 2(10), now in these terms:

"(10) In time of war, persons serving with or accompanying an armed force in the field." See *supra*, p. 219.

[55] These figures and the ones that follow rest on detailed data very generously made available by Mr. Barnett, the Judge Advocate General. Actually, only 94 individuals were involved, because two, one man and one woman, were each tried for a second offense.

second instance was mitigated to ten years; the woman found guilty of abusing the child was sentenced to one year's imprisonment, subsequently mitigated to ninety-one days; and the woman convicted of infanticide was sentenced to confinement for one day. This last result followed from the terms of the Infanticide Act 1938.[56]

(A similar modern, humane, and thoroughly sensible enactment would have precluded the sentence to life imprisonment imposed by American military justice on the English wife of an American soldier for a similar offense.[57] The latter tragic instance actually represented the *reductio ad absurdum* of the American military jurisdiction over accompanying civilians, for since the poor woman was an alien who had committed an offense involving moral turpitude, she was not eligible for admission to the United States—until she was paroled by the Attorney General in order that she might serve her sentence in the Federal Reformatory for Women in West Virginia! [58] This particular case led to questions in Parliament,[59] nor was the grotesque tragicomedy concluded until, shortly after the second decision in *Reid* v. *Covert*,[60] mitigating circumstances not theretofore evident suddenly appeared, with the result that the accused was released.) [61]

The remainder of the civilians tried by British courts-martial between January 1957 and the end of July 1966, some seventy-eight individuals (including thirty-two women), were tried by

---

[56] 1 & 2 Geo. VI c. 36.

[57] *United States* v. *Brillhart*, CM 376967, petition for grant of review denied, 6 USCMA 808.

[58] Ineligibility for admission, 8 U.S.C. §1182(a) (9); parole by Attorney General, 8 U.S.C. §1182(d) (5).

[59] 544 H.C. Deb. (5th Series) Written Answers to Questions, 205–206; 546 *id.* 201–202.

[60] 354 U.S. 1.

[61] In all fairness it must be pointed out that at least a substantial share of the responsibility for this unedifying proceeding rests with the British diplomatic representatives to whose attention the incident was first brought. The offense was committed in Eritrea, a part of Ethiopia; the American military offered to turn the accused over to the British; but the latter refused, waiving their "jurisdiction" while expressing grave doubts whether they had any. In so doing, they overlooked §9 of the Offences against the Person Act 1861 (24 & 25 Vict. c. 100), which renders homicide committed anywhere in the world by a British subject triable in a British court. See *Regina* v. *Azzopardi*, 1 Car. & K. 203 (decision under predecessor statute). Accordingly, it would have been entirely possible to have tried the accused in England, where she would have had the benefit of the Infanticide Act 1938—a course that the American military authorities would have welcomed. (They also were unaware of the 1861 enactment, but somewhat more excusably, because it was not their law.)

district court-martial.[62] Interestingly enough, all but four of these thirty-two women were tried for stealing—a bizarre example of historical continuity over the centuries. H.R.H. William Augustus Duke of Cumberland would have been perfectly at home with this means of dealing with any larcenous ladies following in the train of the troops, though undoubtedly he would have considered his own remedy of a hundred lashes or so well laid on a more effective deterrent than the fines, averaging £13 10s., that were being imposed in the British Army of the Rhine upon women found guilty of theft following trial by court-martial two hundred years afterwards.[63]

One of the sixteen civilians tried by general court-martial was acquitted, while nine out of eighty trials of civilians before district courts-martial similarly resulted in findings of not guilty. Of those convicted, four presented petitions to the Courts-Martial Appeal Court. Only one of these petitions was allowed, and in that single case the conviction was quashed.[64]

Summary trials under §§82 and 83 of the 1955 Acts and the Summary Jurisdiction Regulations were even fewer in number. There are records of twenty-one such proceedings in the Army during this same nine-and-a-half-year period. The available Royal Air Force records cover only the years 1962 through July 1966; there were only seven summary trials in that interval.

In short, whatever may be their deterrent effects, and assuredly those should not be underestimated, the actual impact of the 1955 provisions has been in practice essentially minimal.

The Royal Navy now also has, under §118 and the Second Schedule of the Naval Discipline Act 1957,[65] a jurisdiction over accompanying civilians similar in every respect to that conferred by the Army and Air Force Acts 1955. But there have been no trials under these provisions, a consequence primarily of the smaller percentage of civilians with the Royal Navy on foreign stations.[66]

---

[62] As has been indicated, one man and one woman were tried for second offenses.

[63] One of the women was tried twice for separate thefts, receiving a more severe sentence the second time. The fines ranged from £2 10s. to £40, ten of them being in the sum of £5. One woman, not the recidivist, was sentenced to 84 days' imprisonment.

[64] *Regina* v. *Rees,* CM(A) 533; see Supplement to *Justice of the Peace* for 7 Jan. 1961.

[65] 5 & 6 Eliz. II c. 53.

[66] Information very kindly supplied by the Hon. Ewen E. S. Montagu, C.B.E., Q.C., D.L., the Judge-Advocate of the Fleet.

It may be, of course, that the deterrent aspects of the jurisdiction have had more effect on naval followers than on those in the train of the Army or the RAF. It may be, also, that the civilians who accompany the Royal Navy are better behaved than the others; this is a matter that anyone lacking blue-water background is hardly competent to judge.

And with that comment, which concludes the account of the British military and naval jurisdiction over accompanying civilians presently in force, we have come to the end—for the time being—of the more than 275-year-long story of Civilians under Military Justice.

ILLUSTRATIVE DOCUMENTS

NOTE: Matter in the original appearing to have been deliberately written in script of larger size is reproduced in small capitals.

A. MILITARY JURISDICTION OVER HOMICIDE IN ABSENCE OF CIVIL COMPLAINT WITHIN EIGHT DAYS

Law Officers' Report (Sir R. Raymond and Sir P. Yorke), 19 November 1720 [WO 30/25/158; side-note omitted].

TO THE KINGS MOST EXCELLENT MAJESTY

May it please your Majesty

In Obedience to the Commands of the late Lords Justices of Great Britain during your Majesty's Absence Signifyed to us by Mr Delafaye by his letter of the 27th of October last, taking Notice that upon reading to the Lords Justices the proceedings of a Court Martial held at Edinburgh the 8th day of the said Month, by wch Thomas Berriesford a Soldier was Condemned to be shot for Murder; a Doubt arising whether that Crime was within the Cognizance of the said Court, Their Excellencys commanded him to send Us an Extract of the said proceedings so far as relates to that Matter, and to Signify to Us Their Directions, that we should consider the Same and Report whether a Court Martial can lawfully proceed upon a Tryal for Murder or Manslaughter and whether the Tyral and Sentence of the said Berriesford was according to Law.

We have Considered thereof, and we most humbly certify your Majesty that by an Act pass'd in the last Session of Parliament Intituled an Act for Punishing Mutiny and Desertion, and for the better Payment of the Army and their Quarters Page (120) It is enacted that if any Officer, Non-Commiss^n Officer or Soldier shall be Accused of any Capital Crime or of any Violence or Offence against the Person Estate or property of any of the Subjects of this Kingdom which is punishable by the Laws of the Land, the Commanding Officer or Officers of every Regiment, Troop or Company or Party is and are required upon application made to the then

Commanding Officer on behalf of the Party Injured to use his utmost endeavour to deliver over such accused person to the Civill Magistrate, and shall also be aiding & assisting to the Officers of Justice in the Seizing and apprehending such Offender, in Order to bring him to Tyral; & the Officer to whom such application shall be made or any other Officer shall not proceed to the Tyral of such Offender or Offenders by a Court Martial, within the Space of 8 days after the Offence committed, unless at the desire of the Person or Persons injured; But after 8 days expired, in Case the Person injured shall not in that time have made application to such Commanding Officer nor proceeded to the prosecution of such Offender or Offenders before a Civil Court or Magistrate, and given notice thereof to such Commanding Officer, such Offender may be tryed by a Court Martial for any of the said Capital Crimes, Violences or Offences.

By Virtue of which Clause althô if an Officer or Soldier is accused of any Capital Crime, the Commanding Officer of that Regim^t, Troop or Company, is required upon Application made to him on behalf of the Party Injured to deliver over the Person accused to the Civil Magistrate, and not to proceed to Tryal of such Offend^r by a Court Martial within 8 days after the Offence Committed unless at the desire of the Person injured; Yet Thereby after 8 days Expired, if no such Application has been made to the Commanding Officer nor any prosecution begun before the Civill Magistrate and Notice thereof given to the Commanding Officer such Offender may by the Express Words of the Act be tryed by a Court Martial for any of the said Capital Crimes; And therefore We are humbly of Opinion that a Court Martial may lawfully proceed to the Tyral of Murder or Manslaughter committed by an Officer, Non-Commission Officer or Soldier, in Case the Requisites of this Clause have been duly Observed.

We have perused also the annext Extract of the proceedings of the Court Martial held the 8th of October last at Edinburgh against the said Thomas Berrisfoord a Soldier in Capt Moore's Company of Granadiers of Col^o Clayton's Regim^t for killing of Joseph Dint a Soldier of the same Company on the 16th of July last and upon Consideration of the Evidence therein mention'd to have been given at the Tyral We apprehend that the said Thomas Berriesford was guilty of that Crime which by the Law of England is called Murder (thô we have been informed that by the Law of Scotland where this fact was Committed there is no such distinction as that of Murder & Manslaughter) and therefore as far as appears to Us We humbly apprehend that the Tyral and Sentence of the said Berriesfoord was according to Law.

All which is most humbly Submitted to
Your Majesty's Great Wisdom & Judgem^t

Robt Raymond
Ph: Yorke
Novr 19th 1720.

B. MILITARY JURISDICTION OVER ARTILLERY

Edward Hughes, JAG, to the Rt. Hon. Earl of Cadogan, 3 February 1724 [WO 81/2/43].

Horse Guards. 3^d Feb^{ye} 1723

My Lord.

In Obedience to Your L^{dps} Comands, I have considered the Act of Mutiny & Desertion & how far it doth Extend to the Tryal of the Officers & Gunners in the Train of Altillery & find THAT IF ANY PERSON BEING MUSTERED, OR IN PAY AS AN OFFICER, OR WHO SHALL BE INLISTED OR IN PAY AS A SOLDIER, SHALL DESERT, SHALL SUFFER DEATH OR SUCH OTHER PUNISHMENT AS A COURT MARTIAL SHALL INFLICT. and whereas the said Act Authorises his Matie to make Articles of War for the better Governm^t of His Forces. In the 45th Article His Matie Directs that his Company of Gunners, and other Military Officers of his Train of Altillery are to observe the Rules, & Articles of War, in the same Manner, as by all other Officers, & sold^{rs} in his Service.

I am therefore humbly of Opinion, That the standing General Warr^t appointing Maj^r Genl Tatton President of the Courts Martial to be held at the Horse Guard, is sufficient to try the Gunner Yo^r L^{dp} acquainted me has Deserted.

I humbly offer it as my Opinion that an equal Number of the Officers of the Train be su^{m}oned on this Court Martial, as of the Foot Guards if Your Lord^p is pleased to have a particular Warr^t the Enclosed form Yo^r L^p may think proper,

I am

My L^d

Yo^r L^{ps} most obed^t humble Servt

E. H.

The R^t Hono^{ble} Earl
of Cadogan.

C. MILITARY JURISDICTION OVER CLERK OF THE WORKS AT GIBRALTAR

1. *Lt.-Gen. Thomas Fowke, Governor of Gibraltar, to the Rt. Hon. Henry Fox, SW, 19 September 1755* [WO 81/7/11].

Gilbraltar 19th September 1755.

Sir,

An Accident lately happened here in which I am somewhat dubious how to behave till I have troubled You with the Story and am honoured with Your Directions. It is, and for many Years has been, a standing Order in this Garrison, that no Person, except the Military and Civil Officers, shall be suffered to embark or disembark without the Governors Permit; and a few days ago a Young Gentleman named Mr Delves, who was lately appointed Clerk of the Works by the Board of Ordnance, went aboard a Vessel at the Water Port, without being observed by the Officer of the Guard; and at his Return, the Officer not knowing the Station he was in, asked him by what Leave or Authority he went aboard, and he behaving (as the Officer Says) in a very haughty insolent manner, the Officer sent him Prisoner to me, marching him through the Streets with six Men with fixt Bayonets; upon which finding who he was I immediately released him, and sent to acquaint the Officer that he had committed a Mistake, and that Mr Delves, as one of the Officers of the Board of Ordnance on the Establishment of this Garrison, had a Right to go aboard whenever his Occasions required. The Manner of the Officers sending Mr Delves Prisoner I greatly disapproved of, but was in hopes that I should not have heard any more of the Affair; however, two days afterwards Mr Delves went to the Parade, which was then crowded with Officers & others, & in the face of them all struck the Officer several blows with a Stick, and some of the Gentlemen present interfering he was prevented making any return: As soon as this was Reported to me, I ordered Mr Delves under an Arrest, where he still continues; and after having endeavoured to compose the matter in a private manner, which I found could not be done, I had some thoughts of bringing it before a General Court Martial, but on having recourse to the Articles of War, a Doubt has arisen whether Mr Delves, being an Officer of the Civil Branch of the Board of Ordnance, is subject to the Military Law; especially as the Article of War seems confined to Officers and others receiving Pay or Hire *in the Service of His Majesty's Artillery;* and it is alledged that the Officers of Artillery, & the Civil Officers of the Ordnance, are distinct Branches, and that Mr Delves (who by his Station is one of the respective Officers of the Board of Ordnance in this Garrison) is by no means in the Service or Pay of the Artillery, or within the Description of the Article of War. This being a nice Distinction, and such an one as I never met with an Instance of before, I consulted the Field Officers, and though some of them were of Opinion with myself that he was subject to the Articles of War, Yet others being of a different opinion, It was upon the whole thought most prudent to postpone any publick Trial or Enquiry, till I should lay the Case before You, and have the honor of receiving Your Commands thereon.

I must add, Sir, that if Mr Delves and the other Civil Officers of the Ordnance are deemed Members of the Garrison, and are not subject to the Military Law, they are not liable to be called to an Account here for any thing they may do; the Court of Civil Judicature in this place being expressly forbid, by His Majesty's Patent, to try any Person in actual Pay as a Member of the Garrison; and whatever may be the Construction of the Letter of the Law, I am persuaded it never was His Majesty's Intention that any particular Set of His Officers, or Subjects in this Garrison, should be exempt from the Ordinary Methods of Trial & Punishment (in case of Offending) to which the Generality are liable.

I have the Honour to be
Sir,
Your most Obedient & most
Humble Servant.
Tho: Fowke

Right Honᵇᵉble Henry Fox.

2. *Charles Gould, DJAG, to the Rt. Hon. Henry Fox, SW, 18 October 1775* [WO 81/7/13].

Privy Garden 18ᵗʰ October 1755.

Sir,

I have considered with Attention the Doubt Stated in the enclosed Letter, upon which You was pleased to desire an Opinion, and from the best Judgment I have been capable of forming, am inclined to think that a Clerk of the Works under the Board of Ordnance is not within the Cognizance of a Court Martial, nor comprised in the Act for Punishing Mutiny & Desertion. For, if he is not (as I hardly conceive him to be) within the Clause particularly relating to those employed in the Train of Artillery, and the Article of War explanatory of the said Clause, since it was deemed a Doubt, whether the Officers of the Train were included, unless declared subject to Military Discipline by such a Special Proviso, much greater will the Doubt be in the present Case. And that a Clerk of the Works &cᵃ is not within the said Clause, or Article, may possibly be collected from hence; that he is (if I am rightly inform'd) intirely unconnected with and independent of the Train; has no Duty in Common; and neither gives nor receives Orders from any in that Corps. Whereas the Words of the Clause are, "Persons employ'd in the Trains of Artillery," and those of the Article, "Persons receiving Pay or Hire in the Service of the Artillery."

Another Argument is, that Clerks of the Works &cᵃ have no Commissions, but only an Appointment from the Board; nor do they, as I apprehend, claim any kind of Rank; insomuch that no legal Command would devolve upon them over the Garrison or Soldiers at any Event. (And here it may just be noted, that in some Cases it might be doubtfull, under what Class or Denomination they should be proceeded against; as *Commission Officers* evidently they could not; and that they should be considered as Non Commissioned Officers, or Private Men is a Construction scarcely to be intended.)

And the Distinction of the Civil and Military Branch of the Ordnance, tho' not decisive, will certainly have its Weight; because in new Cases and Matters of Difficulty recourse will necessarily be had to Terms which seem in any measure declaratory of a received Opinion.

Lastly, as all the Powers given by Penal Laws are construed Strictly, and

Nothing is to be presumed, which is not expressed, or will not at least fall exactly within the same reason, the better & safer Opinion seems to be, that the Civil Officers of the Ordnance are not an Object of the Mutiny Act & Articles of War; and that whatever Provision might have been made by Parliament, if the Doubt had occurred, Yet, as the Law now stands, it is a Case omitted.

As to the Objection, that the Civil Officers of the Ordnance will not be liable to be called to an Account at Gibraltar for anything they do, the Court of Civil Judicature there being expressly forbid, by His Majesty's Patent to Try any Person in actual Pay, *as a Member* of the Garrison; nothing can be said with Certainty on that head without Consulting the Tenor of the Patent, but it should seem, that the same reasoning, which exempts them from the Cognizance of the Military Law, should take them out of this Exception and leave them under the Civil Authority; for many Persons may be Supposed by their Office resident within a Garrison & receive a Salary for executing their employ and Yet not be Members of the Garrison within the Meaning of that Exception; and the one Jurisdiction should seem to me to begin precisely where the other ends, and that to prevent their interfering or Clashing with each other. But however that may be, the Civil Officers of the Ordnance will not be dispunishable, as they will be responsible for Misbehaviour to those who appointed them, and liable to Amoval from their Office; and in case of Atrocious Misdemeanors the Governor is armed with a discretionary Power of preventing any breach of Peace or good Order within the Garrison by a proper Confinement, untill some other Course can be taken.

I am with great Respect,

Sir,

Your most Obedient & most humble

Servant

Charles Gould.

Right Hoñble Henry Fox. &cᵃ &cᵃ

D. MILITARY JURISDICTION OVER CIVILIANS IN OCCUPIED CANADA

1. *Charles Gould, DJAG, to Hector Theophilus Cramahé, DJA at Quebec, 11 August 1763* [WO 81/10/204].

Judge Advocate's Office

11ᵗʰ August 1763.

Sir,

I am in the absence of the Judge Advocate General to acknowledge the receipt of your letter of the 30ᵗʰ April last, together with the Copy of the Proceedings of a General Court Martial held on Staatin Island the 24ᵗʰ October 1761, as also the Copies of one held at Crown Point the 14ᵗʰ Novʳ 1762, and of another held at Louisbourg the 31ˢᵗ January following. The same Packet inclosed likewise a Copy of the Proceedings of a General

Court Martial held at Quebec the 29th March, as also of the Declarations and Depositions, which occasioned a second Court Martial upon the 15th of April last, a Copy whereof was likewise transmitted. I have wrote by this Opportunity to Governor Murray the King's Pleasure concerning the Prisoners reprieved by him, untill His Majesty's farther Commands should be known: and have only to hint to you a doubt which is entertained with regard to the Trial of Persons not Military, by Courts Martial, not withstanding the last Article of War, which provides for the punishment of Civil Offences, where no Civil Judicature is in force: the Expression of *All Persons* being to be understood only of All Persons Subject to those Articles. I only mean this hint for your own private information, in case such question should at any time hereafter arise. I am with much truth and regard

Sir,

Your most obedient
humble Servant,
Charles Gould.

Hector Theophilus Cramahé, Esqr Judge Advocate.

2. *Charles Gould, DJAG, to Governor Murray of Quebec, 11 August 1763* [WO 72/5].

Judge Advocate's Offices,
11 August 1763

Sir,

At the same time, that I have the honour of Signifying the Kings Pleasure upon the Sentences of Jacob Ritter and Godfrey Eighorn Soldiers in your Battalion of the Royal American Regiment for Robbery, I beg leave to acquaint you, that a Pardon is passing the Great Seal of Great Britain (and will be forwarded to you by the very first opportunity) for Joseph Corriveaux, as Accessary to the Murder of Louis Helene Dodier at St. Vallier.

I thought it proper to make this the Subject of a Separate Letter, not choosing that any thing should appear officially concerning his Case, as the King's Pardon Signified by the Judge Advocate would not be effectual, and as the Court Martial appear to have exceeded their Jurisdiction in his trial as well as in those of *Marie Josephe Corriveaux* for the same Murder, and of Isabella Silvain for Perjury; neither of them being military Persons, nor Subject to the Mutiny Act or Articles of War. I was in hopes, it might have been expedited, so as to be transmitted herewith; but the Lord Privy Seal, Lord Chancellor, and others, thro' whom Pardons of this nature necessarily pass, being out of Town, the delay occasioned by sending it to their respective Seats has made it impracticable. I took the liberty of mentioning my thoughts to Lord Egremont, who saw the Matter in the same light; and his Lordship, to whose Province it belonged to move His Majesty for the Pardon, preferred it's passing in a private manner through me, rather than Signifying the King's Commands from his Office. Although there has been no Substantial injustice done in this case,—on the contrary the Guilt of the Person, who has suffered, was evident, and the necessity of Example great,—Nevertheless you are so well apprised, how many there are in this Kingdom, who view the Military Arm with a jealous Eye and are ever ready to take advantage of the least mistaken excess of Power, though proceeding from the best intention, that I persuade myself, you will not think the delicacy used upon this occasion unnecessary, and that what I have thought it my duty to Suggest will meet with your candid Acceptance.

Permit me to offer my best Congratulation on your Appointment to the Government of Canada,[1] and to Subscribe myself, with much truth and esteem,

Sir,

Your most obedient
and most humble Servant,
Charles Gould

3. *Governor Murray of Quebec to Charles Gould, DJAG, 12 November 1763* [WO 72/5].

Quebec 12th Novr 1763

Sir!

I cannot delay, a moment, to return Thanks for your Favor of the 11th August. I must forever think myself greatly obliged to you for the tenderness, and delicacy you have shewn in the Business of Josephe Corrivaux &c. &c:: You must be persuaded that tho' we have erred, our Intentions were most Upright, and I declare to You, I think it was lucky we did not know, how limited our Jurisdiction has been here for four years past. His Majesty's new Subjects, already prejudiced against us by every popish Art, must have conceived a Strange Opinion of their new Masters, who had no Law to punish the most notorious Murder, that perhaps has ever been committed.

I understand a civil Jurisdiction will soon be established here, when that happens, we can no longer be at a loss, in the mean Time, I have communicated to the Governors of Trois Rivieres, and Montreal, the Knowledge I have learnt from your Letter; I am confident the Information was as necessary for them, as it was for me, and I am astonished I was not apprised of the irregularity of our proceedings in time to have prevented

---

[1] On 21 Nov. 1763, Gen. Murray was appointed Captain General and Governor in Chief of the new Province of Quebec, created by the Proclamation of the preceding month. Shortt and Doughty 173–181. But neither the Proclamation nor the appointment took effect until 10 Aug. 1764, the end of the 18-month period prescribed by the Treaty of Paris; not until then did the *Règne Militaire* end and the civil government begin to function. See *supra*, pp. 52, 63.

them, as I am certain it is near three years ago, since two Canadians (*not Soldiers, nor in any respect subject to a military jurisdiction, according to your Explanation of the Articles of War,*) were hanged at Montreal, agreeable to the Sentence of a General Court Martial, approven of by Major General Gage, the Governor of that place, to which I add, the Paragraph, of the Secretary of States Letter quoted to you by Mr Cramahé; I certainly must do you the Justice to believe that the Proceedings of that Court Marshal were never sent to Your Office, but I can with difficulty reconcile Lord Egremonts Letter, to His Lordships seeing the Affair of Corrivaux in the same light that you do.

If, Sir! I can be of any Service to you in this part of the world, I shall be happy in receiving and executing your commands for I am with great Truth and Regard

Sir!

Your most obedient, and
most humble Servant
Ja: Murray

Charles Gould Esqr

4. *Draft of Letter, Charles Gould, DJAG, to Governor Murray of Quebec, 14 January 1764* [WO 72/6; crossed out matter in brackets].

Horse Guards 14th Jan:^{ry} 1764

Sir,

I have the honour of your Letter of the 12th November last, and am happy, that the Thoughts, which I took the liberty of Suggesting have been received in the manner I meant and wished. Though my Opinion is still the same, as to the Strict legality,—I must agree with you, that it may have been better in it's Consequences that you should have exceeded in this particular, than that the King's new Subjects should have taken up an Opinion, that Crimes of such enormous Nature might pass unpunished. [At the same time that I must admit, that the Extract of Lord Egremont's Letter might reasonably be thought to extend]

I have looked into the [Proceedings] Entries of Courts Martial in this office, and find the Proceedings had at Montreal, to which your Letter referrs me, [and find them duly Entered, and] to have been exactly similar. [to the present.] Whether they were opened by the Judge Advocate General, or me, I cannot pretend to say, but [they were] with the Sentences appearing upon the face of them to be Confirmed abroad, and no Act remaining to be done thereupon in Britain, they must [were] certainly have been delivered over with several others under the same Predicament, to the Clerks to be Entered and safely deposited in the Office. Had any observation from the Judge Advocate, who transmitted them, led me to look into them, I should [doubtless] have taken the liberty of writing to General Gage thereupon. However with this one and the other they have had their good effect, and that they may have no other, I shall endeavor as far as in me lies, by [not pointing] keeping [out the inaccuracy] the matter [inaccuracy] to myself.

I have the honour to be with much truth & regard,

> Sir,
>> Your most obedient
>> and most humble Servant,

His Excellency Governor Murray.

5. *Charles Gould, DJAG, to General Thomas Gage, C. in C. North America, late Governor of Montreal, 11 February 1764* [Gage MSS., WLCL].

> Horse Guards 11ᵗʰ Febrỹ 1764.

Sir,

I persuade myself from your Candour, that you will excuse the trouble of this Letter from one, who has not the honour of being personally known to you, and that, even should you incline to a different opinion, my intentions will nevertheless be favourably interpreted. Upon looking into some late Proceedings of General Courts Martial transmitted by Captain Falconer Judge Advocate, I observe some Trials, and those in capital cases, of Persons confessedly not Military. These in my humble apprehension (and indeed it does not rest upon my private opinion only) are not strictly warranted in Law: (though, far from controverting the utility of such Proceeding, where no Civil Judicature was in force, I can easily conceive it to have been of the highest import to His Majesty's Service, that some Examples should be held forth to deterr others.) Nor can the last Section of the Articles of War, though worded in general Terms, be taken to extend to any other Persons, than those, who are the Object of those Articles.

You will do me the justice to believe, that I have a proper Sense of the delicacy, which it becomes me to use upon this occasion; and that I should not have observed upon Proceedings, which had received your Confirmation, had not I thought it my Duty to Suggest so much for your consideration in future.

> I am with respect,
>> Sir,
>>> Your most Obedient
>>> and most humble Servant
>>> Charles Gould.

His Excellency General Gage.

6. *General Thomas Gage, C. in C. North America, to Charles Gould, DJAG, 10 April 1764* [WO 72/6].

> New York April 10th 1764

Sir,

I am obliged to you for your Favor of the 11th Febry, in which you are pleased to make some observations on the Proceedings of the Genˡ Courts

Martial which have been held at Montreal; and till the Receipt of your Letter, I must own to you, I had not the smallest Doubt of their being consistent with Law. The utility of such Proceedings you are sensible of, where no Civil Judicature was in Force; you must therefore be sensible of the Necessity of passing Laws for the Direction of Officers in such Circumstances, to prevent Anarchy & Confusion, Murder, Robbery, & every heinous Crime being committed, without Restraint or Controul.

These Matters have been debated here; we have been told in Gen[l], That it is a Maxim held by all Civilians That no Government can subsist without Law, That in Conquered Countrys, The Laws of Such Countrys Subsist, till it shall please the Conqueror to give Them new Laws. In Canada, all Justice ceased upon the Conquest, for every Court of Civil or Criminal Judicature left the Country. The Gen[l] therefore constituted new Courts of Judicature, and Criminal Cases were ordered to be tried by Gen[l] Courts Martial only. This Method was approved of by the King, and was accordingly followed.

If this Method was not strictly Warranted in Law, I should think it worth asking the opinion & advice of the Heads of the Law, how Canada in such Circumstances, ought to be governed, or whether any Difference could be made in the Government of the Canadians, and the British Subjects who came into Canada. The Canadians alledged their Laws were not changed, the British Subjects, that they were to be tryed by English Laws only, and were not Subject to the Canadian Laws, tho' in Canada. Canadians were appointed by the Authority of the Gen[l] to compose Civil Courts, but the British Subjects would not acknowledge their Authority. The Lawyers here have been divided in their opinions, about these Affairs; all agree some Justice must take Place, but differ widely as to the Courts of Judicature.

I tell you what has passed, and the Difficultys and Questions which have been started. What ought to have been done, or what ought not to have been done, I must leave to your better Judgement, as I am not ashamed to own myself at a Loss in a matter, which has puzzled those, who should be more knowing in these Affairs.

Civil Judges we hear are appointed for Canada, It's to be hoped they will arrive soon, and put an End to the Trouble and Perplexity, which the Governors have undergone ever Since the Capitulation of Montreal, I am,
> Sir,

> Your most obedient
> humble Servant
> Tho[s] Gage

7. *Charles Gould, DJAG, to Hunter Sedgwick, Esq.,*[2] *30 May 1764* [WO 81/11/12].

---

[2] Undoubtedly a clerk in the Secretary of State's Office and perhaps a relative of Edward Sedgwick, who was Undersecretary for American Affairs. See 1 *Cal. Home Office Pap., 1760–1765,* p. 529.

Judge Advocate's Office
30th May 1764

Sir,

I think it my Duty to communicate to my Lord Halifax the Contents of a Letter from General Gage, in answer to some Remarks, which I had, to prevent any inconvenience in future, taken the liberty of Suggesting with regard to Proceedings had by Courts Martial against Persons not Military, and particularly in some cases of consequence: and am therefore to desire you will please to lay the inclosed Copy of the General's Letter before his Lordship, that I may have the honour of receiving his Commands thereupon.

In whatever light this Matter may appear to his Lordship, I am hopeful he will not disapprove my having submitted my Sentiments to the Commander in Chief upon a point of that Consequence and delicacy, as I had no other view than to prevent any Proceeding being inadvertently had, of which (however expedient under those particular circumstances) advantage might possibly thereafter have been taken, as not being warranted in Law.

I am Sir,

Your most Obedient and
most humble Servant
Charles Gould.

Hunter Sedgwick Esqr

8. *Charles Gould, DJAG, to General Thomas Gage, C. in C. North America, 7 June 1764* [WO 81/11/14].

Judge Advocate's Office
7th June 1764

Sir,

I was honoured with your Letter of the 10th April last, which from the apparent necessity of some speedy Provision under the circumstances represented in your said Letter, I thought it my Duty to communicate to the Earl of Halifax for his Consideration. Since which I have received by his Lordship's Order Extracts of the Commission and Instructions to Governor Murray containing a Power to establish a Civil Government and to constitute proper Courts of Judicature, and with them an answer from his Lordship dated the 5th Inst: to the following effect, "That, as His Majesty's Commission and Instructions to Governor Murray, which were sent to him a considerable time ago, and must e'er now have reached his hands, contain full Powers to constitute Courts of Justice for the hearing and determining of all Causes as well Criminal as Civil, there can be no doubt, but that the Practice of Proceeding against Persons not Military by Courts Martial will be put an end to, and the Doubts and Difficulties Set forth by General Gage effectually removed."

This makes it unnecessary for me to trouble you with a more particular answer to your Letter; but I cannot conclude without returning my best thanks for your candid reception of the thoughts, which I had Suggested, and for the trouble you was pleased to take in Stating the Matter so fully and in so obliging a manner. I am with respect

Sir, Your most obedient
and most humble Servt
Charles Gould.

His Excellency General Gage.

9. *Extract from letter, Colonel Ralph Burton, Governor at Montreal, late Governor of Trois Rivières, to Charles Gould, DJAG, 3 July 1764* [WO 72/6].

I am gratefully to acknowledge the Contents of your kind letter, of the same date [14 Apr. 1764]; and I do most thankfully receive the observations upon that Court-Martial you have been pleased to communicate to me.

I am very sensible, that the Defect of a Civil Government, not being established in this Conquered Country, must have embarrassed the administration of Justice, with some irregularities; but to me out [?] of Government, being indispensably necessary, at the Conquest of the Country, for the good of the Service; and the Orders, and Instructions, relative thereto, and hitherto followed, having met with His Majesty's most gracious Approbation, it is to be hoped that in case any Sentence given here, should come to be litigated in Great Britain, the Circumstances of these Governments and the good Intentions of those, who carry on that part of the Service, will be taken into Consideration.

E. MILITARY JURISDICTION OVER A MEMBER OF THE ROYAL NAVY

1. *Charles Gould, DJAG, to the Rt. Hon. Welbore Ellis, SW, 2 June 1763* [WO 81/10/169].

Judge Advocate's Office
2^d June 1763.

Sir,

Having perused the Proceedings of a General Court Martial held in the Island of Martinique on the 18th and continued by adjournment to the 22^d of March last upon the Trial of Daniel McDonald Boatswain of His Majesty's Ship Foudroyant for the Murder of William Sampey late Soldier in the 76th Regiment of Foot, I think it my duty to submit my Opinion, that the Prisoner not belonging to His Majesty's Army, the Court Martial had not cognizance of his Offence, and consequently their whole Proceedings from a defect of Jurisdiction are null and void, nor can the Sentence receive His Majesty's Confirmation. For though the words of the Article, under which the Court has proceeded, are General,—"Where there is no form of Our Civil Judicature in Force, General Courts Martial are to try *all Persons* guilty of Wilful Murder, Theft, &c^a"—Yet this expression must be understood of such Persons, as are the objects of Military Law and Articles of War. And indeed the recital at the beginning of the Article Marks this limitation;—"Notwithstanding its being directed in the 11th Section of these Our Rules and Articles, that every Commanding Officer is required to deliver up to the Civil Magistrate all such Persons *under his Command,* who shall be accused of any Crimes punishable by the known Laws of the Land,"—and if we referr to that 11th Section, it will be found, that the Persons so to be secured and delivered up are there described to be *"any Officer or Soldier,* who shall be accused of any Capital Crime &c^a punishable by the known Laws of the Land"—But I even go a Step farther, and should humbly apprehend, that, if the words of the Article were clearly extended to all Persons Civil, as well as Military, nevertheless this would not conferr a Legal Jurisdiction over the former, because they have never done any Act, nor entered into any engagement, which Subjects them to the Articles of War, nor are they bound to take notice of them.

In justice to the Court however it must be observed, that the Evidence has been taken with great accuracy and care, and possibly upon His Majesty's being informed, that, from a State of the matter therein contained, it appears that this unhappy Stroke was given on a sudden quarrell and in the heat of Passion from a blow received and not from any premeditated Malice, other than, that which the Law implies from the use of such a Weapon, His Majesty may be Graciously pleased to grant his Royal Pardon to the Prisoner. But, if His Majesty shall not think fit, upon a Charge Murder, to extend his Mercy, untill the Offence shall have been tried by a Court having a competent Jurisdiction, I conceive, it will be advisable, that the Prisoner be sent over to England in order to his being tried by a Jury upon an Indictment to be preferred in the King's Bench.

I rely intirely upon your candid acceptance and representation of these imperfect thoughts, and have the honour to be,

Sir,

Your most obedient and
most humble Servant,
Charles Gould.

Right Hoñble Welbore Ellis.

2. *Charles Gould, DJAG, to O.C. in C. Antigua, 23 July 1763* [WO 81/10/198].

Judge Advocate's Office
23^d July 1763

Sir,

I beg leave to inclose for your information the Duplicate of a Letter to Governor Rufane, which I have little or no expectation, can have reached him before the Troops Sailed from Martinique. In that case, it is uncertain, whether he may have ordered the Prisoner Daniel McDonald on board with the Forces bound to England, or whether he may have thought proper to send him to Antigua, or some other of His Majesty's Islands untill the King's Pleasure should be known concerning him. If the Prisoner should be left at Antigua or in Charge with any of the Forces under your Command, I am to desire, you will be pleased to send him to England by the first safe opportunity, or give such other orders as you shall judge most effectual towards carrying His Majesty's Pleasure into execution. I am

Sir, Your most obedient
humble Servant,
Charles Gould.

The Officer Commanding
in Chief at Antigua.

3. *Charles Gould, DJAG, to Philip Stephens, Esq., Secretary of the Admiralty, 23 July 1763* [WO 81/10/199].

Judge Advocate's Office
23^d July 1763.

Sir,

Permit me to intreat your favour in forwarding by the first conveyance the inclosed Letter for the Commanding Officer in the Island of Antigua; which Signifies, His Majesty's Pleasure, that Daniel Macdonald late Boatswain of His Majesty's Ship Foudroyant should, if a Prisoner in that Island or in Charge of any of the Forces under his Command, be sent to England by the first safe conveyance in order to take his Trial in one of His Majesty's Courts of Civil Judicature for the Murder of William Sampey, Soldier in the 76th Regiment of Foot, wherewith he is charged and for which some Proceedings have been erroneously had against him by a Court Martial composed of Officers in the Army. The Kings Pleasure to the like effect was Signified in a Letter to the Governor of Martinique, but I have very little expectation of the Letter having reached him before the Troops left that Island: which makes it doubtful, whether the Governor may have caused the Prisoner McDonald to be embarked with the Forces destined to England, or has sent him to Antigua or some of the other Islands. If application should be made to the Captains of any of His Majesty's Ships for the more safe conveyance of the Prisoner, I make no doubt he will give permission: but if you think any application necessary to the Lords Commissioners of the Admiralty, you will be kind enough to move their Lordship's in that behalf,

I am

Sir, Your most obedient and
obliged humble Servant,
Charles Gould.

Philip Stephens Esqr

4. *Charles Gould, DJAG, to the Hon. Capt. Perceval, R.N., 26 August 1763* [WO 81/10/219].

Judge Advocate's Office

Horse Guards 26th August 1763

Sir,

The trouble I am about to give you respects Daniel McDonald late Boatswain of His Majesty's Ship Foudroyant who I learn by a Letter from Colonel Rufane is brought to England Prisoner in the Aquilon. As some doubts have arisen with regard to the Proceedings against him by a Court Martial for the Murder, wherewith he is charged, it has been thought advisable, that he should be carryed before Lord Chief Justice Mansfield by Virtue of a Writ of Habeas Corpus, to be disposed of, as his Lordship shall see fit; when probably, in respect of his long Confinement and some favourable circumstances in his Case, he may be admitted to Bail, but that will be in his Lordship's Judgment. That Writ I am informed from the regular course of Process, will be Served upon you, as Commander of the Ship, on board which he is detained, directing you to produce the Prisoner, before the Chief Justice, and to Set forth the Cause of his Confinement. In consequence of the former part of the Precept you will be pleased to cause the Prisoner to be delivered into the Custody of those, who will be appointed to receive him from the Ship, in order to his being produced; and I hope you will have but little trouble in regard to the latter, as I shall direct the Solicitor for the Crown (from the best information I am possessed of)—to prepare a return to the Writ, which I hope will prove such, as will only require your Signing it: but if you see occasion to vary it in any respect, you will please to make the necessary Alteration. I thought it a respect due to you, to give you this previous information, that you might not be surprised with the unexpected Service of the Writ, in a Matter which ought not to be attended with any trouble to you.

I have the honour to be

Sir,

Your most obedient and
most humble Servant,
Charles Gould.

The Honble Captain Perceval.

5. *Charles Gould, DJAG, to Mr. Francis,*[3] *31 August 1763* [WO 81/10/222].

Horse Guards 31ˢᵗ August 1763

Sir,

I am to desire, that Mʳ Attorney General may be attended with the inclosed Letter, and that you will receive his Instructions concerning the Prisoner, who is to be brought by Habeas Corpus before Lord Mansfield. You will be pleased to mention, that the only occasion of the delay herein arises from the Ship, which has the Prisoner on board, being ordered

---

[3] Quite probably Philip Francis (1740–1818), first clerk at the War Office 1762–1772, reputed author of the *Letters of Junius,* and later knighted.

round from Spithead to the Nore, and till there is an Account of her being arrived at the latter, it is in vain to send down the Writ.

I am

Sir,

Your most obedient Servant,

Charles Gould.

Mr Francis.

F. MILITARY JURISDICTION OVER CIVILIANS ON MINORCA

1. *Charles Gould, DJAG, to the Earl of Halifax, SS, 7 March 1765* [WO 81/11/66].

Horse Guards 7th March 1765

My Lord,

I think it my Duty to acquaint your Lordship, that by the Proceedings of a General Court Martial held in the Island of Minorca in the Month of January last, and which have been lately transmitted to the Judge Advocate's Office it appears, that John McLearen and William Rogers, two Soldiers of the 11th Regiment of Foot together with Mary Rogers were Capitally Convicted of the Murder and Roberry of Joseph Peloutier a French Shop keeper at Ciudadella on the 25th of December 1764, and that the two Soldiers were ordered for Execution, but Mary Rogers on account of certain circumstances in her favour was thought a proper Object of Mercy.

In the Trial of the Soldiers I presume the Court Martial was regular and warrented by the Provisions made by the Articles of War, but with respect to the Woman or any Person not Military I should humbly conceive a Court Martial had not a competent Jurisdiction, and that the Pardon of the Commanding Officer Granted upon a Supposition of his having Authority to Confirm or remit the Sentences of Courts Martial is mistaken and insufficient. It is therefore with great deference Submitted, whether your Lordship may not think it advisable under all the circumstances of this case to move His Majesty to extend his most Gracious Pardon to the said Mary Rogers, who is represented to have made the first discovery of the Murder and of the persons concerned in it; and the rather, as She does not appear, tho' present in Company with her Husband, to have been actually assisting in the perpetration of the Murder.

I am with great respect

My Lord,

Your Lordship's most humble

and most obedient Servant

Charles Gould

The Earl of Halifax,
His Majesty's Principal
Secretary of State.

2. *Charles Gould, DJAG, to Col. Townshend, Governor of Minorca, 28 March 1765* [WO 81/11/67].

Horse Guards 28th March 1765

Sir

Upon looking into the Proceedings of a General Court Martial held at St Philip's Castle on the 14th day of January last, as transmitted by Mr Smith Judge Advocate, to see, whether the Sentences had been approved, or whether any of them required to be laid before His Majesty, I observed that two Persons Convicted of a Murder and Roberry had been Ordered for Execution, but that you had (for proper reasons assigned) Granted a Pardon to Mary Rogers, a third Person concerned therein. You will, I am sure, easily forgive a remark, which suggested itself to me upon the Proceedings, and your Candour, should you even differ in opinion, will not disapprove the Steps, which it appeared to me advisable to take in consequence thereof. The Trial and Condemnation of the two Men, being Soldiers, and the Execution of the Sentence (taking it for granted, that you had express Authority by your Commission or Warrant under the Sign Manual for that purpose) I conceive to be well warranted under the Articles of War; but in the Trial of Mary Rogers, I apprehend the Court Martial have exceeded their Jurisdiction, none but Military Persons being amesnable thereto: for tho' the words of the Article, which may have been thought to warrant this Proceeding are general, "Courts Martial are to Try *all Persons* Guilty of Wilfull Murder, Roberry" &c^a yet this must be understood only of Persons, who are Subject to the Articles of War, and who have Sworn or Subscribed to their observance:—and even supposing this Woman to have been considered in some Sort, as a part of the Garrison and attached to the Corps, which she followed, and that instances might be produced of Courts Martial animadverting upon some irregularities committed by Persons within that description, but which is perhaps connived at, rather than expressly warranted, I think no Usage or Construction can be supported in that latitude as to punish Capitally, and upon a Charge purely Civil. As the Trial was, in this view irregular, so also is the Pardon granted by you ineffectual, as even the Royal Pardon would be, Signified thro' the Military Channel. Under this Persuasion, and thinking it necessary upon every account to provide, that the Woman should not by any possibility be again called to answer for the same fact, I judged it most proper to apply to Lord Halifax and desire his Lordship, in whose province it laid, to move His Majesty for a Pardon under the Great Seal upon the general circumstances of the Case without reciting any Proceedings had by a Court Martial, to which His Majesty has been graciously pleased to assent: And His Lordship approved the method suggested by me of the Pardon passing through my hands, as upon a private Sollicitation, rather than that he should Signify The King's Commands to you officially, as Secretary of State. The Pardon will be expedited thro' the several Offices and I will transmit it to you by the next opportunity, that Mary Rogers may receive it at your hands, as the Royal Confirmation obtained by you of the Pardon, which you had in the King's Name assured her of.—Though nothing has been done in this case repugnant to Equity (on the contrary, the heinousness of the Crime called for speedy Justice, which, from the defect of Civil Judicature, could not otherways be obtained, and the Suspension of the Sentence, though it could not extend to a legal Pardon, has prevented every inconvenience) you are nevertheless aware, how many Persons in this Kingdom are ever ready to censure the least mistaken excess of Military Jurisdiction,—however well intentioned, and I trust therefore, you will think the delicacy used upon this occasion not affected or unnecessary, and that you will believe me to be with great truth,

Sir,

Your most obedient
and most humble
Servant.

Charles Gould.

Colonel Townshend.

3. *Copy of Royal Pardon for Mary Rogers, 20 April 1765* [WO 72/6].

GEORGE THE THIRD BY THE GRACE OF GOD of Great Britain France and Ireland King Defender of the Faith and So forth, To all to whom these presents shall come, Greeting. Whereas It has been humbly Represented unto Us, that Mary Rogers stands charged with the Murder and Roberry of Joseph Peloutier a French Shopkeeper in Ciudadolla in Our Island of Minorca on the Twenty fifth day of December last, for which John McLearen and William Rogers have been already Executed, And We having thought fit upon Consideration of certain Circumstances attending the Case of the said Mary Rogers to Extend Our Grace and Mercy to her, Now KNOW YE, that we being moved with Compassion of Our Especial Grace certain Knowledge and mere Motion Have Pardoned Remitted and Released, and by these presents for Us Our Heirs and successors do Pardon Remitt and Release the said Mary Rogers, or by whatever other Name or Sir Name or Addition of Name or Sirname Profession Place or Mistery the said Mary Rogers might be deemed called or known or was lately deemed called or known the Murder & Robbery of the said Joseph Peloutier Committed by the said Mary Rogers alone or with any other Person or Persons whatsoever whensoever or wheresoever done Committed or Perpretrated, with which she stands Charged as above mentioned, and her flying for the same thereupon, And also all and Singular Indictments, Inquisitions, Judgments, Prosecutions, Convictions, Attainders, Condemnations, Executions, Pains of death, Pains Corporal, Imprisonments, Punishments, Forfeitures, and all other Pains and Penalties whatsoever had made given or adjudged or hereafter to be had made given or Adjudged, upon or against the said Mary Rogers for the Murder and Robbery of the said Joseph Peloutier, and also all and Singular Outlawrys Promulgated or had or to be promulgated or had against the said Mary Rogers by reason of the Premisses or any of them And all manner of Suits, Plaints, Impeachments, Judgments, and demands whatsoever, which We, Our Heirs or Successors, now have or have had or in any manner hereafter may have against the said Mary Rogers for the Murder and Robbery of the said Joseph Peloutier, And by these presents We do give and grant to her Our firm Peace by reason thereof Forbidding, that the said Mary Rogers be Molested, Impeached, disturbed, or in any wise Aggrieved by the Justices Sherriffs Bayliffs or other Ministers of US, Our Heirs or Successors or any of them, by reason of the Premisses or any of them, So that Nevertheless she may stand right in Court, if any one will Prosecute or Implead her concerning the Premisses, or any of them. AND FURTHER We will Grant for Us Our Heirs and Successors, that these Our Letters Patent of Pardon and all and Singular matters and things therein Contained shall be and remain good Firm valid Sufficient and effectual in the Law and shall be taken in the most favourable and beneficial Sense for the Advantage of the said Mary Rogers for the discharging and acquitting her for and concerning the Premisses and shall be taken Adjudged Pleaded and allowed in all Our Courts and elsewhere without any writ of allowance, or other Warrant first obtained or to be obtained in that behalf, and that for the future the said Mary Rogers shall not be Arrested, Prosecuted, Impeached, Imprisoned, or in any manner Molested for or concerning the Premisses or any of them, any Misrecital Repugnancy or Contrariety in these presents contained or any other Matter Cause or thing whatsoever to the Contrary thereof in any wise Notwithstanding. In Witness whereof We have caused these Our Letters to be made Patent. Witness Ourself at Westminster the Twentieth day of April in the Fifth Year of Our Reign

By Writ of Privy Seal————Yorke & Yorke

4. *Extract from letter, Charles Gould, JAG, to Capt. Henry Schomberg, DJA at Minorca, 22 September 1770* [WO 72/6].

With regard to your fourth Query, I should by no means recommend the Trial of a Woman, Wife to a Soldier, by a Court Martial for Felony. You mention their being included in the Mutiny Act; but I do not recollect any Clause which extends to such. And the Article of War, which says, that, in the Island of Minorca and other places specified, All *Persons* guilty of Murder, Robbery, &ca—are to be tried by Courts Martial, must necessarily be understood to speak of Military Persons.

5. *Charles Gould, JAG, to Joseph Collins, DJA at Minorca, 23 September 1777* [WO 81/13/157].

Horse Guards 23ᵈ September 1777.

Sir,

In answer to the favor of your Letter of the 10ᵗʰ August last, I cannot offer to you any better opinion, than that which General Murray⁴ has

---

⁴ Gen. James Murray, Governor of Quebec 1759–1764 and Governor in Chief of Canada 1764–1768, was named Governor of Minorca in 1774. In 1782, after a long siege, he surrendered the island. See Mahon, chs. XVII–XIX.

himself suggested. The Storekeepers, Clerks, and Artificers of the Ordnance not comprehended within the provisions of the Mutiny Acts and Articles of War are clearly not amesnable to Courts Martial in respect of any Assaults or disorders amongst themselves: for if those Courts have not Jurisdiction over them in Matters which respect the public Service, much less can they be supposed to have cognizance or inferior Offences, originating from disputes of a personal or private Nature.

If the several persons in the Service or employ of the Ordnance in Minorca are desirous of being considered as Military, and to be alike Subject to discipline and triable by Courts Martial, it is probable, a representation through the Master and Principal Officers would be attended to; but that they should be amesnable to those Courts in some cases and exempt in others will scarcely be deemed expedient.

I must desire, you will be pleased to present my best respects to General Murray; and am, with much regard,

Sir,

Your very faithful
and Obedient Servant
Charles Gould.

Joseph Collins Esqr

G. MILITARY JURISDICTION OVER INHABITANTS IN NEW YORK DURING THE WAR OF AMERICAN INDEPENDENCE

1. *Charles Gould, JAG, to Gen. Sir William Howe, C. in C. North America, 20 June 1777* [WO 72/8].

Horse Guards 20th June 1777

Sir,

At the same time that I have the honor to Signify to your Excellency the King's Pleasure respecting the Sentences of several Courts Martial, which your Letters to Lord George Germain expressed to have been respited, untill His Majesty's determination should be known, I take the liberty of submitting to your consideration, whether Courts Martial are well founded in the Jurisdiction exercised by them in the Trial of persons, who are in no sort belonging to the Army. I am very sensible of the necessity of executing speedy Justice upon signal Offenders, as an Example to deter others, nor have I a doubt, that the Prisoners will have as fair and candid a Trial by Courts Martial, as before a Civil Tribunal: I mean only to point out a material distinction, as to the Authority vested in Courts Martial, between Military persons, who are the proper and immediate objects of the Articles of War, and Civil persons, who are certainly not within the purview of them. Perhaps therefore it might have been advisable, if in any case from the evident necessity of present and exemplary punishment Courts Martial have been induced to exceed the limits of their ordinary Jurisdiction, not to call the attention to any of the Articles of War in the penning of their Sentence.

One other circumstance I will offer to your Excellency's consideration, Whether upon any military person being convicted of Crimes, which the Law of the Land deems to be *Capital*, the Court is not bound to give Judgment of Death. The conclusion of the 2ᵈ Article of War of the 20ᵗʰ Section, which directs Courts Martial "to punish Offenders with Death or otherwise, as the Nature of their Crimes shall deserve," has manifest reference to the precedent Words, "Capital Crimes or other Offences"—And the natural Construction of the whole Article taken together seems to be, that Capital Crimes shall be punished with Death, and inferior Offences, with such other punishment as the Law may have specially prescribed, and, in cases where no special punishment is provided, *then* at the discretion of the Court Martial.

These are delicate Subjects, and I shall therefore not presume to suggest my thoughts upon them to the Judge Advocate acting in America, but through your Excellency.

I have the honor to be,

Sir,

your Excellency's most
Obedient and most humble
Servant,
Charles Gould.

His Excellency The Honble Sir William Howe, &cᵃ &cᵃ &cᵃ

2. *Report of the Magistrates of Police at New York to Gen. Sir Henry Clinton, C. in C. North America, 4 December 1781* [CO 5/104/166].

REPORT of the Magistrates of the POLICE, made in compliance with His Excellency Lieut: General Robertsons [5] Letter of the 29ᵗʰ Novʳ: 1781 in which was enclosed His Excellency Sir Henry Clinton's Letter of the 28ᵗʰ November with the Memorial of George Folliott Esquire to Their Excellencies His Majesty's Commissioners

From Sir William Howe's taking Possession of New York in September 1776 untill May 1778, The Police of New York was solely conducted and executed by the Commandant of the City assisted by the Mayor; the great increase of the Returning Inhabitants, Traders and Itinerants of the Army, then called for a further Assistance, and at same time made it necessary to adopt such Regulations for the Security of the Property and Persons of the Civil, as could be admitted of by the Military Government under which this Garrison has continued ever since Sir William Howe's first taking Possession.

Upon these Principles, General Daniel Jones, Commandant of the City, had Orders from the Commander in Chief to establish the Police, which was accordingly done by Proclamation in May 1778. The Commandant

---

[5] Lt.-Gen. James Robertson, at this time the Civil Governor of the Province of New York. See *supra*, pp. 98–99, 119.

and the Magistrates of Police (who were appointed as his Assistants) were to draw a Line of Conduct in regard to Matters connected with the Civil, (every Military Concern in the Garrison continuing under the direction of the Commandant) upon the following Plan;

N° 1.. Inhabitants not to be confined in the Main Guard, but by Orders from Head Quarters, the Commandant or the Police.

N° 2.. The Board of Police to hear all disputes that might daily arise either between the Military and the Civil or amongst the Inhabitants themselves.

N° 3.. All Controversies respecting Trade, or disputes regarding Payment of Debts that had not originated before May 1777, to be brought before the Police.

N° 4.. The Board of Police to grant Passes in some instances, and to recommend to the Commandant in others.

N° 5.. The Police to administer the Oaths of Allegiance and grant Certificates to Persons admitted as Inhabitants.

N° 6.. The Police to Recomend to the Commandant necessary Regulations for the good of the Town, and when adopted by him to see the same duly complied with.

N° 7.. The Officers of the Police had Salaries appointed, with Orders not to receive any Fee or Gratuity whatever in the execution of their duty.

In conformity to the above Plan, with the Approbation of the Commandant, the Police have proceeded Viz^t

N° 1. . Whenever it is found necessary that Inhabitants for their Crimes or Misdemeanors should be confined in the Main Guard, if not done by the Two Superior Powers, the Police issue a Warrant which is executed by the Serjeant of the Police; This Regulation has freed the Inhabitants from much Oppression. Committments to the Provost either of Military or Civil Persons, are made solely by Orders from Head Quarters or the Commandant; The Prisoners of the Main Guard, are examined by the Police every day between Eleven and Twelve O'Clock, they Report the Examination to The Commandant, and recomend the Prisoner to be sent to the Provost if his Crime merits his being brought before a Garrison Court Martial, or that he be discharged on Bail if necessary to be held on Bail (which is given at the Police) or if a consistent attonement can be made to the Complainant, that the Prisoner be immediately discharged; with these Recommendations from the Police the Commandant immediately complys or calls the Parties before himself, by which means the Main Guard is cleared of Prisoners every day. Corporal Punishments or Fines are ordered by Court Martials only.

N° 2. . When disputes arise between an Officer and an Inhabitant, the Commandant orders the matter before a Board of Enquiry, which sits once a week or oftner if necessary, consisting of Three Field Officers and Two of the Magistrates of Police; this Board reports to the Commandant, who enforces their decree if they give one, or follows their directions to dismiss the Matter or bring it before a Court Martial; The same Mode is pursued with the consent of the Naval Commander here when an Officer of the Navy and an Inhabitant have a dispute.

When any Inhabitant complains of another for Trespass or Breach of the Peace, the Parties and their Evidences are summonsed before the Police, in the first instance, the Matter is determined by the Opinion of the Police or by Arbitration as the Case may require; in the Second, the Agressor is reported to the Commandant for a Court Martial if the Matter will not admit of a Compromise between the Parties.

N° 3. . When any dispute in any wise relating to Trade is brought before the Police, the Parties appear at the Board, deliver in their Papers respecting the Matter in question and at same time Sign an Obligation to abide by the Award of the Chamber of Commerce; The Police then enclose the Papers to the Monthly Committee of the Chamber of Commerce who set every Evening for the purpose of determining all Mercantil disputes, the Parties are heard by the Committee, their Papers examined, and the decision of the Committee Reported to the Police, Copies of which are by the Police sent to the Parties with Orders to conform to the Same; in case of non compliance, the Police report to the Commandant, who orders the Delinquent to the Provost, untill he complys with his Obligation. The Commandant has not been obliged to exert his Authority in this manner above once or twice, as the compliance has been so general, the mode of adjustment being so agreable to the Inhabitants; When the dispute is of Magnitude, an Appeal from the decision of the Committee may be had through the Commandant to the Chamber at Large.

> NB.   The Chamber of Commerce was incorporated by
>   Charter before the Rebellion, and consists of
>   the principal Merchants of the Place.

As Mercantil disputes even when the Courts of Law are open are often determined by a Jury of Merchants, this Mode of Referrance to the Chamber of Commerce was readily agreed to by the Commander in Chief as it was the earnest wish of all Persons concerned in Trade: but when the Parties prefer a Referrance to Individuals, their Choice is agreed to by the Police under the same Obligation as to the Chamber of Commerce.

Bonds, Obligations, Book debts, House-Rent and other matters of debt contracted since May 1777 in which there is no dispute, the Payment is ordered by the Police, often with the consent of the Creditor at certain Periods as the Circumstances of the Debtor may require, and in case of non compliance with the order of the Police, the Commandant enforces by Imprisonment: NB. Tavern debts are never attended to, of which the Tavern keepers are informed when they get their License; the good Consequences resulting from this Exception has been felt and acknowledged by the whole Garrison.

The Commander in Chief in Establishing the Police Assistants to the

Commandant, granted to the Inhabitants a temporary relief for the Want of Civil Government in order to give every consistent Security in his Power to the Persons and Property of such Inhabitants as might choose to live in this Garrison under Military Authority; In this Light it was viewed and Received—but the continuance of the War, which has kept dormant Civil Government creates a Wish in those whose Interests it may suit, to have the Powers of this Temporary Establishment made competent to Courts of Law and Chancery—for without such Powers, it would be impossible without throwing Real Property into the greatest confusion and often doing injustice to Creditors, to have a Retrospect to Bonds Mortgages Obligations or other Debts contracted either when the Royal Government, or the Rebel Usurpation were in force in this Province; And indeed such will be the complicated consequences of the Continental Circulation &ca, that additional Laws will be necessary to come from Provincial Assemblies when legally convened, to determine what is right in many instances;

Had the Payment of former Obligations been enforced, many Loyalists now under Protection, would have been deterr'd from leaving their Property amongst the Rebels to be sold and disposed of, if the small Pittance they had in this City and Environs on which they were to depend when they took Refuge here, had been liable to be taken from them for old Debts; In some particular instances, perhaps such Payments might have been properly exacted, but in a Matter of such Moment, a general Line became absolutely necessary; It is however to be regretted, that where Ability admits the payment of old debts there should be any instances where compulsion is wanted and advantage taken of the present Situation of Affairs. Call on Persons in all Conditions or Circumstances who stand bound in any such Obligations for debt, they will immediately point out, that their Situation is as hard as the Person's to whom they are indebted, either by large Real Estates being amongst the Rebels confiscated and sold, or by numbers of Bonds out amongst them, or by Fire perhaps suffered in Property in this City; Besides, if any Authority had ordered the Payment of Old Debts, the Debtors (and there are many such) in whose hands there are large Sums of Provincial Assembly Money, which tho issued under the Royal Instructions is at present out of Circulation, would be apt to complain if obliged to pay off a Bond in Gold and Silver, when they have by them Sums of that very Species of Currency which they received from the Creditor, and for which they can never expect Interest; Creditors in like manner would be apt to complain were they ordered to receive such Money: And the allowing of the Circulation of such Currency would have made the whole Emissions (for the redemption of which the Province is Security) center in this City, and fall into the Hands of Government for Bills, and of the British Merchants for Manufactures &ca.

The Rebels in different Provinces, have after pretended Confiscation Sold much Real Property belonging to the Loyalists; No Act of Parliament having passed to confiscate the Property of the Rebels, every attention has been paid to keep the Real Property of Rebels within these Lines in such a Situation, that the Benefits held up by Proclamations might be complied with in restoring Property to those returning to their Allegiance, that the Creditors in Great Britain might not be cut off from their Securities, And at same time that at the Settlement of the Rebellion disputes about Real Property might be prevented; Neither of which could have been the case had Mortgages been allowed to be Foreclosed, as in some instances was attempted; It was also judged improper to allow the Possessors of the Mortgages of Homes and Estates belonging to Rebels, to receive the Rents of the Mortgaged Property within the British Lines, as these Rents of course must have been accounted for at a future day to the Rebel Proprietors as Interest received on the Mortgage or as part payment of the Principal Sum where the Rents received exceeded the Interest due on the Mortgage; And what would still have added to the impropriety, Government would have paid the greatest part of this Interest, as the whole of the Rebel Homes and Estates within the Lines are necessarily occupied by the Officers, Troops, Publick Departments, or assigned by the order of Government for supporting the Families of distressed Refugees, excepting a certain number of Houses the Property of Rebels, the Rents of which are appropriated by order of the Commander in Chief, to the Support of an Alms House, in which there is generally near Three hundred Indigent Poor many of which are from the Army and Navy, and also for the necessary Repairs and Exigencies of the City; No Tax of any kind being raised in the Garrison, this appropriation became absolutely necessary; the Management of which with a City Treasurer is now conducted by Forty of the Principal Gentlemen of the City.

The preceeding Observations We flatter ourselves will speak fully to Mr Folliotts Memorial, whose case we sincerely commiserate as we do that of Thousands of other Loyalists, who are suffering precisely in the same Situation with Mr Folliott, from the unhappy Effects of Rebellion; but who we hope in a future day will reap the benefit of the Attention paid to Real Property, as it makes Securities within the British Lines much more valuable than Bonds or Real Estate among the Rebels.

N° 4. All Persons leaving the City, obtain Papers from the Commandant by recomendation of the Police; such as have been in Business are obliged to Advertise their intended departure; the Police grant Papers to known Persons that supply the Markets of the City with Provisions from the Rebel Shore of New Jersey.

N° 5. . All Persons coming within the Lines must Report themselves at the Commandants Office, a Certificate of which they lodge at the Police, where the Oaths of Allegiance are administered to them, and the Places of their abode put on Record; by this means Suspicious Persons are readily apprehended, and almost every Robbery of any consequence that has been committed, has been detected.

N° 6. . Various Regulations are adopted as Circumstances and Events require; Bread is Assized Monthly by the Reports from the Chamber of Commerce of the average price of Flour, an Inspector and Weigher employed; To prevent collusive or fraudulent Sales, and to secure to the Merchant payment of Sales, a Bond of Five Thousand Pounds with three Securities is given by every Vendue Master; Persons keeping Taverns obtain Licenses for that purpose which are renewed every Six Months upon the Recommendation of Three responsible Inhabitants; these Licenses raise a Small Revenue, which under the direction of the before mentioned Gentlemen & Treasurer, is applied to the paying of City Officers &ca &ca. The Regulation of Markets, Ferries, Pumps, Fire Engines, Fire Companies, Cartmen and City Watch are also under the inspection of the Police.

N° 7. . The Officers of the Police have Salaries appointed them by The Commander in Chief, and ordered not to receive any Fee or Reward in the Execution of their duty, so that this Temporary Institution is no Tax upon the People; The Magistrates of the Police attend the Office from Eleven O'Clock till Three every day, Sunday excepted.

Andrew Elliot
Sup' G¹
Mathews Mayor
Wm Walton
Magist° of Police

Police Office New York
4 December 1781.

3. *Excerpt from the record of trial by general court-martial of Capt. Richard Lippincott of the Associated Loyalists, May and June 1782* [WO 71/95/324–332].

"BE IT REMEMBERED, that on this Sixth day of May, One thousand seven hundred and Eighty two, Richard Lippincott of the City and Province of New York, Gentleman, being charged by His Majesty's Deputy Judge Advocate, with the Murder of Joshua Huddy, a Prisoner of War to the Associated Loyalists, and being brought before this General Court Martial to be tried and Adjudged upon the Said Charge, he, the said Richard Lippincott, here in his own Person, and under Military Arrest, saith, that he is not bound by the Laws of that part of Great Britain called England, nor by the Laws of this Province, Province of New York, to make issuable defence against the supposed Crime charged as aforesaid against him, for the following reasons.

"Because the said Richard Lippincott is not an Enlisted Soldier, nor paid nor Mustered as a Soldier, nor is he an Officer in Pay and with Rank, and therefore he saith, that he is not triable by any Court Martial for the said supposed Crime.

"Also because the said Richard Lippincott is an Inhabitant and Citizen of New York aforesaid, a part of His Majesty's American Dominions, where Civil Government is by Law established; and that he being now, and having ever been, a Liege Subject of His said Majesty, and his Royal

Predecessor, is intitled to all and singular the Rights and Priviledges of a subject of that part of Great Britain called England, and to all and singular the Rights and Priviledges that His Majesty's Subjects ever had, or ought to have, in this said Province of New York;—that a Trial according to the Ordinary course of Common Law Proceedings being one of those essential Rights and Priviledges, and he being a Citizen as aforesaid, he is legally held to answer, for the said supposed Offence, before a Court of Common Law Cognizance, and not elsewhere.

"Also because it is expressly stipulated in the Articles of Association, to which the said Richard Lippincott became a Party by subscribing his Name thereto, that the Associators should not be viewed in the light of Enlisted Soldiers; which said Articles had been previously sanctioned and consented to by His Excellency Sir Henry Clinton, Knight of the Most Honorable Order of the Bath, then General and Commander in Chief of all His Majesty's Forces, &cᵃ, &cᵃ, &cᵃ.

"Wherefore he, the said Richard Lippincott, doth hereby decline the Jurisdiction of this Court Martial, as being altogether incompetent by Law to hold him to Answer to the aforesaid Charge.

"But if the said Plea to the Jurisdiction of this Court Martial should be over-ruled, and they sustain their Jurisdiction over the said supposed Crime, as a Court competent to try the same, he, the said Richard Lippincott, doth hereby declare and aver, that any Plea that he may hereafter make thereto, other than this present one, will be the result of the alternative imposed upon him, either of answering over, or of suffering the consequences of making no defence at all."

This Plea to the Jurisdiction of the Court being accordingly read, and the Court cleared, they took the same into consideration, as also the Commission (hereunto annexed) granted by the Commander in Chief to, and accepted of, by the Prisoner, together with the Instructions given to the Board of Associated Loyalists under whose immediate Orders the Prisoner Acted, and came to the following Resolution and Opinion—That an Act of Parliament having passed on the 24ᵗʰ day of March 1781, entitled "An Act for punishing Mutiny and Desertion and for the better payment of the Army and their Quarters" And which Act is by the 85ᵗʰ Clause thereof declared, to be and continue in force, within the Island of Minorca and Garrison of Gibraltar and in His Majesty's other Dominions beyond the Seas, untill the 25ᵗʰ day of March 1783;—by which Act His Majesty is empowered to make Articles of War and constitute Courts Martial; and His Majesty having by Virtue and Authority of this said Act, been pleased amongst other Articles to constitute and form one vizᵗ the Second Article of the 20ᵗʰ Section of the Articles of War wherein it is declared that, "Notwithstanding it's being directed in the Eleventh Section of these our Rules and Articles that every Commanding Officer is required to deliver up to the Civil Magistrate all such Persons under his Command who shall be accused of any Crimes which are punishable by the known laws of the

Land; Yet in our Garrison of Gibraltar, and Island of Minorca, where our Forces now are, or in any other place beyond the Seas, to which any of our Troops are or may be hereafter Commanded, and where there is no form of our Civil Judicature in force, the Generals or Governors, or Commanders respectively, are to appoint General Courts Martial to be held, who are to try all Persons guilty of Wilfull Murder, Theft, Robbery, Rapes, Coining or Clipping the Coin of Great Britain, or of any Foreign Coin Current in the County or Garrison, and all other Capital Crimes, or other Offences, and punish Offenders with Death, or otherwise, as the nature of their Crimes shall deserve."

THE COURT being clearly of Opinion, that Captain Lippincot, circumstanced as he is, came under their Jurisdiction, they therefore Authorized the Deputy Judge Advocate to communicate this opinion and call on him to plead the General Issue of Guilty or Not Guilty.

THE PRISONER being again brought into Court, and informed of their Opinion, he requested that the Court would indulge him with some little further time to consider, whether he should make any other or further Plea, and upon what grounds to rest his Defence; In consequence hereof the Court Adjourned till 10 o'Clock the next Morning, previously informing the Prisoner, thro' the Judge Advocate, that they should then expect an explicit Answer to the Plea of Guilty or Not Guilty, and proceed on the Trial accordingly.

BUT other Public Services intervening, which called for the attendance of some of the Members, the Court was occasionally ADJOURNED 'till Thursday the 23ᵈ Instant.

THURSDAY MAY 23ᵈ 1782.

THE COURT again Assembled pursuant to an Order of the following tenor and date, issued by His Excellency Sir Guy Carleton, K.B. Commander in Chief: &c, &c, &c.

Head Quarters New York 17ᵗʰ May 1782.

"The Meeting of the General Court Martial of which Major General Paterson is President is put off 'till Thursday the 23ᵈ Instant, on which day it will Assemble at the City Hall in New York at 10 o'Clock in the Morning."

BUT THE COURT, in consequence of the following Letter from Lieut. Colonel Delancey Adjutant General, to Major General Paterson President, again ADJOURNED, *Sine die*, Viz.ᵗ

New York 22ᵈ May 1782.

Sir,

"I am directed by the Commander in Chief to inform you the Board of Directors of Associated Loyalists, as well as the Prisoner Captain Lippincott who was to be tried, have objected to the competency of the General

Court Martial of which you are President for such purpose His Excellency has laid their Objections before His Majesty's Attorney General for his Opinion, and in the mean time he directs that all Proceedings in the Trial of Captain Lippincott, may be suspended 'till he has made his Report."

I have the Honor to be,
Sir,
Your most obedient Humble Servant.
OL. Delancey

Major General Paterson.

Adj. Gen[1]

THURSDAY JUNE 13th 1782.

THE PRESIDENT and Members (Brigadier General Skinner and Colonel Beverly Robinson excepted) reassembled, in consequence of the following Public Order issued by His Excellency the Commander in Chief.

General Orders 5th June 1782.

"The Proceedings of the General Court Martial of which Major General Paterson is President having been suspended in consequence of the Prisoner Captain Richard Lippincott pleading against the legality of the Court; the Commander in Chief after the most mature consultation and deliberation, finding that there is no other Method of obtaining Justice, has thought proper to Order that the said Court shall Assemble on Thursday the 13th Instant at 10 o'Clock in the Morning at the City Hall in New York and proceed in the Trial of the said Captain Richard Lippincott."

COLONEL BEVERLY ROBINSON having in a Letter to the Deputy Judge Advocate which was laid before the Court, declared his inability to attend from a fit of illness, the Court came to a Resolution to proceed without him, there being still a sufficiency of Members to constitute a Court, but not knowing how to Account for the Non Attendance of Brigadier General Skinner and unwilling to proceed till it was known, whether he would be able to take his place as a Member,

THE COURT ADJOURNED 'till
next Morning at 10 o'Clock.

FRIDAY JUNE 14th 1782.

THE COURT (including Brigadier General Skinner, who had been prevented by other Public duty from attending the day before) being Met pursuant to Adjournment, the Deputy Judge Advocate laid before them the following Letter from the Adjutant General, together with the Enclosure, containing the case stated to the Chief Justice and Attorney General of the Province of New York, together with their Opinion which are as follows, vizt

"Head Quarters June 12th 1782.

"Sir,

"I am directed by the Commander in Chief to inform you, that in consequence of the Prisoner, Captain Richard Lippincott having pleaded against the Competency of the General Court Martial, by which he was to be tried; His Excellency had thought proper to suspend the Proceedings, untill he had taken the opinion of His Majesty's Law Officers on the subject, for which purpose, they were immediately furnished with the Papers put into his hands in behalf of the Prisoner, and after time sufficient for considering a Case of that importance the matter was debated before the Commander in Chief; the Admiral, the Governor of this Province, the Governor of New Jersey, and some principal Persons; a Case was in consequence thereof stated and their Opinion desired to be put into Writing, that the Court Martial might be informed of it in their own Words, which case and their Answer, I have the honor to enclose to you Sir, with the Commander in Chief's direction that they may be entered in the Proceedings of the Court, which is to go on, in the Trial of the said Captain Richard Lippincott."

I have the honor to be
Sir
Your most Obed^t Humble Servt

Capt. Adye D.J.A.   Ol. DeLancey
&c.   Adj^t Genl"

"RICHARD LIPPINCOTT having been Charged with the Murder of Huddy, within the Province of New Jersey, a Court Martial was Constituted to try and Adjudge the fact: But the said Richard Lippincott having alledged that he is not subject to Martial Law, it is thereupon referred by the Commander in Chief to the Honb^{le} William Smith, Chief Justice of this Province, and to John Tabor Kempe, His Majesty's Attorney General, to consider and report, if the said Richard Lippincott can be tried within the Island of New York for the alledged Offence in any Civil Court now subsisting within the said Island upon the strict rules of Law, and with that effect, which a Crime contrary both to the first principles of Civil Society and the Law of Arms necessarily demands; and if not, whether a Court Martial ought not to proceed, and try and Adjudge the said Richard Lippincott, upon such principles of substantial Justice, as the nature of the Case seems to require.

"UPON the Case as above stated in the Paper received Yesterday, and independent of any other Facts than it Communicates, We Report with great Submission and Respect to His Excellency the Commander in Chief.

"That by the non Revival of the exercise of the Civil Authority of the Crown in this Province, the recovered Counties still remain under the Government of Military Discretion, with the King's Courts of Justice all shut up. And we are of opinion that if they were opened; they would only be competent for our own internal Jurisdiction, and that they could not take Cognizance of such a Felony, as the Case supposes to have been committed in the Province of New Jersey.

"That such Offences in the Plantations in general, can be tried according to the course of the Common Law, only in the Province, and by a Jury of the County where it was perpetrated, unless a Provision be made for that purpose by some future Act of Parliament or by a Law of the Colony.

"That Antecedent to the Statute of 3ᵈ of King Charles I, commonly called the Petition of Rights,[6] there had been Trials in England by the Law Martial, and that it seems to be the better opinion since the passing of that Statute, that necessity so impelling, Offences may still be punished by the indulged Proceeding stiled Martial Law, in times of War, Rebellion and Invasion, when the Courts are shut and the regular Administration of Justice cannot be carried on.

"But as it would be a question of Fact, whether the necessity that would authorize a Tribunal for the Trial and Punishment here, of Murder committed in New Jersey now exists, subject as the British Provinces are to a double Legislature as above alluded to, and unacquainted as we must be supposed to be, with all those great and profound Considerations of Policy upon which it turns, it becomes us to be silent.

"Upon every Question of Law, with which it may be connected, and on every occasion in which our Services can be made useful to the Crown we are chearfully disposed to contribute all the Aid in our Power."

(Signed)
Wᵐ SMITH
J. T. KEMPE"

"City of New York 9ᵗʰ June 1782"

CAPTAIN RICHARD LIPPINCOTT being then Arraigned upon the Charge of having been guilty of the Murder of Joshua Huddy, a Prisoner of War to the Associated Loyalists, by hanging or causing him to be hanged, by the Neck untill he was dead, he (Lippincott) having received the said Huddy into his Custody for the purpose of Exchanging him for another Prisoner of War, by Virtue of an Order from the Honorable Board of Directors of the Associated Loyalists dated April 8ᵗʰ 1782—and he having Pleaded *Not Guilty*, the Deputy Judge Advocate Addressed the Court as follows.

---

[6] So in original.

TRIALS OF CIVILIANS BY BRITISH
GENERAL COURTS-MARTIAL
DURING THE WAR OF
AMERICAN INDEPENDENCE

Below are listed, alphabetically by the name of the accused, every trial of a civilian by British general court-martial during the War of American Independence of which a reliable official record has been found. Trials of garrison courts-martial are accordingly excluded, likewise trials by general courts-martial mentioned only in the monthly returns of prisoners made by the provost marshal at New York (*supra*, pp. 134, 138).

All entries being severely abbreviated, the following explanation of the symbols used becomes necessary.

Accused: "NSI," no status indicated; "F/A," follower of the Army; "R/A," "R/C," retainer to the Army or to the camp, "SrW," soldier's wife. "Inhab" will be understood as Inhabitant. Inconsistency in description reflects the state of the official records.

Record references: Whenever the trial is one recorded in the War Office court-martial books, the group preface "WO 71" is omitted. Thus "85/442" means "WO 71/85/442."

Order books are cited by the commander's initials; Generals Gage, Howe, Clinton, and Carleton thus become, respectively, TG, WH, HC, and GC; and consequently "HC 6 Aug 78" means "Clinton OB, 6 August 1778." (The Wray OB is cited as "W.") Where an order book reference is available, the date of trial is not specially given, as it normally preceded the order book entry by only a few days.

Geographical abbreviations: Familiarity with standard abbreviations for the States of the Union is assumed; others in the present category are: "SI," Staten Island, NY; "LI," Long Island, NY; "WI," West Indies; "Bo," Boston; "Phila," Philadelphia. "Ft K" means Fort Knyphausen, on the northern end of Manhattan Island; this had been Fort Washington before its capture in November 1776; it was then renamed in honor of the senior

Hessian general; its site is in the part of the present City of New York that is still known as the Fort Washington area.

Charge: Generally summarized.

Result: "G" and "NG" of course mean Guilty and Not Guilty.

Sentences: Generally summarized; "conf," confinement; "L," lashes; "SGB," security for good behavior; "MOW," man of war; "AP," Act of Parliament. No attempt has been made to differentiate between Sterling and New York currency where fines were adjudged or restitution was ordered.

Cross-references: When several civilians were tried together, cross-references are given, likewise when the trial of one bore an obvious relationship to another, as when one person was charged with theft and another with receiving the same stolen goods. But unless two accused are listed in sequence, references to date and place of trial and to the official record are repeated, to spare the reader the frustrating paper-chase that would otherwise result.

No.	Accused	Trial	Charge	Result
1.	ABRAHAMS, MOSES Inhab With Nos. 69 & 155	NY 23 Oct 80 92/381	Burglary	Death
2.	ADAMS, JOSEPH Inhab	NY 23 June 77 83/420	Embezzlement	£10 fine & conf until paid
3.	AGNEW, THOMAS NSI With Nos. 67, 73, & 176	NY HC 12 Mar 79 88/241	Many robberies	Death; recommended for mercy; apparently executed
4.	AIKEN, JAMES Inhab of Newark, NJ With No. 9	NY GC 21 Sept 83	Piratically carrying away sloop	G, but not piratically; Death, but pardoned on SGB
5.	ALGER, ISAAC Refugee With No. 166	NY GC 21 Aug 83	Robbing dwelling house	Death
6.	ARMSTRONG HENRY Mariner With No. 196	NY WH 14 Apr 77 83/340	1, Forcing safe-guard; 2, Murder	1, G; 2, NG; Death; Respited WH 22 Apr 77; pardoned WH 12 Oct 77
7.	ARROWLENGTH, THOMAS Ship's Carpenter With Nos. 49 & 157	Brooklyn HC 11 Sept 78 87/20	Plundering	NG, but G of secreting HM's stores; 100 L & service in HM's Navy

No.	Accused	Trial	Charge	Result
8.	BAITON, ROBERT Mariner With No. 84	NY 16 Nov 79 91/10	Receiving stolen goods	NG
9.	BALDWIN, LUTHER Inhab of Newark, NJ With No. 4	NY GC 21 Sept 83	Piratically carrying away sloop	G only of boarding. Death, but pardoned on SGB
10.	BANTER, BRISTOL Negro & F/A With Nos. 25, 60, 93, 134, 186, 204, 208, and 218	NY GC 23 Aug 82 96/126	Murder	NG, but to be sent to WI
11.	BASFORD, MARY Negro With Nos. 97 & 114	NY HC 1 Dec 78 88/50	Murder	NG
12.	BENNETT, THUENESS Inhab With Nos. 150 & 207	NY GC 21 Aug 83	Carrying soldiers to NJ, enticing soldiers to desert	NG
13.	BISHOP, EDWARD Mariner on Army victualling ship With Nos. 38, 168, & 172	Phila WH 18 Feb 78 85/272	Embezzling part of cargo	NG
14.	BISHOP, THOMAS "of the Navy"	NY 16 Nov 79 91/1	Murder	NG
15.	BLACK, DAVID Trader	NY HC 8 Aug 79 89/194	1, Attempting to ship goods from NY without permit; 2, Obtaining goods fraudulently from auctioneer, refusing to pay purchase money	G; to pay £93 5s., amount of purchase money; conf until paid and until SGB
16.	BRIGGS, GEORGE Inhab	NY GC 3 Mar 83	Aiding & abetting in entering in conditions of a treasonable nature with HM's enemies	6 mos conf, then to be turned out of the lines

No.	Accused	Trial	Charge	Result
17.	BROWN, RICHARD Inhab on SI With No. 53	SI HC 17 Aug 79 89/389	Cutting down timber without proprietor's leave	NG
18.	BROWN, ROBERT Waggoner in QMGD With No. 57	Phila WH 11 Jan 78 85/203	1, Robbery; 2, Ill using 2 women	1, NG; 2, G; 1,000 L, to be drummed through town with rope around neck, then turned out of lines
19.	BROWNDIDGE, GILBERT NSI With Nos. 96, 165, & 202	NY GC 21 Aug 83	Burglary	NG
20.	BUCK, THOMAS Boatswain of the ship Rose	Phila WH 16 Mar 78 85/285	Enticing RN sailor to desert	To serve on board MOW
21.	BURNE, GERALD R/A	NY 2 Oct 76 83/26	Stealing horse	NG
22.	BUSH, GARRET Inhab of SI	NY 16 Nov 79 91/19	Aiding rebels, acting as guide	NG, because of compulsion
23.	BUTLER, CHADLOCK NSI	Freehold, NJ 27 June 78 86/151	Stealing horse	NG
24.	BUTLER, JAMES "a Negroe Man"	Cooper's Ferry 16 May 78 86/148	Robbery	1,000 L, & drummed out of lines
25.	CADMUS, THOMAS Negro & F/A With Nos. 10, 60, 93, 134, 186, 204, 208, & 218	NY GC 23 Aug 82 96/126	Murder	Death
26.	CAMERON, JOHN Officer's servant	NY HC 12 Mar 79 88/258	Assault and attempt to murder	3 mos conf then to be sent on board MOW
27.	CAMPBELL, JOHN Inhab	NY HC 23 Dec 80 92/327	Stealing horse	500 L, remitted, to be turned out of lines
28.	CANE, PETER F/A	NY WH 3 Apr 77 83/251	Theft	NG

No.	Accused	Trial	Charge	Result
29.	CARLE, PHINEAS Inhab With No. 224	NY GC 17 Oct 83	Burglary	NG
30.	CARROL, DAVID Inhab With Nos. 85, 104, 137, 169, 213, & 214	NY HC 15 Aug 80 91/154	Robbery	Death
31.	CARROLL, PHINEAS NSI With No. 225	NY GC 15 Oct 83	Burglary	NG
32.	CARY, REBECCA Follower of or wife of soldier of Bucks County Volunteers	NY 4 Sept 80 92/339	Murder	NG
33.	CARTY, SAMUEL Waggoner With No. 78	SI HC 17 Aug 79 89/416	Robbery	NG
34.	CHANDLER, SOLOMON Inhab With Nos. 59 & 185	NY GC 21 Aug 83	Taking property from a ship	Death
35.	CLARKE, CALEB NSI	NY 7 Oct 77 84/354	Sheep stealing	NG
36.	CLARKE, ELIZABETH F/A With No. 39	Freehold, NJ HC 3 July 78 86/156	Plundering	100 L
37.	CLARKE, LEWIS LATHAM Clerk of HM's Provision stores at RI	RI 13 Nov 78 87/416	Embezzling the King's stores & defrauding the Troops of their due	NG
38.	COATES, JAMES Mariner on Army victualling ship With Nos. 13, 168, & 172	Phila WH 18 Feb 78 85/272	Embezzling part of the cargo	NG
39.	COLETHRATE, MARY F/A With No. 36	Freehold, NJ HC 3 July 78 86/156	Plundering	NG

No.	Accused	Trial	Charge	Result
40.	COLLINS, JOHN Inhab	NY GC 16 Aug 83	Stealing watch	NG
41.	COLLINS, MARY NSI With Nos. 42 & 128(1)	Phila WH 19 Apr 78 86/70	Receiving stolen goods	NG
42.	COLLINS, RICHARD NSI With Nos. 41 & 128(1)	See No. 41, just above	Burglary	Death
43.	COOMBS, ROBERT Inhab	NY GC 22 Mar 83	Murder	NG
44.	COOPER, THOMAS Mariner	NY HC 12 Mar 79 88/289	Embezzling goods	200 L, & to serve on board MOW
45.	CORNELL, JOHN NSI With No. 46	NY HC 11 July 79	Assisting rebels	NG
46.	CORNELL, WILLIAM NSI With No. 45	See No. 45, just above	Assisting rebels	£1,000 fine, conf until paid, then banished from lines
47.	COURTNEY, THOMAS Tailor	NY HC 12 Mar 79 88/279	Enticing seamen to desert	£20 fine for each of the 3 seamen as directed by AP
48.	COX, WILLIAM Mate, RN With Nos. 90, 92, 141, & 191	NY GC 22 Mar 83	Murder	NG
49.	CREIGHTON, JAMES Gunner of a ship With Nos. 7 & 157	Brooklyn HC 11 Sept 78 87/20	Plundering	G only of secreting HM's stores; 100 L, & service on board HM's Navy
50.	CRISPIN, SILVER Ship's Carpenter With No. 164	Phila WH 7 Mar 78 85/367	Knocking down Lt White	NG; complaint frivolous
51.	CROSSING, WILLIAM F/A	NY 19 Feb 81 93/201	Assaulting inhabitant	Pay fine of £20 to victim, & SGB
52.	CUFFEY, PRIMUS A Negro and F/A	Mt. Holly, NJ 21 June 78 87/205	Plundering	500 L

No.	Accused	Trial	Charge	Result
53.	DAVIS, ELIJAH Inhab on SI With No. 17	SI HC 17 Aug 79 89/389	Cutting down timber without proprietor's leave	NG
53A.	DELANCEY, JAMES NSI	NY HC 20 Aug 79	Insulting & assaulting Lt-Col Emerich	3 mos conf & apology, conf remitted on ct's recommendation
54.	DELANCEY, OLIVER Inhab of West Chester, NY	NY HC 20 Aug 79	Insulting Lt- Col Emerich	Apology
55.	DERRY, ADAM Driver in QMGD With No. 167	Freehold, NJ HC 3 July 78 86/154	Arson	NG
56.	DICK A Negro With Nos. 79 & 115	NY GC 25 Feb 83	Arson	NG
57.	DILLON, JOHN Waggoner in QMGD With No. 18	Phila WH 11 Jan 78 85/203	1, Robbery; 2, Ill using 2 women	G of both; 1,000 L, then drummed through town with rope around neck, then turned out of lines
58.	DONNAHY, JOHN Master of a sloop	NY GC 8 July 83	Assisting Hessian soldiers to desert	NG
59.	DONNALY, CORNELIUS Mariner With Nos. 34 & 185	NY GC 21 Aug 83	Taking property from a ship	Death
60.	DOREMUS, SAMUEL Negro & F/A With Nos. 10, 25, 93, 134, 186, 204, 208, & 218	NY GC 23 Aug 82 96/126	Murder	NG, but to be sent to WI
61.	DOWNING, TIMOTHY Asst Commissary of Forage	NY 6 Nov 77 84/411	Embezzling the King's stores	Dismissal; make good the loss; £100 fine; & conf as directed in AP

No.	Accused	Trial	Charge	Result
62.	DUNCAN, JAMES Master of the ship *Rose*	Phila WH 15 Mar 78 85/284	Enlisting sailors from MOW	To pay £20 for each seaman, as directed by 6 Anne, c. 37
63.	DURYEE, JACOB Inhab With Nos. 70 & 203	NY GC 22 July 83 97/320	Carrying off a Negro	Fine 50 Gs & expulsion; remitted on condition of reasonable bail
64.	ELLIS, LUCRETIA (*alias* McNICOLL) NSI	Brooklyn HC 6 Aug 78 86/230	Murder	NG
65.	EMERSON, JOHN In the Provision Train With Nos. 177 & 211	Germantown, Pa WH 8 Oct 77	Plundering	NG
66.	ESLING, RANDOLPH Rope-maker With Nos. 99 & 194	Phila WH 11 Nov 77 84/432	1, Attempt to kill Capt Stewart; 2, Stealing & killing cattle	NG as to both
67.	FARREN, JOHN NSI With Nos. 3, 73, & 176	NY HC 12 Mar 79 88/241	Many robberies	Death
68.	FERNE, ELENOR NSI With No. 163; cf. No. 69	NY 23 Oct 80 92/393	Receiving stolen goods	1 mo conf
69.	FERNE, JOHN Inhab With Nos. 1 & 155; cf. No. 68	NY 23 Oct 80 92/381	Burglary	Death
70.	FIGHLIMAN, FREDERICK Inhab With Nos. 63 & 203	NY GC 22 July 83 97/321	Aiding & abetting in carrying off Negro	One hr in stocks; pardoned
71.	FITZPATRICK, BERNARD F/A	Phila 28 Apr 78 86/109	Stealing a watch	NG

No.	Accused	Trial	Charge	Result
72.	FLYNN, DENNIS Inhab With Nos. 132, 138, 158, 159, & 175	NY GC 26 Aug 83 97/386, also WO 71/155	Conspiracy to make & utter counterfeit US notes	NG
73.	FOGWELL, GEORGE (alias WILSON) NSI With Nos. 3, 67, & 176	NY HC 12 Mar 79 88/241	Many robberies	Death
74.	FORD, WILLIAM Inhab	NY GC 21 Sept 83	Murder of wife	G of manslaughter only; punishment provided by law; pardoned on condition of transporting self to WI
75.	FORSTER, NATHANIEL Inhab on LI With No. 76	NY HC 8 Aug 79 89/261	Murder	NG
76.	FORSTER, SAMUEL Inhab on LI With No. 75	See No. 75, just above	Murder	NG
77.	FOSNER, ANDREW Inhab	NY GC 8 July 83	Burglary	NG
78.	FRANK A Negro Man With No. 33	SI HC 17 Aug 79 89/416	Robbery	1,000 L
79.	FRANK A Negro With Nos. 56 & 115	NY GC 25 Feb 83	Arson	NG
80.	FULLER, SILVESTER Inhab	NY HC 28 Aug 79 90/108	1, Assisting Hessians to desert; 2, Purchasing provisions from soldiers; 3, Insulting officer; 4, "For speaking often in a very Rebellious manner, against HM's Army & Government"	NG; "prosecution has been Vexatious, Malicious & groundless"

No.	*Accused*	*Trial*	*Charge*	*Result*
81.	FURMAN, WILLIAM Inhab of LI	Flushing Fly, LI HC 24 Oct 78 87/183	Endeavoring to assist desertion	Fine of £40 to be paid in 4 days, else 1,000 L
82.	FYGIS, MARY Spinster	Phila WH 29 Mar 78 85/442	Perjury	Turned out of lines; in case of return, ½ hr in pillory & 6 mos conf
83.	GARRETSON, JOHN R/A With Nos. 87 & 209	NY WH 24 Mar 77 83/220	Robbery	Death
84.	GATH, GEORGE Mariner With No. 8	NY 16 Nov 79 91/10	Receiving stolen goods	NG
85.	GELLIN, JOHN Inhab With Nos. 30, 104, 137, 169, 213, & 214	NY HC 15 Aug 80 91/154	Robbery	Death
86.	GIBBONS, MARY NSI	NY 4 Sept 77 84/243	Stealing	300 L at 3 different times, & conf until 2 Gs stolen repaid
87.	GIBSON, THOMAS R/A With Nos. 83 & 209	NY WH 24 Mar 77 83/220	Robbery	1,000 L Pardoned, WH 22 Apr 77
88.	GOODRICH, JAMES Inhab of SI With No. 89	NY 27 Aug 81 94/418	Assault & battery on servants in employ of Supt of Hospitals	£5 fine & £500 SGB for 12 mos
89.	GOODRICH, JOHN Inhab of SI With No. 88	See No. 88, just above	Same as No. 88, just above	Same as No. 88, just above
90.	GORDON, ROBERT Mariner, RN With Nos. 48, 92, 141, & 191	NY GC 22 Mar 83	Murder	NG
91.	GORMON, THOMAS Mariner	Brooklyn HC 6 Aug 78 86/170	Rape	NG

No.	Accused	Trial	Charge	Result
92.	GRANT, JOHN Midshipman, RN With Nos. 48, 90, 141, & 191	NY GC 22 Mar 83	Murder	NG
93.	GRANT, WILLIAM Negro & F/A With Nos. 10, 25, 60, 134, 186, 204, 208, & 218	NY GC 23 Aug 82 96/126	Murder	NG, but to be sent to WI
94.	GREEN, ISAAC Negro [F/A, in view of refer- ence to Art. 23 of §14] With No. 173	Darby, Pa WH 27 Dec 77 85/186	Plundering	1,000 L
95.	GREEN, THOMAS Inhab	NY GC 16 Aug 83	Stealing	Transportation to some place within HM's Dominions beyond Sea
96.	GREGORY, RICHARD NSI With Nos. 19, 165, & 202	NY GC 21 Aug 83	Burglary	NG
97.	GROVES, MARY A Negro With Nos. 11 & 114	NY HC 1 Dec 78 88/50	Murder	NG
98.	GUFFIE, JAMES Conductor in QMGD	NY 9 Aug 81 94/303	Murder	Death
99.	GUSSELL, CHARLES Mariner With Nos. 66 & 194	Phila WH 11 Nov 77 84/432	1, Attempt to kill Capt Stewart; 2, Stealing & killing cattle	1, NG; 2, G; 1,000 L
100.	HALFPENNY, PATRICK Mariner	NY GC 22 Jun 83	Forging name of Wm Fowler Esq Naval Store- keeper at NY to Bills of Exchange drawn on Treas- urer of RN	NG

No.	Accused	Trial	Charge	Result
101.	HALLY, PETER A Mulatto	Brooklyn HC 6 Aug 78 86/218	Stealing (1) horse, (2) 3 lambs, & (3) a pig	1, NG; 2, G; 3, G; to be drummed out of lines
102.	HAMILL, JAMES Inhab of Phila	Derby, Pa WH 27 Dec 77 85/189	Plundering	1,000 L
103.	HAMILTON, JAMES Refugee	SC W 12 June 80	Stealing cattle, selling them to butcher & not giving them to Com- missary of Captives as directed	G only of selling cattle & applying proceeds to own use; 300 L, & to refund proceeds
104.	HARDING, JESSE Inhab With Nos. 30, 85, 137, 169, 213, & 214	NY HC 15 Aug 80 91/154	Robbery	Death
105.	HARRISON, NATHANIEL Inhab With Nos. 171, 178, 188, 189, & 192	NY GC 17 Oct 83	Burglary & Robbery	NG
106.	HAYES, JAMES Owner of the True Blue Privateer	NY 17 July 81 94/251	1, Fitting out vessel without register; 2, Sending out vessel without pass; 3, Exercis- ing unlawful authority in said vessel	No jurisdiction; court adhered to opinion
107.	HENNESEY, ANN SrW	Boston WH 3 Jan 76 82/235	Breaking & entering	NG
108.	HETFIELD, CORNELIUS Inhab of NJ	NY 8–27 Sept 83 4 HMC Am. MSS 376–377	Breaking & entering; robbery of inmates	NG; prosecution groundless and malicious

No.	Accused	Trial	Charge	Result
109.	HEYDON, JOSEPH Inhab With No. 111	NY GC 21 Feb 83	Counterfeiting Spanish Dollars	NG
110.	HILL, JOHN NSI	NY HC 12 Mar 79 88/295	1, Robbery; 2, Assault with dangerous weapon	1, G; 2, NG; 3 mos conf
111.	HORTON, NATHAN Inhab With No. 109	NY GC 21 Feb 83	Counterfeiting Spanish Dollars	NG
112.	HUBBS, SELAH NSI With Nos. 113 & 210	NY HC 12 Mar 79 88/306	Holding corre- spondence with rebels	NG
113.	HUBBS, URIAH NSI With Nos. 112 & 210	See No. 112, just above	Same as No. 112, just above	NG
114.	JACKSON, ELIZABETH Negro With Nos. 11 & 97	NY HC 1 Dec 78 88/50	Murder	NG
115.	JAMES A Negro With Nos. 56 & 79	NY GC 25 Feb 83	Arson	6 mos conf, & 600 L, 100 at a time, 1 mo in between
116.	JEFFERIES, MARY F/A	Brooklyn 24 July 78 86/174	Persuading soldier to desert	NG
117.	JEFFERS, JOHN Inhab	NY 6 Nov 77 84/416	Stealing out of HM's stores	1,000 L
118.	JOHNSTON, BENJAMIN Mariner	NY GC 17 Oct 83	Stealing chest from sloop	600 L
119.	JOHNSTON, GEORGE Inhab	NY GC 16 Aug 83	Robbery	Death; on 30 Aug, respited to 29 Oct; on 1 Nov, still in conf
120.	JOHNSTONE, WILLIAM Mariner	NY 4 Mar 77 83/168	Robbery	200 L
121.	JONES, CHARLES Inhab	NY GC 16 Aug 83	1, Assault; 2, Stealing	1, G; 2, NG; to be sent on board ship

No.	Accused	Trial	Charge	Result
122.	JOYCE, MATTHEW Inhab	Phila 12 Feb 78 85/277	Breaking into house of Town Adjt	NG
123.	KENNET, CRADDOCK Lieut of privateer	NY HC 12 Mar 79 88/285	Concealing seamen belonging to Army victualler	NG
124.	KENNY, JOHN F/A	Brooklyn HC 6 Aug 78 86/180	Assault with intent to commit robbery	1,000 L, & then to be drummed out of lines with Halter about Neck
125.	KING, WILLIAM F/A	Phila HC 7 June 78 86/311	Advising desertion	NG
126.	KNAPP, TITUS Inhab	NY GC 8 July 83	Assault & attempted robbery	500 L
127.	KNOTT, RICHARD Of the City of NY	NY HC 11 July & 15 Sept 79 89/2	Murder	G of manslaughter. Burning in hand & forfeiture; remitted on condi- tion of paying widow £300
128(1).	LAMB, THOMAS NSI	Phila WH 19 Apr 78 86/70	Burglary	NG
128(2).	Same	Phila WH 22 & 24 Apr 78 86/78–83	Accessory to same burglary	Death; respited; pardoned by King
129.	LEASEY, HERMAN Inhab	NY GC 21 Aug 83	Carrying Hessian soldier to NJ	NG
130.	LEE, JAMES (alias MARTIN) Mariner	NY HC 21 Apr 79 88/414	Enticing soldiers to desert	£5 penalty for each of 2 soldiers; if no payment within 4 days, then 500 L
131.	LIPPINCOTT, RICHARD Captain, Asso- ciated Loyalists	NY May-June 82 Not in GC 95/321–408	Murder of Joshua Huddy, Prisoner of War	NG because acting under orders

No.	Accused	Trial	Charge	Result
132.	Lyon, Sylvanus NSI With Nos. 72, 138, 158, 159, & 175	NY GC 26 Aug 83 97/386, also WO 71/155	Conspiracy to make & utter counterfeit US notes	NG
133.	Macdonald, Charles "Mr.," late of the 84th Regt	SC W 12 June 80	Disobeying orders in enlisting Rebel prisoners in the Legion	NG
134.	Maffis, Daniel Negro & F/A With Nos. 10, 25, 60, 93, 186, 204, 208, & 218	NY GC 23 Aug 82 96/126	Murder	Death
135.	Maltbie, David Inhab of Stamford, Conn	NY GC 21 Feb 83	Robbery	NG, but to be sent out of lines
136.	Martin, Samuel A Negro F/A With No. 174	Mt Holly, NJ HC 21 June 78 87/207	Plundering	NG
137.	Mason, John Inhab With Nos. 30, 85, 104, 169, 213, & 214	NY HC 15 Aug 80 91/154	Robbery	Death
138.	May, William NSI With Nos. 72, 132, 158, 159, & 175	NY 13 Aug 83 WO 71/155	Conspiracy to make & utter counterfeit US notes	Special verdict, only in WO 71/155, not in GC 26 Aug 83 nor in 97/386; banished beyond lines
139.	McAlpine, Daniel Inhab	NY 4 Sept 1780 92/333	Carrying naval deserter to NJ	G, but no knowledge. 2 mos conf & £200 SGB
140.	McCowan, Winifred R/C	Boston TG 25 Sept 75 81/393	Stealing and killing the Town Bull	100 L & 3 mos conf
141.	McGee, Catherine Inhab With Nos. 48, 90, 92, & 191	NY GC 22 Mar 83	Murder	NG, but to be turned out of lines

No.	Accused	Trial	Charge	Result
142.	McGINNES, PHILIP F/A	Brooklyn HC 6 Aug 78 86/212	Robbery	NG
143.	McINTIRE, JOHN Inhab of NY	NY HC 1 Dec 78 88/7	Stealing	Death
144.	McLAUGHLIN, ROBERT Inhab With No. 197	NY GC 16 Aug 83	Stealing	NG
145.	McMAHAN, ISABELLA SrW	Boston WH 3 Jan 76 82/207	Receiving stolen goods	100 L &3 mos conf
146.	McNEAL, MARY Inhab	NY GC 8 July 83	Burglary	Death
147.	McTAGGART, JOHN Late Master of Privateer With No. 153	Jamaica, LI, 16 Jan 79 88/131	Enticing seaman from HMS *Perseus*	Penalty of £20 as directed by AP
148.	MERRIL, JOHN Inhab of SI	SI 2 Feb 78 85/241	Being a guide & conductor to the Rebels	NG because forced
149.	MESNARD, THOMAS Supercargo	NY HC 8 & 15 Aug 79 89/293	Secreting letters	£200 fine, conf until paid, then to serve on board HM's ships; penalties remitted because of ignorance
150.	MILLER, GEORGE Inhab With Nos. 12 & 207	NY GC 21 Aug 83	Carrying soldiers to NJ, enticing soldiers to desert	£40 fine for enticing
151.	MONK, JOHN Waggoner in QMGD	Brooklyn HC 11 Sept 78 87/10	Stealing	1,000 L
152.	MORGAN, JOHN Ship's Surgeon	Brooklyn HC 11 Sept 78 87/16	Plundering	NG
153.	MURRAY, ROBERT Inhab With No. 147	Jamaica, LI, 16 Jan 79 88/131	Enticing & concealing RN sailor to serve on privateer	NG

No.	Accused	Trial	Charge	Result
154.	MYERS, JACOB Inhab	NY 7 Oct 77 84/353	Sheep stealing	1,000 L & 12 mos conf
155.	MYERS, MARCUS Inhab With Nos. 1 & 69	NY 23 Oct 80 92/381	Burglary	NG
156.	NED A Negro Man, F/A	Darby, Pa WH 27 Dec 77 85/185	Stealing a horse	NG
157.	NETHERSHALL, JOHN Mate of a ship With Nos. 7 & 49	Brooklyn HC 11 Sept 78 87/20	Plundering	NG, but G of secret- ing HM's stores; 500 L, then to serve in HM'S Navy
158.	NICHOLS, LEMUEL NSI With Nos. 72, 132, 138, 159, & 175	NY GC 26 Aug 83 97/386, also WO71/ 155	Conspiracy to make & utter counterfeit US notes	NG
159.	NICHOLS, WILLIAM NSI With Nos. 72, 132, 138, 158, & 175	See No. 158, just above	Same as No. 158, just above	NG
160.	NITZER, MARK Inhab	NY HC 1 Dec 78	Murder	NG
161.	NORMAN, ISAAC Mate of HMS *Adamant*	NY 2 June 81 94/74	Murder of sailor from HMS *Confederate*	Death
162.	OBRIAN, JAMES Inhab of Phila	Phila WH 15 Mar 78 85/287	Concealing deserters from HM's ships	500 L, then to be sent out of lines or on board MOW as the C in C may direct [OB simply says "Approved"]
163.	OBRIEN CATHERINE NSI With No. 68; cf. No. 69	NY 23 Oct 80 92/393	Receiving stolen goods	NG
164.	O'HARA, MARY NSI With No. 50	Phila WH 3 Mar 78 85/367	Assisting in knocking down Lt White	NG; complaint frivolous

No.	Accused	Trial	Charge	Result
165.	OUTHOUSE, SIMON NSI With Nos. 19, 96, & 202	NY GC 21 Aug 83	Burglary	NG
166.	PARKER, NATHANIEL Refugee With No. 5	NY GC 21 Aug 83	Robbing dwell- ing house	Death
167.	PEPPERLY, MICHAEL Driver in QMGD With No. 55	Freehold, NJ HC 3 July 78 86/154	Arson	NG
168.	PHILIPS, JOHN Mate of an Army victualing ship With Nos. 13, 38, & 172	Phila WH 18 Feb 78 85/272	Embezzling part of cargo	NG
169.	PIGOT, HITIBEL NSI With Nos. 30, 85, 104, 137, 213, & 214	NY 26 Jan 80 Not named in HC 15 Aug 80 91/154	Robbery	NG
170.	PLATO A Negro Man	NY WH 3 Apr 77 83/245	Theft	NG
171.	PLATT, ANANIAS Inhab With Nos.105, 178, 188, 189, & 192	NY GC 17 Oct 83	Burglary & Robbery	£1,000 fine, or 1,000 L if not paid before evacuation
172.	PORTER, FRANCIS Mariner on Army victualing ship With Nos. 13, 38, & 168	Phila 12 Feb 78 85/272 (Not in WH)	Embezzling part of cargo	NG
173.	POWER, JAMES Inhab of Phila With No. 94	Darby, Pa WH 27 Dec 77 85/186	Plundering	NG
174.	POWER, JAMES A Negro F/A With No. 136	Mt Holly NJ HC 21 June 78 87/207	Plundering	NG

No.	Accused	Trial	Charge	Result
175.	POWER, JOHN NSI With Nos. 72, 132, 138, 158, & 159	NY 13 Aug 83 WO 71/155	Conspiracy to make & utter counterfeit US notes	Special verdict, only in WO 71/ 155, not in GC 26 Aug 83 nor in 97/386; SGB
176.	PURDY, JOHN NSI With Nos. 3, 67, & 73	NY HC 12 Mar 79 88/241	Many robberies	Death
177.	RAKE, CHARLES Conductor of Artillery Stores With Nos. 65 & 211	Germantown, Pa WH 8 Oct 77	Plundering	NG
178.	RALPH, DAVID Inhab With Nos. 105, 171, 188, 189, & 192	NY GC 17 Oct 83	Burglary & Robbery	£1,000 fine, or 1,000 L if not paid before evacuation
179.	RANDEN, THOMAS Mariner from transport	NY WH 24 Mar 77	Robbery	Death
180.	REID, ROBERT Inhab of Phillipsburg NY	Ft K HC 30 Aug 79 90/210	Selling rum to soldiers, pur- chasing their necessaries, enticing desertion	G of 1 & 2, NG of 3; 50 L & £5 penalty
181.	RICHARDSON, ISAAC Negro	NY HC 1 Dec 78 88/48	Murder	NG
182.	RIGBY, AGNES Inhab With No. 183	NY GC 25 Feb 83	Burglary	NG
183.	RIGBY, JAMES Inhab With No. 182	See No. 182, just above	Burglary	NG
184.	ROACH, JAMES Inhab	NY HC 8 Aug 79 89/248	Attempt to murder & robbery	Death

No.	Accused	Trial	Charge	Result
185.	SATE, MARY Inhab With Nos. 34 & 59	NY GC 21 Aug 83	Taking prop- erty from a ship	NG
186.	SCOBEY, HARRY Negro and F/A With Nos. 10, 25, 60, 93, 134, 204, 208, & 218	NY GC 23 Aug 82 96/126	Murder	NG, but to be sent to **WI**
187.	SCOTT, JOHN Cooper on store ship Cf. No. 200	NY HC 7 Sept 79 90/219	Stealing wine from ship	500 L
188.	SCUDDER, NATHANIEL Inhab With Nos. 105, 171, 178, 189 & 192	NY GC 17 Oct 83	Burglary & robbery	£1,000 fine, or 1,000 L if not paid before evacuation
189.	SIMMIS, SILAS Inhab With Nos. 105, 171, 178, 188 & 192	NY GC 17 Oct 83	Burglary & robbery	NG
190.	SINCLAIR, SOPHIE SrW	NY 16 Nov 79 91/22	Murder on board transport	NG
191.	SMITH, DAVID Mate, RN With Nos. 48, 90, 92, & 141	NY GC 22 Mar 83	Murder	NG
192.	SMITH, JOHN Inhab With Nos. 105, 171, 178, 188, & 189	NY GC 17 Oct 83	Burglary & robbery	£1,000 fine, or 1,000 L if not paid before evacuation
193.	SMITH, THOMAS Inhab	NY 6 Nov 77 84/414	Buying HM's stores from soldier	£50 fine & 500 L
194.	SPENCER, EDWARD Mariner With Nos. 66 & 99	Phila WH 11 Nov 77 84/432	1, Attempt to kill Capt. Stewart; 2, Stealing & killing cattle	1, NG; 2, NG
195.	STANLEY, THOMAS Volunteer	Ft K 4 Feb 78 85/262	Stealing cattle	1,000 L

No.	Accused	Trial	Charge	Result
196.	STEELE, JOHN Carpenter of a transport With No. 6	NY WH 14 Apr 77 83/340	1, Forcing safe- guard; 2, Murder	1, NG; 2, NG
197.	STEWART, JAMES Inhab With No. 144	NY GC 16 Aug 83	Stealing	NG
198.	STEWART, JOHN Inhab of NY	NY HC 12 Mar 79	Enticing soldier to desert	NG
199.	SWEEZY, ISAAC Inhab	NY GC 8 July 83	Burglary	NG
200.	SYMMONS, THOMAS Steward on store ship	NY HC 7 Sept 79 90/223	Receiving goods stolen by Scott, No. 187	500 L, remitted on recommendation of court
201.	TAYLOR, ROBERT Shopkeeper late of Phila	NY 5 Feb 79 88/268	1, Holding corre- spondence with rebels; 2, Attempting to go to them with arms & clothing	1, NG; 2, G: "To be imprisoned in some one of HM's Gaols during the present Rebellion."
202.	TEID, ISAAC NSI With Nos. 19, 96, & 165	NY GC 21 Aug 83	Burglary	NG
203.	TODD, ADAM Mariner With Nos. 63 & 70	NY GC 22 July 83 97/321	Aiding & abetting in carrying off Negro	NG
204.	TOTTEN, CAESAR Negro and F/A With Nos. 10, 25, 60, 93, 134, 186, 208, & 218	NY GC 23 Aug 83 96/126	Murder	Death
205.	VAN BLACK, JOSEPH Negro; inhab With Nos. 216 & 217	NY 12 Feb 77 83/173	Theft of Crown property	300 L
206.	VAN DYKE, NICHOLAS Inhab	NY 7 Oct 77 84/352	Sheep stealing	NG

No.	*Accused*	*Trial*	*Charge*	*Result*
207.	VAN PELT, THUENESS Inhab With Nos. 12 & 150	NY GC 21 Aug 83	Carrying soldiers to NJ, enticing them to desert	NG
208.	VAN RIPER, WILLIAM Negro & F/A With Nos. 10, 25, 60, 93, 134, 186, 204, & 218	NY GC 23 Aug 82 96/126	Murder	Death, but recommended as subject of mercy; pardoned on condition of going to WI
209.	VAN TASSELL, JACOB R/A With Nos. 83 & 87	NY WH 24 Mar & 22 Apr 77 83/220, 239	Robbery	Death; respited; granted King's free pardon, see WH 12 Oct 77
210.	VEAL, JOHN NSI With Nos. 112 & 113	NY HC 12 Mar 79 88/306	Holding correspondence and trading with rebels	NG
211.	WALKER, GEORGE Conductor in the QMGD With Nos. 65 & 177	Germantown, Pa WH 8 Oct 77	Plundering	NG
212.	WALL, THOMAS Inhab	NY 29 Aug 77 84/187	Stealing	1,000 L, & conf until amount of theft, £67 6s. 3d., is restored
213.	WALLER, CATHARINE NSI With Nos. 30, 85, 104, 137, 169, & 214	NY 26 Jan 80 (Not named in HC) 91/154	Robbery	NG
214.	WALLER, JOSEPH NSI With Nos. 30, 85, 104, 137, 169, & 213	NY 26 Jan 80 (Not named in HC) 91/154	Robbery	NG
215.	WALN, JESSE Inhab	NY 3 Sept, 2 Nov, & 13	Carrying on correspondence with the enemy	NG

No.	Accused	Trial	Charge	Result
215—Continued		Dec 81, & 14 Jan 82 HC 9 Feb 82 95/1–103		
216.	WALSH, CATHERINE Inhab With Nos. 205 & 217	NY 12 Feb 77 83/173	Theft of Crown property	NG
217.	WALSH, WILLIAM Inhab With Nos. 205 & 216	NY 12 Feb 77 83/173	Theft of Crown property	NG
218.	WALTER, REUBEN Negro & F/A With Nos. 10, 25, 60, 93, 134, 186, 204, & 208	NY GC 23 Aug 82 96/126	Murder	NG, but to be sent to WI
219.	WARD, JOHN Driver in QMGD	Ft K HC 23 Aug 79 88/519	Stealing a horse	NG
220.	WEAVER, WILLIAM NSI	NY HC 8 Aug 79 89/237	Clandestine going to enemy's country	1 mo conf, recommended to mercy, pardoned
221.	WEBB, ELEANOR SrW	Ft K 19 Dec 79 91/47	Receiving & secreting stolen goods	"to be Drumm'd out of the Lines with a Rope about her Neck"
222.	WELSH, JAMES Laborer	NY GC 21 Feb 83	Robbery	500 L, then to be sent to WI
223.	WHITE, ALEXANDER Asst Barrack Master	NY HC 15 Aug 80 91/430	1. Disobedience orders. 2. Making false reports	Suspended from pay 14 days; remitted
224.	WHITEMAN, ISIAN Inhab With No. 29	NY GC 17 Oct 83	Burglary	NG
225.	WHITTLE, JOSHUA NSI With No. 31	NY GC 15 Oct 83	Burglary	NG
226.	WILLIAM A Negro Man	NY HC 6 Nov 78	Stealing a horse	500 L

No.	*Accused*	*Trial*	*Charge*	*Result*
227.	WILLIS, THOMAS Employee of the Magistrate of Police	NY GC 11 May 83	Abusing a Negro	300 L, rec. to mercy; remitted on condition of leaving country
228.	WILSON, JOHN Mariner	NY 17 July 81 94/253	Rape	NG

TRIALS OF CIVILIANS BY GENERAL COURTS-MARTIAL NOTED IN WELLINGTON'S GENERAL ORDERS, 1809–1818

The scheme of this list, and most of the abbreviations, are identical with that of the preceding Appendix. The principal variant is that the references to the trials are to the date, the volume, and the page of Wellington's General Orders. The only new abbreviation is "SRP," suspension from rank and pay.

Absence of the Christian name of any accused indicates that none was shown in the order. Where, however, the Christian name or initials of the accused appear in brackets, the omission has been remedied through the kindness of Mr. S. G. P. Ward, author of *Wellington's Headquarters*.

No.	Accused	Trial	Charge	Result
1.	ANTENOSA, JOSE F/A With No. 5	23 Dec 13 5:400	1, Robbery; 2, shooting at inhab	1,000 L
2.	ARMSTRONG, JAMES Conductor of stores	7 Feb 11 3:28	1, Disturbing peace; 2, insubordinate conduct; 3, breach of military disc	Dismissal
3.	BACH, WILLIAM Surgeon	7 July 11 3:130	1, Conduct unbecoming &c; 2, highly unmilitary conduct	SRP 3 mos
4.	BEGER, JOHN Butcher & F/A	2 Mar 13 5:73	Killing woman by firing into house	1,000 L
5.	BERNADOS, JOSE F/A With No. 1	23 Dec 13 5:400	1, Robbery; 2, shooting at inhab	Death

No.	Accused	Trial	Charge	Result
6.	BISSON, WILLIAM Conductor of Stores in Dept of RE	6 Feb 14 6:45	Gross misconduct & neglect of duty	Cashiered
7.	BOUBIER, FRANCISCO F/A With No. 29	24 Apr 14 6:124	Breaking into room & stealing	Death
8.	BUXTON, ISAAC Paymaster	13 Nov 09 1:216	AWOL; proceeding to rear	Cashiered; but pardoned
9.	CHRESTO, JOSEPH Driver in Commissariat Train & serving with army	2 June 16 8:141	1, Desertion; 2, taking away horse	1, NG; 2, G; 500 L
10.	DALHUNTY, MARCUS Paymaster	26 Sept 09 1:186	AWOL; going to rear	Reprimand
11.	DAY, ELISHA Dep Asst Commissary Gen	8 July 12 4:117	Highly outrageous conduct	NG
12.	DOUGAN, BRIDGET Follower of 87th Regt	22 Mar 13 5:145	1, firing & breaking into house; 2, drunken & mutinous behavior	1, NG; 2, NG because not applicable
13.	DRAKE, JOHN Dep Commissary Gen	20 May 13 5:195	Conduct unbecoming	NG
14.	DURAND, FREDERIC HOLLAND Paymaster	8 Jan 16 8:20	1, conduct unbecoming; 2, neglect of duty	Dismissal
15.	FAY, ELIZABETH SrW	22 Apr 13 5:148	Accessory to stealing & receiving stolen goods	NG
16.	FORD, THOMAS Storekeeper	30 Apr 16 8:111	Embezzlement & other irregularities (6 charges)	6 mos conf and cashiering
17.	HAFLART, FRANCIS Driver of Commissariat Waggon Train	17 Apr 16 8:102	1, burglary; 2, possession of stolen goods	1, NG; 2, G; 900 L
18.	HARDING, [GEORGE] Commissariat Clerk	22 June 16 8:152	Embezzlement (2 charges)	NG
19.	HICKSON, —— Asst Surgeon	19 Dec 09 1:253	AWOL	SRP, 6 mos; pardoned
02.	JOLY, [F. C.] Dep Asst Commissary Gen	16 Nov 11 3:243	Insubordination (6 charges)	SRP, 3 mos; severe reprimand

No.	Accused	Trial	Charge	Result
21.	KRECH, AUGUSTUS Hospital Mate	1 Sept 10 2:154	1, disobedience; 2, disrespectful conduct	SRP, 6 mos; remitted
22.	LEWIS, JOHN Apothecary to the Forces	19 Feb 11 3:35	Highly unmilitary conduct	SRP, 3 mos; remitted
23.	LYONS, WILLIAM Apothecary to the Forces	18 Feb 18 10:11	1, disobedience; 2 appearing out of quarters without sidearms & hat	Reprimand
24.	M'DONALD, PETER F/A	9 Mar 14 6:62	1, breaking open chests; 2, concealing the stolen property	NG
25.	McNAUGHTON, [A.] Dep Asst Commissary Gen	25 June 13 5:214	Conduct unbecoming	Discharged
26.	MOORE, [J. J.] Asst Commissary Gen	23 May 14 6:156	1, neglect of duty 2, "conduct most unbecoming his character as a Commissariat officer"	NG
27.	MUCKLOW, JOHN Commissariat Clerk	3 Feb 13 5:40	Conduct unbecoming	Suspension & public reprimand
28.	NASALIA, JOSEPH Sutler & F/A	14 Oct 11 3:213	Sodomy	NG
29.	PALACIAN, MACHAL F/A With No. 7	24 Apr 14 6:124	Breaking into room & stealing	Death
30.	PEREIRO, JOSEPH Private servant	16 Apr 17 9:57	1, drunk & absent from quarters; 2, assault on woman & her prop- erty; 3, forcibly entering house & stealing	NG
31.	POOLE, EDWARD F/A	29 Jan 10 2:13	. . . . . .	[Direction that the court-martial is to reassemble]
32.	POOLER, JOHN Surgeon to the Forces	14 Mar 13 5:95	Employing soldier as a servant	Suspended from appointment & pay, 4 mos; returned to duty

No.	Accused	Trial	Charge	Result
33.	RICHARDS, JANE S&W	26 Feb 16 8:65	Entering church, & stealing from it & damaging it	NG
34.	RICHARDSON, THOMAS Late Clerk in Commissariat Dept	1 June 10 2:85	Embezzlement	Conf 3 mos, & cashiered
35.	SMYTH, THOMAS Servant to Asst Commissary & F/A	17 Aug 10 2:135	Robbery	Death
36.	SOARE, CHARLES Deputy Purveyor	13 Jan 14 6:15	Gross neglect of duty; disobedience	SRP, 3 mos
37.	TALLACHER, —— Hospital Mate	27 Jan 14 6:32	Unofficerlike conduct	SRP, 3 mos
38.	THOMSON, JAMES Commissariat Clerk	20 Jan 13 5:23	Causing a Portuguese to be publicly flogged	NG
39.	TONNERE, ANDREW Asst Surgeon	11 Feb 14 6:50	Improper conduct	SRP, 6 mos
40.	WALSH, [JOHN HUTCHINSON] Asst Surgeon	29 Sept 12 4:173	Conduct unbecoming	Dismissal
41.	WARD, WILLIAM GORDON Commissariat Clerk	13 June 17 9:86	Embezzlement	Conf 3 mos, & cashiering
42.	WELSH, GEORGE Hospital Mate	19 Dec 09 1:251	1, drawing sword; 2, improper language; 3, disobedience; 4, neglect of duty	Dismissal
43.	WILKINSON, JOHN Conductor of stores	27 Aug 09 1:137	Absenting self from duty during action	Cashiering

RISE AND FALL OF THE AMERICAN MILITARY JURISDICTION OVER CIVILIANS ACCOMPANYING THE FORCES OVERSEAS IN TIME OF PEACE, A JURISDICTION ADVISEDLY COPIED IN THE ARMY AND AIR FORCE ACTS 1955

As the text of Chapter X indicates, the framers of the Army and Air Force Acts 1955 drew upon and copied the existing American military jurisdiction that was then being exercised over accompanying overseas civilians pursuant to Art. 2(11) UCMJ, the successor to AW 2(d) of 1916; the latter had remained in force until 1951. Here will be traced the rise and fall of that American jurisdiction.

Briefly, the American legislation fell because the doctrinal assumptions of 1916 on which it had been based had been rejected in a series of other decisions from 1922 through 1955.

General Crowder's proposal for an expanded jurisdiction over accompanying civilians overseas in time of peace, contained in his 1916 draft of AW 2(d) that Congress adopted without change—and without discussion—appears to have been triggered by an incident which arose during the American intervention in Cuba in 1906–1909. This concerned a thieving quartermaster clerk who was not subject to military law as it then stood, who could not be tried in any American civil court for what he had done in Cuba, and who ultimately escaped punishment altogether because of Cuban amnesty legislation that was enacted after the intervention ended (Sen. Rep. 130, 64th Cong., 1st sess., p. 38).

Perhaps, then, General Crowder's proposal was born of pique. At any rate, he rested it on two assumptions, which, though not articulated in detail, are nonetheless clearly discernible in his explanations. One was that the "cases arising in the land or naval forces" clause of the Fifth Amendment constituted a source of military jurisdiction, the other that the protections of the Constitution did not extend overseas. These two assumptions will be considered in order.

1. *The Fifth Amendment as a source of military jurisdiction.* The Constitution of the United States in Article I, Section 8, Clause 14, confers upon Congress the power "To make Rules for the Government and Regulation of the land and naval Forces." The Fifth Amendment to the Constitution provides, so far as here pertinent, that "No person shall be held to answer for a capital, or otherwise infamous crime, unless on a presentment or indictment of a Grand Jury except in cases arising in the land or naval forces. . . ."

It was assumed that, by reason of the quoted language of the Fifth Amendment, the test of military jurisdiction was, not whether the particular person tried by court-martial was a member of the land and naval forces, but whether the case on trial had arisen in those forces. That assumption, which indeed regarded the Fifth Amendment as a fountainhead of military jurisdiction, rested on judicial decisions (*In re Bogart*, 2 Sawy. 396, Fed. Case No. 1596 [C. C. D. Calif.]; *Ex parte Wildman*, Fed. Case No. 17,653a [D. Kan.]; *In re Craig*, 70 Fed. 969 [C. C. D. Kan.]), and on an opinion of the Attorney General (16 Op. Atty. Gen. 292). Moreover the United States Army's *Manual for Courts-Martial*, for many years and through many editions published under varying auspices—first privately (3d ed. by Lt. Murray, 1893, p. 2), next by the Secretary of War (1895, p. 4; 1901, p. 6; 1905, p. 6; 1908, p. 6), and finally promulgated by the President (¶1 in editions of 1917, 1921, 1928, and 1949; and, for all the armed forces of the United States, in 1951)—consistently pointed to the Fifth Amendment as a source of military jurisdiction.

Here again, down to the time that General Crowder appeared before Congress in 1916, the authorities supported his test of military jurisdiction, which was, quite simply, whether a particular case did or did not arise in the land and naval forces (Sen. Rep. No. 130, 64th Cong., 1st sess., p. 70).

The same assumption underlay judicial opinions subsequent to General Crowder's testimony. *Kahn* v. *Anderson*, 255 U.S. 1 (citation of earlier decisions, noted above, to sustain jurisdiction over dishonorably discharged military prisoner); *Kronberg* v. *Hale*, 180 F.2d 128 (C.A. 9), certiorari denied, 339 U.S. 969; *U.S. ex rel. Pasela* v. *Fenno*, 167 F.2d 593 (C.A. 2), certiorari granted, 334 U.S. 857, and dismissed pursuant to stipulation, 335 U.S. 806; *Talbott* v. *United States*, 215 F.2d 22 (D.C. Cir.) (the *Toth* case below). And commentators purporting to be knowledgeable in the law military gravely repeated the same views. See E. M. Morgan, *Court-Martial Jurisdiction over Non-Military Persons under the Articles of War*, 4 Minn. L. Rev. 79, 107; L. K. Underhill, *Jurisdiction of Military Tribunals in the United States over Civilians*, 12 Calif. L. Rev. 75). (The present author, who faithfully repeated the learning of his elders, is assuredly estopped from casting stones. *A Practical Manual of Martial Law* [Harrisburg, 1940] §§129–130.)

The only contrary view ever expressed was by Winthrop, who wrote (*52–53) that "The 5th Amendment of the Constitution . . . has also sometimes been viewed as a source of authority for courts-martial. . . . In view of the author, the Amendment, in the particular indicated, is rather a *declaratory recognition and sanction* of an existing military jurisdiction than an original provision initiating such a jurisdiction."

But since Winthrop openly disagreed with both judicial opinions and statutes that were admittedly contrary to his own strict views of the extent of military jurisdiction (*144–146), the foregoing observation went unheeded, and the assumption that the Fifth Amendment constituted a grant of military jurisdiction, on which General Crowder rested his AW 2(d) innovations, was never seriously in question until the *Toth* case reached the Supreme Court.

This was a proceeding that Toth, a discharged American airman, brought against the Secretary of the Air Force to prevent his return to Korea for trial by court-martial there on a charge of premeditated murder; his complicity in the killing of a Korean civilian in Korea was not discovered until after his own return to the United States, where he had been honorably discharged. When he was thereafter apprehended in the United States, under the recapture provision of the Uniform Code of Military Justice, he sought habeas corpus.

Under a decision antedating the Uniform Code, the fact of discharge had been held, on non-constitutional grounds, to terminate further military jurisdiction (*United States* v. *Cooke*, 336 U.S. 210). To plug this gap, Article 3(a) UCMJ provided that, subject to the statute of limitations, anyone committing an offense against the Code while in a status subject thereto, which was punishable by five years' confinement or more, and for which he could not be tried in the United States by any State or Federal court, "shall not be relieved from amenability to trial by court-martial by reason of the termination of said status." So far as the statutory language was concerned, these provisions fitted Toth's case in every particular; now there was raised the overriding question whether they squared with the Constitution.

If General Crowder, the judicial pronouncements before and after his proposal, the several commentators, and the nearly unanimous thinking of military lawyers were severally correct, then, so far as the Constitution was concerned, Toth was triable by court-martial, for, very plainly, his case had arisen in the land and naval forces. Contrariwise, if Colonel Winthrop, who had refused ever to concede the soundness of the earlier decisions, was justified in asserting that the Fifth Amendment "is rather a *declaratory recognition and sanction* of an existing military jurisdiction than an original provision initiating such a jurisdiction" (p. *53), then Toth, once become a civilian, was no longer amenable to military law: After his discharge, plainly enough, he was no longer a part of the "land and naval Forces" that the Constitution empowered Congress to govern.

Toth faced an uphill fight in three respects. First, to turn him loose would mean that he would go without punishment in respect of participation in a murder for which the two others concerned had already been convicted (*United States* v. *Schreiber*, 5 USCMA 602, 18 CMR 226; *United States* v. *Kinder*, 14 CMR 742). Second, the recapture provision of the Uniform Code, Art. 3(a), had been expressly enacted by Congress in order to overcome the holding in the *Hirshberg* case (*United States* v. *Cooke*, 336 U.S. 210) that the fact of discharge terminated military jurisdiction. See H.R. Rep. 491, 81st Cong., 1st sess., p. 11, and Sen. Rep. 486, 81st Cong., 1st sess., p. 8. Third, the decisions were unanimous against Toth in respect of the reasoning of "cases arising in the land and naval forces," and, in addition, all but one of the holdings under earlier recapture provisions were similarly adverse. *In re Bogart*, 2 Sawy. 396, Fed. Case No. 1596 (C. C. D. Cal.); *Ex parte Joly*, 290 Fed. 858 (S.D. N.Y.); *Terry* v. *United States*, 2 F. Supp. 962 (W.D. Wash.); *U.S. ex rel. Marino* v. *Hildreth*, 61 F. Supp. 667 (E.D. N.Y.); *Kronberg* v. *Hale*, 180 F.2d 128 (C.A. 9), certiorari denied, 339 U.S. 969; *U.S. ex rel. Flannery* v. *Commanding General*, 69 F. Supp. 661 (S.D. N.Y.) (*contra*, then reversed by stipulation, C.A. 2, No. 20235, 18 Apr. 1946).

It should therefore not occasion surprise that the *Toth* case seesawed back and forth as its issues were fought through the several stages of the judicial hierarchy. The district court first ordered Toth returned to Washington from Korea, to which place he had been brought for trial shortly after his apprehension in the United States (*Toth* v. *Talbott*, 113 F. Supp. 330 [D.D.C.]). Next, after a hearing, the district court issued the writ and ordered Toth released. *Toth* v. *Talbott*, 114 F. Supp. 468 (D.D.C.).

On the government's appeal, the district court's judgment was reversed, *Talbott* v. *United States*, 215 F.2d 22 (D.C. Cir.), after which the Supreme Court granted certiorari. In the latter court, the case was not only argued twice (see 349 U.S. 949 for the order directing reargument), but the marks of the sharp differences of opinion that it evoked are still visible today. For it is clear from internal evidence that what became the dissenting opinion (350 U.S. at 23–44) was originally prepared as the opinion of the Court (see particularly pp. 24–26). This circumstance doubtless explains the footnote position of the controlling passage in the ultimately prevailing opinion (*Toth* v. *Quarles*, 350 U.S. 11, 14, n 5.):

"The Fifth Amendment . . . does not grant court-martial power to Congress; it merely makes clear that there need be no indictment for such military offenses as Congress can authorize military tribunals to try under its Article I power to make rules to govern the armed forces."

There can be no doubt, however, that the result finally reached was correct. For virtually all the materials bearing on the scope of the Fifth Amendment support the conclusion reached by the Supreme Court—the purpose of the Bill of Rights as a limitation on the central government (*Barron* v. *Baltimore*, 7 Pet. 243, 250, *per* Marshall C.J.); the textual history of the amendment (1 Elliot's *Debates* 323, 326, 328, 334; 2 *id.* 177; 3 *id.* 658; 4 *id.* 243); the strong anti-military feeling generally prevalent at the time the amendment was adopted. After all, the Bill of Rights was not only designed to curb the powers of the then newly created Federal government, assurances of its adoption were an integral part of the process of ratifying the Constitution. Consequently to find in the Fifth Amendment a source of military power, not only expanding the grant of the Constitution proper but actually narrowing the scope of the Sixth Amendment's guaranty of jury trial, was plainly to do violence to the intent and to the understanding of the Framers.

In any event, it is the fact that the *Toth* case undermined and indeed destroyed the doctrinal foundation on which General Crowder had rested AW 2(d), and on which all who followed him had justified the exercise of military jurisdiction over overseas civilians, namely, that theirs were cases arising in the land and naval forces. The way was therefore clear to challenge that jurisdiction, a challenge that Mrs. Covert made just ten days after the *Toth* case was decided.

(It may or may not be significant in this connection that the Solicitor General had argued in *Toth* [Resp. Br., No. 150, Oct. T. 1954, p. 31, n. 14], "Indeed, we think the constitutional case is, if anything, clearer for the court-martial of Toth, who was a soldier at the time of his offense, than it is for a civilian accompanying the armed forces." This concession did not go unnoticed by counsel for the relators in the later cases of Mrs. Covert and Mrs. Smith, and ultimately it attained the honor—a doubtful one in the circumstances—of quotation by the Supreme Court in the opinion that set those women free. *Reid* v. *Covert*, 354 U.S. 1, 32, n. 58.)

Interestingly enough, the old notion of the Fifth Amendment as a source of jurisdiction was never revived, even in the first *Krueger* and *Covert* opinions that were adverse to the relators in those cases, opinions that were later withdrawn. Those trials by court-martial were originally sustained, as it were, *in vacuo*. The Court did not turn to the Fifth Amendment as a source of power; that strange assumption had been exploded for all time by *Toth*. Nor did the Court rest the result on Article I, Section 8, Clause 14; it said there was no need to consider that clause.

(Mr. Justice Frankfurter, reserving judgment, said with reference to the Court's disclaimer of any need to examine the scope of that obviously relevant constitutional provision, "The plain inference from this is that the Court is not prepared to support the constitutional basis upon which the Covert and Smith courts-martial were instituted and the convictions were secured" [351 U.S. at 481]. Or, put somewhat more pithily, there were lacking the necessary votes to hold that the Constitutional words, "land and naval Forces," were broad enough to include and encompass dependent wives.)

Clause 14 having been thus necessarily brushed to one side, the Court sustained the exercise of military jurisdiction over the two women on the footing that Congress had power to erect legislative courts for the trial of persons outside the United States, in which it was not required to provide a jury trial.

That holding directly and inescapably involved—and adopted—General Crowder's second assumption, which will now be discussed.

2. *The Constitution stops at the water's edge.* In the early 1890's, when the non-contiguous territory of the United States was limited to the sparsely settled pre-Klondike-gold-rush District of Alaska (constituted as such by the Act of May 17, 1884, c. 53, 23 Stat. 24) and to uninhabited guano islands (see *Jones* v. *United States*, 137 U.S. 202), the Supreme Court dealt with the case of John M. Ross, a sailor on an American ship—though probably not an American himself—who in 1880 killed a shipmate while their vessel was anchored in Yokohama harbor. At this time the United States and the larger European powers still enjoyed extraterritoriality in Japan, in consequence of which Ross was tried for murder before the American Consul, convicted, and sentenced to death. On recommendation of the American Minister, this was commuted by the President to life imprisonment, and Ross was returned to the United States to serve his time. After ten years in prison he sought habeas corpus, and then appealed to the Supreme Court from a denial of the writ.

There he received short shrift, not only because the consular jurisdiction was by then a well-established one, but more fundamentally because "The Constitution can have no operation in another country" (*In re Ross*, 140 U.S. 453, 464)—a proposition which, if literally true, quite failed to explain the source of the consul's authority to try and to convict the prisoner.

A decade thereafter, following American acquisition of the Philippines, Porto Rico (later, from 1932, called Puerto Rico), and Hawaii, the status of those areas came before the Supreme Court in the so-called *Insular Cases*, a series of decisions on various issues wherein a 5–4 majority formulated two principles: First, the Court looked to see whether Congress had incorporated the new territory into the United States. If so, the Constitution applied *ex proprio vigore*. If not, then the Court looked, second, to see what provisions of the Constitution were "applicable." Here only such of the *Insular Cases* as dealt with the right to indictment by grand jury and to trial by petit jury are relevant.

a) In the interval between the annexation of Hawaii in 1898 and the effective date of the Hawaiian Organic Act in 1900, one Mankichi was by information charged with murder, and was convicted of manslaughter by the verdict of 9 out of 12 jurors in the Circuit Court of Hawaii. Non-unanimous jury verdicts and prosecutions by information in Hawaii dated from the 1840's. The Resolution of Annexation passed by Congress in 1898 had continued in force most local laws insofar as they were "not inconsistent with this joint resolution nor contrary to the Constitution of the United States." Did the latter phrase mean that the requirements for indictment in the Fifth Amendment and for a traditional common law jury trial in the Sixth automatically uprooted institutions native to Hawaii? *Held* no, by 5–4 (*Hawaii* v. *Mankichi*, 190 U.S. 197).

b) Two American citizens resident in the Philippines were tried and convicted by the Court of First Instance of the City of Manila, sitting without a jury, on a charge of criminal libel. *Held,* with only a single dissent, that since the Philippine Islands were not incorporated territory, the constitutional provisions for grand juries and petit juries were inapplicable (*Dorr* v. *United States,* 195 U.S. 138).

c) In 1900 Congress enacted a Code of Laws for Alaska that provided for a 6-man jury for the trial of misdemeanors, a provision perfectly proper if adopted by a State of the Union (*Maxwell* v. *Dow,* 176 U.S. 581). But this was Congressional legislation for a Territory, which the Supreme Court held to be an incorporated Territory, a circumstance from which it followed that the Sixth Amendment, which guaranteed a trial by jury as that institution had developed at common law, rendered the trial unconstitutional (*Rassmussen* v. *United States,* 197 U.S. 516).

The foregoing decisions represented the state of the law when General Crowder appeared before Congress in support of AW 2(d), and said that, once civilians went overseas, "without the territorial jurisdiction of the United States" as AW 2(d) phrased it, they were "away from the protection of constitutionally guaranteed rights" (Sen. Rep. No. 130, 64th Cong., 1st sess., p. 32).

Accordingly, on the law as it stood in 1916, it cannot be contended for a moment that General Crowder was wrong in saying what he did. But, a few years later, significant qualifications made their appearance.

In 1922, the Supreme Court once more decided that, in Puerto Rico, a criminal conviction by a court sitting without a jury was perfectly constitutional. But the Court undercut its former statement in the *Ross* case about the inapplicability of the Constitution overseas, declaring this time that "The Constitution of the United States is in force in Porto Rico as it is wherever and whenever the sovereign power of that government is exerted" (*Balzac* v. *Porto Rico,* 258 U.S. 298, 312).

On three subsequent occasions the Supreme Court had also declared—italics added—that "Neither the Constitution nor the laws passed in pursuance of it have any force in foreign territory *unless in respect of our own citizens*" (*United States* v. *Curtiss-Wright Corp.,* 299 U.S. 304, 318; *United States* v. *Belmont,* 301 U.S. 324, 332; *United States* v. *Pink,* 315 U.S. 203, 226). And, after the Second World War, the Government's argument that any part of the Bill of Rights was inapplicable to Hawaii was emphatically rejected in the martial law cases that had arisen there (*Duncan* v. *Kahanamoku,* 327 U.S. 304).

Consequently the second doctrine on which General Crowder had relied in 1916, that constitutional protections stopped at the water's edge, had been significantly qualified by the time the *Toth, Covert,* and *Krueger* cases were decided, at the 1955 Term.

That second doctrine was not discussed in *Toth,* however much it may have been involved *sub silentio*—after all it was proposed to try Toth in Korea, not in the United States. But it reappeared in its original form, stripped of all subsequent qualifications, in the first opinions on courts-martial of civilians; the Court in *Kinsella* v. *Krueger*, 351 U.S. 470, relied very strongly on *In re Ross*, 140 U.S. 453.

Those first opinions represented a notably short-lived victory for the revived notion of the three-mile limit on the protections of the Constitution. The different result reached on the rehearing of the *Covert* and *Krueger* cases involved, not indeed an overruling of the *Ross* case, but a decisive rejection of its teaching. This later approach was, without question, a consequence of the circumstance that, in the interval between the first and second court-martial decisions, there had been abolished the last remaining vestiges of the consular jurisdiction that had been considered and sustained in *Ross* (Act of August 1, 1956, Pub. L. 84–856, 70 Stat. 773; 35 Dept. of State Bull. 844). Or, as the matter was put in the brief filed on rehearing on behalf of the convicted women (p. 67), "It is thus a paradox, not without irony, that in the very same year that the Congress and the President acting jointly have abolished the consular jurisdiction, essentially because it was unsuited to present day world conditions, this Court should have relied upon that same 'moribund historical jurisdiction' [M.O. Hudson, *The Thirty-First Year of the World Court*, 47 Am. J. Int. L. 1, 15] to justify trials by court-martial that it was not prepared to rest on the power to govern the armed forces."

Sequel to Reid v. Covert II. In the second decision involving the two convicted women (*Reid* v. *Covert*, 354 U.S. 1) four opinions were written, but none for the Court, inasmuch as a majority of the sitting Justices were not in agreement (see, e.g., *United States* v. *Pink*, 315 U.S. 203, 216). The actual holding was in consequence a narrow one, limited to the proposition that in time of peace civilian dependents accompanying the forces overseas could not be tried by court-martial for capital offenses.

For a time it appeared that the services would construe the second *Covert* decision broadly; certainly they failed to seek further review of at least three rulings that did: (1) *U.S. ex rel. Louise Smith* v. *Kinsella*, H.C. No. 1963, S.D. W.Va., civilian dependent convicted by court-martial of non-capital offense released on habeas corpus; no appeal. (2) *United States* v. *Tyler*, CM 396739, holding by Army Board of Review that conviction of civilian dependent for capital offense could not be sustained even where convening authority had ordered case treated as non-capital for depositions pursuant to Art. 49(f) UCMJ; case not certified to Court of Military Appeals under Art. 67(b)(2) UCMJ. (3) *Cheaves* v. *Brucker*, H.C. No. 100–58, D. D.C., woman charged with non-capital offense, released from military custody on habeas corpus, thereafter turned over to authorities of Federal Republic of Germany, and tried in German court.

Not only that, but in *Wilson* v. *Girard*, 354 U.S. 524, the Government had succeeded in establishing its power to waive its jurisdiction over a soldier stationed in Japan—not a mere civilian employee or dependent—

and then to turn over that soldier to the Japanese authorities for trial in a Japanese court, under the provisions of the amended Administrative Agreement that adopted the jurisdictional features of the NATO Status of Forces arrangement (TIAS 2848, 4 U.S. Treaties 1846).

Before long, however, the intransigence that seems to be inevitable in bureaucratic thinking made its appearance, with the result that, at its October 1959 Term, the Supreme Court heard argument in a quartet of cases involving the exercise of military jurisdiction in time of peace over civilians in all of the situations not specifically embraced within its earlier holding. One of these cases involved a civilian dependent convicted by court-martial of a non-capital offense (*Kinsella* v. *Singleton*, 361 U.S. 234), one dealt with a civilian employee similarly convicted of a capital offense (*Grisham* v. *Hagan*, 361 U.S. 278), while the other two involved civilian employees found guilty by court-martial of committing non-capital offenses (*McElroy* v. *Guagliardo* and *Wilson* v. *Bohlender*, 361 U.S. 281).

In each instance, the military jurisdiction was struck down; in each instance, military jurisdiction except in time of war was said to depend upon the military status of the accused; and, in each instance, the opinion was delivered by the same Justice who in June 1956 had written for the Court in sustaining the jurisdiction in the first *Covert* and *Krueger* cases. Here, once again, there was paradox and irony. Today, therefore, civilians not in the actual theater of a war cannot be constitutionally tried by an American court-martial—although Arts. 2(11) and 2(12) UCMJ, which solemnly assert the contrary, remain on the books.

To the foregoing generalization there exists at this time one minor exception, one that appears to be doctrinally inconsistent with the Supreme Court's last decisions on military jurisdiction; that exception concerns the trial by court-martial of dishonorably discharged military prisoners. Such individuals, who have been effectively and indeed ignominiously separated from the service, would plainly seem to be no longer members of the land and naval forces, however much they may still be in the custody of those forces. Winthrop, accordingly, was strongly of the view that they were civilians, no longer subject to military trial, and that any statute (such as R.S. §1361) purporting to render them thus triable was plainly unconstitutional (pp. *144–146). Successive Judge Advocates General of the Army consistently ruled to the same effect (Dig. Op. JAG, 1880, pp. 212–214; *id.*, 1895, pp. 326–327; *id.*, 1901, p. 294).

Thereafter, however, Congress several times reaffirmed the military jurisdiction over military prisoners (Sec. 5 of the Act of June 18, 1898, c. 469, 30 Stat. 483, 484; AW 2(e) of 1916, 1920, and 1948), and the Supreme Court, first by way of dictum (*Carter* v. *McClaughry*, 183 U.S. 365, 383) and then in a square decision (*Kahn* v. *Anderson*, 255 U.S. 1), sustained the exercise of military jurisdiction over dishonorably discharged prisoners.

The case last cited, decided in 1921, was based on the then generally accepted assumption that the Fifth Amendment constituted a source of military power. Nonetheless, despite the circumstance that this concept of the Fifth Amendment was rejected in *Toth* in 1955, despite the further circumstance that the final decisions on military trials of all other civilians in 1960 were strongly the other way in nearly every facet of their reasoning, the Supreme Court has up to now refused to review rulings of lower courts that still felt themselves bound by, even though they now doubted the result in, *Kahn* v. *Anderson*, 255 U.S. 1, with respect to jurisdiction over discharged military prisoners. *Simcox* v. *Madigan*, 298 F. 2d 742 (C.A. 9), certiorari denied, 370 U.S. 964; *Ragan* v. *Cox*, 320 F. 2d 815 (C.A. 10), certiorari denied, 375 U.S. 981.

BIBLIOGRAPHY

I. PRINCIPAL MANUSCRIPT SOURCES CONSULTED

Court-martial records: The basic documents on which the present study of British court-martial jurisdiction rests are, understandably enough, the actual records of trials by court-martial, in three categories.

1. *Proceedings*. These are the MS records of trial by general court-martial, prepared under the direction of the DJA who officiated at the trial, and by him forwarded to the JAG in London. They contain the evidence adduced on both sides, most generally summarized but frequently set forth at least in part in question and answer form, together with exhibits and, very frequently, the prisoner's written defense. Once the proceedings were received, they were laboriously copied into the court-martial books. In view of this identity the proceedings do not justify independent examination except in very unusual instances. The only proceedings examined were WO 71/155, for the year 1783; and WO 71/244 and 71/245, for the year 1816. The first bore on the problem of the New York evacuation (*supra*, pp. 134–140), the other two on the case of Jane Richards (*supra*, pp. 204–205).

2. *Court-martial books*. The following were carefully searched: WO 71/37 through 71/62, Home and Foreign Stations, and WO 71/65 through 71/97, Marching Regiments. Once it was ascertained that WO 71/13 through 71/33 contained only the records of general courts-martial held at the Horse Guards in London, those volumes were not intensively examined.

3. *Order books*. The headquarters order book of the field commander who referred the case for trial and then acted on the proceedings sets forth the name and status of the accused; the charges made; the findings and sentence of the court-martial; and the convening authority's action, i.e., approval, disapproval, mitigation or remission, or pardon. No evidence appears in the order books, which thus are less informative concerning the trial itself than are the court-martial books. But the order books frequently contain entries showing subsequent mitigation or pardon that are never copied into the court-martial books. And, on occasion, as in New York in 1783, the order books announce the results of trials that do not appear either in the proceedings or in the court-martial books. The order books that were examined are listed in Part II of this Bibliography.

The substance of the foregoing detailed listings is simply this: meticulous examination of the available court-martial records has for the most part been limited to the period 1745 through 1783; the first year represents the approximate date of the first camp follower article, the second the end of the War of American Independence, after which the British practice loses its significance for purposes of American constitutional law.

Records of garrison courts-martial. No proceedings have been found, and the results are noted only in occasional order books, duly listed below.

JAG correspondence. Out-letters, other than those deemed confidential, were copied into the Judge Advocate General's Letter Books, the WO 81 group; volumes 1–16, covering the period through 1783, have been examined.

In-letters, together with copies of confidential out-letters, are in the WO 72 group; bundles 1 and 3 through 11, again through the year 1783, were examined. (WO 72/2 contains the MS Articles of War.)

Other War Office correspondence. A few headquarters records of interest were found in WO 28 (includes two Carleton order books) and in WO 36 (includes the Haldimand-Gage Order Book).

The Amherst Papers (WO 34), which Professor Willcox characterized as "an enormous deposit of sediment holding just enough gold to justify the dreary work of sifting it," have not been systematically searched in the present connection.

The Carleton Papers (see HMC Am. MSS. below) were calendared in four volumes in 1904–1909 while in the possession of the Royal Institution. Then, after many years and interesting vicissitudes—purchased by Dr. A. S. W. Rosenbach in 1929 for £ 30,000 (then $145,800), sold by him to Mr. John D. Rockefeller, Jr., in 1930 for $467,500, arranged and numbered at the New York Public Library, presented to Colonial Williamsburg in 1935, and by it given to H.M. Queen Elizabeth II in 1957—they are once more back in London, but at the Public Record Office (PRO 30/55). See E. Wolf 2d, *Rosenbach: A Biography* (Cleveland, 1960) 315, 321, 328–329, 335, 338–340. Where the printed calendars of the Carleton Papers were inadequate, as was the case in respect of the trials by court-martial held in New York in 1782–1783, the underlying documents were examined, and these are cited by number whenever necessary to an understanding of the proceedings.

No other WO group appeared to be particularly helpful. The Secretary at War's Out-Letters (WO 4) were examined on a sampling basis; they yielded up too little to justify an extended search. The Miscellany Books (WO 26 and WO 30) appeared to be promising in the earlier period (e.g., WO 26/16–25; WO 30/18, 25, 29), but thereafter they contain simply formal warrants (e.g., WO 26/29–32).

The Secretary at War's In-Letters (WO 1) occasionally contain an item of interest. Unfortunately, many communications in that category were later transferred to and bound in the CO 5 group, i.e., classified according to locality. All too frequently, a letter of transmittal appears in WO 1, its acknowledgment can be found in WO 4—but the actual document transmitted is not in any WO series.

It should be added that no effort has been made to examine the 1,450 or so volumes and bundles in the CO 5 series (America and West Indies, 1606–1807). Those sources have been sufficiently copied, quoted, and summarized by a spate of historians—some able, some unable, and some alas lamentable—hardly any of whom in any classification appear to have had the least concern with or interest in court-martial jurisdiction.

Other repositories. Not systematically combed; only particular items, all of which have been duly cited, were examined. Once more to quote Mr. Justice Holmes (M. D. Howe, ed., *The Occasional Speeches of Justice Oliver Wendell Holmes* [Cambridge, Mass., 1962] 114), "One has to try to strike the jugular and let the rest go."

Perhaps the most significant single MS item not otherwise classified is the William Smith Diary in the New York Public Library; the entries read cover the period April to June 1782 and July to November 1783; they are quite indispensable to an appreciation of the trials of Lippincott, Hetfield, and the counterfeiters.

Finally, in the endeavor to ascertain the fate of the prisoners remaining in the New York provost after that city was evacuated on 25 November 1783 (*supra,* pp. 134–140), the following records of the civil courts that were reconstituted immediately afterwards were examined: Minute Book of the Court of Oyer and Terminer and General Gaol Delivery, 1784–1796, and all indictments returned to that court that are now contained in the metal box marked "Indictments, 1784–1786." Both items are in the Office of the Clerk of the Criminal Division of the Supreme Court of the State of New York for New York County, 10th Floor Criminal Courts Building, 100 Centre Street, New York City.

II. ORDER BOOKS, PRINTED AND MANUSCRIPT

In the eighteenth century, every military unit had an order book, in which were written down the orders issued by its commanding officer and some at least of the orders issued by his superiors in command.

Differences in the several versions of the same orders stem from the method of their preparation, namely, that the orderly serjeants of each unit would take down what was dictated by the adjutant or the serjeant-major at orderly time. C. James, *Military Dictionary* (London, 1802) *s.v.* "Orderly non-commissioned officers." Accuracy in consequence varied with the ability, the literacy, and the phonetic imagination of the soldier actually pushing the pen.

Accordingly, in the trials by court-martial noted in the text, order book variants have been disregarded, and the name of the accused appears as it is spelled in the court-martial books in the PRO (WO 71 group), except only when the London clerk was confused by Yankee names like Uriah and Duryee and has by obvious error rendered them as Urih and Duyree.

Citations in the present work are to the order book of the commander concerned, e.g., "Gage OB, 25 Sept. 1775," and this is so even when the order in question is found only in the order book of a subordinate commander. Thus, the entry in question, which records the trial of Winifred McCowan for doing in Boston's town bull (*supra*, pp. 84–85), is cited to the Gage OB, even though General Gage's orders for that period appear only in (1) the printed order book of General Howe (which contains General Gage's headquarters orders as long as that officer was in command, as well as General Howe's orders when the latter was still a subordinate commanding only at Charlestown Heights), and (2) in Adjutant Waller's orderly book, which includes General Gage's Boston headquarters orders, General Howe's Charlestown Heights orders, and the battalion orders of the Royal Marines that concerned only Adjutant Waller's unit.

A. Headquarters Order Books of the British Army in North America

1. *Amherst.* There are no order books as such in the voluminous Amherst Papers (PRO, WO 34).

2. *Gage.* The Gage Papers in the WLCL do not include any order books. But General Gage's orders from his resumption of command at Salem, Massachusetts, on 10 June 1774, until his departure from Boston on 10 October 1775, appear in a number of places.

a) Extracts of orders given to the British Army in America (PRO WO 36/1). Extracts from 10 June 1773 to 10 January 1776; but this volume is far from complete.

b) Orders by His Excellency the Hon'ble Thomas Gage, General & Commander in Chief, &c, &c, &c (MS, NYHS). Extends from 10 July 1774 through 9 December 1774.

c) General Orders by His Excellency the Hoñble Thomas Gage, General & Commander in Chief, &c. &c. &c. From 10th Dec. 1774, to 6th June 1775 (MS, Boston Public Library).

d) Lieutenant and Adjutant Waller's Orderly Book Commencing Boston the 22d May and Ending the Twenty Sixth day of January 1776 (MS, MHS). Covers the gap between items (*c*) and (*e*); cited as "Waller OB."

e) B. F. Stevens, ed., *Sir William Howe's Orderly Book at Charlestown, Boston and Halifax, 17 June 1775–26 May 1776* (London, 1890). Includes General Gage's orders from 17 June through 9 October 1775.

3. *Howe.* No substantial collection of Howe papers is known to exist.

a) Stevens' printed version (item 2*e*, just above), contains General Howe's headquarters orders from his assumption of command on 10 October 1775, through 26 May 1776.

b) Howe Order Book (MS, WLCL). Extends from 9 March 1776 through 6 April 1778. Professor Peckham, Director of the Clements Library, classifies it as a brigade order book. The advantage of this circumstance is that it includes the results of numerous trials by garrison court-martial, which do not appear anywhere else. The disadvantages are that it does not record the results of any trials by general court-martial held in the New York area while General Howe was in Philadelphia, and that it does not include the orders for the last seven weeks of that officer's command.

c) Howe's General Orders Written by Capt. Henry Knight (MS, NYHS). Kept by an ADC, from 26 September 1776 to 2 June 1777. Incomplete.

d) Kemble 251–585 contains incomplete entries from General Howe's headquarters orders from 15 November 1775 to 29 June 1776 and from 6 October 1776 to 23 May 1778. (Major and Brevet Lt.-Col. Stephen Kemble of New Jersey, General Gage's brother-in-law [Alden *Gage* 44, 249], was DAG until 23 October 1779, when he was succeeded by Major John André. In 1780–1781, Kemble, then a Brigadier General, commanded the expedition to Nicaragua. 2 Kemble 67 *et seq.;* Alden *Gage* 290–291; 3 Fortescue 345–346).

e) Not infrequently, fragments from the Howe OB are encountered in the order books of subordinate units. E.g., *Orderly Book of the Three Battalions of Loyalists Commanded by Brigadier-General Oliver De Lancey* (NYHS, 1917); Order Book of the 17th Regiment of Foot, 11 Oct.–28 Dec. 1776, Lt. Col. Charles Mawhood Commanding (MS, NYHS). But no effort has been made to run down all such similar secondary references.

4. *Clinton.*

a) The Clinton Papers in the WLCL contain what are undoubtedly General Clinton's own original order books, entitled General Orders from the Commencement of His Excellency Sir Henry Clinton's Command. These four MS volumes cover the period while he was Commander in Chief in America, 24 May 1778 to 9 May 1782.

b) Some of Clinton's earlier orders are also entered in Kemble.

c) The following MS order books in the NYHS have also been examined; they are essentially fragmentary. British Guards Order Book, New York City, August–December 1778; British Order Book, Staten Island, 26 April–3 August 1781; another Staten Island OB, 1 August 1781–20 February 1782.

5. *Carleton.*

a) Carleton Orders (Mackenzie Papers, Item F; MS, WLCL). Mackenzie was General Carleton's DAG, and these orders extend from 8 May 1782 through 2 December 1783, covering General Carleton's entire period of command at New York.

b) His Excellency General Sir Guy Carleton's Orders, New York, Wednesday 8th May 1782 (PRO WO 28/1, pp. 306v–482). Last entry is on p. 482, "After Orders 23d November 1783." This volume also contains some garrison orders.

B. Burgoyne's Campaign

1. E. B. O'Callaghan, ed., *Orderly Book of Lieut. Gen. John Burgoyne* (Albany, 1860). The headquarters orders, cited "Burgoyne OB," with

entries from 20 June to 17 October 1777, the last one reading simply "Treaty of Convention signed."

2. Order Book of the Battalion of Grenadiers (MS, NYHS), cited "Grenadier OB," entries from 7 June to 3 July 1777, only.

3. W. L. Stone, ed., *Orderly Book of Sir John Johnson during the Oriskany Campaign, 1776–1777* (Albany, 1882).

4. Hadden includes an orderly book as well as a journal.

5. G. F. G. Stanley, ed., *For Want of a Horse, being a Journal of the Campaigns against the Americans in 1776 and 1777 conducted from Canada, by an officer who served with Lt. Gen. Burgoyne* (Sackville, N.B., 1961). The author was on the staff of General Fraser's brigade (p. 3). Cited as "Stanley's OB."

C. Cornwallis' Campaigns

1. A. R. Newsome, ed., *A British Orderly Book, 1780–1781*, 9 N.C. Hist. Rev. 57, 163, 273, 366. Entries from 28 August 1780 to 20 March 1781 while under the command of Major-General Alexander Leslie, later Lord Cornwallis' successor in command at Charleston, S.C.; but this is a brigade order book.

2. Orderly Book, 28 June to 19 October 1781 (MS, Boston Public Library). A battalion order book for the light companies, fantastically and indeed pathetically illiterate—"A wiman . . . haveng lattley bin detacted Selling lickerr . . . Should aney Solders wiff . . . Sell licker after this Order Shee will be sent out of the linns and Niver after wards be Admited"—but contains the dignified farewell orders of Lieutenant-Colonel Abercrombie and of Lord Cornwallis after the surrender. Records appointments of some regimental courts-martial, but no results of trials.

D. Siege of Savannah

Regimental Orderly Book, 2 July–2 October 1779 (MS, LC). No results of trials.

E. Other Order Books Cited or Examined

1. A. N. C. Maclachlan, *William Augustus, Duke of Cumberland* (London, 1876). Contains the Duke of Cumberland's General Orders from the Orderly Books of Lieutenant Archibald Campbell, 3d King's Own Dragoons, ADC to General Bland and Judge Advocate, 23 April 1745–6 December 1746, and April–June 1747. Unhappily, the order book entries as printed in this distinctly discursive compilation are neither complete nor consecutive. Cited as "Maclachlan."

2. *Major-General Edward Braddock's Orderly Books, from February 26 to June 17, 1755* (Cumberland, Md., 1880).

3. Orderly book of Major Alexander Monypenny, 24 [?] March 1758 to 6 May 1759 (MS, Fort Ticonderoga, N.Y.). Monypenny was successively major of brigade to Generals Abercromby and Amherst.

4. *Commissary Wilson's Orderly Book* (Albany, 1857). Entries from 22 May to 3 November 1759. "Expedition of the British and Provincial

Army, under Maj. Gen. Jeffrey Amherst, against Ticonderoga and Crown Point."

5. *Military Order Books, 1758–1759,* 8 HMC Var. Coll. 418–568. Contains the orders of the British Army in Germany, 30 July 1758 through 28 April 1759.

6. E. G. Williams, ed., *The Orderly Book of Colonel Henry Bouquet's Expedition against the Ohio Indians, 1764* (Pittsburgh, 1940). Entries from 2 October through 9 November 1764.

F. Wellington's General Orders

In ten volumes, as follows: 1. Spain and Portugal, 27 April–28 December 1809 (London, 1811). 2. Spain and Portugal, 2 January–29 December 1810 (London, 1811). 3. Spain and Portugal, 1 January–31 December 1811 (London, 1812). 4. Spain and Portugal, 1 January–30 December 1812 (London, 1813). 5. Spain and France, 7 January–28 December 1813 (London, 1814). 6. France, 1814 (London, 1817). 7. Flanders and France, 11 April–31 December 1815 (Paris, 1815). 8. France, 1816 (Hq. of the Army, 1816). 9. France, 1817 (Hq. of the Army, 1817). 10. France, 1818 (Hq. of the Army, 1818).

Cited as "Well. G.O."

G. Concordance between Order Books and Court-Martial Books

Ideally, every trial by general court-martial is noted in the commander's order book and is recorded in the court-martial book; each complements the other; the first notes subsequent action by way of remission or pardon, the second supplies the date of trial and summarizes the evidence adduced. But with disappointing frequency this ideal remains unrealized, for a number of reasons:

1. A trial recorded in the order book does not appear in the court-martial book. This may reflect the fact that the original proceedings may have miscarried, or, as was probably the case with most of the trials held in New York in 1783, that (in view of the impending evacuation) they were never sent home.

2. A trial recorded in the court-martial book does not appear in the order books. This happens because the latter are not complete, and seem moreover to have been regarded as private rather than public records. The Mutiny Act required all court-martial proceedings to be sent to the JAG. Also, in some instances of trials of a large number of accused persons, the names of some of those acquitted were simply not entered in the order books and are listed only in the court-martial books.

3. It remains to note what doubtless will be obvious, namely, that the possibility of occasional lapses by the present author in connection with both sets of records cannot be entirely excluded.

III. NEWSPAPERS

Contemporary newspapers have been intensively examined in only two instances, in both of which all other sources appeared inadequate.

1. In order to ascertain the details of the British occupation of three American cities, the Loyalist journals published there during that period were searched; examination was restricted to the Library of Congress runs, which are substantially complete, and accordingly quite sufficed for present purposes:

Newport Gazette, 16 January 1777 through 6 October 1779.

Philadelphia Ledger; or, The Weekly Advertiser, 10 October 1777 through 16 May 1778.

South Carolina Royal Gazette, 3 March 1781 through 7 August 1782.

2. In the effort to determine the disposition ultimately made of the civil prisoners left in the provost when the British evacuated New York on 25 November 1783, every New York newspaper from October 1783 through April 1784 that was available in either the Library of Congress, the New York Public Library, or the New-York Historical Society has been consulted.

IV. SHORT-TITLE INDEX OF WORKS FREQUENTLY CITED

[NOTE: Printed Order Books already listed in Part II are excluded.]

Abbott—W. C. Abbott. *New York in the American Revolution*. New York, 1929.

Adams D. & A.—L. H. Butterfield, ed. *Diary and Autobiography of John Adams*. Cambridge, Mass., 1961.

Adams *Leg. Pap.*—L. K. Wroth and H. B. Zobel, eds. *Legal Papers of John Adams*. Cambridge, Mass., 1965.

Adye—S. P. Adye. *A Treatise on Courts Martial*. 1st ed., New York, 1769; 2d ed., London, 1778; 3d ed., Philadelphia, 1779; 8th ed., London, 1810.

Alden A.R.—J. R. Alden. *The American Revolution, 1775–1783*. New York, 1954.

Alden *Gage*—J. R. Alden. *General Gage in America*. Baton Rouge, 1948.

Anburey—T. Anburey. *Travels through the Interior Parts of America*. London, 1789.

André—H. C. Lodge, ed. *André Journal*. Boston, 1903.

Andrews—*Letters of John Andrews, Esq., of Boston, 1772–1776*, 8 MHS Proc. 316.

Aspinall—A. Aspinall, ed. *The Later Correspondence of George III*. Cambridge, 1962——.

Barck—O. T. Barck, Jr. *New York City during the War for Independence*. New York, 1931.

Barker—J. Barker. *The British in Boston*. Cambridge, Mass., 1924.

Baurmeister—B. A. Uhlendorf and E. Vesper, eds. *Letters from Major Baurmeister*. Philadelphia, 1937.

Bridenbaugh—C. Bridenbaugh. *Cities in Revolt: Urban Life in America, 1743–1776*. New York, 1955.

Burgoyne—J. Burgoyne. *A State of the Expedition from Canada.* Two eds., London, 1780. References in the text are to the 1st (quarto) edition.

Burt—A. L. Burt. *The Old Province of Quebec.* Toronto and Minneapolis, 1933.

Carey—R. Carey. *Military Law and Discipline.* London, 1877.

Carter *Illinois*—C. E. Carter. *Great Britain and the Illinois Country 1763–1774.* Washington, 1910.

W. Carter—W. Carter. *A Genuine Detail of the Several Engagements, Positions, and Movements of the Royal and American Armies.* London, 1784.

Cheever—*William Cheever's Diary, 1775–1776,* 60 MHS Proc. 91.

G. Clinton—*Public Papers of George Clinton.* Albany, 1899–1914.

H. Clinton—H. Clinton. *The American Rebellion.* Edited by W. B. Willcox. New Haven, 1954.

Clode M.F.—M. F. Clode. *The Military Forces of the Crown.* London, 1869.

Clode M.L.—M. F. Clode. *The Administration of Justice under Military and Martial Law.* 2d ed., London, 1874.

Connolly—T. W. J. Connolly. *The History of the Corps of Royal Sappers and Miners.* London, 1855.

Coote—C. Coote. *Sketches of the Lives of Eminent English Civilians.* London, 1804.

Cowper—L. I. Cowper. *The King's Own: The Story of a Royal Regiment.* Oxford, 1939.

Cuneo—J. R. Cuneo. *Robert Rogers of the Rangers.* New York, 1959.

Davies C. G.—G. Davies. *The Early History of the Coldstream Guards.* Oxford, 1924.

Dawson—H. B. Dawson, ed. *New York City during the American Revolution.* New York, 1861.

De Fonblanque *Admin.*—E. B. de Fonblanque. *Treatise on the Administration and Organisation of the British Army.* London, 1858.

Digby—J. P. Baxter, ed. *Journal of Lieut. William Digby.* Albany, 1887.

Doughty—A. G. Doughty. *Report of the Public Archives for the Year 1918.* Ottawa, 1920.

Drinker—*Journal of Mrs. Henry Drinker,* 13 PMHB 298.

Duncan—F. Duncan. *History of the Royal Regiment of Artillery.* 3d ed., London, 1879.

Du Roi—C. S. J. Epping, ed. *Journal of Du Roi the Elder.* New York, 1911.

Edes—S. L. Boardman, ed. *Peter Edes and His Diary.* Bangor, Me., 1921.

Evelyn—*Memoirs and Letters of Captain W. Glanville Evelyn.* Oxford, 1879.

Fisher—S. Fisher. *A Diary of Trifling Occurrences,* 82 PMHB 411.

Force—P. Force. *American Archives*. Washington, 1837–1853. Cited by series, volume, and column.

Fortescue—J. W. Fortescue. *A History of the British Army*. London, 1899–1930.

Freeman—D. S. Freeman. *George Washington*. New York, 1948–1957.

French F.Y.—A. French. *The First Year of the American Revolution*. Boston and New York, 1934.

Frothingham—R. Frothingham. *History of the Siege of Boston*. 2d ed., Boston, 1851.

Gage *Corr.*—C. E. Carter, ed. *The Correspondence of General Thomas Gage*. New Haven, 1931 and 1933.

Gaine—P. L. Ford, ed. *The Journals of Hugh Gaine, Printer*. New York, 1902.

Geo. III *Corr.*—J. W. Fortescue, ed. *The Correspondence of King George the Third*. London, 1928.

Gipson B.E.—L. H. Gipson. *The British Empire before the American Revolution*. Vols. 1–3, rev. ed., New York, 1958–1960; vols. 4–13, New York, 1939–1967; vol. 14, Bibliography, to follow.

Gipson C.R.—L. H. Gipson. *The Coming of the Revolution, 1763–1775*. New York, 1954.

Glover—R. Glover. *Peninsular Preparation: The Reform of the British Army 1795–1809*. Cambridge, 1963.

Goebel—J. Goebel, ed. 1 *The Law Practice of Alexander Hamilton*. New York and London, 1964.

Hadden—*Hadden's Journal and Orderly Books*. Albany, 1884.

Hervey—*Journal of the Hon. William Hervey, 1755–1815*. Suffolk Green Books No. XIV. Bury St. Edmunds, 1906.

Heuston—R. F. V. Heuston. *Lives of the Lord Chancellors 1885–1940*. Oxford, 1964.

Hist. Parl. H.C.—L. B. Namier and J. Brooke. *The House of Commons 1754–1790*. History of Parliament Trust. New York, 1964.

HMC Am. MSS.—HMC. *Report of American Manuscripts in the Royal Institution of Great Britain*. London, 1904–1909.

HMC Rutland—HMC. *Manuscripts of the Duke of Rutland, K. G.* London, 1889–1905.

HMC *Var. Coll.*—HMC. *Report on Manuscripts in Various Collections*. 1901–1913.

Holdsworth—W. S. Holdsworth. *A History of English Law*. London, 1922–1966.

James—T. James. *The History of the Herculean Straits*. London, 1771.

Johnson—*The Papers of Sir William Johnson*. Albany, 1921–1962.

Jones—T. Jones. *History of New York during the Revolutionary War.* Edited by E. F. de Lancey. New York, 1879.

Kemble—*The Kemble Papers.* NYHS Coll., 1883.

Kennedy—W. P. M. Kennedy. *The Constitution of Canada.* 2d ed., London, 1938.

Kimball—G. S. Kimball. *Correspondence of William Pitt.* New York and London, 1906.

Kingsford—W. Kingsford. *The History of Canada.* Toronto and London, 1887–1898.

Knox—A. G. Doughty, ed. *An Historical Journal of the Campaigns in North America by Captain John Knox.* Toronto, 1914. Annotated edition of the original, which was published in London in 1769.

Larpent—G. Larpent, ed. *The Private Journal of Judge-Advocate Larpent.* 3d ed., London, 1854.

Leach—*A Journal Kept by John Leach, during His Confinement by the British, in Boston Goal, in 1775,* 19 NEHGR 255.

Luttrell—N. Luttrell. *A Brief Historical Relation of State Affairs.* Oxford, 1857.

Mackenzie—*Diary of Frederick Mackenzie.* Cambridge, Mass., 1930.

Maclachlan—A. N. C. Maclachlan. *William Augustus, Duke of Cumberland.* London, 1876.

MAFL—Air Ministry (currently the Ministry of Defence). *Manual of Air Force Law.* Four editions to date, 1921, 1933, 1956, and 1964. Part II contains material less likely to be in daily use by those concerned with the administration of air force law.

Mahon—R. H. Mahon. *Life of General the Hon. James Murray, a Builder of Canada.* London, 1921.

Mante—T. Mante. *The History of the Late War in North-America.* London, 1772.

Martin—R. M. Martin. *History of the British Possessions in the Mediterranean.* London, 1844.

McArthur—J. McArthur. *Principles and Practice of Naval and Military Courts Martial.* 2d ed., London, 1805.

McCrady—E. McCrady. *The History of South Carolina in the Revolution.* Vol. 1, *1775–1780.* New York, 1901. Vol. 2, *1780–1783.* New York, 1902.

Mil. L. Eng.—[R. B. Scott?]. *The Military Law of England.* London, 1810.

H. Miller—H. Miller, ed. *Treaties and Other International Acts of the United States of America.* Washington, 1931——.

MML—War Office (currently the Ministry of Defence). *Manual of Military Law.* Eleven editions, the first in 1884, the last up to now in 1965. Part II, first appearing as a supplement to MML 1951, is published as a series of pamphlets; these deal with matters less immediately concerned with the administration of military law, and are cited by the date of each pamphlet. Part III of the current MML "deals with that part of international law known as the law of war on land."

Montrésor—*The Montrésor Journals.* NYHS Coll., 1881.

Morgan—E. S. and H. M. Morgan. *The Stamp Act Crisis.* Chapel Hill, 1953.

Murray Journal—*Governor Murray's Journal of Quebec.* 3d series, Hist. Docs., Lit. & Hist. Soc. of Quebec. Quebec, 1871. A continuation is at 3 Knox 306–334.

N.Y. Col. Doc.—E. B. O'Callaghan, ed. *Documents Relative to the Colonial History of the State of New York.* Albany, 1853–1857.

N.Y. State Doc.—E. B. O'Callaghan, ed. *The Documentary History of the State of New York.* Albany, 1849–1851.

Newell—T. Newell. *A Journal Kept during the Time Boston Was Shut up in 1775–6,* MHS Coll., 4:1:261.

O'Conor—N. J. O'Conor. *A Servant of the Crown.* New York, 1938.

Ogborn—M. E. Ogborn. *Equitable Assurances: The Story of Life Assurance in the Experience of The Equitable Life Assurance Society 1762–1962.* London, 1962.

Onderdonk—H. Onderdonk, Jr. *Revolutionary Incidents of Suffolk and Kings Counties.* New York, 1849.

Oppenheim—H. Lauterpacht. *Oppenheim's International Law.* 7th ed., London and New York, 1952.

Pargellis *Loudoun*—S. M. Pargellis. *Lord Loudoun in North America.* New Haven, 1933.

Parkman H.C.C.—F. Parkman. *A Half-Century of Conflict.* London, 1892.

Pattison—*Letters of James Pattison.* NYHS Coll., 1879.

Pausch—*Journal of Captain Georg Pausch.* Albany, 1886.

Peckham C.W.—H. H. Peckham. *The Colonial Wars, 1689–1762.* Chicago, 1964.

Pettengill—R. W. Pettengill. *Letters from America 1776–1779.* Boston and New York, 1924.

Popp—*Popp's Journal, 1777–1783,* 26 PMHB 25, 245.

Porter—W. Porter. *History of the Corps of Royal Engineers.* London, 1889.

Preston—R. A. Preston. *Gibraltar, Colony and Fortress,* 27 Can. Hist. Rev. 402.

Prichard—M. J. Prichard. *The Army Act and Murder Abroad,* [1954] Camb. L. J. 232.

Radzinowicz—L. Radzinowicz. *A History of English Criminal Law and Its Administration from 1750.* London, 1948–1956.

Ramsay, HSC—D. Ramsay. *The History of South-Carolina.* Charleston, 1809.

Riddell *Br. Cts.*—W. R. Riddell. *The First British Courts in Canada*, 33 Yale L. J. 571.

Riddell *Mich.*—W. R. Riddell. *Michigan under British Rule: Law and Law Courts 1760–1796*. Lansing, 1926.

Riedesel—W. L. Stone, tr. *Memoirs and Letters and Journals of Major General Riedesel during His Residence in America*. Albany, 1868.

Baroness Riedesel—M. L. Brown, Jr., tr. *Baroness von Riedesel and the American Revolution*. Chapel Hill, 1965.

Sabine—L. Sabine. *Biographical Sketches of Loyalists of the American Revolution*. Boston, 1864.

Savory—R. Savory. *His Britannic Majesty's Army in Germany during the Seven Years War*. Oxford, 1966.

Sayer—F. Sayer. *The History of Gibraltar*. 2d. ed., London, 1865.

Schaukirk—*Pastor Schaukirk's Diary: Occupation of New York City by the British*, 1 PMHB 133.

Scouller—R. E. Scouller, *The Armies of Queen Anne*. Oxford, 1966.

Sewall—*Letters from Jonathan Sewall*, 30 MHS Proc. 407.

Shortt and Doughty—A. Shortt and A. G. Doughty, eds. *Documents Relating to the Constitutional History of Canada, 1759–1791*. 2d rev. ed., Ottawa, 1918.

Shy—J. Shy. *Toward Lexington: The Role of the British Army in the Coming of the American Revolution*. Princeton, 1965.

Simmons—T. F. Simmons. *The Constitution and Practice of Courts Martial*. 7th ed., London, 1875.

Simms—W. G. Simms. *The History of South Carolina*. Charleston, 1840.

Smith L. & R.—P. H. Smith. *Loyalists and Redcoats*. Chapel Hill, 1964.

Sosin—J. M. Sosin. *Whitehall and the Wilderness*. Lincoln, Neb., 1961.

Sparks, *Wash.*—J. Sparks, ed. *The Writings of George Washington*. Boston, 1835.

Stanley—G. F. G. Stanley. *Canada's Soldiers, 1604–1954*. Toronto, 1954.

Stedman—C. Stedman. *History of the Origin, Progress, and Termination of the American War*. London, 1794.

Stevens—J. A. Stevens. *Colonial Records of the New York Chamber of Commerce*. New York, 1867.

Stokes—I. N. P. Stokes. *The Iconography of Manhattan Island*. New York, 1915–1928.

Sullivan—R. J. Sullivan. *Thoughts on Martial Law*. 2d ed., London, 1784.

Valentine—A. Valentine. *Lord George Germain*. Oxford, 1962.

Van Doren *Franklin*—C. Van Doren. *Benjamin Franklin*. New York, 1938.

Van Doren S.H.—C. Van Doren. *Secret History of the American Revolution*. New York, 1941.

Viger—J. Viger, *Règne Militaire en Canada, ou Administration Judiciaire de ce Pays par les Anglais du 8 Septembre 1760 au 10 Août 1764*. Mémoires de la Société Historique de Montréal, vol. 5. 1870.

Walton—C. Walton. *History of the British Standing Army, 1660–1700*. London, 1894.

C. Ward—C. Ward. *The War of the Revolution*. New York, 1952.

S. G. P. Ward—S. G. P. Ward. *Wellington's Headquarters*. Oxford, 1957.

Washington—*Writings of Washington*. Edited by J. C. Fitzpatrick. Washington, 1931–1944.

Watson *Geo. III*—J. S. Watson. *The Reign of George III, 1760–1815*. Oxford, 1960.

Well. *Disp.*—*The Dispatches of Field Marshal the Duke of Wellington during His Various Campaigns*. Edited by J. Gurwood. London 1844–1845.

Wertenbaker—T. J. Wertenbaker. *Father Knickerbocker Rebels*. New York, 1948.

Whitworth—R. Whitworth. *Field Marshal Lord Ligonier*. Oxford, 1958.

Willard—M. W. Willard, ed. *Letters on the American Revolution 1774–1776*. Boston and New York, 1925.

Willcox—W. B. Willcox. *Portrait of a General*. New York, 1964.

Williams *Whig Sup.*—B. Williams. *The Whig Supremacy, 1714–1760*. 2d ed., Oxford, 1962.

Winthrop—W. Winthrop. *Military Law and Precedents*. 2d ed., Boston, 1896; reprinted with starred page numbers indicating pagination of that edition, Washington, 1920, 1942.

V. OTHER PRINTED WORKS CITED

[NOTE: Order Books already listed in Part II are not again set forth below.]

Abridgment, An, of the English Military Discipline. London, 1682.

Adams, C. F., ed. *Memoirs of John Quincy Adams*. Boston, 1874.

Allen, James, Diary of, 9 PMHB 176.

Amherst, Jeffery, The Journal of. Edited by J. C. Webster. Toronto and Chicago, 1931.

Anderson, T. S. *The Command of the Howe Brothers*. New York, 1936.

Armstrong, J. *The History of the Island of Minorca*. London, 1752.

Baldry, W. Y. *Early Articles of War*, 4 JSAHR 166, 6 *id.* 188.

Baldwin, E. H. *Joseph Galloway, the Loyalist Politician*, 26 PMHB 161, 289, 417.

Barber, J. W., and Howe, H. *Historical Collections of the State of New Jersey*. New York, 1846.

Barnwell, J. W. *The Evacuation of Charleston by the British in 1782,* 11 SCHGM 1.

Bartlett, J. R. *History of the Wanton Family of Newport, R. I.* Providence, 1878.

Barton, G. P. *Foreign Armed Forces: Immunity from Criminal Jurisdiction,* 27 Br. Y. B. Int. L. 186.

———. *Foreign Armed Forces: Immunity from Supervisory Jurisdiction,* 26 Br. Y. B. Int. L. 380.

Batchelder, S. F. *Bits of Cambridge History.* Cambridge, Mass., 1930.

Becker, C. L. *The History of Political Parties in the Province of New York, 1760–1776.* Madison, 1909.

Belcher, H. *The First American Civil War.* London, 1911.

Bell, J. *The History of Gibraltar.* London, 1845.

Bemis, S. F. *The Diplomacy of the American Revolution.* 4th ed., Bloomington, Ind., 1957.

———. *Jay's Treaty.* Rev. ed., New Haven, 1962.

Berry, W. *Pedigrees of Hertfordshire Families.* London, 1842.

Bird, H. *March to Saratoga.* New York, 1963.

Black, J. D., and Roelker, W. G., eds. *A Rhode Island Chaplain in the Revolution.* Providence, 1949.

Blumenthal, W. H. *Women Camp Followers of the American Revolution.* Philadelphia, 1952.

Bouquet Papers, 19 MPHC 27.

Boutell's Heraldry. Rev. ed. by C. W. Scott-Giles and J. P. Brooke-Little. London, 1963.

Bowen, C. W. *The History of Woodstock, Connecticut.* Norwood, Mass., 1930.

Boyd, J. P. *Anglo-American Union: Joseph Galloway's Plan to Preserve the British Empire, 1774–1778.* Philadelphia, 1941.

Boyle's Journal of Occurrences in Boston, 85 NEHGR 5, 117.

Bradley, A. G. *Lord Dorchester.* London and Toronto, 1926.

British Regime in Wisconsin, The, 18 Wis. Hist. Soc. Coll. 223.

Broadsides, Ballads, &c. Printed in Massachusetts, 1639–1800. MHS Coll., vol. 75. 1922.

Brown, A. S. *The British Peace Offer of 1778: A Study in Ministerial Confusion,* 40 Pap. Mich. Acad. Sci. Arts & Ltrs. 249.

Brown, G. S. *The American Secretary: The Colonial Policy of Lord George Germain, 1775–1778.* Ann Arbor, 1963.

———. *The Court-Martial of Lord George Sackville, Whipping Boy of the Revolutionary War,* Wm. & Mary Q., 3:9:317.

Brown, W. A. *Empire or Independence.* University, La., 1941.

Burpee, L. J. and Doughty, A. G., eds. *Index and Dictionary of Canadian History*. Toronto, 1911.

Butler, L. *The Annals of the King's Royal Rifle Corps*. London, 1913.

Butterfield, L. H., *et al.*, eds. *Adams Family Correspondence*. Cambridge, Mass., 1963.

Cam, H. M, ed. *Selected Historical Essays of F. W. Maitland*. Cambridge, 1957.

Carter, C. E. *The Significance of the Military Office in America, 1763–1765*, 28 Am. Hist. Rev. 475.

Cary, A. D. L., and McCance, S. *Regimental Records of the Royal Welch Fusiliers*. London, 1923.

Chalmers, G. *Opinions of Eminent Lawyers*. London, 1814.

Channing, E. *The War for Southern Independence*. New York, 1930.

Christie, I. R. *The End of North's Ministry, 1790–1782*. London, 1958.

Churchill, W. S. *A History of the English-Speaking Peoples*. New York, 1956–1958.

Clark, G. *The Later Stuarts, 1660–1714*. 2d ed., Oxford, 1955.

Clemensha, H. W. *A History of Preston in Amounderness*. Manchester, 1912.

Coleman, K. *The American Revolution in Georgia, 1763–1789*. Athens, Ga., 1958.

Commager, H. S., and Morris, R. B., eds. *The Spirit of 'Seventy-Six*. Indianapolis and New York, 1958.

Concord Fight: The Narrative of Jeremy Lister. Cambridge, Mass., 1931.

Conn, S. *Gibraltar in British Diplomacy in the Eighteenth Century*. New Haven, 1942.

Coupland, R. *The Quebec Act: A Study in Statesmanship*. Oxford, 1925.

Cresswell, Nicholas, The Journal of. 2d ed., New York, 1928.

Cruickshank, C. G. *Elizabeth's Army*. 2d ed., Oxford, 1966.

Curtis, E. E. *The Organization of the British Army in the American Revolution*. New Haven, 1926.

Cushing, J. D. *The Cushing Court and the Abolition of Slavery in Massachusetts: More Notes on the "Quock Walker Case,"* 5 Am. J. Leg. Hist. 118.

Dabney, W. M. *After Saratoga: The Story of the Convention Army*. Albuquerque, 1954.

Dalton, C. *English Army Lists and Commission Registers, 1661–1715*. London, 1892.

Davies, G. *The Early Stuarts, 1603–1660*. 2d ed., Oxford, 1959.

Davies, J. D. Griffith. *Honest George Monck*. London, 1936.

de Fonblanque, E. B. *Political and Military Episodes . . . from the Life and Correspondence of the Rt. Hon. John Burgoyne.* London, 1876.

de Gaspé, P. A. *Les Anciens Canadiens.* Montreal and Paris, 1961 reprint of 2d Montreal ed., 1864.

Devereux, E. *Andrew Elliot, Lieutenant-Governor of the Province of New York,* 11 PMHB 129.

De Watteville, H. *The British Soldier.* London, 1955.

Dicey, A. V. *The Law of the Constitution.* 8th ed., London, 1915.

Dobson, W. *History of the Parliamentary Representation of Preston.* 2d ed., Preston, 1868.

Dodd, C. *The Case of Marais,* 18 L.Q.R. 143.

Draper, G. I. A. D. *Civilians and the NATO Status of Forces Agreements.* Leyden, 1966.

———. *The Red Cross Conventions.* London and New York, 1958.

Elliot, Andrew, to Governor Robertson, January 19, 1781, Letter from Lieutenant Governor, 37 PMHB 480.

Ellis, G. E. "Chronicle of the Siege," in *Centennial Anniversary of the Evacuation of Boston.* Boston, 1876.

Fairman, C. *The Law of Martial Rule.* Chicago, 1930.

Firth, C. H. *Cromwell's Army.* 4th ed., London, 1962.

———, ed. *The Clarke Papers.* Vol. 4. Camden Soc. vol. 62. London, 1901.

Fleming, T. J. *Now We Are Enemies.* London and New York, 1960.

French, A. *The Taking of Ticonderoga in 1775.* Cambridge, Mass., 1928.

French, G. *The Martyrdom of Admiral Byng.* Glasgow, 1961.

Fortescue, J. W. *Following the Drum.* Edinburgh and London, 1931.

———. *The Royal Army Service Corps.* Cambridge, 1930.

Gage, General Thomas, Some Letters & Papers of, John P. Branch Hist. Pap. of Randolph-Macon College, 4:2:86.

Gibbes, R. W. *Documentary History of the American Revolution . . . in 1781 and 1782.* Columbia, S.C., 1853.

Gladwin Manuscripts, The, 27 MPHC 605.

Gordon, H. *The War Office.* London, 1935.

Greene, E. B., and Harrington, V. D. *American Population before the Federal Census of 1790.* New York, 1932.

Greenspan, M. *The Modern Law of Land Warfare.* Berkeley and Los Angeles, 1959.

Gretton, G. leM. *The Campaigns and History of the Royal Irish Regiment.* Edinburgh and London, 1911.

Grose, F. *Military Antiquities.* 2d ed., London, 1812.

Grotius, H. *De Jure Belli ac Pacis.* 1646. Translated by F. W. Kelsey. Oxford, 1925.

Hale, M. *The History of the Common Law of England*. 6th ed., London, 1820.

———. *Pleas of the Crown*. 7th ed., London, 1773.

Hamilton, E. P. *Fort Ticonderoga: Key to a Continent*. Boston, 1964.

Hamilton, F. W. *The Origin and History of the First or Grenadier Guards*. London, 1874.

Hawkins, W. *A Summary of Crown Law*. London, 1770.

Hayes, J. *The Royal House of Hanover and the British Army, 1714–1760*, 40 Bull. J. Rylands Lib. 328.

Hedges, J. B. *The Browns of Providence Plantations*. Cambridge, Mass., 1952.

Heinrichs, Capt., Extracts from the Letter-Book of, 22 PMHB 137.

HMC. *Report on the Manuscripts of F. W. Leyborne-Popham, Esq.* Norwich, 1899.

Hogg, O. F. G. *English Artillery, 1326–1716*. London, 1963.

Holdsworth, W. S. *Martial Law Historically Considered*, 18 L.Q.R. 117.

Holmes, O. W. *Collected Legal Papers*. New York, 1921.

Hough, W. *Precedents in Military Law*. London, 1855.

Howard, C. N. *The British Development of West Florida 1763–1769*. Berkeley and Los Angeles, 1947.

———. *The Military Occupation of British West Florida 1763*, 17 Fla. Hist. Q. 181.

Howe, M. D., ed. *Holmes-Pollock Letters*. Cambridge, Mass., 1941.

———, ed. *The Occasional Speeches of Justice Oliver Wendell Holmes*. Cambridge, Mass., 1962.

Howe, Lieut. Gen. Sir William, The Narrative of. London, 1780.

Hyde, C. C. *International Law Chiefly as Interpreted and Applied by the United States*. 2d ed., Boston, 1945.

Jacobsen, G. A. *William Blathwayt*. New Haven, 1932.

James, C. *Military Dictionary*. London, 1802.

James, E. R. "A List of Legal Treatises Printed in the British Colonies and the American States before 1801," in *Harvard Legal Essays*. Cambridge, Mass., 1934.

Johnson, C. *British West Florida 1763–1783*. New Haven, 1943.

Johnston, H. P. *Observations on Judge Jones' Loyalist History*. New York, 1880.

Jones, E. A., ed. *The Journal of Alexander Chesney*. Columbus, Ohio, 1921.

Kellogg, L. P. *The British Regime in Wisconsin and the Northwest*. Madison, 1935.

———. *A Footnote to the Quebec Act*, 13 Can. Hist. Rev. 147.

Koke, R. J. *Washington and Captain Joshua Huddy*, 41 NYHS Q. 335.

Kuntzleman, O. C. *Joseph Galloway, Loyalist*. Philadelphia, 1941.

Lawrence, A. A. *Storm over Savannah*. Athens, Ga., 1951.

Leach, Christiana, Diary of, 35 PMHB 343.

LeMoine, J. M. *Quebec, Past and Present*. Quebec, 1876.

Leslie, J. H., ed. *A General Court Martial in 1708*, 4 JASHR 161.

Letters Illustrating the Siege of Boston, 14 MHS Proc. 276.

Letters Written from Boston, during Its Occupation by the British Troops, 16 MHS Proc. 182.

Lieber, F. *Instructions for the Government of Armies of the United States in the Field*. Washington, 1863.

List, A, of the Officers of the Army, serving in North-America, Under the Command of his Excellency General Sir Guy Carleton, K.B. New York, 1783.

Lockmiller, D. A. *Enoch H. Crowder: Soldier, Lawyer, Statesman*. Columbia, Mo., 1955.

Long, J. C. *Lord Jeffery Amherst: A Soldier of the King*. New York, 1933.

Lovejoy, D. S. *Rhode Island Politics and the American Revolution, 1760–1776*. Providence, 1958.

Lydenberg, H. M., ed. *Archibald Robertson, Lieutenant-General Royal Engineers: His Diaries and Sketches in America, 1762–1780*. New York, 1930.

Lyman, E. B. *A Reminiscence of Newport before and during the Revolutionary War*. Newport, R.I., 1906.

Lysons, D. *The Environs of London*. 2d ed., London, 1810.

Macaulay, Lord, The Works of. Edited by Lady Trevelyan. London and Bombay, 1897.

Macaulay's, Lord, History of England. Edited by C. H. Firth. London, 1914.

Madison, James, The Papers of. Edited by W. T. Hutchinson and W. M. E. Rachal. Vol. 4. Chicago, 1965.

Maitland, F. W. *The Constitutional History of England*. Cambridge, 1908.

Martin, E. J. *Women's War Work with the Army*, 23 JSAHR 54; 25 *id.* 21.

Massé, C. H. *The Predecessors of the Royal Army Service Corps*. Aldershot, 1948.

Masson, D. *The Life of John Milton*. London, 1877.

Maurer, M. *The Court-Martialing of Camp Followers, World War I*, 9 Am. J. Leg. Hist. 203.

Mayo, K. *General Washington's Dilemma*. New York, 1938.

McManus, E. J. *A History of Negro Slavery in New York*. Syracuse, 1966.

Mishoff, W. O. *Business in Philadelphia during the British Occupation, 1777–1778*, 61 PMHB 165.

Mississippi Provincial Archives, 1763–1766. Edited by D. Rowland. Nashville, 1911.

Morgan, E. M. *Court-Martial Jurisdiction over Non-Military Persons under the Articles of War,* 4 Minn. L. Rev. 79.

Morison, S. E. *The Oxford History of the American People.* New York, 1965.

Morris, R. B. *The Peacemakers.* New York, 1965.

Morton, D. B. *Philip Skene of Skenesborough.* Granville, N.Y., 1959.

Mowat, C. L. *East Florida as a British Province 1763–1784.* Berkeley and Los Angeles, 1943.

Murray, G., ed. *The Letters and Dispatches of John Churchill, the first Duke of Marlborough from 1702–1712.* London, 1845.

Neale, E. *The Life of Field-Marshal H.R.H. Edward, Duke of Kent.* 2d ed., London, 1850.

Nevins, A. *The American States during and after the Revolution, 1775–1789.* New York, 1924.

Nickerson, H. *The Turning Point of the Revolution.* Boston and New York, 1928.

Nys, E. *Le Droit Romain, le Droit des Gens et le Collège des Docteurs en Droit Civil.* Brussels, 1910.

Ogg, D. *England in the Reign of Charles II.* 2d ed., Oxford, 1956.

———. *England in the Reigns of James II and William III.* Rev. ed., Oxford, 1963.

Oman, C. *Wellington's Army.* London, 1913.

Onderdonk, H., Jr. "A Brief Sketch of the British Prisons in New-York during the Revolutionary War," in *Manual of the Common Council of the City of New York* (1849) 372.

"Papers Relating to the Evacuation of New York, in the Year 1783," in *Manual of the Common Council of the City of New York* (1870) 772–844.

Pargellis, S. M. "The Four Independent Companies of New York," in *Essays in Colonial History Presented to Charles McLean Andrews by His Students.* New Haven, 1931.

———. *Military Affairs in North America, 1748–1765.* New York, 1936.

Parkman, F. *History of the Conspiracy of Pontiac.* 6th ed., Boston, 1870.

Partridge, B. *Sir Billy Howe.* New York, 1932.

Peckham, H. H. *Pontiac and the Indian Uprising.* Chicago, 1947.

Perkins, W. T. *Denial of Empire: The United States and its Dependencies.* Leyden, 1962.

Philalethes. *Gibraltar a Bulwark of Great Britain.* London, 1725.

Pintard, J. "The Old Jail," 9 *The New-York Mirror* 73 (Sept. 10, 1831).

Pollock, F. *What is Martial Law?* 18 L.Q.R. 152.

Pollock, F., and Maitland, F. W. *History of English Law.* 2d ed., Cambridge, 1898.

Pope, D. *At Twelve Mr. Byng Was Shot.* Philadelphia and New York, 1962.

Porter, Captain David, *Minutes of Proceedings of the Courts of Inquiry and Court Martial, in Relation to.* Washington, 1825.

Proceedings of a Board of General Officers of the British Army at New York, 1781. NYHS Coll., 1916.

"Providence Lawyers in Colony Times, Something About," in 7 S. S. Rider, ed., *Book Notes* 133. Providence, 1890.

Rainsford's, Commissary, Journal of Transactions, 1776–1778. NYHS Coll., 1879.

Ramsay, D. *The History of the American Revolution.* London, 1793.

Richards, H. E. *Martial Law,* 18 L.Q.R. 133.

Richmond, H. W., ed. *Papers Relating to the Loss of Minorca in 1756.* Nav. Rec. Soc., vol. 42. 1913.

Riker, J. *"Evacuation Day,"* 1783. New York, 1883.

Ritchie, C. I. A., ed. *A New York Diary of the Revolutionary War,* 50 NYHS Q. 221, 401.

Robson, E. *The Expedition to the Southern Colonies, 1775–1776,* 66 Eng. Hist. Rev. 535.

Russell, N. V. *The British Regime in Michigan and the Old Northwest 1760–1796.* Northfield, Minn., 1939.

Sack, A. N. *Punishment of War Criminals and the Defence of Superior Order,* 60 L.Q.R. 63.

Sackville, Lord George, Proceedings of a General Court-Martial held . . . upon the Trial of. London, 1760.

Samuel, E. *An Historical Account of the British Army, and of the Law Military.* London, 1816.

Scharf, J. T., and Westcott, T. *History of Philadelphia, 1609–1884.* Philadelphia, 1884.

Scott, K. *Counterfeiting in New York during the Revolution,* 42 NYHS Q. 221.

Semmel, B. *The Governor Eyre Controversy.* London, 1962.

Sheppard, E. *H.R.H. George Duke of Cambridge.* London, 1906.

Shirley, William, Correspondence of. Edited by C. H. Lincoln. New York, 1912.

Shortt, A., et al., eds. *Documents Relating to Currency, Exchange and Finance in Nova Scotia, 1675–1758.* Ottawa, 1933.

Siebert, W. H. *How the Spanish Evacuated Pensacola in 1763.* 11 Fla. Hist. Q. 48.

Siebert, W. H. *Loyalist Troops of New England,* 4 New Eng. Q. 108.

Smelser, M. *The Campaign for the Sugar Islands, 1759.* Chapel Hill, 1955.

Smith's, Josiah, Diary, 1780–1781, 33 SCHGM 1, 79, 197, 281; 34 *id.* 31, 67, 138, 194.

Squibb, G. D. *The High Court of Chivalry.* Oxford, 1958.

Staples, W. R. *Annals of Providence.* Providence, 1843.

Stenton, D. M., ed. *Rolls of the Justices in Eyre for Yorkshire 1218–19.* Selden Soc., vol. 56. London, 1937.

Stirling, A. M. W. *Annals of a Yorkshire House.* London, 1911.

Stoesen, A. R. *The British Occupation of Charleston, 1780–1782,* 63 S.C. Hist. Mag. 63.

Stokes, Anthony, A Narrative of the Official Conduct of. London, 1784.

Story, G. *An Impartial History of the Wars of Ireland.* London, 1693.

Sulte, B. *Le Régime Militaire 1760–1764,* Proc. & Trans. Roy. Soc. Can., 2:xi:xxvii.

Sulte, M., Les Histories de: Protestation par J. C. Taché. Montreal, 1883.

Sutcliffe, M. *The Practice, Proceedings, and Lawes of Armes.* London, 1593.

Tatum, E. H., ed. *The American Journal of Ambrose Serle.* San Marino, Calif., 1940.

Three Letters relating to the Navy, Gibraltar, and Portmahon. London, 1757.

Tunstall, W. C. B. *Admiral Byng and the Loss of Minorca.* London, 1928.

Tytler, A. F. *An Essay on Military Law, and the Practice of Courts Martial.* 1st ed., London, 1800; 2d ed., London, 1806.

Uhlendorf, B. A. ed. *The Siege of Charleston.* Ann Arbor, 1938.

Underhill, L. K. *Jurisdiction of Military Tribunals in the United States over Civilians,* 12 Calif. L. Rev. 75.

Updike, W. *Memoirs of the Rhode Island Bar.* Boston, 1842.

Upton, L. F. S., ed. *The Diary of . . . Chief Justice William Smith 1784–1793.* Toronto, 1963.

Vattel, E. de. *The Law of Nations.* 1758. Translated by C. G. Fenwick. Washington, 1916.

Wall, A. J. *The Story of the Convention Army,* 11 NYHS Q. Bull. 67.

Wallace, J. W. *The Reporters.* Heard's 4th ed., Boston, 1882.

Warren-Adams Letters. MHS Coll., vol. 73. 1925.

Watson, J. F. *Annals of Philadelphia and Pennsylvania.* Philadelphia, 1870.

Webb, H. J. *Elizabethan Military Science.* Madison, 1965.

Whitehead, W. A. *A Biographical Sketch of William Franklin, Governor from 1763–1776.* New Jersey Hist. Soc. 1848.

Wiener, F. B. *History Vindicates the Supreme Court's Rulings on Military Jurisdiction*, 51 Am. Bar. Assn. J. 1127.

———. *A Practical Manual of Martial Law*. Harrisburg, 1940.

Williams, B. *The Life of William Pitt*. London, 1913.

Williams, E. N. *The Eighteenth Century Constitution, 1688–1815*. Cambridge, 1960.

Windeyer, W. J. V., *"A Birthright and Inheritance". The Establishment of the Rule of Law in Australia*, 1 Tasmanian Univ. L. Rev. 635.

Winslow Papers, A.D. 1776–1825. Edited by W. O. Raymond. St. John, N.B., 1901.

Wolf, E., 2d. *Rosenbach: A Biography*. Cleveland, 1960.

Wraxall, Sir N. W., The Historical and the Posthumous Memoirs of. Edited by H. B. Wheatley. London, 1884.

Zouche, R. *Law between Nations*. 1650. Translated by J. L. Brierly. Washington, 1911.

INDEX

Active service, on, 212, 218–219, 227

Adams, John: drafts American AWs, 22–23 n. 82; mentioned, 93 n. 36

Ayde, Stephen Payne, DJA: author of *A Treatise on Courts-Martial*, 182–183; career of, 182–188; participation in trials of counterfeiters, 124–126, 128, of Hetfield, 132, of Lamb, 149; of Lippincott, 116, 120, 121; views of, on double jeopardy, 148–150, on no-form-of-civil-judicature AW, 186–187; mentioned, 112

Air Force Act: originally synthetic legislation, 235; Air Force Act 1955, same as Army Act 1955 in respect of accompanying civilians, 235

Albemarle, George Monck, Duke of, 7, 167

American Civil War, 86, 105–107

American Independence, War of, 11, 86–164, 194

Amherst, Gen. Sir Jeffery: captures Canada, 38; corresponds with Gen. Gage on military jurisdiction in Canada, 50–52, 58; directs court of inquiry to try Indians at Detroit, 43; establishes military government in Canada, 39–41; returns to England, 52; mentioned, 63, 66, 105, 179, 180

Anne, Queen, orders soldiers to draw lots for execution, 20 n. 68

Appy, John, DJA, 178–180

Army Acts: 1881, supersedes Army Discipline and Regulation Act, 215, 217–219; mentioned, 231; 1955, civilians not on active service subjected to terms of, 4–5, 231–236; exercise of jurisdiction under, 240–242; extended on quinquennial rather than annual basis, 236–237

Army Discipline and Regulation Act 1879, superseded annual Mutiny Act and annual AWs, 215–219

Articles of War, American: always legislative, 22; camp follower article, 22–23; civilian jurisdiction under, 218–219; drafted by J. Adams in 1776, 22–23 n. 82; expansion of jurisdiction in 1916, 227–229, 305–306, 310–311; superseded in 1951 by Uniform Code of Military Justice, 72, 230, 232

Articles of War, British:

general: Board of General Officers early drafted, 9–10; "curious cabinet of antiquities," 30–31; impossible to reconstruct complete set, 9; JAG later prepared, 10–11; mechanically repeated, 29–30; promulgation of, ratified, 7–8; reflect vestigial survivals, 29–31; single set for home and abroad, 21–22; statutory rather than prerogative after 1813, 196–197; superseded in fact when military code consolidated, 215–219; two sets in 1742, 16–17; whether competent to expand Mutiny Act, 28–29

specific: camp follower AW, 21–22, 161, 219; no-form-of-civil-judicature AW, 14–15, 23–24, 29, 74, 111, 116–117, 161, 178, 186–187; provost marshal AW, 91, 216–217; relative rank AW, also a survival, 30; rulings on, neither known nor published, 187–188

Artillery: drivers of, militarized, 190–191; first mentioned in Mutiny Act, 11; integrated into army, 12

Asgill, Lt. Charles, 115, 121

Atkins, Pvt. Thomas, first mention of, 77 n.61

Attorney General: of England (*see* Law Officers); of United States, 219, 306

Austrian Succession, War of the, 16, 32

Balfour, Lt.-Col. Nisbct, 156–157

Barrow, Dr. Samuel, JAG 1661–1682, 7–8 n.6, 167–168

Battles: Bennington, 160; Bunker Hill,